Praise for *Anatomy of a Confession*

"Gary Stuart's *Anatomy of a Confession* vividly describes how a 'constitution be damned' detective, a zealous prosecutor, a grossly inexperienced defense attorney, and a trial judge all converge to set in motion the introduction of a 'confession' that was neither appropriately witnessed nor recorded as required by police department policy and the criminal case law. Author Stuart's telling of Debra Milke's more than two decade journey through the American legal system expertly details how assumptions by the very players whose job it was to ensure a legally level playing field did just the opposite. By their ineptitude or callousness, an arguably innocent mother was found guilty of the cold-blooded murder of her four-year-old child. *Anatomy of a Confession* is a story that will enthrall not just law enforcement, lawyers, and the judiciary, but particularly the American people who, as jurors, selflessly serve to make our criminal justice system truly work."

> —*A. Craig Blakey II, Judge (Ret.),*
> *Maricopa County Superior Court*

"Presumed innocent? What does it mean? We all ought to know what it means. After all, the presumption of innocence is central to the American criminal justice system. The Debra Milke story, as carefully traced by Gary Stuart, is a disturbing window into what it means to be presumed guilty, a presumption that invaded every step of her case, beginning with the corrupt detective who claimed she confessed to murdering her child, to the prosecutor who manipulated the grand jury, to the trial court judge who apparently had no presumption in mind other than guilt, to a chain of state court and federal court judges who remained blind to any inkling of innocence, and even at the end to a County Attorney who to this day scoffs at the conclusion that our criminal justice system erred. This is also though a story about what it means to have a few determined, persistent people who believed in the presumption of innocence and were willing to endure the cost of a twenty-five-year war to earn Debra Milke's freedom."

> —*Larry Hammond, Fellow, American College of Trial*
> *Lawyers; Past President, American Judicature Society;*
> *Founder, Arizona Justice Project; U.S. Department of*
> *Justice Exceptional Service Award*

"Gary Stuart has chronicled a riveting account of Debra Milke's odyssey through a flawed criminal justice system that failed until the Ninth Circuit overturned her conviction. Milke spent more than twenty-two years on death row based solely on the false testimony of a corrupt cop that said she confessed to conspiring to kill her four-year-old son. Stuart's book is more than an exciting narrative of Milke's case. His central character is the Fifth Amendment in action and how it protects the individual from government abuse.

"Even though I was one of Debra's federal appellate lawyers and worked on her case for more than thirteen years, Stuart's book gave me a perspective of Debra's case that I had not seen. Because we were in the trenches dealing with the 'tree' we did not see the forest—Gary Stuart shows us the 'forest.'"

—Michael D. Kimerer, Past President, Arizona State Bar Association; Past President, American Board of Criminal Lawyers; Past Chairman, American Bar Association Criminal Justice Section

"A mother is sentenced to death after confessing to killing her four-year-old son by having him shot in the back of the head in a Phoenix desert. But did she confess? That's at the heart of Gary Stuart's real-life drama about the trial and conviction of Debra Milke. He unravels how an Arizona cop worked the system and how a justice bureaucracy failed. In this gripping read, Stuart researched trial transcripts and police reports and conducted many witness interviews. Although she is free, the question remains: Is Debra Milke an innocent mother convicted based on a lying cop's made-up confession or did she conspire with two men to lure her son to the desert and shoot him to death with a promise of a trip to see Santa? This is the true-life tale of a woman who spent many years on death row while her case slowly wound its way through America's flawed legal system."

—Craig Mehrens, Criminal Defense Lawyer, Phoenix, AZ

"Gary Stuart's thorough and exhaustive work relates a story of dishonesty, misconduct, and judicial rubber-stamping causing an innocent person to be condemned to death row. A well-written analysis that rivals Netflix's hit series *Making a Murderer*, it recognizes the diligent post-conviction defense counsel who brought this gross miscarriage of justice to the attention of federal appellate judges who understood and recognized the factual, legal, and moral inadequacies of the case when others chose not to. No stone is left unturned in the author's scrutiny of how and why this injustice occurred. Mr. Stuart's analysis demonstrates that there are no winners in this story unless participants in the criminal justice system learn from it. A work well done."

—Mike Piccaretta, Past President, State Bar of Arizona; Fellow, American College of Trial Lawyers; Fellow, International Academy of Trial Lawyers

"An exhaustively researched, purposefully even-handed, and unsensationalized tome. . . . An invaluable resource, indeed lesson, for all those who participate or aspire to participate in the criminal justice system, whether judges, prosecutors, defense attorneys, or law students. . . . A means for the greater public to better appreciate and understand the inner workings of the criminal justice process, where it can go wrong, and how, in some cases at least, the same process ultimately remedies that wrong.

"Gary is the John Grisham of nonfiction. His writing is brilliant, and his attention to detail is beyond compare. Great read of an actual case."

—*Buddy Rake, Trial Lawyer, Phoenix, AZ*

"Once again, Gary Stuart has demonstrated brilliance in his writing as well as his understanding of the criminal justice system in *Anatomy of a Confession*. However, the title is somewhat of a misnomer, because what Gary Stuart has provided is a comprehensive inside look at the entirety of a high-profile capital murder case, from the crime itself to the investigation, pretrial motions, trial, and the complicated appellate process.

"The book is not about whether Debra Milke is guilty or innocent. Many, including myself, believe she is guilty of some participation in the murder of her child. However, what Gary so eloquently describes is how the justice system failed in not exposing police misconduct of the lead detective and at best prosecutorial indifference or at worst prosecutorial misconduct. Debra Milke and every criminal defendant, whether guilty or not, deserves not only the presumption of innocence, but also a fair investigation and trial. The public and our justice system also deserve a prosecutor who is a minister of justice and not just someone whose goal is to convict, as well as judges who are fair and impartial and don't just brush aside overreach and misconduct. No matter if Debra Milke is guilty or not, she did not receive a fair investigation and trial, and because of that, her case was ultimately dismissed. Ultimately, for the memory of young Christopher Milke, the only one in this sorry saga who we know was innocent, we will never know the whole truth.

"As in his previous writing, Gary Stuart has contributed to the sentinel event review of where the justice system went wrong, and what some remedies are, such as the need to record all suspect statements and interrogations, as well as the obligation of a prosecutor to disclose prior misconduct of its police witnesses. Shining a light on a case gone bad can only help in improving the justice system."

—*Ron Reinstein, Judge, Maricopa County Superior Court, Retired; Judicial Consultant, Arizona Supreme Court; Chair, Arizona Supreme Court Commission on Victims in the Courts and the Arizona Attorney General's Forensic Science Advisory Committee*

"I am very pleased with Gary's book on Debra's case. It sets out the facts accurately and is a compelling read on how a rogue cop and an unscrupulous prosecutor not only stole a young girl's life, but fought to have her executed, based on the police officer's belief he has the infinite wisdom to know who is guilty and will do anything to support his belief and get a conviction."

—*Anders Rosenquist, Criminal Defense Lawyer,*
Phoenix, AZ

"In *Anatomy of a Confession: The Debra Milke Case*, Gary Stuart takes the reader through the long, hard legal battle Debra has somehow amazingly survived. As Debra's appellate attorney for fourteen years throughout her federal capital habeas appeals and her subsequent Arizona state re-trial and appellate proceedings, I can attest to how truly complex and often very intense a lengthy legal fight for a person's life can be. Gary thoroughly conveys the defense team's difficult but ultimately rewarding journey with Debra in a way that will be understandable even to lay readers, but without oversimplifying the capital case and appellate process. What happened in Debra's case should never happen to any American citizen, and I highly recommend *Anatomy of a Confession* to anyone who is interested in learning why her case went so wrong. Only together can we, as a collective, educated and concerned citizenry, help to prevent such travesties of justice in the future."

—*Lori Voepel, Cochair, Appellate Law Department,*
Jones Skelton & Hochuli, PLLC, Phoenix, AZ

"Gary Stuart's *Anatomy of a Confession* is a fascinating, comprehensive, and meticulous telling of the tragedy that led Debra Milke, an innocent woman, to be convicted of a horrific capital murder that she did not commit based on a confession that she never made and spend more than two decades on Arizona's death row as a result. But this story is about more than one person's decades-long wrongful capital conviction and incarceration—it is a systemic indictment of police corruption, prosecutorial misconduct, and judicial arrogance in Arizona. It offers an object lesson for the rest of the nation of what can go wrong in our criminal justice system when the presumption of innocence is turned upside down and becomes a presumption of guilt, fiction is treated as fact, constitutional rights are trampled on, and official misconduct is repeatedly overlooked if not encouraged. Gary Stuart's excellent book is a case study of justice off the rails and a valuable and insightful resource for anyone who wishes to better understand or improve American criminal justice."

—*Richard A. Leo, author of* Police Interrogation and
American Justice *and Hamill Family Professor of*
Law and Psychology, University of San Francisco

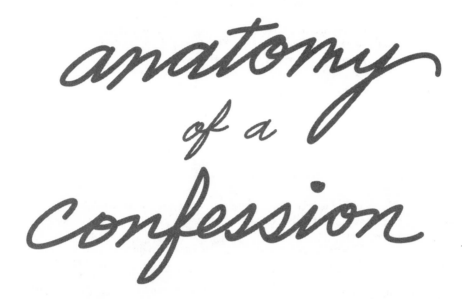

anatomy of a confession

THE DEBRA MILKE CASE

GARY L. STUART

ANKERWYCKE

20 19 18 17 16   5 4 3 2 1

Library of Congress Cataloging-in-Publication Data

Library of Congress Cataloging-in-Publication Data

Stuart, Gary L., 1939– author.
    Anatomy of a confession : the Debra Milke case / Gary L. Stuart.
        pages cm
    ISBN 978-1-63425-273-7 (alk. paper)
    1. Milke, Debra—Trials, litigation, etc. 2. Trials (Murder)—
Arizona. 3. Confessions (Law)—Arizona. I. Title.
    KF224.M55S78 2015
    345.791'02523—dc23
                                        2015034307

Dedication

This book is respectfully dedicated to the following men and women. Each is an Arizona citizen who was charged with a felony, convicted at trial, imprisoned, and later exonerated.[1]

Debra Jean Milke (2015)

Amon-Ra, Nubian (2006)
*Bennett, Donna (2013)
*Castillo, Armando 2013
Cruz, Robert (1995)
Fish, Harold (2009)
*Girdler, Ray, Jr. (1991)
Grannis, David (1996)
Islas, Francisco, Jr. (2013)
*Jordan, Brandon (2013)
Krone, Ray (2002)
*Knapp, John Henry (1992)
*Lacey, Byron
Lewis, Brandon (2014)
*Macumber, Bill (2012)

McCrimmon, Christopher (1997)
Minnitt, Andre (2002)
Peak, Carolyn June (2003)
Prion, Lemuel (2011)
Robison, James Albert (1993)
*Rushdan, Khalil (2011)
Span, Darlene (1996)
Span, Jerry (1996)
Suarez, Rafael (2000)
*Taylor, Louis (2013)
Watkins, John (2010)
*Witt, Drayton (2012)
Youngblood, Larry (2000)

---

1. http://www.law.umich.edu/special/exoneration. This list is compiled and maintained as the *National Registry of Exonerations*. It is a project of the University Of Michigan College Of Law. To be eligible for inclusion, an exonerated defendant must have been convicted of a crime and later was either: (1) declared to be factually innocent by a government official or agency with the authority to make that declaration; or (2) relieved of all the consequences of the criminal conviction by a government official or body with the authority to take that action.

Defendants marked with an * were represented by lawyers associated with the Arizona Justice Project. See, http://azjusticeproject.org.profiles.

CONTENTS

CONTENTS

PROLOGUE—DECEMBER 2, 1989

*T*HE CHAMBER OF COMMERCE HERALDS Phoenix Arizona, a Sonoran desert community of several million people, as "The Valley of the Sun." Larger by far than any other Southwestern city; it boasts a dry heat, fabulous golf resorts, and a big-city police department. And like large cities all over America, it occasionally endures a gruesome and inexplicable murder. Christopher Milke's murder happened in a sparsely populated area that thrives on the harsh conditions of the Sonoran Desert. Phoenix's bi-seasonal rainfall pattern produces more plant species than in any other North American desert area. The flat sandy terrain north of Bell Road (a traditional boundary from busy city to open desert land), supported thickets of agave, palm, cactus, sage brush, and legumes. Critters of all kind called it home—snakes, rodents, wild pigs, and domestic animals.

On Saturday, December 2, 1989, someone took four-year old Christopher from Metrocenter, a large Phoenix shopping mall, to a sparsely populated area called Happy Valley. While kneeling on the warm desert ground, that person fired three-high velocity shots into the back of the small boy's head. He likely died before he hit the ground.

The initial police missing-person report had him disappearing at 2:30 that afternoon. It said he was last seen near a restroom in the Sears store at Metrocenter. An exhaustive search began in and around the shopping mall. Store security personnel, mall security agents, and uniformed officers of the Phoenix Police Department quickly engaged. Radio alerts were broadcast, telegrams and faxes sent, off-duty officers mobilized and all sister law enforcement agencies notified. Police detectives quickly contacted and interviewed the boy's family and family friends. Scores of people helped in the search for and the investigation of his inexplicable disappearance. The Phoenix police department organized a temporary command post in the mall's huge parking lot. By late the next day, they thought they had the crime solved; they found Chris's body about sixteen miles northwest of Metrocenter. The police reports meticulously describe the crime scene's geographical features. The still and video film captures the peace and weather conditions at the crime scene—an abundant and forgiving desert in full winter bloom. The crime scene investigators carefully located, identified, and bagged items that would later become forensic evidence about "where" Christopher Conrad Milke died. The officers and technicians paid careful attention, documenting distances from known landmarks. They created a large, comprehensive, written, and visual record. Like all such reports and photos, these were very clinical, devoid of the human tragedy in that desert wash. They do not describe the split-second terror that the four-year old boy must have felt, or the rush of adrenalin that surely coursed through the shooter triggering three shots into the back of his head, at point blank range.

The killing took place three and one-half miles north of Happy Valley Road, just south of its intersection with Jomax Road. The aerial photos, taken three days later, show a lush and vibrant desert locale, with dry washes and paved roads, interspersed with few houses and large fenced and unfenced areas of raw desert. The killer parked near a "large under-pavement conduit" and took Chris from the car under the guise of "looking for snakes." The crime-scene investigators documented "hooved animal hoof prints" into and out of the wash all the way from the paved road to the "location of the victim's body." And they measured and took plaster casts of "soil disturbances," also known as footprints. There were twelve soil disturbances identified. One , Number 4, had a "recognizable shoe imprint; a waffle type design, similar to those partial imprints found in the area of the body." The footprints and soil disturbances "appeared to circle away and up from the body and back eastwards toward the road." The sketchy trail from the road to the body indicated a general westward track for approximately 100 feet from the paved roadway, out of sight, and down into a dry desert wash on a 20-degree slope. The wash was thick with growth—"Heavy desert type weeds, shrubbery, trees and four large [sic] Sahuaro cacti." The combination of downgrade slope, degraded wash, and the plants made Chris's "body invisible from the road."

Phoenix Police Detective Jim House noted the weather and wind as "cool and clear [with] a slight breeze blowing. However, the wind was not noticeable in the wash [because] the shrubbery and trees were apparently protecting the wash area." His narrative about Chris's body was police-speak, professionally neutral, but chilling. "The body was lying in a fetal position on its left side. The head was to the north, with the feet to the south. The head was tilted down towards the chest. Both legs were bent upward at the knees with the right leg crossed above the wrists with the right arm on top of the left. Both hands were loosely clenched, forming a fist. The body was totally [sic] rigored."

The Maricopa County Medical Examiner confirmed most of the crime scene observations the following day, Monday, December 4, 1989. However, long before the medical examiner released his terse report, the detective's blunt language said all that needed saying. "Two apparent bullet entry wounds were observed on the right rear head. The lowest of these two was located at the base of the skull . . . blood and what appeared to be an abrasion type injury was observed in the left frontal area of the head. The left eye appeared to be swollen and blood was emitting from the nose . . . the body was removed from the scene at approximately 10:30 P.M. and transported to the Office of the Medical Examiner."

Dr. George Bolduc performed the autopsy on Monday, December 4 at "0930 hours," confirming Det. Hamrick crime scene notes. "Cause of death, gunshots to head. Manner of death, Homicide." During the autopsy, a vial of blood was secured for analysis, along with a "jar containing chewing gum from the victim's teeth," and three vials of "bullet fragments from victim's head." Later, the detectives gathered important crime scene evidence from the medical examiner's office. "Victim's shirt, grey long sleeve sweatshirt with a picture of a dinosaur on the chest and blood stains on the back; victim's blue levi jeans and 'Ghostbuster' undershorts; victim's cowboy boots, brown tops with lizard design bottoms and yellow socks; ink impressions of victim's feet."

Dr. Bolduc also documented *three* bullet entry wounds, not two as originally thought at the crime scene: "[The back of the head] "revealed three entry gunshot wounds." The consensus of the medical and investigatory teams was instructive. "There was nothing to indicate that the wounds were contact or even close contact. Dr. Bolduc saw no gunshot residue. One of the bullet wounds was in the upper right portion of the back of the head and the other two bullet holes were in the lower portion of the head just above the neck." During the autopsy, Dr. Bolduc placed trajectory rods placed in the bullet holes to show the probable angle [from which] the bullets were fired." From this, he theorized that the "shooter stood behind and above Christopher. The small depression on the front of his head likely occurred when he fell to the ground from the impact of the first shot." The other two shots, he said, "were just to make sure."

While seemingly unimportant at the time of autopsy, the finding of pizza in the victim's stomach would later match what the boy ate for lunch earlier that Saturday. The raw horror of the killing was manifest in a small detail of the autopsy findings: Christopher "died with chewing gun embedded in his clenched teeth."

1

CHRISTOPHER GOES MISSING

THE OFFICIAL MISSING PERSON REPORT on file at the Phoenix Police Department is a form document filled out by a police officer. A uniformed officer, Jim Corey, took the information by telephone from a man named James Styers. He wrote, "Date of Last Contact: 12-2-89; 1430. Complainant's Name—Jim Lynn Styers."

Styers told Officer Corey that Christopher Milke, the four-year old son of his roommate, walked away from him while he was in one of the toilet stalls in the Sears restroom at the Metrocenter mall. He said he left Christopher "standing directly outside the stall for only several minutes." When he opened the stall door, Christopher was gone. He looked for him in the store and notified the mall security department at Sears. They broadcasted a missing juvenile announcement, Styers said.

More than a dozen police reports were filed in the first 12 hours after Christopher went missing. Taken from a dozen sources, they detailed the people involved, and everything that occurred that morning at 7734 North 12th Street in Phoenix. Jim Styers and his daughter, Wendy, shared the apartment with Debra Milke and her son, Christopher. Wendy was two years old and Christopher four. Styers explained that he offered Debra "the chance to move into the apartment, in separate bedrooms, about three months ago." Jim was 46, and Debra 26. She had a job; he did not. She was vivacious and outgoing. Jim was a loner living on Social Security disability payments. Debra needed a place to stay, at least temporarily, Jim said, "because her ex-husband had kicked her and Christopher out of his apartment."

Christopher got up early, as he usually did, and watched TV until a little after nine, when his mom got up. Styers said he was going out with his friend Roger Scott, and asked Debra if he could borrow her 1986 Toyota Corolla. His car was not working and he wanted to buy a Christmas gift for Wendy. Styers often "babysat" Christopher and seemingly had a good relationship with him. Chris asked Styers if he could please go with him—he wanted to see Santa Claus at the mall. Jim told him to ask his mother, which he did. She said okay. Knowing he would see Santa and probably have his picture taken, Debra dressed her son for the occasion. He wore his new gray snakeskin cowboy boots, a gift from his father. She put fresh underwear on him and bright yellow socks. He wore brand new Levi's jeans and his favorite sweatshirt—the one with the dinosaur on the front.

Debra kissed him good-bye at the door. "I wuv you," he said, as he and Jim walked to her car.

Styers was not good at details. Friends said he had "memory problems." The police said his recitation was "convoluted." He told the Sears employees and the police officers that he'd had lunch with Christopher and his friend Roger Scott before dropping Roger off and coming to Metrocenter. They all ate pizza at the Peter Piper Pizza store at 43rd Avenue and Glendale. Styers was a little sketchy about the exact times things happened, but the pizza parlor was not far from Scott's apartment. Next they visited a Walgreens and a Basha's Food Store. He said that Chris had "to go," so he took him into Basha's because he knew they had a public restroom. Then, he took Roger back to his apartment before he and Chris went to Metrocenter.

Once they got to Metrocenter, Styers had to use the restroom. So, they went into the Sears store. This version is documented in the Missing Person Report Styers gave to Officer Corey over the telephone: "On 12-2-89, at approximately 1430 hours, Christopher Milke (10-2-1985) walked away from Styers while Styers was in one of the toilet stalls in the restroom inside of Sears (10002 N. Metro Parkway)." Styers said he left Christopher standing directly outside of the stall. When he came out, Christopher was not inside the restroom. Styers notified store security and subsequently mall security when efforts failed to locate him inside of Sears. Both Sears and Metrocenter mall security broadcasted "a missing juvenile announcement with a full description of little Christopher." The report notes that "about ten mall security agents and several Sears's agents began searching the store and the rest of the large shopping mall, as well as the many parking lots."

The first person Styers contacted after he said he lost Christopher was Fiona McCormack at Sears, who assisted customers filling out credit applications and processed them for instant credit at Sears. She said Styers came to her desk and asked if she'd seen a little boy with a blue and gray sweatshirt with a dinosaur on the front. She told him no. He left and walked out of Sears down the mall. Five minutes later, he returned, with a can of Pepsi, saying he'd notified mall security. Then he talked to "Budda" in Kitchenwares. A few minutes later Styers told McCormack that mall security "had no luck in locating" the boy. She asked him if he had called the police; he said no. She closed her desk and helped Styers look through the store and then out into the mall. Styers suggested they look in the Tuxedo Shop and then go to the upper level so he could look over the railing, down into the mall. They checked the ice skating rink and Styers went into several restrooms along the way.

While Fiona McCormack was walking back to Sears with Styers, he pointed to a man coming down the mall toward them and said, "Wait a minute, there's a neighbor of mine; maybe we should ask him if he has seen Christopher." It was the man he'd had lunch with a few hours earlier, Roger Scott. Scott told McCormack he was there to meet a friend who didn't show up. He was planning to catch a bus home, he said. It was almost four o'clock by this time; Scott told McCormack he'd been at the mall for two hours. He hadn't seen Christopher, whom he said he knew, or Jim Styers during those two hours. He walked back to Sears with them. When they got there, Styers told them he would check the parking lot. He was gone for five or ten minutes. When he came back, he told McCormack he had checked around his car. "No sign of Chris," he said. The three looked downstairs at Dillard's, where Santa was talking to little children—no sign of Chris.

The police interviewed McCormack two days later. She told Detective Meenk that Styers appeared optimistic and at times had joked about the incident, saying, "You didn't take him, did you?" He told her he hadn't informed "the mother" because there was no way for her to get to Metrocenter—"he had her car." McCormack was clear about Roger Scott: "He never acted concerned and didn't pay much attention to the fact that the [boy] was missing."

Jim Corey, the uniformed officer who filed the initial Missing Person Report, met Styers at Metrocenter around three o'clock; he filed no supplemental report but later wrote a long-hand memo detailing his interactions with and his suspicions of Styers. Officer Corey was "irritated" because when he got to the mall, directly outside Sears on the lower level, he "stood waiting for several minutes before anyone approached him." He'd talked to Styers, but had never seen him. Styers "was standing 10–15 feet away." When Styers finally greeted Corey "with a handshake and a smile," Corey said he was "responding to the missing juvenile call."

Corey asked Styers what happened, to which Styers replied, "I don't know." He repeated what he'd said earlier about using one of the stalls in the Sears restroom and when he came out, "Christopher was gone." He said he checked the other stalls and the store itself. He said he called the police, but not Sears or mall security. With Styers in tow, Corey searched all the restrooms in Sears. He talked to mall security, and each of the Sears security agents. As they walked, Corey asked Styers about his relationship with Christopher's mother. Styers said the mother was a "friend, and they shared an apartment."

Corey's report reveals his growing discomfort with Styers' story. While he didn't suspect "foul play," "he didn't think Styers appeared to be the least bit concerned about Christopher's welfare," or worried about "Debra Milke's predicted emotional reaction to the situation." Corey's report also notes that Styers was not "very emotional" when he said, "Gee, I kind of feel responsible for this whole thing." Corey laid it out: "You are responsible. This shouldn't have happened because

Christopher was your responsibility today." As they walked the mall and the parking lot, Styers continued to talk. Corey said that he "displayed a very obvious artificial concern." He thought it was "a personality defect rather than foul play." Styers was very "uncharacteristic of an individual who had just 'lost' someone's child."

There were dozens of police and mall security officers searching the entire mall and surrounding area as Corey and Styers talked. Unbeknownst to Styers, Sgt. Ontiveros told Corey to stick with Styers and keep him in the parking lot. Corey asked more questions about his past, noting that his driver's license indicated that he was "of age during the Vietnam war era." Styers told Corey that he was a vet, and that there were times when he was in Vietnam that he'd "had to kill women and children in the villages. He also told Corey that people in the states didn't understand why they had to kill them."

When other officers searched his car, Styers asked Corey, "Do they think I did it or something?" Corey told him the search was routine. Styers "looked nervous." One of the mall security officers shared his reaction to Styers' attitude. "You know, if I had lost my kid, I would be very upset; but if I lost someone else's kid, I would be frantic. This guy is too cool about this. There is definitely something wrong."

The temporary command post set up by the Phoenix Police Department at Metrocenter managed the search and the flow of more than a dozen uniformed officers and detectives. The lead detective gave Officer W. Criswell the thankless job of rechecking locations and possible sightings. Because Styers and his friend Scott were the last two people known to have seen Christopher, Criswell talked to clerks and customers at each place where either Styers or Scott said they had been that Saturday. He covered the Osco Drug store at 34th and Glendale, Skipper's Lounge at 6124 N. 43rd Avenue, the Arabian Room at 4318 W. Bethany Home, and the Circle K at 47th Avenue and Bethany Home. By late Saturday afternoon, the police had secured photos of Christopher from his mother, and had taken photos of Styers and Scott during the lengthy interview process. Officer Criswell showed these photos to dozens of employees and customers. Almost everyone recognized the photos of either Scott or Styers, but none recognized Chris or his mother.

Daryl Barkley, an employee at Osco Drug, recognized Scott, was unsure about Styers, and didn't remember the boy being with Scott when he came in on Saturday afternoon. Barkley spent "about 8 to 12 minutes with the customer asking about 'three packs of Yardley soap'. . . . Roger was upset so he asked the manager, Paul Grebba, to speak with him." Mr. Grebba remembered Daryl asking him "to open the perfume case at about noon" for a customer but didn't recall Scott, Styers, or the boy being in the store. Trini Stern, another Osco employee, remembered that Scott was there on Saturday "at about 1:15 to 1:20 P.M. in the liquor department." She told Criswell she "was concerned that he was going to steal liquor." But she didn't remember a young boy or another man being with him.

Eileen Doberstein, the bartender at Skipper's Lounge, knew Roger Scott. She picked his photo out, but didn't recognize Styers, or the boy in the third photo. "Roger," she said, "came in Friday evening, maybe about 8:30 P.M., . . . looked around and left." She was certain he was not in on Saturday night.

Officer Criswell checked out the Arabian Room by talking to the owner, George Callahan. He remembered seeing both Styers and Scott in his bar before, "especially this guy," pointing at Roger's picture. But he wasn't in the bar "last night," and "he was definitely not in here after 5:15 P.M. yesterday." However, Bonnie Engstrom, the daytime bartender, remembered Roger. She said, "He's been here before and was here yesterday. He sat at the bar . . . for 15 to 20 minutes." She didn't see him leave and wasn't sure of the exact time he arrived but it "was between 1:30 and 2:00 P.M. . . . he entered the bar alone and left alone . . . the guy was kind of quiet, he was not nervous, and he did not talk to anyone."

Criswell's last stop in checking out Roger's story was the Circle K store. Maxine Edwards, the manager, didn't recognize the photos of Chris or Jim Styers, but she pointed at Roger Scott's photo. "He comes in here all of the time . . . he was in here yesterday afternoon. He purchased a can of Shasta pop and stood outside the door of the store for a short time. He came back inside and asked if I knew if there was a nice bar nearby. . . [I told] him about the Arabian Room being close, but did not know how nice it was . . . he was wearing a red plaid shirt and a ball cap."

In addition to the search at Metrocenter and the ongoing interviews of Styers and Scott, the lead detective dispatched several detectives to Debra Milke's apartment. They spent most of Saturday, and stayed into the early hours of Sunday morning. Their cumulative reports indicated the last officer left the apartment mid-day on Sunday afternoon, after talking to Christopher's mother, other members of his immediate family, and neighbors. Detective Davis was one of those officers. He wrote a six-page report summarizing the Milke family's complex dynamics. The police effort was tactical and strategic: advance the search for Chris *and* explore the possibility of family involvement in his disappearance. When Detective Davis arrived at the apartment Debra shared with Jim Styers, Detective Judy Townsend briefed him; she had been there most of the day. Debra, her stepmother Maureen Kay Sadeik, and "two or three other females that were either relatives or friends were present." Detective Davis introduced himself to Debra as a member of the "active investigation team." He asked if he could speak to her alone. Debra's stepmother and the other women stepped out while Detectives Davis and Townsend engaged Debra in a lengthy conversation about her personal history, her son, and their relationship with Jim Styers.

Debra asked how long this would take because "she wanted to leave for Florence to see her father." It would take a long time, but they didn't tell her that. They started with questions about her ex-husband, Mark Milke.

She told them that Mark was in Fort Hood, Texas. He'd gone there on November 28 "to get a Texas driver's license," she said. Mark got a "D.W.I. and lost his Arizona license." She explained that he probably wouldn't use his real name to get it. She gave them contact names and numbers for Mark's mother, Ilse Milke, his brother, Harold Milke, and information about the car he was driving. She told them she had left Mark in 1986 and divorced him in 1988; he was "a drug addict and an alcoholic." After leaving him, she moved in with her sister, Sandy Peckinpaugh, age 23. Sandy "now lives in Wyoming."

Has Mark ever tried to "take Christopher," they asked. "Yes, in July, when we were at his mother's and he asked [me] to give him a ride home. I told him I was not his taxi, but finally agreed to take him home. When [we] arrived at his house, he pulled the keys out and told [me] to get out and walk home. It is five miles away. Mark told [me], until you give me what I want, I'll have the car, it's my mother's car . . . He wanted the divorce papers changed . . . it would be a big mistake if [I] tried to take Christopher . . . Christopher was kicking him . . . [I] started crying . . . Mark hollered at [me] . . . take your fucking kid." She got the police to go back with her and get the keys to the car. He threw them at her. She got a restraining order on him. "They ordered him to stay away from me . . . Christopher's name was not on it but [I] felt it covered both of [us]." What about child support? "He's never paid child support. We did go to a justice of the peace when Mark contested the restraining order. At the court, Mark convinced the judge he should have visitation. [I] asked about child support. The judge said it was not his jurisdiction; they would have to go to Superior Court for that. [I] didn't go [because] it would be a waste of my time to leave work and go fill out the papers for child support . . . Mark would not pay anyway."

"Did Mark take Christopher?" they asked. "You know, it's really strange. But Mark said he would never go back to prison again. He said he was going to Texas to get a driver's license; he uses different names, and probably will get the license under another name. I think, yes, maybe Mark would take Christopher."

The two detectives changed the subject to Jim Styers. She met him in 1987. He lived in the "same apartment complex that my sister did. We were on the third floor and he was on the second . . . [I] often saw Jim sitting outside his apartment drinking Pepsi. . . ." Then she told them about moving into Susie Stinson's house until August of 1988, when she moved to Loveland, Colorado because Mark was "harassing her." She flew back to Phoenix in October of 1988 to "finalize the divorce." Styers "went with her to the divorce proceedings." When she came back from Colorado, she and Christopher lived with her mother-in-law, Ilse Milke, until July 1989, when she moved into the extra room at Jim's apartment. In the interim, Mark got out of prison, and "lived with some crack-head and got caught quickly. . . . [So] he joined a rehabilitation center to keep from going back to prison." They asked her if Mark ever accused her of sleeping with Jim Styers. "Not to me, but maybe to Jim," she answered. She told them that Mark has "joint custody" and that when she came back from Colorado, "he was trying to take Chris." Jim advised her that "she should get away from them [Ilse and Mark] and offered for her to come to his apartment." So, she did. "Mark has resented [me] ever since [I] left him."

Moving to Christopher, the detectives asked Debra what sort of child he was. "He has a hard time listening," she said. "He is tossed back and forth with Mark's visitations." As a tactical maneuver, the detectives switched from one friend or family member to another. Instead of following up on Christopher, they switched to Jim Styers and "the type of person he is." He's "a nice guy and goes to Valley Cathedral 3 or 4 times per week. He is attending minister school . . . has a 2-year old daughter he is trying to get custody of . . . Jim is a good father and has spoiled Wendy . . . he is very patient and has taken care of her sister's baby . . . he was in the Marines . . . he never flipped out. . . ." Jim is "good with kids and does change their clothing. He does everything for Wendy and when [I'm] at work, he does everything for Christopher. He started babysitting [for me] full time to save [me] babysitting money." He has no job because "of a disability."

Jim is the "type of person that when he buys his daughter Wendy a toy, he also buys for Christopher . . . he buys clothing . . . reads him stories . . . takes Christopher places in my car . . . we go out and eat tacos . . . Christopher has never complained about Jim . . . Jim corrects Christopher, but he doesn't yell, he just talks. He will stand Christopher in front of him and tell him he should act like a little man and if he can't do that, he would have to go to his room."

Does Christopher sleep with Jim, they asked. "Christopher sleeps with me," she said. Does Jim date anybody? "Not that I recall," she said. When they go out, "[h]e dances with other girls . . . he hasn't spent a night away since I've been here [at his apartment]."

Does he drink, they asked. Debra said that "he is not the bar type . . . he is not a recovering alcoholic." "[Jim and I are] good friends . . . he is the first person I could ever really talk to about my marriage and my going through hell." He doesn't talk about his personal life; he is a "very considerate person." How does he dress, they asked. "When he's at home, he is either dressed, or has a bathrobe on."

They asked about Jim's military service. "One night," she said, "Jim showed [me] some pictures of when he was in the service . . . he had written a story about the Vietnam war . . . he is into church stuff and always tells me to have faith . . . he is really into God." They asked if Jim had guns. "I think he has one gun," she said. Can we see it, they asked. She went to another room and returned with a revolver in a brown leather holster. It was German made, "initials EIG model E15, .22 caliber 6-shot revolver, serial number 247137." Does he take the gun out into the desert to shoot it, "or any location to shoot it"? She answered, "He has talked about shooting snakes and cans and so forth but [I don't] know where."

Detectives Davis and Townsend changed the subject to Jim's friend, Roger Scott. "I met Roger a few months back." How many times, they asked. "From about the first of August, we have gone out twice and I've seen him about five times at the apartment for a total of seven times . . . [I] think he is a nice guy . . . he yacks and yacks and it takes him forever to get out a sentence . . . Roger and Jim mostly talk about old days when they were 17 or 18 years old and racing their 1957 Chevrolets. . . ." Was Roger in the service? "I don't think he was in the war." What do they talk about, the detectives asked. "They just sit around and talk." Do they drink? "Maybe once or twice but Jim is not a drinker. If he does have a drink, it's usually rum and Coke . . . Roger is [not] much of a drinker either."

Could they have anything to do with Christopher going missing? "I don't think Jim or Roger could hurt my little boy."

"Could Mark?"

"Yes, I think Mark would."

She told them about some of Mark's friends—"ones that wear bandanas—have a history of assaults—surfer types. Mark has been on [my] mind for the last couple of months. Christopher has been telling me things Mark has said. One day [when] I told Christopher to pick up his toys, he said no and said his daddy told him he didn't have to. Christopher also called me a baby killer. [Mark] told everybody at

O'Brien's that [I] was a baby killer." Christopher also told her that "his daddy spanks him a lot . . . one day Christopher had a black and blue mark on his head . . . Mark said he had fallen . . . one day Christopher asked [me] why don't you get some cowboy boots so we can go over to Daddy's and kick him . . . maybe he'd pierce [Christopher's] ears because he liked Mark's earrings. . . ."

The detectives asked hundreds of questions about Christopher. Most were open-ended and broad, seeking background information for the ongoing search. But some were narrow, getting down to motive and foul play. "Would he walk away with anybody?" Debra answered warily, "He was so infatuated with Santa Claus, if anybody tried to bribe him with the right thing, he would go . . . [he] is not afraid of anybody . . . he is independent . . . he might go with a stranger [but I] have taught him not to take candy from a stranger." Moving to the Metrocenter visit, they asked if he were left alone, "[would] he wander over and look at toys." "Yes, he would go look at the toys, he's a very touching person; he likes to touch things."

What would a person have to say to Christopher to get him to go with them, the detectives asked. "I think they would have to tell Christopher that Santa Claus is outside and ask him if he wanted to go see him." Has he seen Santa Claus recently? "I think Christopher saw him Friday night when he was with Jim at Metrocenter. That's when Jim bought the remote control car that one of your officers has taken," Debra answered. "[Chris] told me that he talked to Santa Claus and said he should call me at work Monday." Did Jim tell you about the Friday night visit? "No, he did not," she said.

They asked her about the day before when Jim and Christopher left the apartment to go to Metrocenter. "It was between 10:30 and 11:00 A.M. . . . I was tired and Christopher wanted to get up. Jim told him to let his mom sleep and they would watch cartoons. Later, Jim asked if he could use [my] car to go Christmas shopping for his daughter Wendy. Christopher wanted to go. I said [Jim] takes care of you all week and probably wants to go by himself. Jim, however, said it was okay and they left . . . after Jim left [I] took a shower and went out to get the mail. It was around 2:45 P.M. that [I] got a phone call from Jim. [He] asked if anyone had called [me] and said 'they had Christopher'

. . . Jim explained that he had a security guard and they can't find Christopher. [I] got hysterical and told him to call the police."

When the detectives asked her about dating other men, she told them about Ernie Sweat. She used to work with him and "really likes him." She hadn't seen him for two weeks. She added that she wanted to go to Florence to see her dad. They concluded this series of interviews, and Debra left the apartment in a Ford F-150, with a white and blue camper shell. They took down the license number of the truck.

—

WHILE DETECTIVES TOWNSEND AND DAVIS were at Debra's apartment, Detective F. Dimodica was talking to Ilse Milke about her son, Mark Milke. She said her son was in Texas staying with his brother, Harold. He would fly back to Phoenix that day, December 3, 1989. She called her son and let the detective speak with him. Mark Milke told Dimodica that the military police at Fort Hood had just contacted him in person and advised him of Christopher's disappearance. He confirmed that he'd been in Texas since November 28. He said he "knows James and does not think he would be involved in foul play." But, he said, "James does have some friends that [I] do not trust . . . [one of them is] Roger. Roger had once taken Deborah's [sic] car without permission." Milke assured Detective Dimodica that he did not "have" Christopher and that he'd be returning to Phoenix on December 4 in the early afternoon.

Detective H.E. Hamrick interviewed Karen Smith shortly after he talked to her father, Richard Sadeik. Karen and Debra Milke are stepsisters, the daughters of Richard Sadeik. Karen said that she and Debra were not close and had different "lifestyles." She said that while she was with Debra on Saturday night and into the early hours on Sunday, "Debra did not seem overly concerned that Christopher still had not been located." She "was more concerned with the fact that Jim was being held by the police and this upset her greatly." Karen thought, "Everyone worried more about Christopher than Debra [did]." She told Detective Hamrick that while she and Debra were driving from Phoenix to Florence, Debra made several statements about Christopher. "I just know a stranger has him. I just know he's dead." She said that instead of having "a memorial service, she was going to cremate Christopher and spread his ashes over her parent's backyard." In Karen Smith's opinion, this meant that Debra already knew that Christopher was dead.

Detective J.A. Yost talked to Deidra Strickland at the Sears store on Saturday night at 10:20 P.M. She was a long-time family friend of the Milkes and a friend of Jim Styers. She was at Metrocenter trying to help in the search for Christopher. She said Christopher "has been known to run off before . . . not actually running away, but that he would just forget to come home when he was playing and would stay away too long. His mother and James would have to search through the apartment complex where they live to find him."

—

AT 11:15 P.M. ON SATURDAY night, Ron Jones, another detective, went to the apartment and spoke with Debra, again asking for a complete physical description of Christopher. She said she'd given it numerous times during the day. He said he understood that, but he needed it again. She repeated everything from the brand name on his underwear ("Hanes") to the way he styled his hair ("upward in the front and longer as it goes down the neck"). She described his two scars ("the first being hardly visible on the inside of the right eyebrow and the second being a one-inch horizontal scar on the front of the neck to the right side of the throat—from surgery as an infant"). She repeated what she'd told the other detectives about Jim and Christopher going to the mall at about 11 o'clock that morning. This conversation continued until 12:30 A.M., at which time Detective McElvain arrived. He took over the ongoing interview. Detective Jones went back at the temporary command post at Metrocenter.

McElvain got a little new information from Debra—most of it was about her ex-husband, Mark. Debra recalled an odd thing that happened a week earlier, on November 26, 1989. She said that Mark had Chris for the day and brought him back that night. At 8:00 P.M., Mark knocked on the door and brought Chris into the apartment.

Jim Styers had apparently been outside when Mark and his girlfriend, Terry, drove up with Chris. Jim told her that he'd heard Mark tell his girlfriend, "we can't do it now." Debra didn't know Terry's last name, but knew that she lived in Mesa. Debra also told Detective McElvain that Mark had gone to Texas on November 28 to get a Texas driver's license because the MVD suspended his Arizona license. She didn't know whether he was back yet. She gave McElvain a phone number for Mark's mother, Ilse Milke.

After interviewing Debra, McElvain contacted Henry Milke, Mark's father and Christopher's grandfather. He told Henry about Christopher's disappearance at Metrocenter earlier that day. Henry hadn't seen his grandson for about four weeks. He confirmed that Mark was in Texas, staying with his other son, Harold. He told McElvain, "[Mark] would have no reason to come back to town and take Christopher." He said that "he didn't keep in touch with Deborah [sic] and was not aware she was currently living with a man." And he told McElvain about an odd occurrence that day. Someone had called him about 5:00 P.M. earlier that day and asked for Mark. Henry "did not recognize the voice and would not tell the man where Mark was." An hour later, Henry said, "an unidentified woman called him and asked for Mark. She said that James was in trouble and needed some advice from him [meaning Mark]." Henry refused to give her any information about Mark. At the end of the interview, Henry said he would have Mark call the "missing person's detectives . . . when he returns from Texas."

2

MOUNTING SUSPICIONS

THE FIRST DETECTIVE TO INTERVIEW Roger Scott was Detective J.A. Yost. Yost had been interviewing Jim Styers and learned that he'd seen Roger Scott both on Saturday morning, and later, after Christopher disappeared, at Sears. Accordingly, Detective Yost took Styers with him to find Scott and get his version of the day's events. They arrived at Scott's apartment in Glendale at "0045 hours." Styers and Scott's mother, Wilma, were present during the interview. Scott confirmed what Styers had already told Yost. "Jim and Chris came over to [my] apartment to drive [me] to a drug store for some prescriptions for my mother. Shortly after 11:00 [we] drove to the Osco drug store . . . [then] to Walgreens . . . [then] to lunch at the Peter Piper Pizza immediately north of Walgreens." Roger said they had lunch at noon and "stayed in the restaurant for approximately 60 to 90 minutes . . . the service was slow."

After lunch, Jim drove him back toward his apartment, but he told Jim to leave him off at 47th Avenue and Rose Lane "to save them some time." He didn't feel like going home "quite yet, [so] he walked over to the Circle K." There, he met an "old acquaintance." Roger said he didn't remember the acquaintance at first, but he introduced himself as "Phil from high school." Phil was "about 40, 5'10", 170, with short brown hair parted on the right side and clean shaven." Roger remembered that Phil "was wearing a dark blue pullover polo shirt with a collar and blue jeans." And, he drove "a medium brown 1970's model Chevrolet 4-door sedan."

Then, Roger said, he and Phil went driving in Phil's car. Phil "wanted some tools so they went to Metrocenter about 1:30 P.M." They walked around the mall, "window shopping and looking at women." But, Phil said, "We got separated and I never saw him again." Then, while he was waiting for Phil outside the Sears store, Roger "found Jim walking with a girl who identified herself as Holly. Jim told [me] they were looking for Christopher [because he] was missing." Roger said he'd "hang around the area and look for Chris as long as he could but that he needed to get back home . . . to his mother."

Roger said he hadn't heard or seen anything after that until Detective Yost and Jim arrived at his mother's apartment. He assured them he had not seen Christopher at the mall.

The second detective to interact with Styers at Metrocenter was Detective C. Masino. He had been briefed on what Styers had told Detective Yost on Saturday afternoon, as well as what Yost had learned from Deidra Strickland, that is, that Chris had been known to wander about the apartment complex on his own, at four years of age. And he knew that an Arizona Department of Public Safety (DPS) officer (Wayne Mitchell) had seen a young boy in the mall wearing gray snakeskin boots in the company of a 50-year old man.

Masino met Styers at the west side entrance to Sears at 1:10 A.M. on Sunday. With the mall closed, and all the customers gone, the mall brimmed with police and security officers searching for Christopher. They started with canines and waited until the dogs and officers completely cleared Sears. Then Detective Masino took Styers back inside. By this time, Masino had spoken with Debra and the other women back at Styers apartment. Masino insisted that Styers walk him through each area of the mall up to the exact moment he "lost" Christopher. They entered the restroom where Styers said Chris disappeared. Styers pointed out the row of stalls where he "last saw Chris."

Masino insisted on details. "Styers pointed to the wall mirror and said he saw Chris in the mirror before he closed the stall door."

"Which stall?" asked Masino. Styers pointed to one against the wall. He said he had "to defecate." Masino opened the stall door and saw that the toilet seat was missing. Styers explained that he "had to go so bad, that he sat on the porcelain bowl without the seat." No one else was in the restroom when they came in, and he didn't hear anyone come in or go out while he "sat on the bare porcelain toilet bowl."

Masino tested the tension on the exit door; it was strong. He asked Styers if he thought Chris could have opened the door. "No, Chris is small." The restroom door was directly next to the toy department. Masino told Styers that if Chris had left the restroom, he would have stopped to play with the toys. "He should have been found," Styers insisted. Masino kept Styers busy searching all the refrigerators and washing machines at Sears. They left the store and returned to the command post the Phoenix PD had set up at the mall. Masino let Styers get in the back seat of his car so he could sleep. But Styers said he didn't need sleep. Thirty minutes later, they walked the perimeter again looking in the bushes for Chris. At one point, Styers "admired my .38 revolver and said he had a handgun, a .22 caliber cowboy type gun." Styers said he "recently was able to fire [it] to see if Vietnam had affected him." But he said, "It didn't cause him problems."

Masino tape-recorded this interview, which was eventually transcribed and filed in the case reports. The transcript is remarkable for, if nothing else, the sheer aplomb with which Styers calmly responded to Masino's mounting suspicions and probing questions. Masino asked Styers to describe exactly what happened in Sears when he and Christopher first arrived at the store. "We're walking in; we're just looking at things off and on all the way through. Got through. The restroom is over by the toy department. We're in the toy department in the corner there so we went into it, and I went into the stall, and in the stall I didn't even look at the seat, I just turned around didn't have time to get up no more. Ahhh, Chris said, I was closing the door, he says are we gonna go see Santa Clause [sic] and I said yes, in just a few minutes when I get done here. That was the last of it. When I got done, it took me maybe 3, 5 minutes, maybe a little longer. I don't estimate the time, right?"

Masino said, "Right."

Styers went on. "And I got done and I got up, opened the door and Christopher was not in there. I started looking for him; do you want me to say what happened through the store?" "Yeah, sure," Masino replied.

"I started looking for him through the toys, in the hardware, in the bicycles, all around the store and could not find him." Styers said it was "two fifteen, maybe." He looked for 10 or 15 minutes. "Then I said, oh, he's probably headed out towards Santa Clause [sic] because he'll go on his own a[t] times anyway. . . . But that's why I went in the restroom but I didn't think he [would] take off out of the restroom. Anyway, so I started walking up there, found one of the mall security guards and he was with a maintenance man, house cleaner or whatever the guy was, talked to him, he suggested I go back to Sears, talk to security because he might still be in the store. We checked that out and I guess they checked out Santa Clause [sic] and they were checking through and they went on and we got some more security involved. I met a girl named Holly . . . she works at Sears . . . she's very nice, we talked and walked and she helped me with that and we walked around for about an hour maybe. We went through all the stores in the skating rink from one end of the place to the other, trying to find Christopher or if anybody had seen him. Talked to a reindeer, talked to a lot of people and we come back. At that time, I said this is it. I'm gonna call the Police."

Masino asked Styers about the parking lots, the bus stop, and Roger. Weren't you surprised that "Roger was there when you'd just left him off"? No, Styers said, "Not with Roger, no."

Styers told Masino about his medications: "My Lithium and my Narvine [Navane]. . . I take 900 milligrams a day . . . I'm suppose to take a double dose, 1,800, but I'd only taken nine 'cause I didn't want to take the other . . . [yes] the Lithium is for depression . . . I guess . . . the Narvine is for my voices that I hear, dreams and things like that." Did he hear the voices during the day or only at night? "Different times, all different times." What kind of voices are they? "There's kids. I can't make out all the time what they're saying . . . some crying noises and all kind of things on that order." Did he hear adults, too, Masino asked. "Yeah, but I don't know if they're Americans or

Vietnamese or what . . . I don't know what they say 'cause you can't understand them. . . ."

Styers said he didn't think he heard "crying" yesterday. "[I just] try to put it out of my mind. That's what the doctor says to do. . . ." Masino said, "Well, obviously it's good for you to put it out of your mind, but tonight might be important. Maybe something else, but you don't hear anything today?"

Styers answered, "I don't know if I heard anything or not 'cause right now I can't think straight."

"Okay, that's all you remember about today?"

"Yeah."

"Okay, ahh, it's about 0438 and I'm just gonna turn off the tape recorder at this time."

—

MEANWHILE, DETECTIVE RON JONES HAD been working on contacting the military police at Fort Hood for assistance in locating Harold Milke, Mark's brother. With that task finished, he checked in with Sgt. Cusson, who told him to go with Detective Yost and conduct a second interview with Roger Scott. He and Yost drove to an apartment at 48th and Bethany Home about 2 A.M. Roger Scott's mother, Wilma Scott, rented it. She met them at the door and "welcomed into the apartment." Yost said they needed to "clarify" some information on his activities that day involving "his friend Phil." Roger "got dressed and volunteered to help [us]." They drove him back to Metrocenter. En route, Roger said he'd taken a bus back home from Metrocenter. They asked him to show them the bus stop where he got off to go home. He pointed to the one at 43rd Avenue and Keim, volunteering that he'd gotten off "at about 5:00 and walked over to Skipper's bar." Once inside the bar, he said he didn't recognize anybody. So, he said, he walked to the Arabian Room, had "a tall rum and coke and was in the bar about 10 minutes." A "white, short, thin waitress" served him. Then he "left for home, about 5:10 to 5:20."

Jones asked Scott whether the lunch at Peter Piper Pizza was accidental or arranged. Scott said Styers had called him about 10 yesterday morning and said he "would probably come by" his place. He did, and Scott repeated his earlier story about going to Osco, then Walgreens, then the pizza parlor for lunch. They asked about lunch. He confirmed what Styers had said. They asked him about "Phil," and Scott added more detail to that story. He said he and Phil talked about old times, old friends, and old places like the "Pacesetter and teenage dance places." He knew Phil from Alhambra High, class of '65 or '66, but couldn't remember Phil's last name. He repeated the story about going to Sears to buy tools and then losing track of Phil but finding Jim.

In this version, Scott told Jones and Yost that he and Styers had gone back into the Sears restroom area around the toys. Then he went to the Metrocenter bus stop "just past 4:00 and checked the schedule and found that the #3 bus would be leaving at 4:21 P.M. He caught the bus and left, which went out to 43rd Avenue down toward Van Buren."

When they got back to Metrocenter, they checked in with Sgt. Cusson and told him what Roger had said. As it happened, Cusson had also gone to Alhambra High during the "Phil" years. He decided to talk to Scott to see if they could come with some common friends and maybe Phil's last name. Sgt. Cusson asked Scott to take a polygraph. He refused. Cusson told Jones to find out why Scott refused. Scott told Jones that he didn't refuse; it was just that he was a nervous person and thought it might not work.

At 3:30 A.M., Jones told Scott that they would be taking him downtown to finish the interview, and that they would "tape his story." Scott agreed. At 4:00 A.M., the command staff ordered all detectives to return to police headquarters. Only uniformed officers would remain at the temporary command post set up at Metrocenter. Styers wanted to go home. But Masino said Chris was still missing and they needed his assistance. He told Styers other detectives would interview him again, on tape. By 5:00 A.M., the detectives had mapped the differences between what Roger Scott said and what Styers said.

They took Scott and Styers to 620 West Washington where Scott gave a taped interview at 4:15 A.M. They took "voluntary" photos of him. Detective Masino was in a separate room interviewing Styers at this time. When he finished, he crossed the hallway and talked to Scott "for some time." Jones next talked to Scott at 6:15 A.M. when

Masino completed his interview. And in this interview, Scott said he "remembered something he had forgotten to say earlier." He explained that "right before he found Jim in the mall, he went into the Sears tool department."

Entirely out of the blue, Jones then asked Scott whether he knew anything about "the disappearance of an 18-month old baby that had been taken from Jim Styers's apartment complex on Friday, December 1st." Scott said he'd been "at Styers apartment that afternoon and saw all the news cameras. The neighbors told him something about kidnapping but he had no further explanation about this child's disappearance."

At the end of this interview, Jones asked Scott to explain why he had been arrested in Glendale "several years ago." Scott indicated that it was a long time ago and at that time he had a drinking problem and really wasn't sure what he had done. He said he "had a bad drinking problem and since has given up drinking." The typed report confirms the interview was "terminated 0645 hours."

ONE OF THE MOST SUCCESSFUL techniques police officers use on reluctant suspects, also known as "investigative leads," is to engage tired suspects in the wee hours of the morning with revolving teams of fresh, fully briefed new officers. It was no surprise that Detective Masino took another crack at Scott that Sunday morning. Detective Masino's supplemental report confirms that he interviewed Scott in the "Auto Theft Sgt's Office in the General Investigations Bureau at 0550 hours." He knew by then that some of Scott's statements contradicted Styers' version. Scott told Masino that he decided *not* to go to Metrocenter with Jim and Chris after their lunch on Saturday morning because he had to go home to see Wilma, his mother. But now he wasn't sure if he went inside to see her before he went to the Circle K, where he met Phil. He said he did go inside but quickly contradicted himself and said he didn't. He also said he called Jim from a pay phone at 10:30 and arranged to have Jim pick him up at 11:00. But Styers' version indicated the meeting with Scott was not preplanned. When

Masino confronted Styers with this, he said that he thought Roger had called him the day before. Scott said he entered the Sears store "alone at 3 o'clock or three thirty to look for Phil, and this was before he knew Chris was missing." Masino countered, saying that he'd already said he had met Holly and she saw him in Sears. Scott had told Jones a different version, one that had him entering Sears after he learned that Chris was missing. Masino also challenged Scott on his interview with Sgt. Cusson at the command post at Sears. Cusson learned Phil's last name from Scott. Scott denied that he told Sgt. Cusson Phil's last name. Detective Masino's report ends cryptically: "Investigation Continuing."

By 11 A.M. on Sunday morning, Scott had been awake all day Saturday and 11 hours on Sunday. Detective Mills, a veteran homicide officer, had been involved early on in the Milke case. Sgt. Cusson briefed Mills on Scott's several prior interviews, just before Masino introduced himself to Scott at the General Investigations Bureau in Phoenix police headquarters at "1100 hours." Scott was "not restrained in any fashion." Mills did not give Scott "his Miranda warnings at this time, as he was *not* a suspect," merely an *investigative lead*. Mills began with the topic *du jour*—the elusive man named "Phil." Scott repeated most of what he'd already said about Phil to Detectives Yost, Masino, and Jones, and Sgt. Cusson. And he brought in a new name. "Jim Wafland, who he said he'd hung out with at Alhambra High, along with Phil." He expanded on the description of Phil's car, saying, "It was an automatic with radio and air conditioning." Mills suggested that maybe Phil was a "transient type person with tools, or mechanic's tools in the car." Scott said he had not looked around in the car carefully.

Mills again brought up Scott's years-old "Public Sexual Indecency Charge." Roger dodged the issue by saying that he had been drinking a lot during those years. He remembered it "was in a book store and there was some other man in there but didn't remember what happened because he was drunk." Mills covered other police interactions with Scott—"a burglary, some thefts, and four DWI charges." On the issue of medications, Scott told Mills he was taking "Dilantin for seizures." He had hurt his neck in 1974 in an automobile accident "and then in succeeding years he had more and more seizures with the last one occurring while he was at Thunderbird Samaritan Hospital approximately four months ago." He was also using an asthma inhaler.

They talked about his work history as a mechanic before his 1974 auto accident. Since then, he'd had "difficulties holding a job." Mills asked about his income. He said he was "living with his mother who was aged 69 and ill and they were living off of her social security." He got "food stamps, and was under AHCCCS medical care, and earned money on the side by doing odd jobs like window washing, weed pulling, lawn mowing, and tree trimming." He'd been married from "approximately 1971 until 1974." His wife was a hairdresser and "made sufficient money to support the both of them."

Mills asked Scott whether he "liked children." Mills' report says, "Roger seemed to perk up" with this question. Scott said that "[h]e liked all kids. There were so many kids in the neighborhood that would come over to his home, or would speak to him when they saw him outside."

Mills asked about Christopher. Roger became "somewhat subdued." He said Christopher was "a hyperactive child and difficult for Debbie to control." He knew this "because he had observed Christopher to be a real active child, but had only been told by Debbie and Jim that he was hard to control." Mills asked how they disciplined Christopher. Scott said, "Jim occasionally whacked him on the butt to get him to do what was requested of him." But as far as he knew, "Debbie did all of the discipline regarding Christopher."

Scott interrupted his interview with Mills several times for "sodas and cigarettes." At 12:15 P.M., Detective Saldate knocked on the door and "indicated that he wanted to speak with Detective Mills." Mills terminated the interview and "went outside into the hallway to speak to Detective Saldate." Then, Mills came back into the interview room, and introduced Saldate to Scott. Saldate took a chair away from the suspect. Mills renewed the interview, under the watchful eye of Saldate. While the police reports are silent about any change in atmosphere, it is safe to assume that Scott sensed that his friendly interview was about to change. The tension must have been patent, with Mills questioning in his calm, almost detached manner, and Saldate studying him, silent, but focused.

Mills went back to questions about Jim Wafland. Scott said Wafland was the head custodian at North High School. He gave Mills a telephone number and a general street location for Wafland's house. Mills asked how often Scott ate at the Peter Piper Pizza parlor and what he would order. At this point, Saldate interrupted by standing up and pulling out a card from his pocket, and reading Scott his Miranda rights. Mills went mute. His report says, "[I] slid my chair back away from Roger."

Saldate immediately challenged Scott. "Your story regarding Phil is a lie. There is no Phil." With that, Saldate employed a classic interrogation technique—both detectives left the room. That would give Scott a little quiet time to consider his situation, and ponder his fate.

While Scott was pondering, Detective R. Kavanagh was interviewing Louis Smith, the Chief of Security and Safety at Alhambra High School. Kavanagh was following up on Scott's claims about "Jim Waffard [sic]," the man Scott had insisted was a former classmate of Scott and "Phil." Kavanagh met with Smith at Alhambra High School at 11:25 that Sunday morning, just 50 minutes before Saldate took on Scott. Smith secured the school's yearbooks for 1964–1967 and gave them to Kavanagh, who gave them to Officer Rubio at police headquarters for "evidence." Apparently, there was no Phil matching Scott's description, and no one named Waffard or Wafland at Alhambra High.

From Alhambra High School, Kavanagh went to the Glendale apartment where Scott's mother lived, and interviewed Wilma Scott about her son. That interview started at 12:15 P.M., just when Saldate was confronting her son. Mrs. Scott repeated her earlier answers about her son's activity the previous day. "He got up at 9:00 and was inside the apartment until 11:15 . . . he did not make or receive any phone calls . . . there is no phone in the apartment . . . Jim came at 11:00 . . . with his young daughter . . . I was in my bedroom the whole time they were here . . . [no] I did not actually see Jim, Christopher or the daughter . . . I heard their voices . . . Jim attended Alhambra High with Scott . . . Christopher and Jim's daughter have been to [my] apartment at least 10 times before . . . Jim babysits Christopher . . . the mother of Christopher has been [here] only once . . . [I] do not know her well enough to express an opinion of the mother . . . [they] left the apartment at approximately 11:15 . . . they were only here for 15 minutes . . . As they were leaving, Roger called to [me], 'See you later.' . . . Jim said they would not be gone long . . . [I] assumed that meant they would be gone 3–4 hours . . . Roger said he'd be home for dinner . . . Before they got here, Roger told [me] Jim was coming over and they were going Christmas shopping."

Kavanagh asked many of the same questions other detectives had asked earlier and got the same answers about Roger going to Walgreens for a prescription, Osco to buy soap, Roger's seizure medicine, and what Roger was wearing that day. Mrs. Scott confirmed Roger's arrival yesterday at home at about 5:20 P.M. and his comment that they had pizza for lunch and he came home on the bus. Roger had not mentioned Metrocenter, or that Christopher was missing. Mrs. Scott said she "was positive that Roger did not mention those items." Roger's attitude and demeanor "was normal both in the morning and evening . . . [he] seemed calm and collected and not nervous."

Kavanagh confirmed that Roger has no car and "normally walks or takes the city bus . . . when his friend, Jim is with Roger, usually Roger will ride with him." Kavanagh asked about Roger's drinking. "He does not drink. He quit over a year ago. Roger is a self-proclaimed alcoholic. Once in a great while, Roger will go to Skipper's or The Arabian Room."

Finally, late in the interview, Mrs. Scott volunteered something about Phil. "Roger only goes to bars to play pool with Phil, a 70-year old man who lives in the apartment complex . . . Roger did not go the bars on 12/2/89. She believes this only because Roger always tells her when he goes and because 'Phil' is about to be hospitalized and cannot play pool."

Kavanagh followed up and learned that "Roger has known Jim Wafland for approximately 25 years. Waffard also is a high school friend of Roger . . . Roger sees Waffard only once every 3 months. He seems to be straight-laced . . . Roger rarely socializes with Phil . . . they play pool together but infrequently . . . Roger has not had a girlfriend for 2 or 3 years. He has no girlfriend currently . . . he was married in 1971 but divorced 3 and ½ years later . . . Roger is not a homosexual . . .

he is very much against homosexuality and often is outspoken when the subject arises . . . Roger refers to homosexuals as 'queers.'"

When Kavanagh asked about Roger's reading habits, Mrs. Scott denied that her son had or read *Playboy*, sex magazines, or pornographic magazines. She said she had a close relationship with her son and that he tells her "about personal problems he has." Kavanagh asked what Mrs. Scott's reaction would be if she heard that Roger molested a young child or a young girl. She said she "would be shocked and there is no way that Roger would do such a thing . . . he likes women his own age."

He asked about any problems Roger might have had with the law. She said the Glendale police once arrested Roger "for urinating in a bush four years ago . . . between 1965–70, he was arrested several times for DWI . . . and about 20–25 years ago, Roger and Jim Styers were arrested for siphoning gasoline." Kavanagh closed the interview by looking at the receipts Mrs. Scott kept from Roger's trip on Saturday. He saw the Walgreens receipt, a pharmacy slip, and a TV Guide book. Kavanagh described Mrs. Scott as "open and honest. She was cooperative and she relies on Roger a great deal."

Not every police supplemental report in the Milke case contains the exact time that an event occurred, although all are dated. Detective Saldate, officially designated as the "case agent," wrote four short reports. He wrote them three or four days after the events described actually occurred. He may have used notes, which he says he always destroys after he dictates his reports. And he never records his interviews. Sometimes he has no outside witnesses in the room, preferring one-on-one confrontations. On December 4, he wrote a supplement describing his "interview" with Roger Scott, which had begun on December 3. Presumably, he wrote this particular supplement the next day based on his general recollection of both what Scott said and how he interpreted it. His reports do not appear to record facts; they offer opinions about facts and interpretations of what witnesses meant to say. His report on Scott is consistent with other investigative leads; he accuses and confronts—there is little conversation.

"At that time [1258 hours] I told Roger I was involved in the victim's disappearance and for that reason I was going to read him his rights. I then removed the Miranda Rights card from my badge case and read the Miranda rights verbatim to him. Roger responded yes to understanding his rights and I began my interview." Sgt. Ontiveros assigned Detective Mills the job of repeating Scott's constitutional rights to him and securing a proper waiver of those rights from him. Another hallmark of Saldate's style was his penchant for getting down to business right away. "I first explained to Roger that he had been telling detectives all this time about a subject named Phil and I did not believe this subject existed. I told Roger that I was just getting involved in the interview because I had been talking to his friend, Jim. I then explained to Roger that I was not going to look for someone that did not exist and that I knew it was difficult on him, that he was going to have to tell me the truth. Roger then began moving his head in and up and down motion, indicating that he would."

And as was often true in Saldate's other cases, his challenge worked. "Roger then told me that I was right and that Phil did not exist. He said the only reason he made up Phil was because he did not want to get involved after Jim told him that Chris was missing." In retrospect, it is remarkable that after intense questioning by Detectives Jones, Masino, and Yost, not to mention his session with Sgt. Cusson, the only man to "break" Scott was Saldate, the man who spent the least amount time with him. Perhaps Saldate was right along—it's a matter of style.

Saldate asked Scott whether he had accompanied Chris and Jim to the mall. Yes, he had. According to Saldate, Scott admitted that "Jim parked the car outside Sears . . . the three of [us] walked into the store . . . stopped momentarily at the tools . . . before he knew it, Jim and Chris had walked away." Scott took some time " . . . looking for Jim . . . could see . . . Jim walking ahead . . . [but in the] large crowd . . . could not get to Jim before [I] lost them . . . did not see Jim again until a little bit after 3:00 P.M. . . . . Jim told [me] Chris was missing." By this admission, Scott implicated himself, at least insofar as participating in "losing" Chris. But he went on to explain, "[I] told Jim that [I] did not want to be involved because [I] had to get home to take care of mother."

Saldate's report says Scott "felt like he was not being believed only because he lied about Phil." That theme recurred several times in the unrecorded conversation with Saldate. Scott insisted, "A Phil does exist, however, he is an elderly man who lives near [my] home and has colon cancer."

No matter, Saldate told him. They already "knew that Chris was dead . . . and sooner or later [you will] have to tell me the truth." At this point in the investigation, no one knew anything of the kind. Most officers were hoping to find Christopher alive, but Saldate knew that telling Scott that he "knew" the boy was dead would worry an already fragile suspect. So, Saldate expanded his version of the truth. "I told him that I strongly believed that he was involved in Chris's disappearance . . . Roger continued to deny it . . . We continued to talk and I told Roger that sooner or later, he would have to tell me what occurred."

In an obvious ploy to gain the suspect's favor, a technique often upheld in court cases, Saldate told Scott, "[You are] not a cold blooded killer. . . ." Saldate's report reflects his signature ability to move any suspect to truthfulness: "I was sure his conscience would not let him continue to lie." Saldate's interview of Scott began at 12:58 P.M. Forty minutes later, Saldate played another proven interrogation card. "I told Roger that I was going to leave him alone in the room for several minutes and that I would be back to continue our conversation."

At 1:52 P.M., Saldate returned to the interview room, "*by myself,*" and continued the interview." This was another confidence-gaining technique—clear the room of everyone except the interrogator and the accused. "Roger and I spoke about his past and his current responsibilities with his mother . . . He also had other responsibilities with neighbors that he also took care of . . . We spoke about . . . his unemployment . . . [how] it [is] important for you to tell me the truth. . . ."

Scott kept denying any involvement in Chris's disappearance, insisting the only reason Saldate thought otherwise was his initial lie about Phil. Saldate was having none of that. "I pointed out to Roger that Jim had told security persons initially he and Chris were by themselves and that did not correspond with his story about telling Jim that he did not want to get involved until 3:00 P.M." Scott couldn't explain that. Maybe Jim was trying to protect him, Scott said. Saldate played a card he'd already used. "I told Roger that we all knew that Chris was already dead and that finding his body was not as important as him telling me the truth."

Saldate's report documents how effective his strategy was. "At approximately 3:05 P.M., I told him 'I will again leave [you] alone with [your] conscience,' but that I would return in a few minutes to continue our conversation. I told him that when I returned we were only going to talk about the truth about what actually happened and that I was not going to listen to any more of his denials, which I knew were lies. Roger then moved his head in an up and down motion indicating that he understood."

Saldate came back at 3:35 P.M. Scott asked for cigarettes and a pop. "In a few minutes," Saldate answered. "But it is necessary for [you] to tell me the entire truth . . . I was not going to tolerate [you] telling me any more lies . . . [you] know where Chris's body was . . . the least [you] can do is tell us so we can recover it. Roger then began moving his head from side to side, indicating no, but would not respond aloud. I told Roger that we were going to send officers to his home to '*speak with his mother.*' He immediately responded that it would kill her. I told him it was going to be necessary since he continued to lie about his involvement and we needed to verify certain things. Roger again asked for a pack of cigarettes and a Mountain Dew, which was obtained for him. I continued to tell Roger that I was there to get the truth and Roger finally told me that he would tell me everything I wanted to know."

Saldate had him. "I asked Roger if he knew where the body of Chris was at and he said he did. I asked him if Chris was dead and Roger responded, 'Jim killed him.' Roger then told me that he didn't think Jim was going to do it and that he had talked him out of it several times. Roger then said that Chris's body was in a wash in the area of 99 Avenue and Jomax Road."

This gave Saldate the location, but he wanted more. He wanted motive, as well as opportunity. So he pressed Roger on *why* this murder occurred. "Roger then told me that Jim had never liked the kid . . . [but] he didn't think that Jim would go through with it." Saldate dug in. "He said that he and Jim had gone out on several occasions with the intentions of killing the kid . . . he would always talk Jim out of it . . . there were too many people around."

Returning to *why* things happened, Saldate queried Scott about the original trip to Metrocenter. "Chris never made it to the Metro Center . . . after Jim killed Chris, [we] did go to Metro Center to create an alibi . . . [I did not want to] build a story but [I] went along with Jim's story because . . . Jim knew more about that kind of stuff."

Saldate asked how they found the place to kill Chris. "[We] drove to a location which [we] had been at before and had pre-selected as the location where [we] were going to kill Chris . . . 99 Avenue and Jomax Road, in a wash that Jim picked out." Probably thinking he had little to lose, "Roger said that he would direct us to that location and would show us where the wash was."

How did Jim do it, Saldate asked. "He shot him . . . Jim parked his car along the roadway on 99th Avenue . . . Jim and Chris got out of the car and walked back into the wash . . . Jim had previously told him that he was going to leave him near the road because he wanted him found right away."

And then, "I drove away, then made a U-turn, and came back . . . Jim was supposed to be waiting by the roadside . . . [I] did not hear any shots and did not see Jim . . . [I] continued past the wash, waited just north of the wash, but again did not see Jim . . . all the windows of the car were down but still could not hear any shots . . . made another U-turn, headed southbound and pulled along the roadway at the opening of the wash . . . began to hit my horn very lightly . . . did not want to attract attention . . . still did not hear any shots . . . did not see Jim . . . drove further south, got out of the car and began to walk towards the wash . . . still not hearing or seeing anything . . . changed my mind . . . walked back to the car . . . made another U-turn . . . headed northbound . . . began to use [my] horn very lightly . . . still did not see anything . . . parked [my] vehicle again northbound across the road . . . headed into the northern section of the wash . . . [I] heard three shots."

Saldate was on a roll; he pressed Scott for incriminating details. "A short time later, [I] saw Jim walking out of the wash on the south side towards the roadway . . . [I] walked back to the car, made another U-turn . . . headed southbound . . . saw Jim with his thumb out as if he was hitchhiking . . . picked up Jim . . . Jim immediately told [me] he had shot Chris three times in the head."

In law enforcement, a confession is the Holy Grail. Getting a confession from a co-conspirator is almost as good. And Roger was coming around to that reality. Saldate's report confirms the connection between shooter and co-conspirator. "Roger then became concerned and said he knew that he was in serious trouble but he was not going to be held responsible for killing Chris because he did not do that." Trying to refocus Scott, Saldate asked about the gun. "Roger paused and then said that Jim gave him the gun to get rid of it, and that he had not. He said that Jim gave him the gun initially, and told him to get rid of it but that Jim also told him that he could keep it if he wanted it. Roger said he kept the gun; it was in his closet at his home."

At this point, Saldate had a confession implicating Scott in Styers' murder of Chris *and* a motive for Styers. But he did not have a motive for Roger's help. So he pressed and Scott told Saldate about his application for Social Security. "They refused me," he said. He had gone to an attorney "who he thought was free, but who later tried to charge him $250.00 before he would file a case. Roger said he only went with Jim because he needed the $250.00 to file the Social Security case. Roger then mentioned that Chris was supposed to have a $5000 life insurance policy and that Jim told him that he would give him $250.00 if he was to help him." Now he had Roger's motive as well.

Saldate asked Roger to show them where the body was. He agreed. Saldate and Detective Mills took Roger from the downtown Phoenix police station to Styers' pre-selected murder site—99th Avenue and Jomax Road. They took Interstate 17, the quickest route, and got there in a little under 35 minutes. The ride gave Saldate a little more time to talk with Scott, without the impediments of tape or notes. Just after leaving the main station, Roger asked "if he could tell us some more while he was in the car, or would we rather wait until we returned." Saldate told him to talk away. Roger volunteered that the detectives "probably felt that he and Jim were the only bad ones in this situation." Were there others in the situation? Scott said he could "tell [them] something about the baby's mother. Roger went on and said that the baby's mother knew all about the killing . . . the only reason that Chris was killed was because the mother wanted it done." This would turn out to be a hotly disputed statement.

Scott expanded his "other people" offering. "Jim came up to [me] several weeks ago and told [me] about this plan to kill Chris . . . Jim told [me] Debbie (Chris's mother) had talked to him about doing it . . . Jim was afraid of doing it by himself . . . Jim asked [me] if [I] would go with him . . . [I] agreed. At first Debbie was not to know that [I] knew anything about it . . . or that [I] was going to accompany Jim when he did it. Later, however, [I] did meet with Debbie on several occasions along with Jim . . . they talked about what they were going to do . . . Jim told [me] that Debbie was pressuring him into doing it quick . . . Jim got upset . . . he told Debbie why didn't she do it . . . Debbie refused . . . Jim told [me] that Debbie did go out with him one time . . . they were going to kill Chris . . . there were too many people . . . they decided to go back home."

At this point in the drive from the main police station downtown to the place where Scott said the body was, they decided to stop at the Phoenix Police Cactus Park Briefing Station to get gas. While there, Saldate called Sgt. Ontiveros and "informed him about the mother's involvement . . . he told me that she was now in Florence." They finished the drive to 99th Avenue and Jomax and as they neared 99th Avenue, they passed a dip in the roadway and a wash; Scott told them that they "just passed it." They made a U-turn and returned to the wash. Saldate summarized the dialogue: "Scott pointed out that Chris should be on the west side of the roadway in the wash not too far beyond the roadway. Roger said Jim wanted to leave him not too far from the roadway so he would be found in just a couple of days and they could collect the insurance money as soon as possible."

Within minutes after reaching what would soon become an active crime scene, two other detectives arrived. Saldate, Detective Mills, Scott, and the two new men walked "down the wash westbound carefully looking for footprints, and mainly staying on the rocky surfaces. We then observed Chris's body lying in the center of the wash. Chris was 'obviously' dead. The area was secured by other officers."

Mills and Saldate left the site, intending to take Scott back to the main station. But Scott was still talking. Saldate was still interpreting. "Jim had taken off a pair of shoes that he supposedly used when he walked Chris into the wash . . . he gave [me] the shoes to get rid of when we arrived at Sears before making the missing person report . . . [I] left the shoes in a planter near where [we] parked the vehicle." With this new information, Saldate changed direction. Instead of going back to the police station, he told Mills to take them to Metrocenter. Once there, Scott showed them where he'd hidden the shoes. They found them "exactly where Roger pointed out. The shoes were retained and identified by Roger as being the same shoes he had placed there." It got better. Scott also told them, "After the shooting, when we were headed to the Metro Center, Jim removed the 6 bullets from the gun he had used to kill Chris and threw them in the desert area on the south side of Union Hills. Jim later gave him the gun, and 6 new bullets which he was either to keep or destroy."

Saldate closed his report by noting that "[a] taped interview of Roger was completed after we returned to the main station. This taped interview was attended by Det. Mills, while I was enroute to Florence to interview the mother." Mills' taped interview was secured without Saldate's aid in guiding Scott's testimony. That makes it important at several levels. It was recorded on audio tape—there is a transcript—and the transcript qualifies as a written waiver of Scott's Fifth Amendment rights.

Mills asked, "You remember sometime around noon or so when Detective Saldate read you your Miranda warnings, right?"

"Yes."

"Okay and those rights were you have the right to remain silent, anything you say can be used against you in a court of law, you have the right to the presence of an attorney to assist you prior to questioning, and to be with you during questioning if you so desire, if you can't afford an attorney you have the right to have an attorney appointed for you prior to questioning, and you understand those rights."

"Yes."

"Were those the same rights that Armando read to you earlier today?"

"Yes."

This Q & A has the force of law—an explicit waiver by Scott of each right, each of which he said he understood. This makes his confession, absent any coercion on the part of the officer taking it, admissible in evidence. The remainder of his taped interview is largely an effort to document in writing what Saldate learned orally, and unwitnessed. Detective Mills documented the following elements of Saldate's earlier off-the-record interviews: "No physical force . . . no one beat me . . . no coercion . . . yes sodas given . . . yes bathroom breaks . . . yes we ate hamburgers together. . . ."

Detective Mills asked Scott to "lay out what you told us earlier." Scott answered, "Jim and I talked about it a few times . . . I was in the car . . . I heard the gun go off three times . . . I picked Jim up . . . then he told security at Metrocenter Chris was lost . . . I'm tired of lying my way out of it . . . created an imaginary friend named Phil . . . after further conversation . . . I admitted that I did know . . . tried to help the detectives by telling the location of the child, the incident, the way it occurred, the route back to Metrocenter, the whole made-up story . . . where the tennis shoes were throw out . . . admitting where the gun had been hidden. . . ."

Mills also asked several questions about "who first approached you about doing away with Christopher." Scott answered, "Jim approached me . . . several weeks ago . . . the kid has to go . . . I just can't stand [him] any more . . . I can't stand him. . . ."

He asked about talking face to face with Debbie. Scott said, "Yes, um, within the last week it was brought up at least twice from her. . . ."

"What did she tell you?"

"That she just had to get away from him and she just wasn't cut out to be a mother and that she wanted us to take care of it."

"How did she say she wanted it done?"

"She just said that she wanted Jim and I to handle it after Jim had purchased the one gun, uh, later on I believe it was 3, 4, days later he purchased another two guns. At first it was planned to be Christopher and his father, but his father went to Texas, but they decided they couldn't wait, that Christopher would just have to disappear . . . that's the idea. . . ."

"Okay, and there was some money involved in this, too, right, in the form of an insurance policy?"

"Yes, of $5000, which would help them to pay off debts that they needed to take care of, their money situation had got out of hand and they offered me money. . . ."

"Okay, how much did they offer you?"

"It was, at first it was $150 . . . then . . . as it went on . . . they wanted to get rid of Chris all the more, it went up to $250."

"Okay, what was your part to be, what were you going to do for that $250?"

"Drive the car."

Mills asked Scott to confirm that Jim had told him "that he had taken Christopher out to 7th Street and Paradise or something like that?"

"Yes . . . they had told me . . . Jimmy said that, uh, he and Debbie were out by 7th Street and Beardsley to start with and then it was Paradise Road and 7th street. . . ."

Scott confirmed that he also had gone to 7th Street and Paradise Road with Jim. Scott said, "Yes . . . he [Jim] was thinking of doing it then but he heard a voice off ahead of him in the dark . . . and it turned out to be a National Guard [unit] out there . . . don't know if they were on maneuvers, or what, but anyway he forgot about it then."

Mills, looking for premeditation evidence, asked what Scott knew *before* he went with Jim on Saturday morning, based on Jim's telephone call to him at 10:30 that morning. Scott answered, "Yes, it had to be done . . . Yes, I was aware it was going to be done . . . on Saturday. . . ."

He asked Scott for details about what happened when he, Jim, and Christopher got out of the car at the wash. Specifically, Mills asked:

"What did he [Jim] tell Christopher about getting out?"

"Let's go look around for snakes and he had some binoculars and uh, let Chris carry the binoculars and look through them to keep his interest. . . ."

"How were they spaced? You know one right after the other or was it . . ."

"Bang, bang, bang."

Mills wanted to know what Jim said when he came out of the wash. Scott answered, "Exact words I can't say, but more or less, well that's done, and let's get out of here."

Mills extracted specific details about the shoes he hid for Styers at Metrocenter, hiding Jim's gun on the bus ride back to his house from Metrocenter, the specifics of the gun, and its exact location at his house. Scott confirmed "Jim and Debbie" had not paid him yet. He signed a consent form to search his house. He said he was there when Jim bought one of the three guns he owned. ". . . The guns were purchased at gun shows . . . out in Mesa . . . they sell guns across the counter like you would go into a Circle K and buy a roll of Certs. You just put the money down and take it with you . . . but that was the first gun . . . not the one at my house."

Mills asked Scott how he was doing with his asthma and about his medications. "I feel better now that I've told you the story . . . I know the consequences but still I do feel better, it's easier on me." After signing the consent to search his house, and confirming on tape that the search was "fully authorized," Mills closed the taped interview.

"Okay, do you have any questions you want to ask me?"

"No, looks like it's been covered."

"Okay. I'll go ahead and shut the tape off again now. It's now 9:17 P.M. by my watch. It's still December 3, 1989."

The transcript confirms the words spoken, but more importantly, it captures the remarkable aplomb of two grown men about to murder a four-year old boy by deceiving him into a walk out into the desert to look for snakes, before he could go see Santa Claus at the mall. That transcript also displays how slavish Scott was to Styers' sinister plan, which he apparently carried out with the coolness of a serial killer. That Styers could, at arm's-length, fire three high-velocity rounds into the back of the head of a boy he'd cared for every day for months is numbing to think about and impossible to imagine. That his motive for such an atrocious, barbaric act was to give him a chance of romance with a young woman who'd rebuffed his advances is almost preposterous. But if Scott is to be believed, this is how and why Christopher Milke was murdered. That singular event, Scott confessing his role, colored everything else in the Phoenix Police Department's investigation. Child murder is always horrific. This one more so because Styers wanted Chris's body found quickly so the insurance money would be quickly paid. It was beyond the pale—below any recognized standard of human decency. And it colored every facet of how Saldate would deal with Debra Milke. From what he saw about the depraved way Chris was murdered, and his grotesque fetal position in the desert wash, Saldate's blood must have boiled. From what Scott told him about Chris's mother, he must have seen her as the worst kind of depraved murderer. All he needed now to cap his career, and start his already announced retirement, was to get her to confess. He knew he could, he'd done it before.

—

ON SUNDAY AFTERNOON AT 2:00 P.M. Detective Judy Townsend went back to the Milke apartment and learned that Debra had just left—driving down to Florence to see her father. But John Ciulla and Patrick Murphy were there. Ciulla said he'd spent the night in the apartment waiting to hear about Christopher. He lived next door and said that he "partyed [sic] two or three times a week with them and knew them very well." He said both Jim and Debra were "heavy drinkers." He and his wife "babysat Christopher many times when she went out with Jim and Roger." Ciulla told Detective Townsend that Roger "would come over to the apartment two-three times per week and also went to the VA Hospital with Jim for treatments. Both men had been in the Marines together back in Vietnam. Roger was a heavy drinker and would get obnoxious sometimes during his visits and Jim would transport him back home."

Detective Townsend questioned Ciulla about guns. He told her he didn't know if Jim and Roger went hunting together, but "Jim had a gun." Ciulla had seen him wearing the gun and asked him why he had it. Jim said because he "felt like wearing it." This was apparently a recent thing. The detective asked whether Jim and Debra were living together as "boyfriend/girlfriend." He said, "Jim wanted it that way, but Debroah [sic] didn't. She had told him that Jim tried to get into bed with her, but she hit him and told him to get out. Jim also told

John if he couldn't have her he was going to go to Wyoming to be with Deborah's sister. He was trying to save $300 to get his car fixed (clutch out) so he could move to Wyoming in January because Deborah told him she was moving closer to her job." John also said that Jim was about $900 in the hole already this month and was cashing bad checks. John thought Christopher was a "real good kid . . . and always good at his house."

The other neighbor, Patrick Murphy, said he "also partyed [sic] with [Debra and Jim] and knew them well." He agreed with what John had already said. Just then, Detective Townsend got a call from Lt. Polk who told her to leave the apartment. "Jim has been released," he said. She left, "securing the door." What she didn't know was that Detective Mills would arrive just minutes later.

Because Jim Styers had said all he was going to say and had cooperated with the search mission, the detectives decided to let him go home. They didn't have Scott's confession yet. But Debra's car had been impounded. So, Detective Mills was tasked with the job of getting Styers out of police headquarters and back to his apartment in North Central Phoenix—7734 N. 12th Street, Apartment No. 5. First, he had to be photographed. Mills found "Jim sitting in an interview room awaiting his ride." Jim asked, "Why am I being photographed?" Mills explained that it was because "we didn't have photographs of his clothing that we may need to show at locations" where he, Roger, and Christopher went the preceding day. Jim consented and volunteered that he "wore a baseball cap which was in the trunk of the car belonging to Debbie Milke." Styers also said, "Christopher was wearing a blue plastic motorcycle helmet." Once the photos were taken, Styers asked whether Mills "still had the form for him to sign authorizing a search of Debra's Toyota." Mills said yes. Styers volunteered to sign it. So, Mills retrieved it "at 2:21 P.M. on the 3rd, [and] Jim signed it and [he] witnessed his signature on that form." Mills escorted Jim out of the building where they found "numerous news reporters and camera men." Jim asked, "Why is the news media here?" Mills said, "They probably want to talk to [you]." Jim asked Mills what he should say. Mills said he "could say anything he wished to." So, Jim consented to an interview, "by numerous members of the news media."

On the drive from the police station in downtown Phoenix to Jim's apartment in North Phoenix, Mills asked Styers for "all the clothing you were wearing yesterday, including his shoes." He explained that when "the suspects are caught in this matter, they may point to [you] as a suspect and if we have your shoes and we were able to find footprints at the scene where Christopher was found, we could eliminate [you] from being a suspect." When they got to Styers' apartment, he changed clothes, and stuffed yesterday's clothes "in a green plastic garbage bag" and gave it to Mills. Mills took the clothes back to police headquarters as "evidence."

It was only after returning to his office, around 3:00 P.M., that Detective Mills learned that Detective Saldate had obtained a confession from Roger and that Roger was willing to take them to the crime scene.

———

STYERS LEFT HIS APARTMENT ABOUT 10:30 on Saturday morning. He reported Christopher missing at 2:30 that afternoon. He spent the next 24 hours either at Metrocenter or at the police station telling his story—over and over again. But he was not officially in custody. He was there to "help find Christopher." Accordingly, when Detective Mills brought him back home at about 2:30 P.M. on Sunday, he likely felt relieved. Debra was gone by then—down to her father's house in Florence. And Roger was still at the police station, or so Styers thought. He didn't know that Saldate had extracted a confession from Scott or that Saldate would soon confront Debra at the Pinal County Sheriff's Station in Florence. And he didn't know that shortly before 5 P.M. officers of the "Special Assignments Unit" had his apartment under surveillance.

Officers T.D. Carey, Janet Dubina, Roy Jacobson, B.T. Soza, and Sgt. M. Sheahan were in place on the street outside the apartment, armed, and waiting for orders. At 5:17 P.M., Lt. Polk gave the order. He then told Styers that they "had probable cause [to pick him] up for homicide." They arrested Styers "without incident," and placed him in Officer Carey's vehicle for transport back down to police headquarters, in handcuffs.

His ex-wife, Karen Kay Styers, had come to the apartment after Detective Mills left and a little before the arrest team got there.

When the officers cuffed Styers and inserted him into the cage in the back of Carey's police car, Styers asked Carey, "If [you] found Christopher . . . I hope you did, but I'm not sure if I want to know, but if you did he's probably dead." Moments later, Sgt. Sheahan approached the vehicle and told Carey to take him to GIB (General Investigations Bureau). Styers looked at Sgt. Sheahan and asked, "Did you find Christopher?" Neither Carey nor Sheahan answered. Neither had to. Styers already knew.

His ex-wife watched him leave, but before she left herself, a detective showed up wanting to talk to her. She told Detective Dennis Olson she'd been there when they arrested Jim. She was happy to answer his questions. She explained that Styers had called her about one o'clock that afternoon from the police station. He was very tired and told her he hadn't been to sleep since five o'clock Saturday morning. He told her about Chris going missing on Saturday and that he'd been helping the police to find him for more than 24 hours. Later that same afternoon, about four o'clock, he called again, and asked her to come over to his apartment. He said he was calling from a neighbor's apartment because "the police had his phone bugged or taped or something like that." He wanted to go to church, so she agreed to come over and take him to Valley Cathedral Church. When she got to his apartment, Jim was on his phone, inside the apartment, "talking to Debbie's sister in Wyoming. Jim was explaining about the disappearance of Chris."

"About this time," Karen said to Detective Olson, "a neighbor came over and said Jim was on TV. Jim hung up and they turned on the TV to watch his interview." Then Jim said he wanted to go to the bathroom and she should wait in the car. She went outside and waited in her car. "When Jim came out of the apartment and got in her vehicle, a car pulled up behind them and blocked them in. Several people jumped out with guns drawn and said they were police officers. These police officers arrested Jim and took him away to the police station." Olson asked what Jim said to her when he was arrested. She answered, "Get an attorney through the church."

Detective Olson continued the interview for another half-hour. Karen told him that Jim had been coming to church "a couple of times a week." He was active in the church "as an usher . . . he also taught the 'junior bible quiz' class on Sunday and Wednesday nights." As far as she knew, Jim had never held a job after the Marines. She had never met Debbie, but had talked to her on the phone a few times. She had met Chris because "Jim brought him to church . . ." and she did know Chris was going through the "terrible fours." She explained that "about four months ago, while they were in church, Chris caused a disturbance inside the class. Chris was disciplined by having to stand in the corner. Jim was upset with Chris. Chris was also upset with Jim and spoke back to him." Detective Olson probed to find out more about this incident, and why it stuck out in her memory. She wasn't sure but said that this didn't seem to be unusual behavior for a four-year old. She said, "It was just being a little boy."

Detective Olson also asked about Roger Scott. He was Jim's only friend that she could think of. They'd gone to high school together, she said. But when she married Jim, he lost contact with Roger for "several years." When Styers called her earlier, he had said "something about Roger but she was not clear on what he said." But she thought it was about "Roger going to a drug store to get something for his mother, but they couldn't find it, so they went to a pizza parlor and then Jim dropped Roger off and took Chris to Metrocenter to see Santa Claus."

Olson asked several questions about her relationship with Styers: "Married Jim on either June 3rd or 4th, 1978 in Phoenix . . . she'd known him for one year . . . met him at a disco bar called The Night Life . . . she knew he'd had an accident in the military . . . head injury . . . he lost consciousness for approximately 3 months and had to learn everything all over again . . . how to talk, eat, and how to use his arms and legs . . . he was discharged from the military in 1976 or 1978 . . . she knew about his seizures . . . he took medication for that . . . phenobarbital, dylatin [sic], and some other type too . . . on disability from the VA Hospital . . . he is untrainable and cannot work . . . married to another woman but divorced . . . two kids—Janet and Susan by his first wife . . . happy marriage at first . . . but he began seeing other girls and decided he did not love her anymore . . . they separated after two and a half years of marriage . . . never got a divorce . . . separated for the last 8 years."

With Jim's background out of the way, Detective Olson asked questions about Styers' current situation. Karen Styers explained that Styers had another child from a previous girlfriend, named Wendy, and that Wendy stayed there at the apartment "quite a bit." Jim, she said, wasn't "depressed and did not resent taking care of Wendy." She hadn't been to Jim's apartment for two or three months. On the last occasion, she brought him some medication.

At the end of the interview, Detective Olson asked whether Styers had ever assaulted her or any of her kids in any way. "[We] never had a domestic violence incident. Jim never assaulted [me], or hit [me] or my kids." She said he did not appear to be depressed recently and did not express any type of resentment toward anyone. She said she did not think that Jim "was in any way responsible for the disappearance of Chris."

3

SALDATE CONFRONTS MILKE

*C*ONFESSIONS ARE TRENCH WARFARE FOR detectives. When they predetermine the suspect's guilt, they ignore the core American presumption of innocence. The combination can be lethal to both the suspect and any hope of a just and fair trial. Some suspects become cannon fodder as seen through the tunnel vision of a cop who knows guilt even before he sees it. Treating suspects as little more than detritus to be broken in custodial interrogation dates back to at least the Middle Ages. Trial by torture and canonical courts of "inquisition" relied heavily on forced, involuntary confessions. For some modern detectives, the only change is substituting psychological tricks for physical torture.

A voluntary confession, fairly and intelligently given, can blow up a case, or the lawyer that offers it in evidence. Sometimes the cop that takes the confession implodes. Murder trials always fascinate the public. The murder trial that offers the jurors a confession is the ideal civic solution. The perpetrator takes responsibility, and the public sleeps soundly. But murder trials rarely examine *how* the confession came into being. Was it the product of the suspect's guilty mind, or of the interrogator's will and perseverance?

Debra Jean Milke was about to face Detective Armando Saldate. Would she profess her innocence? Would he presume it? Or would she be *saldateed*—a made-up verb that aptly describes what was about to happen in Florence, Arizona on Sunday, December 3, 1989. A contest of wills was about to begin. It would test Debra Milke, the suspect. And it would define Armando Saldate, the interrogator. She was eager to talk and he to listen. And not just to what she said; he would divine what she meant.

In his "paraphrased account" of Milke's confession, Saldate said, "On 12-3-89, at approximately 7:45 P.M., the Phoenix Police helicopter landed at Pinal County Hospital with me as a passenger. I was then transported by Pinal County Sheriffs to the County Jail where Debra had been taken to be interviewed." He was fresh off a big victory—he'd broken Roger Scott (confession), and his colleagues had James Styers under lock and key (arrested and booked). The missing piece was the woman he believed to be an active co-conspirator in Christopher's murder—his mother, Debbie Milke.

Saldate was none too happy about flying in a helicopter. His preference would have been to drive the 70 miles from Phoenix to Florence. But time was of the essence—word would leak out. It always did. By the time the ten o'clock news came on in a couple hours, Arizona might know about the discovery of Christopher's body, and that Roger Scott and James Styers were under arrest, charged with murder. If Debra learned that, she might do something fearsome to a police detective—she might lawyer up. Saldate wanted a confession and he knew how to get it. But he knew he had to do it quickly and privately. Time and silence were his enemies and Milke was his target.

Saldate's travel arrangements and a police plan of attack were in place. Pinal County Deputy Sheriff Robert Soules had his orders. At 5:00 P.M., dispatch advised him to contact Sgt. Ontiveros of the Phoenix Police Department. Ontiveros told him two detectives were en route to Florence by car, and a third would come by helicopter. "Could he locate a Debra Milke in the Florence area at her father's house? Her father was a Richard Sadeik; he had a rural route address." Soules said he knew Mr. Sadeik, "and where he lived at." Sgt. Ontiveros told Soules about "the nature of the offense" and told him not "to alert her to the reason they needed to talk to her." Thirty minutes later, Soules arrived at the Sadeik trailer; he talked to Mrs. Sadeik. She said Debra was there and went to get her from a bedroom. Soules told Debra that the Phoenix police needed to talk to her. He offered to "escort her to the station, or if she liked, a family member could drive her. Debra had a friend of the family, Janet Frobe, deliver her into our office." He followed them in. They arrived at 5:44 P.M., as "Phoenix P.D. was pulling in." Soules reported that Debra and her friend "were taken to the Doctor's office in the main jail to await the Phoenix police department detectives who needed to talk to her."

The two officers Soules referred to in his report were Detectives Dimodica and Hamrick. In his report, Dimodica confirmed that he and Ernie Hamrick drove to the Pinal County Jail. Lt. Jahn told them to "stand by at the jail facility until Detective Armando Saldate interviewed Debra Milke, who was waiting at the jail facility." Once Saldate arrived, Dimodica and Hamrick were to return immediately to the Sadeik trailer, "for the purpose of contacting family members . . . and notifying them of the death of Christopher Milke." Soules' instruction was clear—do not interact with the family until Saldate had talked to Debra Milke.

As soon as he walked into the Pinal County Jail facility, Saldate learned that Debra Milke was waiting for him in the medical treatment section of the jail. She was in a small room with "her aunt." Saldate went into the small room and asked the aunt, later identified as Janet Frobe, to leave the room. Debra, thinking he was there to give her new information about the search for Chris, asked, "Who are you?" He identified himself and said, "I'm investigating your son's disappearance."

Saldate's written report is remarkable for the transparency of his language. It was "a *paraphrased account* of her interview." Later, he would call it her *confession*. He maintained that position for years. She denied it for years. But in 1989, by any name, it ultimately proved to be the only evidence against her. There was no physical or forensic evidence to implicate her. Consequently, only Saldate and Milke can ever know what was said in that small, windowless office—even today. The conversation took less than 30 minutes. It was unwitnessed, unrecorded, and unverified. Saldate later said he took notes, but destroyed them three days later. The questions asked and the answers given are not in the paraphrased account. And it was not written until December 6, 1989 at 8:40 A.M. The record says Clerk #A1724 typed it at the GIB facility in Phoenix police headquarters. Saldate's recollections became the only evidence against her. Her recollections became her only defense. There was no other substantive evidence directly implicating her in this or any other crime.

Saldate's paraphrased account states: "At approximately 1953 hrs, I explained to Debra that her son Chris had been found in a desert area and that he had been found shot to death. Debra immediately began to yell 'what, what.' She then started to scream and make noises as if she was crying, but no tears were visible." These three sentences, written mostly in first-person point of view, are illustrative of the whole seven-page, single-spaced document. It is a curious mixture of his opinion of her, and his version of what he says she said. None of his questions is presented as actual dialogue. Her alleged answers to his questions are presented as actual fact. There are only four specific quotes allegedly using her own words, none of which incriminates her. Two quotes implicate Styers. Her emotional state, if he is to be believed, is evident in those first three lines. She burst into tears and screamed at the first two things he said—your son is dead and you are under arrest for murder. Apparently, he did not believe her tears to be genuine (as if she was crying), or her screams meaningful (an observation he may or may not have actually made).

Saldate claims that he said "I would not tolerate her crying. . . ." She became very excited, he says, and "asked why I was doing this." Because, he said, "[You] had been implicated in the murder by Jim, and Roger." In retrospect, it seems unthinkable that after telling her she was under arrest, he would try to silence her, but he did. "I then told her to be quiet, while I removed a rights card from my identification badge case, and read her her Miranda rights verbatim from the card." This clear legal requirement had been the law in America since 1966, because of another Phoenix police officer's interrogation of a suspect in the now famous *Miranda* case. But instead of getting a clear waiver of those rights, in writing, or at the least as recorded on audio or video tape, Saldate relied on his ability to read her physical reactions. "I asked Debra if she understood her rights and she moved her head in an up and down motion indicating yes." Saldate claims, as though it was an afterthought rather than a mandated process under the Fifth Amendment, that he repeated the question, "and she responded, yes." Since he allowed no witness in the room, didn't record it, and because he destroyed his notes, no one can say with certainty what he asked or even whether she answered.

His account, if truthful, paints a picture of how he treated her, but minimizes her mental, emotional, or rational state. Crying, screaming, acting emotional, or refusing to tell the truth were forbidden conduct. His arrogance was manifest. He insisted that "he would not tolerate that type of activity from her." He warned her, "[I]t was very important that she tell the truth." When she asked what he needed to know, he gratuitously said, "Tell me the truth *about [your] involvement* . . . I won't tolerate any lies . . . I don't want [you] to minimize *your involvement. . . .*" His words confirm his mindset—he believed she was involved before he even asked her whether she was. His paraphrased account does not reflect whether she answered him, but nonetheless concludes: "She kept moving her head in an up and down motion as if she was agreeing with me." As if?

Saldate's account condemns Milke for feeling sorry for her son, because of what he had to go through—adding that she told Styers that Chris would probably grow up just like his father, and not be any good. She tried crying again, he said, but again there were no tears. "You're not telling me the truth," he said. Since he did not record the interrogation, his tone of voice is unavailable. But, his version, the words he puts into her mouth, and the words he says he used to get her to confess in less than 30 minutes clarifies two things: one, his presence as an authority figure, and two, her reaction as a bewildered and deeply distressed mother. "I wouldn't tolerate that because I was not here talking to her by accident. I told her I already knew the truth from her standpoint." The account is presented as if the chronological flow of opinions and observations followed on the same timeline as the actual question and answer sequencing. Since he "already knew what had happened, this was her opportunity to tell me the truth." Her response, he said, was, "Look, I just didn't want him to grow up like his father, I'm not a crazy person, I'm not an animal, and I just didn't want him to grow up like that."

According to Saldate, she gave him a fairly detailed social history beginning in high school. He says she talked about her popularity, likeability, friendliness, self-esteem, positive outlook, and love of life. But, he says, she also talked about meeting her ex-husband, Mark, a man involved with drugs and alcohol. Mark, according to Saldate's account, was always putting her down, always telling her she was no good and would never amount to anything. Saldate says she told him Mark was incarcerated several times during their marriage.

A good part of what he says Debra said reads more like a therapy session than a police confession: difficulty with sex—it is a dirty thing to do—Mark was into kinky stuff—into pornographic material—I was taking birth control pills—I knew before Chris I wouldn't be a good mother—I never wanted children—my pregnancy was a mistake—I had tests to ensure Chris was not deformed—I considered an abortion—divorced Mark but he got visitation rights—Mark was always in and out of jails—after visits Chris would act just like Mark. Since these observations on Saldate's part appear on page three of his seven-page report, it is safe to assume this all happened in the first 10 minutes of his 30-minute session with her.

Saldate wrote about Debra's feelings during the session. She "felt very bad about this . . . she had an empty feeling . . . she just wanted God to take care of him . . . she was very scared about what was going to happen. . . ." Her consistent denials that any of this ever happened are a matter of record, as is Saldate's insistence that she "opened up to him." That may explain why she, on page three of the report, allegedly told Saldate the truth that he said he already knew. At first, "she could not tell Jim that she wanted her son Chris killed because it was very hard for her. Finally, she told him it would be better for her son to die than to grow up like her husband, his father. She said Jim agreed to help her and that the only agreement they made was that he would not tell her the specifics about the killing."

Since she had not yet volunteered anything about her real motive, Saldate fed her what Scott fed him—killing for insurance money.

Wasn't there "some insurance she may have had on him"? She said no. Her father had insurance, she didn't. But Saldate explained, "It had been my understanding that Jim and Roger were to receive a partial payment of the $5000 policy which she had on her child's life." She denied that.

Saldate asked if "she, Jim, and Roger talked about how they were going to kill Chris and she told me they had . . . several times with Jim . . . but only one time with Jim and Roger. She did go out with Jim once and Jim was going to do it—kill him—but something happened." She said, according to Saldate, "the plan was for Jim to do it, then go to Metrocenter, and claim that Chris was lost." She never knew, according to Saldate, what "method Jim was going to use to do it."

The last three pages of Saldate's account are consistent with what Scott told Saldate earlier in the day. The only differences are Saldate's take on Debra's feelings about her son, her relationship with Styers, her ex-husband's criminal history, and what happened in the month before the murder. Saldate said she told him about lying in bed next to her son, hearing her son say he missed his father, wanting to know when he'd be home, and feeling disappointed that Jim "had not done it yet." She denied getting angry with Jim, Saldate said, but was disappointed because "the longer he waited, the more influence her ex-husband could put on Chris."

Saldate even managed to get her to talk about God, heaven, hell, and Chris, in that order of priority. That was a remarkable achievement for a man who had only met this woman a few minutes earlier, and after telling her she was under arrest for killing her son. "God," he says she said, "was coming down and going to take him to Heaven. She would see him later in Heaven. When Jim called her in the afternoon on Saturday saying he was at the mall, she immediately realized that he had done it and that her son was now dead." When she hung up the phone, according to Saldate, "she immediately prayed to God to take care of Chris and that she would not be mad at him if he sent her to Hell." Just to make sure that Saldate was listening, he says she also said, "She also prayed to God to do something that would never allow her to have any more kids . . . she was not crazy and hoped no one would think she was . . . she loved her son. . . ."

Debra was worried about her family, he said. "Maybe they would disown her," he said she said. But Saldate, besides his role as interrogator and therapist, also assumed the role of Father Confessor. He "explained to Debra that her family was still her family and they would probably try to help her." "Was she crazy," he says she asked him. He said no. Then she answered her own question, "No, I'm just an emotionally troubled 25-year old girl who needs help dealing with her problems." And in priestly style, on page five of his report, Saldate accounted for how much he could help her deal with those problems. "She then told me that she has had her problems bottled up in her and that she has never been able to express herself from the time she married Mark, *until now*." Debra "asked me how I felt about her." He told her there were other alternatives. She could have given Chris to the grandparents, her sister, or someone else in the family. She said, "I guess I just made a bad judgment call."

The discussion about feelings, remorse, and the future for both the son and his mother took up a good chunk of the report. That makes it remarkable that "Debra kept telling me she felt bad, ashamed, and said that she knew everyone was going to be staring at her because of 'this.'" She said, "I worry about Jim." Saldate asked why. "Well, you know, because he had to be the one to do it." Saldate must have felt sorry for her plight because his report says that they rode back to Phoenix in the back of a uniformed Pinal County sheriff's vehicle. Debra was "not handcuffed. She and I sat in the back." That violated every police protocol.

They kept talking "during the trip back to Phoenix." Debra "kept on asking questions to see if I knew what she was going to get and I told her I did not. Bail? Understanding? An attorney?" When they got to Phoenix, "at approximately 2250 hours . . . booking information was obtained . . . she was given a Pepsi and some cigarettes . . . I called her father for her. . . ."

As part of *his* written paraphrased account, Saldate explained that he told her father she had confessed her involvement in Chris's death. The father asked Saldate if he knew how he felt. Saldate assured him he did. While they were waiting for Debra "to be transported," Debra asked if there "was a possibility she would be released on her own recognizance so she could go back to work." Probably not, he told her. "But," he said she said, "I have never been in any trouble and would not leave the state and would be available for court." Probably not, he said again. "Are you going to call my employer and tell him what happened?" she asked. "No, why should I?" he replied. "Because just in case I get out on bail, or on my own, I'd like to go back to work because [I] really like [my] job."

When they got back to Phoenix, Saldate said, he would have to handcuff her for the first time. So he did, with her hands to her front. Will you go with me, she asked. No, he could not, he said. "She immediately said she was scared." But Saldate now became a father figure—"she would have to face this by herself—she had made an adult decision to do something—and now she had to face the music." Her parting comment: "She had never had anyone that she could speak with before and that this may sound strange but she was starting to feel better and she thought she was getting her self-esteem back."

A different police officer took Debra to the main jail for booking. While waiting in line, within an hour of her arrival at the jail, she agreed to a press interview with Paul Huebl. She didn't face the music. She told a very different version of the Saldate interview, once she was away from him.

4

POLICE INTERROGATIONS, CONFESSIONS, AND THE AMERICAN CRIMINAL JUSTICE SYSTEM

*I*N 2005, PROFESSOR SAUL KASSIN said, "By definition . . . interrogation is a guilt-presumptive process, a theory-driven social interaction led by an authority figure who holds a strong *a priori* belief about the target and who measures success by his or her ability to extract a confession." History is replete with eloquent offerings about the interconnectedness of interrogation and confession. Daniel Webster reminded us, "There is no refuge from confession but suicide and suicide is confession." A Latin writer named Pubilius Syrus clarified how long confession has plagued justice in circa 43 b.c., when he said, "Confession of our faults is the next thing to innocency." But Christopher Marlow said it best: "Confess and be hanged."

Famous judges have weighed in as well. Supreme Court Justice Robert H. Jackson outlined a common path leading from interrogation to confession in Ashcraft v. Tennessee: "A confession is wholly and incontestably voluntary only if a guilty person gives himself up to the law and becomes his own accuser." Chief Justice Earl Warren read aloud the most famous confession case of all time, Miranda v. Arizona, from his center seat on the bench of the United States Supreme Court on June 13, 1966. He said, "At the outset, if a person in custody is to be subjected to interrogation, he must first be informed in clear and unequivocal terms that he has the right to remain silent."

Saldate probably warned Debra Milke when he first confronted her on December 3, 1989. That is perhaps their only area of agreement. She admits he read her rights to her from a little card he had in his pocket. It was undoubtedly the standard Miranda card all Phoenix police officers carried in 1989. But whether she confessed became a swearing contest at her trial. He swore better than she did. Faced with the age-old he said/she said proposition, and unaware of Saldate's history of interrogation misconduct, the jury believed him. She had no expert testimony at her trial. There are well-recognized experts in the science and law of police interrogations and the voluntariness of confessions extracted during custodial interrogation. Her lawyer did not even think about an expert, and the prosecution had Saldate—primed and virtually untouchable, thanks to the judge.

Richard A. Leo is the foremost expert in America on custodial interrogation. In his 2008 book, *Police Interrogation and American Justice*, he catalogued confession science and law from the mid-1960s to 2008, some of which reformed a system that too often produced unreliable, undocumented, but easily believed confessions in swearing contests with ill-prepared and hapless defendants. Dr. Leo described it this way:

> Despite the changes in practice and regulation, though, the adversarial structure of American police interrogation has remained constant. . . . Interrogators continue to assume a partisan role that is often more about case-building and impression management than impartial investigation. They still seek to elicit incriminating statements from a presumed guilty suspect that will help the state prosecute him, weaken his position in plea negotiations, and minimize the possibility of an acquittal. Interrogators still try to "win" cases

by successfully outsmarting the suspect, breaking down his resistance, and eliciting a confession—to secure a conviction.

Professor Leo's assessment applies to the Saldate/Milke confrontation in many respects. But it does not fit what most likely happened during the most important 30 minutes of Debra Milke's life. True, Saldate presumed her guilt. And his goal was to elicit incriminating statements, not information from her. He was confident his efforts would help the state prosecute her and he tried to "win" the case by outsmarting her. He broke down her resistance, but he did *not* elicit a confession. He just made that part up.

5

POLICE INTERVIEWS:
MAUREEN SADEIK, RICHARD SADEIK,
AND JANET FROBE

*A*S PART OF THE POST-INTERROGATION plan following Saldate's confrontation of Debra Milke, Detective Dimodica interviewed Maureen Elizabeth Sadeik at her home in Florence, Arizona. Mrs. Sadeik was Debra's stepmother. He interviewed her right after telling Debra's father and sister about Christopher's murder and Debra's arrest. Dimodica asked Mrs. Sadeik to go over her contacts with Debra on Saturday afternoon. She told Dimodica she'd first learned of Christopher's disappearance "[j]ust shortly after 3:00 P.M. She got a call from her stepdaughter, who sounded very hysterical. Debra told her that Jim had just called and said Chris was missing. Mall security is searching for him." She and Debbie talked on the phone every half-hour about Christopher. Debra had called the police. Maureen told her she "probably ought to go to Metrocenter." But Debra wanted to wait at home "just in case anyone needed to contact her." Maureen didn't want Debra to have to wait alone, so she drove "to Phoenix, arriving at the apartment about 9:00 P.M."

Maureen thought it was "very strange that Debbie did not hug her when she first arrived." Debbie, she said, "did not seem to show the emotions she would have expected in such a circumstance." She also thought it was strange that Debra was "so upset with the police about the questions they were asking her." The police officers "were talking amongst themselves away from her and not telling her everything they knew at that point . . . Debra appeared to be more upset that the police were holding James, than about the fact that Christopher was missing."

"Debra," she said, "appeared to be more at ease than a mother should be in a similar situation." During the evening, Debra said she was sure that Christopher had been molested and was dead. She wanted to have Christopher cremated and wanted to spread his ashes in Maureen's back yard. During the entire course of the evening, Debra was drinking what Maureen believed to be Coke. She later found out through her daughter, Karen, that Debra was mixing rum with the Coke.

Maureen and Karen stayed up all night with Debra and drove back down to Florence on Sunday afternoon with Debra. Dimodica asked about Debra, Christopher, and the father, Mark Milke, before the disappearance. Maureen told him Debra never seemed to show an interest in children. As a child she had no interest in babysitting and didn't like being around children. It was a big surprise when she got pregnant because "Debra told her she didn't want to have children."

Maureen provided some details about the time, in August of 1988, when Debra and Christopher moved to Colorado and moved in with one of Debra's girlfriends. Debra was "always going out, leaving Christopher with the girlfriend for long periods of time. Eventually, Debra's girlfriend became tired of having to watch Christopher so often and she and Debra argued until Debra decided to move out. She moved in with an unknown man in Colorado. The police department in Colorado found Christopher a few blocks away from his home wandering around. When they returned him home, they found Debra lying in bed watching television. Debra did not appear to be very interested in raising Christopher. Then she moved back to Phoenix and moved in with her ex-mother-in-law, Ilse Milke."

According to Maureen, when Debra moved in with Styers, "it was strictly platonic." She described Debra as "a very reliable person, works hard, and always paid her debts. But during the last year she has become less responsible." She lost several jobs and stopped repaying debts. At Thanksgiving, Debra "brought James to dinner" at their house in Florence. James called Debra "dear" and "honey" and it appeared to Maureen that "James felt there was more to the relationship than Debra did." She added, "Debra always had a way of manipulating men to get what she wants from them."

Maureen said Debra had a new boyfriend, named Ernie. She was "very much in love with Ernie . . . and less interested in keeping Christopher . . . Ernie was very career oriented and did not want any children." Mark had been trying to get custody but Debra wouldn't agree. But, "[a]fter Debra met Ernie in April of 1989, Debra began thinking differently." She said Debra was thinking of giving Christopher to Mark. Debra's father became angry when he heard that because he knew that Mark has a problem with drugs and could not believe Debra would allow Christopher to grow up in that environment. Debra changed her mind and did not allow Mark to have custody.

While Debra was with Ernie, "Debra became pregnant. After learning she was pregnant, Debra borrowed some money and had an abortion, due to the fact that Ernie did not want any children."

Dimodica closed his interview by asking whether Maureen believed Debra could have been involved with Christopher's murder. "I do not believe that Debra could do something so horrible as being involved in the murder of her own son," but she had to admit that "it did appear as though Debra was not interested in having children since meeting Ernie."

Detective Hamrick's last interview of the day was with Debra's father, Richard "Sam" Sadeik. In his report, Hamrick confirmed that he had gone to the Sadeik home to tell the family about Christopher's death and Debra's arrest, "and to obtain any background information pertinent to the investigation." After allowing a short time for the family members to "compose themselves, I took Mr. Sadeik away from the other members, to his workshop." After confirming what Mrs. Sadeik had already told him, Hamrick asked about Debra. "She just did not seem remorseful over the disappearance . . . I told myself that was because she was in shock. . . ."

Mr. Sadeik repeated what his wife had already said about Ernie, and said he'd had "bad feelings about Ernie." That stemmed, he said, from a telephone call he'd received from Debra "several months ago." She told him she was "seriously thinking of giving up custody of Christopher and was going to give him back to his father." Sadeik was "very upset" with this suggestion and asked his daughter if she was "going to let a drunk raise his grandson." Sadeik said that he "felt" his daughter's love of Ernie and Ernie's lack of interest in children was "the main reason she was considering giving up custody."

Sadeik said he'd take custody of Christopher himself, but the "phone call got to the point where extremely harsh words were exchanged . . . he made derogatory remarks about her lifestyle and her morals." Sadeik never tried to get legal custody because he "didn't feel the court system would grant custody to a grandparent."

Sadeik only met Jim Styers twice, "once at his birthday party on November the second and the second time at Thanksgiving." Debra had told him "the relationship [with Styers] was strictly monetary . . . just a convenience so they could both meet their expenses." Sadeik that Styers had "been court-martialed out of the U.S. military . . . disabled in Vietnam . . . received a disability pension . . . and was taking Lithium as a treatment for his military related problems."

Hamrick went over Sadeik's understanding of the events surrounding the disappearance. He recounted the first phone call from Debra about 3:30 P.M. on Saturday afternoon. She was "hysterical." Sadeik said that "he just wrote the incident off as a missing child and told her to call mall security." His wife, stepdaughter, and the stepdaughter's boyfriend went to Phoenix to be with Debra, but he had to work. They got back "sometime around 2:30–2:45 P.M., only a guess, and the minute Debra stepped out of the truck, [I] sensed that she was not sincere . . . maybe she was in shock . . . she defended Jim saying he was not involved . . . later finally [she] did make contact with [Jim] and they talked about police harassing him . . . Debbie told Jim he did nothing and for him not to worry . . . that's when Deputy Soules came [here] and asked Debbie to go to the Pinal County Sheriff's office with him."

Hamrick noted in his report that he only questioned Sadeik "briefly about Debra's background." But Sadeik described his daughter as "an unstable child . . . she was high strung and did not like to obey rules."

~

JANET FROBE WAITED AT THE Pinal County Jail until after Saldate finished his interview with Debra and took her to Phoenix. Detective Hamrick interviewed Frobe at 7:55 P.M., "in the visitation section of the jail." Was she related to Debra, he asked. She was not. But her father and Debra's father had worked together at the Arizona Department of Corrections. She's been a friend of the family for many years, she said. She wanted to know what was going on. Hamrick told her they'd found Chris's body in Phoenix. She asked if he was "dead or alive." She asked about Debra. She is being charged as one of three people involved in the murder, he said. Frobe "was completely surprised that Debra had any involvement, but said that the family members had been suspicious of James from the beginning."

Hamrick asked how well she knew Debra and Chris. She explained that as far as she could see, "the relationship was normal." She only saw them on "holiday like occasions." She had heard nothing about Debra "not wanting to have Christopher around." When asked what Debra had said while they waiting for Detective Saldate, Frobe said Debra told her "she thought Chris had been taken by a stranger and that Jim had nothing to do with his disappearance."

Debra had given her purse to Frobe before Saldate arrived at the sheriff's station. She had not seen them take Debra away and was unsure about what to do with the purse. So she took it to Richard Sadeik's house, but he said that nothing that belonged to Debra could stay in his house. So Frobe called the Pinal County Jail at 11:45 P.M. and talked to Deputy Soules. She told him she had Debra's purse but did not want to keep it, and the family didn't want it either. He said she could bring it in to the station and he'd have it sent to the Phoenix

Police Department. She drove back to the sheriff's station and Deputy Soules took the purse from her. He "did an inventory on the contents prior to placing it in a box." Then he called the Phoenix police to tell them what he found inside the purse. They told him to "maintain the purse as evidence for their office. They would arrange to have it picked up." Deputy Soules filled out a "Chain of Custody Log" for the contents of Debra's purse. There were 12 items including car keys, ballpoint pens, hair brushes, and perfume. But, item 2 on the list got the Phoenix Police Department's attention: *"Box of 50 rounds CCI 22 cal. Bullets."* The chain of custody log confirms initial possession by Janet Frobe, then three transfers, from her to Deputy Soules on December 3, 1989, then to an evidence tech on December 27, 1990, and finally to the Phoenix Police Department Evidence section on October 5, 1990. There is no explanation in the record as to why the bullets, described as "evidence," did not surface until almost a month *after* Milke's trial started. No one entered the bullets into evidence in her trial. It seems everyone forgot about them.

6

WHO IS DEBRA MILKE?

*E*LIZABETH HURLEY, A PHOENIX LAWYER, assisted Anders Rosenquist on Milke's *habeas corpus* petition in 2002. She prepared a 93-page social history of Debra Milke to advance Milke's appeal in federal court. Her prologue to that document states that she used excerpts from Milke's 1990 trial testimony, recollections from Debra's family, the Donald Jones family, and other knowledgeable and reliable sources. She did not consult with Debra, or her mother, Renate Janka, in preparing this social history. They were not consulted because this was an independent, objective report designed for admission in evidence in federal court. Portions of a partial history prepared years earlier by Mrs. Janka were considered. This chapter is an abbreviated version of Ms. Hurley's federal court filing.

Debra Jean Milke, née Sadeik, was born on March 10, 1964 in Berlin, Germany to Richard and Renate Seidek. Seidek was an American enlisted man stationed at a United States Air Force base near Berlin. Her mother, Renate Janka, was a German national. Richard was 25 when he met Renate, a bank clerk in Berlin. Richard had been married once before and had a son from that marriage. They seemed an unlikely couple with little in common. Richard was uninterested in sports or social activities, and was not well read or educated, all of which Renate valued highly. Richard had been raised in New Jersey, and was "more than a social drinker." After they were married, Renate learned he spent most of his Air Force salary on alcohol.

Their second child, Sandra, was born on August 9, 1966. In May of 1967, the family was transferred to an Air Force radar site near Atlanta, Georgia, then to Homestead Air Force Base in Florida. Renate spoke enough English to converse with the children and both girls were fluent in German. In October of 1971, the family moved to Phoenix, when Richard was transferred to Luke Air Force Base. He retired from the Air Force in 1975 and took a job in Saudi Arabia in 1977. Renate, Debra, and Sandy stayed home in Phoenix for the next two years.

Debbie was popular in school, and had many friends. She was a good student, earned good grades, and took good care of her appearance. Her mother described her as shy and naïve. Other than outbursts with her sister, Debbie was good to everyone she met. Sandy was "said to be loveable, but life with her was an emotional roller-coaster." Richard became unemployed and did not try to get another job. The family lived on Renate's earnings. She left Richard, but did not immediately seek a divorce, because "the girls were teenagers." He moved to Florence, Arizona, and took a job as a guard at the Arizona State Prison.

After the separation, both girls stayed with their mother, but the rivalry between Debbie and Sandy escalated. They constantly fought and Sandy always felt she could not live up to Debbie's achievements in high school. Other family members described Sandy as a "handful." Renate continued to work at Luke Air Force Base, but she had no benefits and knew her job would eventually be discontinued. Richard visited occasionally, but referred to his daughters as "spoiled brats."

In the spring of 1980, Richard met an old schoolmate from New Jersey, Maureen, who had recently become a widow, with three children. Richard asked Renate for a divorce so he could marry Maureen. In March of 1983, Renate left Phoenix for Germany. Debbie was 19 and Sandy 17. Sandy went to Florence to live with Richard and his new wife, Maureen. Renate gave Debbie her car, her apartment lease, a credit card, and $2000 in cash. She got a good job in Germany and sent money back to the girls in Arizona (Debbie in Phoenix and Sandy in Florence).

Debbie went to Germany in May of 1983 to visit her mother. In June, just before she returned to Phoenix, Debbie told her mother she had "fallen in love with a man named Mark Milke." She showed Renate a picture of Mark; her response was that he looked "shaggy" and "of the type she did not favor." In June of 1983, Sandy reported that her father and Maureen were planning to divorce and were sleeping apart. Maureen was in counseling, but Richard refused to participate. Renate came to Phoenix in August of 1983. She said she came on business, and "to visit her daughters." She met Mark Milke and said he was "all that she had feared for her daughter." He had moved into Debbie's apartment and her two female roommates had moved out. Shortly thereafter, Mark was arrested for possession of cocaine. Debbie had quit college and was working full time. By the fall of 1983, Richard and Maureen had reconciled and Sandy was looking forward to leaving Florence and going back to Phoenix to move in with Debbie and attend beauty school. Renate came to Phoenix in November to see the girls. She said her relationship with Debbie had changed because of Mark. She "tried to hold her tongue" about Mark.

Renate returned to Phoenix in May of 1994 to attend Sandy's high school graduation and visit Debbie. Debbie and Mark had changed apartments and were living with Diane, a friend of Debbie's. Debbie told her mother on this visit she and Mark planned on getting married. Debbie no longer had the car that Renate had left for her because Mark had "demolished it with a baseball bat." He kept a tarantula and a boa constrictor in the apartment as "pets." Renate found Mark's drug paraphernalia but did nothing about it. Mark's father, Henry, told Renate that his son had been using drugs since he was 15. Henry told Renate he had lost his wife, his business, and his son, all due to Mark's drug problems. He advised her to "take Debbie as far away as she could." She tried to talk to Debbie about Mark's drug use, but said her daughter was "in denial." She talked to Richard about Mark but learned that Richard had "found a new friend in Mark, with whom he could drink and go target shooting."

In August 1984, the police raided Debbie and Mark's apartment and arrested everyone present, charging them with possession of marijuana. The court dismissed the charges against Debbie because "she had merely been present." Shortly thereafter, Debbie went to Colorado to see her friend, Dorothy Markwell. In December 1984, Debbie married Mark, and in March of 1985, Debbie told her mother she was pregnant. The next month, Sandy announced she too was pregnant, at 18. Renate flew to Phoenix to see both girls. Richard "disowned" Sandy. Sandy's position was "if Debbie could have a baby with Mark, then she could have one on her own."

Christopher was born on October 2, 1985. Sandy's child, Jason, was born a month later, on November 11. In December, the Maricopa Superior Court sentenced Mark to a six-month jail term. He got out on probation in May 1986, but was arrested a few months later for domestic violence and violating his parole; he went back to jail. Meanwhile, Sandy was going through an "ugly paternity suit" with the father of her child. Through phone calls and letters, Renate learned that Debbie "enjoyed motherhood and marriage, and was considering having another child." Then, in late 1986, Debbie and Christopher moved out because Mark was "abusing drugs again." Christopher was a year old. In October 1987, Mark went back "to prison." Family friends in Phoenix described Christopher as "a handful," but felt that Debbie was always "diplomatic with him, never showing anger, only love." The Donald Jones family reported, "Debbie would never do anything to harm her son."

Debbie was introduced to Jim Styers by her sister, Sandy, since they lived in the same apartment complex in North Phoenix. He always lent Sandy a "helping hand with carrying groceries, carrying the laundry, and helping get the kids and all of their belongings into the apartment." Debbie thought he was kind and polite. Jim watched Sandy's son Jason while Sandy worked, "and Christopher when he was not in pre-school." She learned about Styers' Vietnam War experiences and realized he was "uncomfortable about it." As time went along, Styers became a regular visitor at Debbie and Sandy's apartment. He and his girlfriend Gail often came over for dinner.

During that fall, Debbie attended drug counseling with Mark, as a non-addicted spouse. Her efforts were solely for Christopher's sake. Mark still lived in what they called "the marital residence," even though Debbie was not "with him." She insisted that Christopher grow up in a "two parent household" despite Mark's continued drug problems. In July 1988, after Mark got another DWI, Debbie filed for divorce. The decree was uncontested, with joint custody of Christopher. Debbie was designated "primary caretaker." Mark had unlimited visitation rights. Mark engaged in various acts of "stalking" in 1988, after the divorce petition was filed: there were threatening phone calls, her car was vandalized, and "bikers" (known associates of Mark) began "making themselves visible near Debbie's home." Debbie went to Colorado to stay with her friend Dorothy Markwell. She stayed for a few months and then returned to Arizona.

In December 1988, Debbie found a lump on Christopher's neck, which turned out to be a tumor on his thyroid. He spent three weeks in the hospital. In January 1989, Debbie drove to Florence to pick up Mark, who was being released from prison. The divorce was finalized while he was in prison. He went into drug rehab for six months, but relapsed shortly thereafter. In July 1989, Debbie and Mark's relationship turned "hostile again." He said he was tired of her "over protectiveness toward Christopher—it was her fault he had to go to rehab—he was sick of her compassion." He told her "he would find a way to get Chris back even if it meant killing her."

A few days later, Styers offered Debbie the spare bedroom in his apartment to help her get away from Mark. She and Christopher moved into the apartment the first week of August 1989. She felt it was only an "interim solution until she was at a point where she and Chris could live by themselves close to her work." She made it clear to Styers that the move was only "temporary." Debbie lived in constant fear of Mark, who continued to harass her. She "instructed Jim to call the police [when] Mark appeared while she was at work." In late August 1989, her employer, MeraBank, became insolvent. The once prominent bank laid off every worker. Debbie then got a new job with a health insurance company doing computerized accounting. Styers told Debbie that he loved Sandy, her sister, and was sorry she had married another man and moved to Wyoming. Debbie was not aware, at first, that Styers "suffered from psychological problems from his years in Vietnam." She did not know that he had "killed both women and children." Styers went to church three times a week and was "studying to become a minister." At some point, she also learned that he had suffered a head injury in an incident in Yuma, Arizona. After that, his doctors diagnosed "post-traumatic stress disorder, and treated him [with] counseling and numerous prescription drugs." While the relationship was always platonic, over the next four months Styers became increasingly obsessed with Debbie. He addressed her as "honey or sweetie," but she rebuffed his advances. Mark continued to be hostile toward her. Styers suggested she get a restraining order against Mark, which eventually she did.

A month after moving to Styers' apartment, Debbie met Roger Scott. She was "uncomfortable around him and thought he was strange." She never socialized with him, and disliked him "intensely, because he got upset about Christopher and Wendy." She told Styers she did not want Scott around Christopher. Scott asked her for a loan so he could appeal a denial of his Social Security disability benefits; she said no. However, both Styers and Roger Scott continuously tried to get money from her—she was the only one working.

In September 1989, Debbie met Ernie Sweat while working at Lincoln Insurance Company. She thought he was "intelligent and neat—a breath of fresh air—compared to her relationship with Mark." That same month, her mother came from Germany for a visit. Debbie showed Renate where she worked and told her about her plan to move out of Styers' apartment and get an apartment in Tempe, closer to her job. She showed her the pre-school she had selected for Christopher called "La Petite Academy." During that visit, Renate met Styers. She said she had "a frightening sense of uneasiness about him, but could not bring herself to voice those concerns to Debbie."

Her mother bought her a Toyota Corolla with the understanding that Debbie would make monthly installment payments into Renate's bank account. Debbie agreed because she needed the car to drive to Tempe for her job. Debbie told her mother she enjoyed spending week-ends with Ernie Sweat but that she would not consider moving in with him because "she and Christopher were a package deal and Ernie was not the type for a ready-made family."

Christopher's fourth birthday was October 2, 1989. Debra allowed Mark to see Christopher the day before at Ilse Mark's home. Styers argued with Debbie about her decision to let Mark see the boy for the day. Styers said Mark was a "worthless piece of shit" and "did not deserve to see Christopher." When Mark brought Christopher back home to Styers' apartment that evening, Chris was "overjoyed and had armfuls of presents, which he brought inside to show Jim and his mom." Mark stayed outside, "high on cocaine. Debbie swore at him." They argued and Styers came outside and told Mark to leave. "They argued for several minutes. Debbie thinks this is when Jim began to formulate his plan to murder Christopher."

At Chris's birthday party the next day, Styers told Christopher to stop playing with a truck. When Chris refused, Styers said, "I wish he were dead." Roger Scott also voiced "dislike for Christopher." Debbie saw Scott for the last time in October. Debbie learned on October 11 that a constable had served Mark with the restraining order. They scheduled the hearing for October 24. They told her if she didn't appear for the hearing, the restraining order would be invalid. She went to the hearing; the court issued the order against Mark.

On November 11, 1989, Debbie telephoned her sister in Wyoming to wish Jason, her son, a happy birthday. She was on the phone with Jason when Styers returned to the apartment. After she hung up, Styers told her he had something to show her. He emptied a brown paper bag containing "a gun and two boxes of bullets." The gun was in a holster. Debbie was shocked. He told her he always wanted a gun for "recreational purposes and thought he needed one since Mark was constantly making threats against Debbie." Debbie did not like having a gun in the apartment with the children, but "there was not much she could do about it." Jim put the gun on a shelf "in the back of his closet." Eventually she would learn he had other guns.

On December 2, 1989, when Jim and Christopher were supposedly at the mall, Debra stayed at home to do housework. "She was sitting on the couch folding clothes when she felt something between the seat cushions. She discovered a box of bullets, 'full count.' She felt she had to confront Jim when she saw him, and put the box of bullets in her purse, thinking that a safe place."

She never saw Styers or her son again.

7

WHO IS ROGER SCOTT?

*R*OGER MARK SCOTT WAS A quiet, poorly educated man who lived with his mother, Wilma Scott. She had a small apartment in Glendale, Arizona at the time of his arrest in December of 1989. He was not violent, was thought to be harmless, didn't stand out in any crowd, and cared deeply for his mother. He had only one friend—James Lynn Styers. What little public information about his life prior to December of 1989 comes from a formal presentence report filed in the Maricopa County Superior Court in 1991.

Roger Scott was born June 4, 1948, in Omaha, Nebraska, the younger of two children. He told Mr. Lembo, his probation officer, that his father was an alcoholic who often physically abused various family members. He was about five when his parents separated. Although his mother had a part-time job throughout his formative years, she often depended on other family members for financial assistance. There was an obvious closeness between mother and son—they were all each other had.

He quit school after completing the tenth grade, with average grades and no disciplinary history. He got his G.E.D. in 1971 and participated in the Manpower Development and Training Act program in Phoenix for six months in 1971, doing a little field work in auto mechanics. But he quit the program before earning a completion certificate.

He read "above the sixth grade level." He held a job for six years, but became permanently unemployed in 1977. His last job was a six-month stint as a maintenance worker at the Fountain Apartments in Phoenix. He quit because his boss "harassed" him regarding his work performance. Until he went to jail in 1989, he only found sporadic, part-time employment as an auto and truck mechanic, a wallpaper hanger, and a lawnmower mechanic.

The scant Arizona police records are minimal and bleak. His first arrest occurred on November 4, 1966, for stealing a set of golf clubs from someone's garage. Scott began a 60-day sentence in jail on December 18, 1967 after he was caught siphoning a gallon of gasoline from someone's car. In July of 1968, police discovered him and two friends drinking beer and engaging in disorderly conduct. The Phoenix Municipal Court ultimately dismissed the case for lack of evidence. The Phoenix PD arrested him again on January 24, 1982 for assault, but did not file a complaint in court. On September 27, 1985, a different municipal court fined him $100 on a sexual indecency charge after he was apprehended for sexual contact with another male at an adult bookstore. His presentence report noted that, although there were no confirming police reports, Scott admitted to four DWI arrests between 1972 and 1974. He paid the fines, and followed a court order to attend Alcoholics Anonymous meetings. He also took the standard driver's education course following each arrest. Scott told his probation officer that he started drinking alcohol when he was about 23. He admitted to "abusing alcohol," until he was 33, when he started attending AA meetings. He quit going to meetings in 1974 and had no treatment from then up to his arrest and confession in the Milke murder case. He insisted that he did not "consume alcoholic beverages anymore," and that it wasn't a problem for him "in the last nine years." Marijuana was the only illicit substance he ever used, but he had not used it during the "last fifteen years."

He and Patricia Ann Jackson were married in 1971, divorced in 1974, and had no children. The marriage broke up due to his "wife's infidelity and to the fact that they simply got tired of each other."

His asthma got him classified as 4F, so he never served in the military. He had one car accident, in 1974, which resulted in his suffering from a severe back and neck injury. These injuries, over the years, "handicapped my efforts to secure and maintain stable employment." To complicate matters, he also suffered a seizure disorder in 1983. At the time of his arrest, he was taking Dilantin, an anticonvulsant medication.

After his trial, but before he was sentenced, Dr. Donald Tatro, a jail psychiatrist, examined Scott. Dr. Tatro defined Scott from an intellectual, functional, and personality perspective. "This is a man who cannot make decisions when it comes to even the most trivial of matters. It is difficult to conceive of him conspiring to commit murder, deciding to commit murder, and then, over a protracted period of time, taking the steps necessary to carry out the murder. Since Mr. Scott is not psychotic and, as a consequence, [not] dangerous to either himself or to other people, there is no indication of a need for inpatient treatment. His type of neurotic disorder is classically difficult to treat by means of psychological counseling, since his defenses are so rigid and denial of psychological problems is so essential to the kind of self-image he needs to maintain."

Dr. Alexander Don, another psychiatrist, examined Scott on July 2, 1990. "Mr. Scott has no present difficulty in communicating and is able to provide a coherent account, within the constraints that he has imposed on himself, of the events leading to his arrest, as well as considerable detail relating to his recent and past life circumstances. Roger Scott has no history of prior psychiatric disorder other than alcohol abuse, and in particular has not experienced any mental illness of a psychotic nature which might thus impair his contact with reality."

As is customary in presentence evaluation, Mr. Lembo did a financial status assessment on Scott. He found that Scott had almost nothing of value and no visible means of support. Even so, he recommended a restitution order for $1,772.43 to be paid to Richard Albert Sadeik, Christopher's grandfather, as reimbursement for Christopher's funeral expenses.

The primary job of a probation officer at the presentence phase of any criminal case is to recommend a sentence to the court. Because this is necessarily an "opinion," probation officers usually take care to support their recommendations. Lembo said this about Scott:

"In reviewing the available social and psychological data, it appears that the defendant does not possess a history of severe emotional disorders, is probably more of a follower than a leader, and has found it difficult over the years to 'make decisions when it comes to even the most trivial of matters.' Although the argument could be made that the defendant was the least culpable of the three defendants, he was certainly an active participant in the offense, stood to gain financially from his involvement, and could have prevented the incident from occurring at any given time. Mr. Scott has an apparent history of alcohol abuse, although his past difficulties are dated, and do not appear to be an issue in the matters at hand. As indicated previously, he also has a history of physical and medical disabilities which, seemingly, have prevented him from securing and maintaining stable employment for over the past 15 years. His inability (or unwillingness) to be a productive member of the community and to earn legitimate wages may have, unfortunately, provided him with the necessary incentive to involve himself in this offense. In conclusion, the defendant has certainly demonstrated himself to be a serious risk to the community, as evidenced by the conspiracy and the fatal shooting of four-year-old Christopher Milke. It particularly concerns this writer that the victim was a helpless child who posed no threat to the defendant, and that he apparently committed the offense in expectation of pecuniary gain. It is also noted that, throughout the presentence interview, the defendant seemed to focus his efforts on extricating himself from guilt, showing no signs of concern for the victim, or his surviving family members, in the process. Mr. Scott has been found guilty of murder, conspiracy, and kidnapping charges and the law is specific in providing sentencing ranges for these charges. For the reasons outlined and discussed in this report, aggravated sentences appear appropriate. These factors were considered in making my recommendation: 1. The age and the relative helplessness of the victim. 2. The defendant committed this offense in expectation of pecuniary gain. 3. Although the defendant does not possess any prior felony convictions, he has, nonetheless, had a number of previous encounters with the criminal justice system. 4. Social and psychological data made available on this defendant. 5. The manner in which this offense was executed. 6. Statements from the various references and interested parties, to include those elicited from the victim's family members. 7. The defendant was instrumental in recovering the victim's body."

As to counts I and II, Lembo "[r]espectfully recommended that the defendant be sentenced in accordance with the law and pay a felony penalty assessment in the amount of $200.00, and pay an $8.00 time payment fee per A.R.S. 12-116, unless all penalties, fines, and sanctions are paid in full on this sentencing date. As to count III, it is respectfully recommended that the defendant be committed to the Department of Corrections for a term greater than the presumptive and pay a felony penalty assessment of $100.00. It is also recommended that the defendant pay restitution per the attached ledger sheet. The defendant has served 494 days of presentence incarceration."

Lembo designated Christopher's father, Mark Milke, as a crime victim. As part of the case against Roger Scott, Mark, who later changed his first name to "Arizona," gave a statement summarizing his feelings about Scott's role in his son's murder. "Christopher was the most important thing in my life, and when he was taken away from me, I felt that I myself had died." As part of his victim's statement, "Mr. Milke advised that he is a recovering alcoholic and acknowledges that he has been dealing with the loss of his son through his involvement in Alcoholics Anonymous. He advised that there is little question in his mind that his former wife initiated the conspiracy to have his son killed and that codefendant Styers was equally responsible for causing the son's death. Although Mr. Milke acknowledges Mr. Scott's involvement in this matter as an atrocious act, he does feel that, of the three defendants, Scott should be shown some leniency, as he did lead police to his son's body and was instrumental in solving this case. Mr. Milke commented that if his son's remains were never found, this incident would have proven to be an even greater tragedy. He commented that it was his ex-father-in-law, Richard Sadeik, who was responsible for his son's funeral expenses."

8

WHO IS JAMES LYNN STYERS?

*J*AMES LYNN STYERS LED AN aimless and essentially unex-
amined life prior to December 3, 1989. He rented a modest
apartment in North Phoenix, had few friends, and no job. Some of his
pre-conviction history is contained in various legal briefs filed by his
lawyers, Amy Beth Krauss and Judy Singleton Hall. They filed and
processed a long, complicated *habeas corpus* petition in federal court.
Their briefs revealed for the first time his personal and medical history.
Their careful research and detailed investigation provided insight into
his life before he met Debra Milke and her son in 1988. The synopsis,
prepared years after his state court proceedings were complete, brought
psychological and psychiatric insight into his case for the first time.
Styers was born September 3, 1947, in New Castle, Pennsylvania, the
sixth of seven children. Styers' father, Charles, supported the family
under financially difficult circumstances from his meager earnings as a
maintenance man. His mother, Lois, later supplemented that income
by cleaning motel rooms, leaving the children home to raise themselves.
As a child, Styers suffered from learning disabilities. He consequently
struggled in school, leaving high school in the eleventh grade.

In 1967, when he was 19, Styers "joined the United States Marine
Corps, where he served honorably in the Vietnam theater of combat

operations during 1968–1969. At this young age, during the height of the conflict, Styers participated in at least twelve different combat operations, including those in the northern most portion of the former South Vietnam, Quang Tri Provence. He suffered multiple severe traumas during his war service. He shot and killed a young Vietnamese boy when the boy jumped onto a truck carrying marines. It was common for children to be wired with explosives. Styers could not risk the lives of his fellow soldiers. He was tormented by the belief that he neglected to protect his friend from being shot and killed by the enemy during combat. Styers had the enemy shooter in his sights, but failed to fire his weapon in time to save his friend. He witnessed the killing of another friend near the DMZ in northern South Vietnam in 1969."

Styers left Vietnam a broken man, "plagued by mental illness forever thereafter. Shortly after his transfer to a USMC facility from Vietnam, he began having symptoms of Post-Traumatic Stress Disorder (PTSD). He slept poorly, began experiencing auditory, visual and tactile hallucinations, and dreamed of combat operations nightly. These symptoms never abated after leaving Vietnam."

Not long after his military discharge, Styers attempted suicide. Despite Styers' decades-long effort to obtain help from the VA, his treatment was unsuccessful. He continually suffered from symptoms of PTSD, depression, survivor guilt, anxiety, and ongoing auditory, visual, and tactile hallucinations. Styers' records are replete with evidence of frequent hallucinatory symptoms, recognized as an "ongoing active psychosis," involving "voices and ghostly images, that only he could hear, see, and feel." His appellate lawyers argued that his problems had reached psychotic proportions during the time of Christopher Milke's murder. During the two years immediately preceding December 1989, Styers took two primary drugs: "Navane, an antipsychotic drug for schizophrenia and psychotic thinking, and Lithium for manic bipolar disorder."

His wife left him in 1977 and took his children away. Shortly after, he reported "episodes of loss of contact with the environment." By 1983, he reported more seizure activity. In 1984, he was hospitalized by the Veterans' Administration for four months for treatment of post-traumatic stress disorder. He displayed "residual deficits

. . . compatible with an old head injury—losses in immediate attention span, sustained concentration, incidental and systematic new learning."

In 1985, a decade and a half after he returned from Vietnam, his records display some insight into his thinking. He said, "Most of the time I am in Viet-Nam. Like driving a truck in a convoy and getting into a village and people start shooting at us killing and wounding. Having a kid between eight and ten years-old jump on my truck and me blowing his head off. Or driving down the road and having a bullet come through the windshield while reaching for a can of beer, or having bullets coming through the window while trying to get out the other side of the truck. Or blowing up a truck you are driving killing four people and wounding one and you just get hurt a little. Seeing a friend get killed when I could have stopped it but didn't and not know why."

In response to a question about his current day-to-day functioning in 1985, he said, "Losing sleep because of dreams of Viet-Nam. Seeing kids including my own and wondering if I'm going to do something to hurt them, and remembering the ones I had to kill. Worrying about what I'm going to do when I hear some loud noise. Or, hearing and seeing Vietnamese people when they are arguing, or just messing around. I don't know if I will be able to keep walking away, or if it will happen when I'm already upset and I might do something."

In 1986, he returned to the VA because he wanted to "learn to control his temper so not to hurt his three kids . . . He was afraid of what he might do, and searching for help he never received. Two months later, he reported that he had punched a wall and did not understand 'what makes him do this.'"

Over the next three years, Styers told mental health professionals he did not like to be around people. He was having auditory and tactile hallucinations. In May of 1988, he told doctors that he was "concerned about being upset by daughter's crying. It brings back crying of kids from Nam." He also reported having blackouts. By July of 1988, Styers was "tired of hearing the voices."

His mental health continued spiraling downward, as shown in a report from November 1988: "Sleeping poorly recently. More nightmares also nightly. Feels more depressed. Mother has cancer. Isolating more. Feels total lack of energy. Continues at vet center. Aunt recently died of cancer. 'Increased symptoms.'" On consecutive days in 1988, Styers' mother and his brother Thomas died. Later, the VA medical center "continued to fail to grasp the warning signs of how deep in his illness he was, missing a classic sign of trauma when it callously reported that Mr. Styers 'seems at this time unwilling to "experience" the loss of his mother and brother.'"

By January 1989, Styers felt like he was "battling the world." He was depressed about his isolation and lack of work, and his depression had become more severe since the deaths of his mother and brother. A month later, he shared with his therapy group that he feared "losing control." By June, his visual and auditory hallucinations had him near the breaking point. He told mental health professionals he was "tired of feeling tired." A progress note, made just a few weeks before Christopher Milke's death, says, "Has been irritable and short tempered. These things are getting worse. Sleeps 3–4 hrs/nite. Hears voices regularly. Doesn't pay attention to it. Feels like quitting trying anymore."

A disabling head injury compounded Styers' psychiatric difficulties. After he left Vietnam, while stationed at a USMC base in Yuma, Arizona, he fell from a moving truck, suffering a right occipital skull fracture and a cerebral contusion. Because of these injuries, Styers was declared disabled and discharged from the Marine Corps. His medical record is "replete with evidence of the deleterious effects of these neurological injuries."

Styers' appellate lawyers also defined his legal difficulties. In addition to his psychosis, Styers was afflicted with a dysfunctional lawyer, Jesse Miranda. Miranda, later disbarred, was "becoming a serial violator of Arizona's Rules of Professional Conduct," Krauss argued to a federal judge in 2002. She said, "[M]onths prior to his appointment to represent Mr. Styers, Miranda had been censured by the Arizona Supreme Court's Discipline Commission and placed on probation. In the midst of his representation of Mr. Styers, Miranda was entangled in further disciplinary charges, which included allegations he had violated the terms of his probation. The ultimate decision in that matter found that during August 1988 to March 1990, Miranda had failed to respond to eight letters from Arizona State Bar representatives regarding complaints against him. Because of these further violations, in January 1991, just a few weeks after Mr. Styers's sentencing, Miranda was suspended from the practice of law for a three month period. No sooner was he reinstated, than in May 1991, the Ninth Circuit Court of Appeals ordered Miranda to show cause why sanctions should not be imposed for filing 'a deficient appellate brief' in another criminal case. As a result of this misconduct, the Arizona Supreme Court's Discipline Commission suspended Miranda from the practice of law for an additional seven month period. Ultimately, Miranda was disbarred from the practice of law, upon multiple grounds of misconduct, including dishonesty, fraud and illegal conduct."

Krauss also told the court, "Miranda's troubling record of wrongdoing and professional neglect rifled its way into Mr. Styers's capital proceedings. Throughout his representation of Mr. Styers, Miranda filed only a solitary pre-trial motion, an uncontested motion to sever the co-defendants' trials. Perhaps Miranda's most egregious error, which affected both the guilt phase and the sentencing phase of the proceedings, was his abject failure to develop a defense strategy that incorporated Styers' well-documented mental health issues. Despite testimony about Styers' mental health, the strong antipsychotic medication he was taking, and passing references to his wartime service in Viet Nam, Miranda neglected to secure expert neuropsychological and medical witness testimony to aid the jury in understanding that Mr. Styers' conditions were genuine, chronic, and involuntary. Had Miranda followed through with neuropsychological testing, for example, he might have been able to prove that Mr. Styers suffered from diminished capacity or that he acted impulsively, without premeditation."

Although the state filed a legal memorandum to support the death penalty, "Miranda failed to present any legal arguments responding to the state's memorandum, nor did he file a defense death penalty memorandum, setting forth the factual and legal grounds why the death sentence should not be imposed. In fact, despite the extensive record of Mr. Styers's severe mental illness, and demonstrated neurological disabilities, Miranda failed to properly develop the case for mitigation."

Styers' trial began on October 15, 1990. He testified in his own defense at his trial, indicating that "Roger Scott shot Christopher and then threatened him. After shooting Christopher, Scott pointed the gun at Styers and said, 'I took care of Chris and I'm going to tell you what you're going to do.' Styers testified that in the face of Scott shooting Christopher and then threatening him, he 'went into solid fear.' He could see other children's bodies lying on the desert wash floor, but he never saw Christopher."

The trial transcript confirms an ineffective effort by Styers to explain his position to the jury. "His traumatic reaction to the shooting was compounded by a medical condition that he was being treated for at the VA Hospital, which resulted from his combat experiences in Vietnam, and for which he had been taking prescribed medication for twenty years, since 1970."

Styers' trial lawyer led him through a disjointed explanation of who he was, including his "nightmares and hallucinations, and the consequences of his prior severe head injury." Styers testified that after the shooting, Scott drove Styers to Metrocenter and "instructed [him] to make up the story about Chris getting lost in the mall." Scott left Styers with a warning: "if Styers told the police what happened, Scott would shoot Styers, or Styers' baby daughter Wendy. Out of fear for himself and his family, Styers obeyed Scott's orders, and during the remainder of the day of the shooting and into the following day while dealing with the police investigation he did not have access to his Navane and Lithium medications and his hallucinations worsened.

Styers denied wanting to harm Christopher. He denied cooperating with Christopher's mother or Roger Scott to have Christopher murdered. Besides the history and medical perspectives in legal briefs, there are the many letters Styers wrote to Debra Milke from jail between December 1989 and June 6, 1990. Some of those letters were preserved. When Milke got the first letter, she asked Kirk Fowler, an investigator assisting her trial lawyer, Kenneth Ray, what to do with the letter. He suggested she write back "to find out what really happened in the murder." She gave Kenneth Ray all of the letters. He tried to introduce them as evidence in her trial, but Judge Hendrix rejected all of them.

The first letter, dated December 1989 just 16 days after Christopher's murder, says, "Debra, I lost a friend with Roger. I can't believe what's going on, what he did and the lies he's telling. I pray you will forgive me for bringing him into your life . . . I know about your family and what they did. I'm sorry but there is nothing I can do except to say I will never do that to you."

Milke wrote back on January 4, 1990. "Jim, I have received your letters and I'm not ignoring you. I'm just confused and angry with all that has happened. I feel nothing but contempt for Roger. It's not your fault you brought him into my life. He was a friend of yours. I always thought Roger was weird, but I had no idea he was capable of doing what he did. Jim, I have known you for 3 years and I do not believe that you would do anything like this to hurt me. I know how you felt about Christopher. Roger, on the other hand, did not like me, and especially Christopher. I never imagined myself in jail. I never got into trouble before and now this. My whole life is at stake. I miss my son very much and nothing or anyone will ever bring him back . . . I honestly believe that Roger was behind all of this and just implicated you and me."

Styers' January 11, 1990 response was cryptic. "Debbie, I'm totally confused myself. They want my life for this and I didn't do anything. Roger did it and he's still trying to do the two of us in." Debbie wrote back on January 18, saying, ". . . I've been going through some heavy counseling here. I have so many mixed emotions and it's very hard to maintain myself. All I want to know Jim is what happened? When you left that morning, I thought you were going to the mall with Christopher. When and how did Roger get into the picture . . . If Roger is responsible for this—then how did he do it alone? What kind of transportation did he use and how did Chris get away from you? Is there any way that Mark was involved in this . . . My son is gone and I'll never see him again! Ever! I don't even know if he suffered . . . Can you imagine how I must feel . . . What if it was Wendy . . . please write back and tell me everything you know. . . ."

Styers answered on January 22, 1990. He told her about his pre-trial conference that day and said his lawyer asked for a trial date "as soon as possible, but not on March 5." They wanted to move the trial out of Phoenix. He said "Roger was in court today also . . . tried to get a new lawyer but judge said no . . . My lawyer tells me that the best that Roger can get, if he is lucky, is his life . . . Debbie do you think I did this. Because I did not. I could never do anything to Christopher or to you. Roger did it behind my back."

He wrote again on January 30, rambling about her things at his house that her dad wanted given to Goodwill. So, "your close [Styers' spelling in the letters is left uncorrected] are gone to goodwill or something . . . I had no control over that . . . about Roger I want nothing to do with him . . . he's not only doing this to you but he's doing this to me too . . . Hear is what went on that Sat. We picked up Roger got his prescription and Chris said he wanted something to eat so that's when we got pizza and decided that we would get Wendi and you and go to the mall and look at Lights that night. Roger wanted to go that night and I said no we were going to do something with the kids. To pass time until I could get Wendi we went out to watch the gliders and snakes. Chris thought that was a good idea. We went out there for awhile and I said it was time to go. Chris was right behind me and Roger behind him. I thought the gun was in the car I said no shooting with Christopher along. But Roger had other plans. I have to stop now. Just Remember your not the only one thats out everything. I'm in jail also. Love you. Jim."

He wrote again on February 3 and 11, and talked about their trials, his lawyer, spending money in jail, and other issues not related to the crime. But on February 16, he returned to the crime and Roger. ". . . Now about Roger and his motive. I don't know for sure but I've been thinking about it. I think he done it out of jealousy that I was doing things with you and the kids and not going out with him. That he decided to get Chris to get at you and me. I think he knows that if Wendi would have been there he would have done her in to. He knows that would hurt us more than anything else he could . . . he got us included to hurt us even more. And to get himself out of trouble for doing it himself. After it happened with Roger and Chris, I was in shock and scared and didn't know what to do. So I made a mistake out of fear and stupidity and want to the mall called you and you know the rest now I got to live with this mistake. I offer and hope you will accept my Apology for being so stupid and in sock. I didn't mean to disappoint you but I was in shock myself and didn't know what I was doing. If you want to stay angry at me for it I understand because I am angry with myself . . . this is a hard letter to write because I'm thinking about Chris and it hurts . . . the dog on the envelope was done by a man in hear with me. Love you, Jim."

His next letter, written eight days later on February 24, was also about Roger Scott. "Dear Debbie, were I'm at now is were Roger as been. They moved him out to move me in. I don't know where he's at now. The people here talk about him. How he's afraid that we have someone out to get him. Better yet Roger talked to two guys in hear one told 4 different stories about what went on. But the other said Roger confessed to doing the shooting. And they will testify in court." While the trial record is sketchy, a prisoner named Robert E. Johnson said he had talked to both Scott and Styers. In those talks, Johnson said Scott admitted his guilt in shooting Christopher, while Styers maintained his innocence. Styers offered legal advice to Milke in his February 24 letter. "About your confession when you got arrested talk to your lawer about it. When your hysterical and in shock it's not allowable in court." He also explained how Roger knew of the insurance policy Milke had through her employer. "Your benefits booklet is probably how he got his information but I never saw him look at it. I told him no for the $250 also. He needed it for his social security lawer." He added more about Roger in a March 12 letter: "I thought about Mark and Roger had something going for some time but don't know how to prove it . . . About the gun. I got the gun for Roger you saw it at our house. I took it that Sat to give to him but when Chris and I got to his house he was in the outside and ready to go. So he didn't put the gun in the house. . . ."

On May 5, 1990, Styers wrote to Milke and said, "Roger confessed to a man named Robert Johnson I told my lawyers secretary. Can't get my lawyer to tell him. Your lawyer can get it from my lawyer. No one else is willing to talk in court." He followed that with a June 6, 1990 letter. "The only thing they got on me is one of the letters I wrote to you. The one telling them what happened out there. Then all that tells them is that I was there . . . I'm a little scared of this whole damn thing but I think we will make it through . . . my lawyer thinks you might be using me to cover yourself to keep you from going to jail. He thinks you are covering yourself with my letters. I don't think you are. I think you just want to know what happened. Honey the gun belong to Roger I had given it to him that morning and I thought he left it in the car. I don't know anything about them finding any bullet casings. I don't know anything about what Roger did with them. I had an old pair of tennis shoes in the car but they had nothing to do with anything and I thought they were still in the car. Well its time for bed and they are going to shut us down so I will stop writing for now. I want a Pepsi too. Love you Jim."

That was the last letter from Styers to Milke. The Maricopa County Attorney's Office tried to introduce some of these letters in evidence but Judge Hendrix refused to admit them.

9

WHO IS ARMANDO SALDATE?

*A*RMANDO SALDATE, JR., IS A man whose self-confidence in securing confessions from suspects where others fail is fully justified. His self-made reputation for making people talk earned high-fives from colleagues and promotions from police brass. His many Google images depict an unprepossessing man—size triple XL—a strapping sort of guy that would make you believe you were in real trouble if he sat close enough to you. Over the years, suspects described him as burly, and tried to keep their distance as best they could in a confrontational setting. Small children, looking only at his round face, fuzzy upper lip, and wide-set saucer eyes, might have thought him cuddly. He was definitely not cuddly, though when called for, he had a generous smile. He never used it in an interrogation room. If he confronted you, as he did every suspect he met, and if he sat close enough to put his hands on your knees, which he often did, even with female suspects, you felt his presence loom over you. Some vocally withdrew, sensing the futility of trying to make him listen to their side of things. For others, his menacing air and confident manner stripped what little resolve to maintain their innocence they had when he came into the interrogation room. But with Debra Milke, shy by nature, but outgoing with men, he threatened her when he first opened his mouth. His first few sentences, about death and accusation, put her on the defensive. She stayed that way for the next 30 minutes trying to explain her innocence in a way that only made him more resolute and her continue to babble.

His almost 20 years on the force, doing things his way, gave him a certainty that few cops shared. Cops almost never assume innocence in suspects, but most are at least open to the possibility. Because Saldate relied on his instinct about guilt, he interrogated through a tunnel vision that always narrowed down to certain guilt, harboring no room for denial. When he said "tell me the truth," he meant the truth he came in the room with, not the truth the suspect held onto, which he always took for the lie he knew it was.

His character traits and unconventional interrogation style were widely known within the tight circle of homicide-grade detectives. His habit of grilling suspects over and around the thin thread of Miranda warnings was familiar to the small corps of prosecutors that handled the bulk of Maricopa County capital punishment cases. The police brass counted on him to get the confession, especially when forensic evidence was wanting. The heavy-weight prosecutors counted on him to hold up under cross-examination. But even without help from a quick-to-object prosecutor, or a prosecution-friendly judge, Saldate always intimidated young, inexperienced public defenders. Kenneth Ray was no match for Armando Saldate. And prosecutor Noel Levy knew exactly how to present Saldate to a trusting jury. He felt confident with a judge who had a reputation for protecting prosecution witnesses from their own histories. As the Milke case proved, Kenneth Ray was not the first young defense lawyer to cross-examine Saldate in the dark.

Saldate testified against Milke on seven occasions: (1) her grand jury hearing, (2) her voluntariness hearing, (3) his pretrial interview, (4) her petit jury trial, (5) and at two *habeas corpus* hearings in federal court. Sixteen witnesses contradicted various pieces of Saldate's testimony. Some of the contradictions came out of the trials of Scott and Styers. Some of it came from witnesses in Milke's trial and federal hearings. Her relatives had divergent views about Saldate's credibility and what he told them. Kirk Fowler, Dr. Richard Leo, and Robert Johnson discredited his testimony in supplemental hearings.

Granted, some of the contradictions were variations on a theme—time, place, purpose, motive, etc. But other contradictions were substantive. Whether one believes or doubts witness testimony often turns on whether the witness is "credible." Witnesses often inject attitude, perspective, and selective recall into their testimony. Trial lawyers call that "coloring." It is usually unintentional, often subconscious, and with good background, information often exposed as unreliable. But truth, as opposed to witnesses coloring, is much harder to define and recognize. What people declare to be the "the honest truth" is accepted if it isn't directly and effectively challenged. In a courtroom setting, the only way to challenge what a witness says is "true" is by discrediting the witness. The most effective way to discredit a distrustful witness is to impeach him by casting doubt on his credibility.

No one challenged Saldate's truthfulness about Milke's alleged *confession* for her jury. The jurors did not know about his history of confession and interrogation misconduct. His history was tightly contained inside the law enforcement and prosecution community, until 1995.

The breadth and depth of Saldate's misconduct was on the record in Maricopa County, but not publicly known until Anders Rosenquist took over Milke's defense in 1995. He organized a team of law students, young lawyers, paralegal assistants, and researchers. They combed the Maricopa County Superior Court and Arizona Appellate Court records for instances that might cast doubt on Saldate's credibility under factually and legally apt circumstances. Two members of the team were recent Arizona State University law graduates—Robert Chermak and Terri Capozzi. On September 19, 1995, Chermak wrote an 11-page single-spaced memo to Capozzi summarizing 23 trial court cases over the 11 years immediately preceding the Milke case (1981 to 1990). In each case, Saldate was accused of serious misconduct in how he dealt with suspects. Thirteen involved first-degree murder charges, and five were second-degree murder charges. The other five cases involved lesser felonies. In 19 of the 23 cases, judges questioned Saldate's interrogation practices and Miranda compliance. Saldate's misconduct in handling photo lineup sessions and his false or misleading testimony to grand juries was detailed in the remaining four cases. The U.S. Court of Appeals for the Ninth Circuit ultimately reviewed eight of those cases and a Police Department Internal Affairs report.

The Internal Affairs review was in August 1973. Saldate had stopped a motorist driving a car with a "faulty taillight and possibly an outstanding warrant." The case file confirmed he let her go without checking her warrant. She offered him a kiss, so they found a "less conspicuous place," where he leaned inside the car, kissed her, and "deliberately began making advances and taking liberties." They agreed to meet later for sex. He lied about the incident but his supervisors ordered a polygraph. The Chief of Police and the Phoenix City Manager signed his five-day suspension. It said, "because of this incident, your image of honesty, competency and overall reliability must be questioned."

In State v. Yanes, a 1984 Maricopa County Superior Court case, Saldate admitted interrogating a suspect while he was strapped to a hospital bed. The suspect was "incoherent, and disoriented, following a skull fracture." He did not know his "own name, the year, or the president's name." The prosecution nonetheless "presented the suspect's statement at trial." The court vacated his conviction and ordered a new trial, granting defendant's motion to suppress "statements made by the defendant to Armando Saldate."

Two years later, in 1986, Saldate was accused of "lying under oath." Saldate told a grand jury in State v. Rodriguez that "the victim had been shot four times." The victim was shot only once. The prosecutor blamed it on the court reporter, but the court concluded that "Saldate made a false statement, and ordered a redetermination of probable cause."

Saldate faced another lying under oath charge in 1989 in State v. Reynolds. The court found "Saldate made false statements to a grand jury that undercut the defendant's alibi and made the defendant look more culpable than he otherwise would have." The court held the defendant's "right to due process and a fair and impartial presentation of the evidence [was denied] by the manner in which the Grand Jury proceeding was conducted." The court ordered a new finding of probable cause.

Another 1989 case, State v. Rangel, reviewed a third charge of lying under oath. Saldate, the court said, "testified before the grand jury and omitted some of the defendant's statements in such a way as to make the defendant look more culpable." Saldate "and the prosecutor made the presentation of the evidence to the grand jury less than fair and impartial." This resulted in a denial of a substantial procedural right. The court ordered a new finding of probable cause.

In June 1990, two months before the Milke trial started, Saldate faced another Fifth Amendment violation and a fourth charge of lying under oath. In State v. King, Saldate testified on direct examination that the defendant never indicated that he did not want to answer questions. On cross-examination, defense counsel impeached Saldate with his own report. Saldate admitted the false statement and that he had continued to interrogate the defendant despite defendant's demand to cease questioning. The trial judge held "inadmissible all statements made after the defendant said he wanted to cut off questioning."

State v. Jones was a Fourth Amendment case. In this 1990 case, Saldate ordered a juvenile detained in an interrogation room, handcuffed to a table. The court held there was "no probable cause for detention [of the juvenile] and the police [Saldate] clearly had no information linking him to the murder, or the disappearance of the victim." The judge said "the detention ordered by Saldate [was] a show of flagrant misconduct." It ruled the murder confession suppressed "as the fruit of the illegal arrest."

In 1992, after the Milke trial, but before Debra's appeal, Saldate faced two other appeals. The first was a Fifth Amendment violation in State v. Conde. He had interrogated a defendant in an intensive care room in an Arizona hospital. The patient was intubated, connected to intravenous lines, and was drifting "in and out of consciousness." Saldate read him his Miranda rights and interrogated him even though he "didn't really know whether he [the defendant] wasn't responding because he did not understand his rights because of the medication he was on." Saldate admitted the defendant was in pain and that the nurse told him she could not give him more pain medication until he finished talking. The court ruled that the interrogation was "involuntary and inadmissible."

The Arizona Court of Appeals held in another 1992 case, State v. Mahler, that the defendant had made an "unequivocal invocation" of his right to remain silent to Saldate. But, "instead of stopping the interrogation, Saldate pushed on, telling defendant he did not want an admission but he just wanted [defendant's] side of the story." The court wrote, "Officer Saldate's intent was clear—he wanted additional statements from the defendant. This conduct violated defendant's right to remain silent." The court suppressed all statements the defendant made after he invoked his right to silence.

No one knows whether the 23 trial court cases identified by Saldate's habeas team or the nine cases cited in the federal court review were enough to impeach Saldate's confession "technique," or his interrogation "style." Nonetheless, it is clear that what happened to Milke had happened to at least 31 other defendants in Maricopa County—Saldate misusing his authority during custodial interrogations.

The larger issue in the Milke case became whether that was common knowledge in the Maricopa County Attorney's Office, such that it should have produced those other cases as *Brady* or *Giglio* material at Milke's trial. A side issue was whether the 31 incidents of lying under oath and interrogation misconduct would warrant habeas relief once the federal bench got a glimpse of Saldate's long history of misconduct.

10

THE SECRET TAPE—EXHIBIT #147

*J*URIES OFTEN LISTEN TO TAPES properly admitted in evidence. But the Milke jury listened to one not played in open court, or argued by either lawyer during the case. The tape revealed a conversation between Saldate and Sandy Peckinpaugh, recorded several months after Christopher's murder. The story of what some called "the secret tape—Exhibit #147," was first reported by a freelance reporter, Paul Huebl, eight years *after* the trial. He learned about the tape and its significance from Deanna Krupp, one of the 12 jurors who decided the case in 1990. Huebl had written a good deal about the case and had observed the trial in person. As he recalled it, "The jury deliberation did not produce a quick verdict. The jury was out for several days. We all suspected they were deadlocked. At times there was laughter so loud we could hear it out in the hall. With such a terrible case, I could not imagine what the jury found to be so damned funny."

The jury returned its verdict—guilty on all counts. Huebl described the jury as "a stern, poker-faced group of men and women" when they came into the courtroom to announce their verdict. Judge Hendrix, Huebl recalled later, "[t]hanked the jurors for their service, advising them that the attorneys and media present would like to talk with them, but that they were under no obligation to answer to anyone at all." Huebl and the rest of the "gaggle of other reporters," had many questions. But the jury, he said, "fled the courthouse quicker than [he had] seen happen before or since. No comments, no questions, just silence."

Eight years later, Huebl got another chance to write a follow-up story about the case. He discovered what he dubbed "the secret tape." Judge Hendrix allowed it in evidence at prosecutor Levy's request, as Exhibit #147. Huebl got a list of jurors, located them, found their telephone numbers, and called each one. He told them who he was and why he was calling (to talk about Debra Milke). He recorded each call. "Some hung up on me immediately; others used profanity before they slammed the phone in my ear. Others politely refused comment. The eighth call was to juror Deanna Krupp. She was pleasant and told me, 'I'm sorry Mr. Huebl; we all agreed never to talk about our deliberations. I don't want to break my promise here.'"

Huebl was persistent. "I don't want to ask you the intimate details of what happened. I just want to know what was the single most significant piece of evidence that brought the conviction of Debra Milke?" Ms. Krupp said, "That had to be the tape." Huebl had sat through the entire trial and could not recall a tape recording being played for the jury. Krupp explained that the tape she was talking about "had not been played in the courtroom." Krupp told him that the jury members "found the tape among the evidence in the boxes brought to them to examine in the jury room."

Krupp's explanation was fascinating. "Since the jury was deadlocked . . . the prosecutor, Noel Levy, had told [us] to look carefully at each and every piece of evidence . . . we would find answers to [our] questions. [We] searched once again and found that tape, requested the bailiff get a player for it, and [we] listened to the tape intently. It was a conversation between Saldate and Debra Milke's younger sister Sandy. Saldate was interviewing Sandy in Wyoming in connection with the murder investigation. Saldate did not bring a tape recorder, but Milke's sister wanted this taped and produced her own to make a record of the interview."

Huebl reported in his 1998 story that Armando Saldate told Sandy, on the 1990 tape, that "Debra Milke flashed her breasts during his interview, trying to seduce him. He went on to say Milke confessed to him that she failed in an earlier attempt to murder Christopher by putting cyanide in his cereal. Saldate told Milke's sister he had this confession all on tape."

According to Huebl, Sandy Peckinpaugh sent her tape to the "prosecutors at their request. A copy was turned over by prosecutors to defense lawyer Ken Ray. Ray made a clumsy . . . and unsuccessful attempt to play it in court during his closing argument. But his recorder/player wouldn't work. Ray put the tape aside and it never resurfaced because it was simply forgotten."

Anders Rosenquist, Milke's lawyer at the post-conviction review stage, confirmed that Levy had offered Exhibit #147 in evidence, without objection by Ray. But, if Huebl's report is correct, that tape broke the deadlock, permitting the jury to return a unanimous verdict. It was based on their belief that what Saldate told Sandy Peckinpaugh was true—Debra Milke had "flashed her breasts at him, trying to seduce him, *and* he had her confession on tape." No one, not even the prosecution, believed Saldate's claim about Milke's behavior during the interrogation. No one could imagine her trying to seduce him, then or at any other time. And no one ever suggested that he had taped the interview. But Saldate's word was apparently good enough for Milke's sister.

11

THE SALDATE SYNOPSIS

A SYNOPSIS IS A CONDENSED STATEMENT or outline. When used by law enforcement, it should mean an abstract of the case. But Armando Saldate used the term "synopsis" to identify the supplemental report he wrote on December 7, 1989, the day after he dictated the infamous "paraphrased account" of Milke's interrogation. The second document is a stream of consciousness narrative containing unedited, random thoughts that presumably went through his mind before they became comprehensible. His synopsis "indexes" three suspects (Roger Mark Scott, James Lynn Styers, and Debra Jean Milke) in standard police demographic terms (Race/Gender/DOB/Height/ Weight/Hair and Eye Color/Telephone Number/Social Security Number/Street Address/Employment Status/Booking Number). It "catalogues" what Saldate presumably thought was the hard, or tangible evidence in the case: 1. R&G .22 caliber revolver SN #358440, blue steel, brown plastic grips. Fully loaded with six silver cased copper plated hollow point cartridges. 2. Audio tape confession by Roger Scott on 12/3/89. 3. Three spent .22 caliber casings (found on West Union Hills Drive). 4. One live .22 caliber cartridge.

Telling by its absence is any reference to Milke's alleged confession, as "evidence." Yet, it was the only evidentiary connection between her son's murder and the charges against her. Saldate identified two support personnel (Dennis Degler, a crime lab photographer, and Noel Levy, a prosecutor). He also named himself and six other police officers as "investigators" (Robert Mills, Jim House, Russ Davis, Sgt. S. Ontiveros, Charles Masino, and Sgt. Henry Cusson). He attached crime scene diagrams to his synopsis, two search warrants for 4818 W. Bethany #120 and 7734 N. 12th Street #5), and a "vehicle."

The narrative portion of the synopsis is a scant two pages written in language that is conclusory, unreferenced, and tightly focused on his role rather than the case itself. He begins by concluding that Styers and Scott took Christopher to the crime scene on "12/2/89 between 1100 hours and 1430 hours . . . while there Styers shot and killed the victim and left him in the desert area . . . the murder had been arranged by the victim's mother . . . after the murder Styers and Scott went to Metrocenter and claimed the victim was missing and possibly kidnapped as pre-arranged during the conspiracy."

His third paragraph is an abstract digesting "my interview with Styers." It reads like a short travelogue of Styers' auto trip from his apartment to Scott's apartment, then to a pizza parlor, followed by a stop at a shopping mall so "the victim could see Santa Claus," ending with a two-sentence description of Styers "and the victim stopping by the bathroom at the Sears store . . . Styers coming out of the stall . . . could not find Chris . . . Styers denied any knowledge about Chris' disappearance and was later released."

Saldate next summarizes what Scott "[t]old Det. Bob Mills . . . [He was] dropped off at home before Styers went to Metrocenter with Chris . . . lost touch of Phil . . . ran into my friend Jim . . . looked for Chris for a short time . . . had to go home to take care of mother."

The narrative drills down to solving the crime. "At approximately 1258 hours, I began the interview of Roger . . . I immediately read him his rights . . . he admitted he had not gone to Sears . . . only lied because he did not want to get involved . . . Roger finally admitted that Jim had shot and killed the victim . . . Roger admitted conspiring not only with Jim but the victim's mother to kill her son . . . their motivation was a $5000 life insurance policy."

He deals summarily with Styers: "Jim was arrested and interviewed however he refused to comment and later booked in the County Jail for 1st degree murder and conspiracy to commit murder."

He allocates only three sentences to Debra Milke: "Debra Milke, the victim's mother, was interviewed in Florence Arizona by me and read her Miranda warnings which she understood. She later admitted conspiring with Jim Styers and Roger Scott to have her son killed. She said her motivation was that she did not want her son to grow up like his father and become an alcoholic and drug abuser."

Saldate summarizes his role in acquiring the physical evidence: "During his interview Roger indicated where the three empty shell casings and three live rounds were thrown out of the car by Jim . . . a search team found them . . . along with one live round . . . the murder weapon was at his home and later recovered by virtue of a search warrant."

He ends tersely: "All three suspects were booked and officially charged with murder in the first-degree, conspiracy to commit murder first-degree, kidnapping, and child abuse . . . Therefore, this case is cleared by arrest."

12

FIRST DOUBTS ABOUT MILKE'S ALLEGED CONFESSION

*I*N WHAT WOULD BECOME A widely published breaking-news story, Paul Huebl, an investigative reporter, recorded a jailhouse interview with Debra Milke shortly after Saldate turned her over to the jailers on the night of December 3, 1989. Huebl, a former Cook County and Chicago police officer, worked for local and national TV news organizations. As news spread of Milke's arrest on police scanners, KSAZ-TV (Channel 10) sent Huebl to get an interview with Debra Milke. He hoped to "capture" incriminating statements from her for the "dinner hour newscast." Instead, he found her "distraught" and "adamant" about her denial of any involvement in her son's murder. She was "astonished" and "confused when he told her the police were saying she 'confessed.'" Huebl found her perplexed state and denial of any confession "genuine." From a timing perspective (minutes after she got away from Saldate) and as an independent witness (a reporter with nothing to gain if she had not confessed), Huebl's assessment was highly relevant and strong corroboration of Milke's version of what happened at the Pinal County Jail earlier that evening. From a legal standpoint, evidence that is highly probative, because it matches a defendant's account of what happened, provides insight into a defendant's demeanor following a custodial interrogation. As it turned out, Huebl's tape-recorded interview with Milke at the Maricopa County Jail was the only interview she gave that night. While Milke's trial judge ignored him, and his testimony, her appellate judges did not. Huebl interviewed her within "hours of her arrival at the Madison Street jail with a hidden tape recorder." He recalled that she was "still wearing the same clothes she'd worn when they arrested her in Florence."

Based on his 20 years in law enforcement, and assuming she'd confessed, he thought she would continue to incriminate herself on "his" tape. And he was surprised to learn that he had the *only* tape-recorded interview that day. His experience suggested that defendants confess "out of guilt feelings, or hopes of obtaining a reduced sentence." But Debra appeared "astonished" when he told her that she'd already confessed. To Huebl, her "perplexed state appeared genuine. She had no concept of how the interview with Saldate could be viewed as a confession. He tested her by telling her the police said the motive was to collect insurance. Debra responded, 'That's off the wall, who told you that?'"

Besides his taped interview and his sworn affidavit, Huebl also testified in the U.S. District Court habeas proceedings as a witness for the petitioner. He testified at length, and under oath, about the most important question and answer on his tape. "Did you tell the police that you had anything to do with the death of your son?" "That's crazy. Who told you that? I had nothing to do with the death of my son."

Huebl testified: "She looked me right in the eye. She was sane-looking. She was sober-looking. She was dead serious. I was serious. I thought it was a serious question. And I felt I was getting a freak answer . . . I took it over to Channel 10, to the news room . . . the 6:00 broadcast was by Mary Cox . . . she broadcast it to over a million people."

Later, before her trial, Huebl said that Debra's lawyer Ken Ray caught him in a hallway and said, "'You're the man that interviewed Debra. Don't you dare talk to my client ever again.' He scolded me. He was angry. But he never asked me what she said." Nor did he call Paul Huebl as a defense witness at her trial.

13

THE 116TH MARICOPA COUNTY GRAND JURY

IVE DAYS AFTER THEIR ARRESTS, the Maricopa County Grand Jury indicted Milke, Styers, and Scott. As is almost always the case in homicide investigations, the grand jury only heard one side. The basis for the case comes from the police department's investigation and the county attorney's prosecutorial discretion. A grand jury indictment is a formal accusation that a person committed a crime. The grand jury does not decide guilt or innocence. It only expresses a collective belief there was *probable cause* to believe Milke, Styers, and Scott killed Christopher Milke.

Grand jury proceedings are always secret, private matters. The grand jury members act only on prosecutor's information. They neither ask for, nor accept input from, the individuals against whom an indictment is sought. The Maricopa County Attorney's Office convinced the grand jury there was enough evidence to show that all three defendants probably committed Christopher Milke's murder and should be formally accused of it.

A *grand* jury differs from a *petit* jury. Grand juries determine whether a person may be tried for a crime. Petit juries listen to the evidence at the trial and determine guilt. Petit is the French word for "small." Petit juries usually comprise 12 jurors in criminal cases. Grand is the French word for "large." Grand juries have from 10 to 25 jurors.

The Milke grand jury had 14. Deputy County Attorney Miles Nelson told the grand jury, "This investigation involves an alleged homicide, an alleged conspiracy to commit homicide, an alleged child abuse and an alleged kidnapping, on December 2, 1989 in Phoenix, Maricopa County." He gave them copies of the Arizona Revised Statutes regarding the legal standard (probable cause). He read aloud the substantive sections of Arizona law defining premeditation, homicide, first-degree murder, second-degree murder, manslaughter, and negligent homicide. He also talked about the general legal concepts covering sexual assault or molestation of minors, child abuse, physical injury, conspiracy, and culpable mental state. Detective Armando Saldate was the sole witness called to testify before the grand jury. They never saw his reports. No physical evidence was documented, other than by reference from one of the prosecutors or Saldate.

Nelson said the alleged victim was Christopher Milke. He reminded the jurors they had "to make a decision in the investigation based solely and exclusively on the evidence presented. . . ." He said there had been media coverage of the crime. Every juror was a long-time resident, and presumably a "good citizen." By definition, that means they were the kind of people interested in and caretakers of their communities, including the city of Phoenix. Nelson likely assumed his next question was easy to answer in the affirmative: "Have any of you heard, read, or seen anything with respect to the case that would in any way interfere, or prevent you from acting as a fair and impartial juror during the course of this investigation?" Apparently, there was no physical or visible response from them. He continued, "I take it from your silence that each of you would be able to make a decision in this investigation based solely and exclusively on the evidence presented to you during the course of this hearing."

He never gave them the chance to say that yes, they knew about the case from the massive press coverage for the last six days. The headlines and above-the-fold news stories had focused on the horrific murder of a four-old boy. There had been scores of print stories and anchor-level broadcasts on the crime, the arrests, and at least one interview of Debra Milke. In that interview, Milke vigorously denied ever confessing to Saldate, or any involvement in the murder of her son. Pictures of all three defendants blanketed the valley for a week. With that perfunctory assessment of bias out of the way, as though it were mere housekeeping, Noel Levy called Armando Saldate, Jr., to the grand jury's witness box.

~

AFTER INTRODUCING SALDATE AS THE "case agent," Levy asked his star witness to confirm basic case facts. The murder occurred between 11:00 A.M. and 2:30 P.M. on December 2, 1989. He had read the entire police report in both the missing person investigation and the homicide case. He was asked to step into the case because of his expertise as a homicide detective and his interaction with suspects. There had been 40 to 50 officers involved *before* "he was called in on Sunday morning, at 8:45." Saldate summarized the story Styers had first told the police. Then he told them Scott's first story. He assured them Styers and Scott had initially "helped" the police and were "free to come and go at any time before they were arrested later" on Sunday afternoon. He said other officers briefed him on the case at 10:00 that morning "so that he could confront Scott." That confrontation occurred at 12:50 P.M.

Within "a short period of time . . . he indicated that he [Scott] had not told the truth initially . . . in my interview with him he corrected his story . . . there was no Phil . . . later in our interview he indicated that he knew where the child's body was at . . . he would take me to that child's body . . . he also indicated that Mr. Styers had shot the child three times in the head."

"Okay," Nelson added to Saldate's narrative, "you gave him his rights. You brought up the discrepancies. . . ."

"That's correct."

"I believe," Nelson said, taking over the presentation, "did he tell you that he later saw, according to this story, later saw Styers there, and so forth, and then you said you left him alone. Didn't you tell him, well, you didn't feel he was telling the truth, something to that effect, left him alone, you came back, and then he started telling you the facts of the . . . that the child was dead and where the body was?"

"That's correct."

By answering, "That's correct" two consecutive times, Saldate established a pattern of responding to lawyer-speak, by labeling the questions as *correct*.

The story, as corrected by Scott, and as posed by Saldate, with a lot of help from Nelson, eventually included the logistics of the crime scene, what Scott heard happen from his vantage point in the car, when Styers returned from the wash, and how he removed bullets from his small .22 caliber revolver. He testified, as though he had been there, about how the bullets were thrown out of the car on the south side of Union Hills Drive on the way back to Metrocenter. He explained finding the shells, "along with a live round, which is right now being analyzed."

Nelson interrupted for clarity, "So the analysis isn't complete, but does it fit with at least the area that Scott told you about?"

"That's correct."

Nelson and Saldate informed the jurors about small details—Styers' tennis shoes, and how and where Scott got rid of them at Metrocenter. Saldate said he did "a search warrant on Scott's home and did find a .22 caliber weapon, inside a box in his closet." He did not say it was the murder weapon and none of the jurors was curious enough to ask how it related to the crime.

Through the orchestrated Q & A, the jury learned the details of Dr. Bolduc's autopsy on December 4, 1989. Nelson asked Saldate if the bullets and fragments Dr. Bolduc removed were "consistent with a .22 caliber-type of lead bullet."

"That's correct."

Nelson circled back to Saldate and his interaction with Scott. "Now with reference to the allegation of a conspiracy, did you have further discussion with Roger Scott concerning whether this had been a pre-planned event, and if so, with whom, and when, and from whom did it originate?"

Saldate said Scott was involved, Styers was involved and " . . . he and Jim Styers had conspired with the mother of the child, Debra Milke . . . Debra Milke wanted it done . . . later, he with Jim Styers, met with Debra at least on several occasions to plan this murder out . . . he indicated that Debra was disappointed, in fact angry at them on several occasions because they had taken the child out on several occasions to do the murder, but had brought him back for several reasons. The reasons—basically because there were too many people around or the plan could not be carried out as they wished."

"Was the plan to kill the child and then go to Metrocenter and report the child missing?"

"That's correct."

"Did he explain whether or not there was any money aspect involved, or an insurance policy with reference to murdering the child as discussed?"

"Yes, he indicated the child, as told to them by Debra, that the child had a $5000 life insurance policy and that Debra would give them money after the child was dead. . . ."

Nelson moved back to Scott's actual participation. "And on the particular occasion of the Saturday afternoon, December 2, did he indicate, Scott, that he merely drove, let them out, drove back and forth, then heard shots, so forth? In other words, he wasn't actually present at the site of the killing *per se*?"

"That's correct."

The balance of Saldate's testimony related to Debra Milke. Nelson's first question on this aspect of the case was telling. "Now, fortified with the information from Mr. Scott, and having gone through, found the body, and also items, did you then have an opportunity to interview Debra Milke?"

Asking whether Saldate was "fortified" with Scott's information foreshadowed how Saldate approached his "interview" with Milke. But the grand jury likely thought little about his tunnel vision. Saldate explained that shortly after finding the body, he went to Florence and contacted Debra. "She was in Florence visiting her father, on Sunday evening. She came down to the station voluntarily and waited for me until I arrived."

"And when you arrived, did you give her her Miranda rights?"

"Yes, I did."

"And what did you tell her and what was her reaction?"

"I told her that her son had been found . . . he was shot . . . she immediately began to yell and cry and scream. I told her I wouldn't tolerate that. I told her she was under arrest for murder, and she again began to yell and scream, and again I told her I would not tolerate that and wanted to speak to her and interview her in regards to her involvement in the murder, which we did."

"And so, did she voluntarily agree to discuss the situation with you?"

"Yes, she did."

"What did she tell you, in essence?"

"She told me that she had gotten the idea at approximately one month ago about killing the child. She said that at first she thought about suicide, but had decided not to because the child would then be released to her husband. She said she wanted the child killed because he was starting to act like her husband, would be just like her husband. She said she loved the child and wanted him to go up with God and not have to live in the house that her husband did. She indicated that she talked to Jim Styers, her roommate, told him about it, and that he agreed to do it. Later, she said, Styers got in touch with Roger Scott . . . all three of them discussed doing this . . . she said her motivation was that she wanted her child killed . . . but she did not want to collect the insurance . . . that may have been their motivation [but not hers. . . .]"

"On . . . Saturday, was she aware that James Styers was taking the child, and was she aware that the plan was to kill him that day?"

"That's correct."

"According to her statements to you?"

"Yes, that morning she woke up, she dressed the child. She knew that they were going to do it that day, or were planning to do it that day. They told him that he was going to see Santa Claus . . . they took him . . . she knew the plan was to take him out to the location, kill him, and then go back to the Sears, Metrocenter Mall and claim the child had disappeared. . . ."

"And whose vehicle was utilized?"

"Her vehicle was utilized. She lent Jim her vehicle."

Apparently, the deputy county attorneys in the room assumed the jury now had enough questions to pose to the witness. Nelson turned to the jurors and asked, "Does the Grand Jury have any questions?"

One juror asked whether footprints were found near the body. Another asked if the prints matched the tennis shoes. Saldate told them "the analysis is being completed at this time." Another juror asked whether the child was found wearing snakeskin boots, which was apparently confusing, given Saldate's answers about tennis shoes. That question likely came from TV news stories, which had widely reported Chris's snakeskin boots. Saldate clarified, "Styers wore tennis shoes and the child wore snakeskin boots."

Noel Levy jumped back in.

"Wait a minute, Detective Saldate; we don't know that as a fact. That's what Mr. Scott said."

A different juror asked whether Styers had been questioned. Nelson answered that by rephrasing the juror's question to Saldate.

"Other than those statements that you're already presented to the Grand Jury, you obtained no other additional statements from Mr. Styers. Is that correct?"

That was not correct. Styers consistently made exculpatory statements. But Saldate may have assumed the grand jury would only want to hear about incriminating statements. His answer was, "That's correct."

Another juror asked, "So am I to understand then, Mr. Styers then has not been arrested on this charge, if he hasn't been . . ."

Nelson cut the juror off. "The question as to whether he's been arrested would not be relevant to your determination whether there's been probable cause."

Since there is no judge or defense lawyer in the room, the prosecutor has the luxury of objecting to jurors' questions and ruling on his own objection, by not permitting the question to be asked of his own witness. But here, they faced a determined juror. "Well, let me rephrase it then. He then has not been asked questions about the child's murder, just the fact that the child is still missing, am I understanding that correctly?"

Levy jumped on this one. Turning to Saldate, he said, "Let me ask the detective this way. Has what you've gone through, is that what Mr. Styers explained to you about the missing child?"

But Saldate didn't quite get it. "Regarding the missing child?" he asked Levy.

"Yes," Levy answered.

Saldate got it this time. "That is correct."

The juror was not satisfied. "May I, just to get this straight in my own mind then . . . Debra Jean Milke has been, or is in custody, and knows that the child has been murdered through you by Scott's testimony to you; is that correct?"

Nelson seemed worried. "Is this a question you're asking the detective?"

The juror responded, "I'm trying to get in my mind here a situation, because when Debra was summoned to the police station and was told of the death of the child by Officer Saldate here, she is aware that the child is dead?"

Nelson gave up. Turning to Saldate, he said, "You can answer that question."

Saldate said, "Yes."

The juror tried again. "Right. And she knows Styers is the one, or she knows that you know that Styers is the one that shot the child, from what Roger Scott told you."

Levy, apparently worried about where this was going, interrupted. "Detective Saldate, that calls for an opinion."

Nelson to the rescue. "Let me put it this way, Detective, can you answer that question?"

Levy objected to Nelson's question. "In a factual setting with reference to . . ."

But Saldate gave the wrong answer: "No."

Levy clarified, "Persons making statements?"

Nelson asked, "You don't know what she knows then?"

Finally, Saldate got back with the program. "I don't know what she knows until she tells me."

But the juror was on a roll. "I thought you told me you had told her the child had been murdered?"

"Yes, I did tell her that."

"And there was some discussion about not tolerating her behavior or something and I was under the impression that she was aware of the premeditation. I mean she related the story to you, that yes, they had planned this, she had gone about it a month ago, and all these things?"

"That's correct."

There is an old saying that a good prosecutor could indict a hamburger. But this juror was no hamburger. "So, I'm a little confused. I'm trying to put this into simple terms in my mind. Basically, in layman's terms here, Styers is the only one that doesn't know that you folks know that he's the one that killed him?"

Levy tried to save Saldate as best he could. "What he knows would be calling for speculation. I don't think Detective Saldate can answer what's in his mind."

The juror wasn't having it. "In other words, he has not been informed—I mean—is life going on normal here? I mean Milke and Styers are living together, right?"

Nelson turned up the heat. "Detective. You can ask [sic] the question, does Mr. Styers know he's being investigated for the murder of the child."

But the juror was not satisfied and turned to Saldate, "So Styers is aware that he is a chief suspect in this investigation."

"Yes," Saldate answered.

The juror pressed on. "And Scott is still in custody?"

There were no cameras or audio recordings. No one can know how exasperated or frustrated Nelson might have been, but he gave it one more try with this rebellious juror. "The question of whether or not a person is in custody is totally irrelevant to your determination as to whether there's probable cause."

"Oh. Okay. So what are we trying to determine here?"

Nelson ducked. Turning to the full panel of jurors, he asked, "Are there any additional questions?"

"Yes," a different juror said. "Debra Milke has been charged with the murder. You told her that she was charged with murder when you read her her Miranda rights and stuff like that when she was screaming her head off, you told her to knock it off. She started screaming again. You told her to knock it off. She was charged with murder."

Saldate, "I told her she was under arrest for murder."

"Right."

Now another juror joined the fray. "I was wondering if Ms. Milke told you that her husband had a mental condition, or what it was that she didn't want this child to grow up like him. Was there some definite thing that you're able to tell us like that, or just generalism [sic] she didn't want him to grow up?"

Levy gave Saldate permission: "I think you can answer that."

"She told me that her husband was a heavy drinker, a drug user, had spent time in prison, and that she didn't want him to grow up with that."

In what might have looked to Levy and Nelson like a full-fledged jury revolt, a new juror popped up. "Has it been determined who the owner of the gun was? Is there a registered owner of the gun, or who bought and purchased the gun?"

These grand jurors were definitely not acting like hamburgers. They seemed interested in actual facts, not police rubber stamps to prosecutor's theories.

"That takes some time and that has not been done. And that's being done."

Nelson tried again. "Are there any further questions? . . . There being no further questions . . ."

Levy said, "Well before we break, in summary, then, Detective Saldate[, what we have] is that both Debra Milke and Roger Scott have indicated that they, including Styers, agreed to . . . that the child should be killed. Is that correct?"

"That's correct."

"And then the child was taken out, put into Roger Scott's car, shot by, according to Roger Scott, shot by Jim Styers, because he heard three shots, and James Styers said he shot the child. Is that correct?"

"That is correct."

Apparently, Levy was not as fully briefed as one might have wished. It was not Roger Scott's car. Roger Scott did not say it was his car. And Styers never said he shot he child. But Saldate presumably chose not to correct Levy.

"That is correct."

Levy continued to lead the witness. "And on autopsy the child was found with three bullet holes in the back of the head purporting to be .22 caliber, is that correct?"

"That is correct."

"And then you found a .22 caliber gun that he said that Styers gave him to get rid of in his house?"

"That is also correct."

Levy plowed thrice-plowed ground. He went back and asked Saldate questions about the tennis shoes in the bushes; the child's alleged disappearance in the bathroom; the time frame that Scott gave him indicating that the child had already been killed when the Metrocenter search was started; the alleged fact that Styers was "living with" Milke; her admission that she knew Styers took the child and understood it was "to kill the child"; and Roger Scott's "knowledge they would kill the child that day." He got affirmative answers from Saldate. Then he asked, "Any other questions?"

A juror asked, "Have you been able to ascertain the time of death?"

Saldate said he had not, but "the doctor I don't believe can."

A different juror asked, "And has there been a record of a phone call at that particular timeframe determined in that time span?"

No one understood the question; so the juror rephrased, "The time span from the time they supposedly left the scene of the crime, arrived at Metrocenter, and placed a call to Debra Milke?"

Saldate answered, "There is [sic] no records for any public phones that someone uses to call someone else. There is no record of it unless it's a toll call."

"Oh, but I thought she was in Florence."

Levy to the rescue again. "She went to Florence later."

"She went to Florence after the disappearance of her son?"

"That is correct."

A different juror modified the question. "So, after Jim's call?"

"That is correct."

Nelson kept trying to end the questions. "Are there any further questions?"

An inquisitive juror spoke up. "Who did Scott say drove the car out to the desert area?"

Saldate answered. "He said he drove part way and Mr. Styers also drove part of the way. The last part he drove. Styers took the child from the car."

Levy: "Any other questions?"

Nelson: "There being no other questions, Detective, you are excused. Arizona law prohibits you from discussing your testimony here with anyone other than the prosecution. Would you please remain outside in the witness room?"

When Saldate left, Nelson asked the jury members whether they had any "legal" questions. Hearing none, he said, "There being no legal questions at this time, I'll remind you of your options. We'll leave the room to allow you time to consider those options."

The official court record contains the reporter's official note: "Thereupon, the Deputy County Attorney and the Court Reporter were excused from the Grand Jury Room, were subsequently recalled into the Grand Jury Room, and the following proceedings took place."

The foreman of the grand jury: "The jury has voted and directs the County Attorney to prepare a draft indictment for our consideration."

Nelson was ready. "I have prepared a draft indictment for you to consider."

The court reporter noted, "Thereupon, the Deputy County Attorney and the Court Reporter were excused from the Grand Jury Room, were subsequently recalled into the Grand Jury Room, and the following proceedings took place."

The jury foreman: "The clerk will read the Grand Jury findings."

The clerk: "The grand jury with 14 members present and only members of the Grand Jury present, deliberated upon evidence, and with 14 jurors voting by a vote of 14 to 0, returned a true bill."

The term "true bill" means an indictment, as in: "The grand jury impaneled in Maricopa County returned a true bill indicting Debra Milke, James Styers, and Roger Scott for first-degree murder." While thought quaint by many, charges are handed *down*, but a true bill of indictment is handed *up*. Historically, that's because in days of yore, judges who handed them down from the bench made charges. But these days, grand juries hand their indictments *up* to the bench.

At that point, Superior Court Commissioner Patrick O'Neil entered the courtroom. The grand jury foreman addressed the court. "Your Honor, case 116 GJ 83, a true bill. My signature appears on the indictment endorsing it as a true bill."

Deputy County Attorney Kmiec said, "This is an NSI [Notice of a Supervening Indictment]? All defendants are non-bindable on Count 1 and Mr. Levy will give you the factual basis and the information on Counts 2, 3, and 4."

Levy: "Your Honor, Count 1 is murder. Count 2 is conspiracy to commit murder, first-degree. Count 3 is child abuse. Count 4 is kidnapping, both counts 3 and 4 are alleged as dangerous crimes against children. I have the warrant fact sheets here. The way I read the statute of 13-3961 B and E as to counts 2 and 3 being dangerous crimes against children, that they are not bailable, and also on count 1 we're alleging that it is a capital case on the basis that there is a child that was killed under the age of 15 years, which is an aggravated factor. Pecuniary gain at least as to two of the defendants, Scott and Styers. As to the purported, there in fact was an insurance policy $5000 on the child's life payable to Debra Milke, so there are factors that make this a capital case."

Levy went on at some length, arguing that none of the defendants should be granted bail on any of the counts.

Commissioner O'Neil asked, "Do you want to place anything on the record so that I can find that the *proof is evident, presumption great?*"

The phrase "proof is evident, presumption great" is a historic idiom of American law. The Arizona Constitution provides that all persons accused of a capital offense shall be bailable unless "the proof is evident, or the presumption great" that they committed the offense. A defendant is constitutionally and statutorily entitled to both the presumption of innocence at every stage of a criminal proceeding and the presumption that bail will be granted. The judge was signaling Levy that he had forgotten to justify the state's request to withhold bail for these defendants. Levy got it.

"Okay," Levy said. "Defendant stated, after Miranda rights, so forth, that there was a conspiracy to commit to murder the child involving the mother [who] wanted the child killed. Styers who lived with her, was to kill the child, and he drove them out to the desert where the child was killed. Debra Milke, also after Miranda, talks that she wanted the child killed; she wanted James Styers to do it. She knew that he wanted Scott to be involved with him, and they tried to do it several times before. On the day in question, she knew they were going to take the child out to kill the child and confirmed about the insurance policy, and when Styers called her later that afternoon and said he was at Metrocenter, so forth, she knew the child had been killed because that was part of the plot, to say the child had become missing from Metrocenter."

Commissioner O'Neill: "And that last information was obtained from Defendant C?"

"Yes. And then, of course, there's physical evidence. Three shots to the back of the child's head. Casing. Gun. Bullets, those sorts of things."

With that unscripted, 150-word, spontaneous statement, based entirely on inadmissible third-party hearsay, the judge accepted the magic words in capital litigation—*proof is evident, presumption great.*

Commissioner O'Neill: "It's ordered assigning this cause a criminal number."

Deputy County Attorney Kmiec corrected Deputy County Attorney Levy. "The paperwork does not read as Mr. Levy just stated."

"Yes. Do you want a chance to read that to change it or what are you proposing?"

"Your Honor, I believe that the court clerk can change the paperwork on those issues."

And with that administrative assignment, the court clerk was handed the *proof is evident, presumption great* paperwork assignment in a capital murder case.

Commissioner O'Neill had a short discussion with the prosecutors about warrants, ordered a new warrant, and a new supervening indictment. He told the prosecutors to issue his order, and serve copies on the parties confirming "release or custody. . . ."

Kmiec interrupted, speaking in prosecutor-to-judge jargon. "They're NSI, non-bondable on one two, warrant on Counts 3 and 4."

The court commissioner, well versed in grand jury jargon, ordered all three defendants subject to prior court orders relating to "custody status." Repeating the magic words, he stated his finding: "The proof is evident, presumption great that the requirements of our laws and Constitution have been satisfied at least at this time." Combining jargon with constitutional law, this meant that he refused bail in all three cases. In capital cases, it is legally acceptable for the court to deny bail on a low standard of evidence. If the judge makes a perfunctory finding that the crime is evident, *or* the presumption is great that the crime alleged has occurred, and the prosecution asks that the defendant be held without bail, the court always honors the request. The bail burden then shifts to the defendant, who may file a written motion asking that bail be set, alleging "proof is *not* evident or that the presumption is *not* great." That is often called a "Simpson hearing" in Arizona.

14

ARRESTS AND SEARCH WARRANTS

ETECTIVES OLSON AND KAVANAGH WENT to Judge Les
Anderson's home at 11:55 P.M. on Sunday night to get a
search warrant. They gave him the paperwork and a detailed explanation of the legal and factual basis for two warrants—one for Debra
Milke's car and the other for James Styers' apartment.

Judge Anderson swore Detective Olson as a witness to make the
case for searching Styers' apartment. He told Judge Anderson they
had good legal reason to believe they would find a ".22 caliber revolver
handgun, insurance papers on Christopher Milke, and other evidence
that tends to show that the crime of murder occurred and that James
Styers and Roger Scott committed the crime of murder and conspiracy
at 7734 North 12th Street, Apartment #5." Judge Olson signed the
warrant. On December 4, at 12:30 A.M., Detectives Olson, Kavanagh,
Mills, and Sgt. Ontiveros entered Styers' apartment "without problems . . . completed a systematic search . . . Det. Kavanagh seized
several items of evidence . . . investigation continuing." They found a
.22 caliber handgun in Scott's apartment, just where he said it would
be. From there, Detective Mills went to the police impound lot to
search Milke's white Toyota Corolla, which he erroneously presumed
was titled in her name; title was held in her mother's name, Renate

Janka. Styers' signed consent is attached to the booking slip. It allowed the Phoenix Police Department to search "a 1986 Toyota White 4D." Detective Mills witnessed, signed, and dated the form, "12-3-89 at 2:21 A.M." They had no legal basis to search it because Styers had no authority to grant permission to search a vehicle Debra Milke's mother owned. But no one contested the search. He found some incriminating evidence and a good deal of circumstantial evidence: "(1) Pair of brown leather like gloves with paint and possible blood. (2) Spectrum 1 brand binoculars in black vinyl case, (3) a yellow child's hard hat w/"Shocking" label on front, and (4) a camouflage baseball cap w/Marine emblem, discharge pin and rank insignia on front—name of Jim Styers written on inside." He found the following on the front seat of the car: "(5) Sunglasses w/rope found on transmission hump in front of gear shift. (6) Red child size Phoenix Cardinal shirt w/tag attached, (7) one plastic box of CCI brand .22 cal. ammunition. Head stamp "C" silver casing with copper plated hollow point bullets. 18 missing from box of 50, K-mart sale tag reading $2.19—Key 7/." Each item would eventually be introduced as evidence in three separate trials. The police also found a bag of grapefruit, which was impounded, but not marked as evidence. That report authorizes the release of the car "to the mother, Debra Milke." Neither the bag of grapefruit nor the car was ever returned.

Styers' "official" Arrest/Booking Record in the Phoenix Police Department's files identifies the arresting officers as D. Armitage and T. Carey. The charge was one count of first-degree murder and one count of conspiracy to commit first-degree murder. After handcuffing Styers, they searched him and found $2.20 in currency and change, a wallet, four keys on a ring, a watch, and a change purse. T.D. Carey, a uniformed officer, wrote the official arrest report. Carey also transported Styers by police car from his apartment to jail. On the way, Styers asked Carey "if [you] had found Christopher . . . I hope you did, but I'm not sure if I want to know, but if you did, he's probably dead." Carey took Styers to 620 West Washington, police headquarters, and turned him over to Detective Olson.

Scott's "official" Arrest/Booking Record identifies the arresting officer as Detective R. Mills. The charge is one count of first-degree murder under the same statute assigned to Styers and an identical count of conspiracy to commit first-degree murder. Scott had $118.29 in currency and change, along with a watch, keys on a fob, a wallet with ID, a black comb, Marlboro 100's, a lighter, and a brown belt. Attached to his booking slip is Scott's signed consent allowing the police to search his mother's apartment. Detective Mills witnessed his signature.

Milke's "official" Arrest/Booking Record identifies the arresting officer as Detective A. Saldate. She was charged with the same crimes, in the same priority, as Styers and Scott. Her belongings were described as "zero currency and change, a woman's watch, and a Cortez High School class ring."

Detective Saldate summarized the evidence on December 7, 1989 at 0030 hours: "A R&G .22 caliber revolver SN #58440, blue steel, brown plastic grips. Fully loaded with six silver cased copper plated hollow point cartridges. Audio tape confession by Roger Scott on 12/3/89. Three spent .22 caliber casings (found on West Union Hills Drive). One live .22 caliber cartridge." That's it—that was all the evidence Saldate said supported his case against Milke.

On January 31, 1990, almost two months after the arrests of all three suspects, Detective Mills tracked down one final piece of incriminating evidence against Styers. He interviewed a man named Steven Hicks who confirmed he had sold Jim Styers "two guns in mid-November." He remembered Styers gave him a check and asked him to hold the check for two weeks—he "post-dated it." One of the guns was an "RG model 14 short barrel .22." Hicks purchased the gun at Hudson Auction some months earlier; he could not remember the serial number. He sold the guns to Styers at a VFW hall in Mesa. The other gun was a single action western style revolver owned by a friend named "Bill." Hicks cashed the check later and used a portion "of the $80.00 check when it finally cleared the bank in early December."

15

MILKE'S SUPPRESSION HEARING

*I*N ARIZONA, PROSECUTORS CANNOT TALK about a defendant's confession to the jury until the trial judge conducts a voluntariness hearing, outside the presence of the jury. The judge hears what the defendant told the police and the circumstances under which her statements were made. Then, the judge makes two important pretrial decisions. First, were the defendant's statements voluntary, under a test called the "totality of the circumstances"? If the statements were voluntary, then the judge must make a second decision. Were the statements given after proper Miranda warnings, or was Miranda violated?

The voluntariness hearing conducted by Judge Cheryl Hendrix on September 10, 1990 was a *pro forma* affair. Nothing about Judge Hendrix's judicial career, her prosecutorial favoritism, or her rulings remotely indicated that she might suppress the confession. The hearing was a two-day affair and conducted entirely "for the record," given the certainty that Judge Hendrix would formally admit the confession in evidence the first chance she had. That would come two days later, once the jury was empaneled and in the box, ready to listen carefully to Saldate's version. But in Milke's pretrial suppression hearing, the parties called other witnesses besides the arresting officer.

Since Milke had moved to suppress the confession, Judge Hendrix permitted Kenneth Ray to call the first witness.

"Call Dr. Martin Kassell to the stand."

Judge Hendrix asked whether Mr. Ray would be "kind enough to go out and get him." When the doctor came into the courtroom, ushered by the defense lawyer, she said, "Dr. Kassell, please come forward. Come up to the clerk, this young lady right here, give her your name and be sworn."

He took the stand, confirmed his name for the record, and said he was employed by Maricopa County. He was the psychiatrist "in charge of the psychiatric unit at the Durango Jail." Over the space of a few minutes, Dr. Kassell outlined his credentials. He was board certified in psychiatry, had been an assistant professor of psychiatry at the Thomas Jefferson University School of Medicine in Philadelphia, and had been the clinical director at the Arizona State Mental Hospital in Phoenix, before accepting his current job with Maricopa County. He was a recognized court expert on psychiatric issues. His office was designated as D-2, one of the houses at the Durango Jail, where Milke was incarcerated pending the outcome of her case.

Ray began his examination with the seemingly obvious question, "Is there anyone in this courtroom who has been housed in that facility?"

"Yes."

"Who is that, sir?"

"The patient, my patient who sits beside you, your client."

"Debra Jean Milke?"

Dr. Kassell confirmed the obvious, saying that he'd known her "since she was first brought into the jail." He admitted to Ray he "had occasion to meet and converse and discuss various psychiatric matters with her in connection with psychiatric examination and monitoring as well as her psychiatric problems." As a matter of foundation, since the entire point of the hearing was to create an appellate record, Ray asked Dr. Kassell about the documents he'd reviewed. Dr. Kassell listed them, including a "narrative supplement police report authored by Detective Saldate." He also reviewed a transcript of an interview with Detective

Saldate dated June 16, 1990, and a tape recording of that interview. He said he read and listened to these items because he wanted "to form some general opinions as to what was happening in this interview. Then [I] met Ms. Milke, who gave [me] a copy of the report."

"Did you talk to her about the report?"

"Yes. I read the report and talked to her about the interview, not so much to validate the specifics of the things mentioned but to get a flavor for why certain bits of information were included in the interview, which I initially felt rather inappropriate for this kind of interview . . . and in the course of my interview with her, she explained from her perspective what had transpired in the interview. Thereafter I was in a position of having heard her version and having heard Detective Saldate's version and tried to put them together in some fashion that would make sense to me."

"From a psychological standpoint," Ray asked.

"Strictly from a psychological standpoint. I was not interested in the least as to whether somebody was innocent or guilty. Sort of a legalistic panoply from a psychological point of view that went on in that interview."

Ray asked whether the doctor had formed any opinions "to a reasonable degree of psychiatric and medical certainty." Dr. Kassell said he had. Noel Levy objected and asked the court for permission to "*voir dire*" the witness, which Judge Hendrix quickly granted. Inexplicably, Levy asked Kassell what Milke told him about the interview. "She told me that when the detective came in the first thing he told her, in very short order, was that her son had been found, that he was dead, that he had been murdered, and she was being arrested for complicity in the case, and that she then became quite hysterical and Officer Saldate told her that he wouldn't tolerate her crying and wouldn't tolerate her screaming and she was to speak quietly and that he was there to ascertain the truth; that he then Mirandized her and she . . . , in her words, she did not fully comprehend what was being said because she was too involved with absorbing the information that her son was killed."

The judge suggested that he was getting a little afield of *voir dire* and said that he could ask more questions on cross-examination. Levy backed off and Kenneth Ray resumed his place at the podium.

"Doctor, I believe my question to you was, 'What opinions did you reach in connection with your examination of these documents coupled with the recorded interview that you had with Debra?'"

"I gave considerable thought to the task that you gave to me and, having read the report several times, and had the specifics of his testimony in front of me and listened to the tape and listened to Debra . . . I put it in global perspective at first. Then, working from there, the thing that impressed me most in Detective Saldate's report was that much of what he states there are . . . impressions, assumptions, but he doesn't validate these assumptions with facts. He doesn't validate by asking questions that would perhaps give him an insight as to whether he was on the track or not. He uses a lot of assumptions but no facts to substantiate them. In listening to Debra and her testimony, her opinions [of] what happened there . . . I arrived at the conclusion that much of what I was reading, much of what I was seeing were assumptions and conclusions that [were] not based upon fact[s] that I could see in the report."

Ray asked, "You have reached certain conclusions from at least partially a psychological standpoint that the conclusions reached are illogical conclusions, is that correct?"

"Yes."

"Based upon your analysis of the writings, do you have any opinion as to whether or not there is a psychological or psychiatric explanation for the writings in the condition that they are?"

"Oh, there are a number of explanations for this, but these are strictly theoretical, tentative. This kind of an interview would tend to make me suspicious that the individual is rather arrogant. It's a little like, psychologically speaking, a paranoid personality disorder where they are always right and other people, therefore, are always wrong . . . I was struck by the fact that Detective Saldate kept repeating that. And Ms. Milke also told me what happened during the interview, that he had moved his chair directly in front of her . . . he says in his report that he stared face to face, looked into her eyes and she looked into his eyes, and that he told her that she could trust him. And I said to myself, that sounds somewhat faintly familiar. And suddenly I recalled what it sounded like. And I call that the *Svengali* phenomenon where a

Svengali individual says look at me, look in my eyes, listen to me, do as I say, tell me the truth. Essentially this is what Detective Saldate says that he did. He made her look at him. They were in eye-to-eye contact . . . throughout the entire interview . . . he told her to stop crying and told her to stop being excited and to stop shouting and to trust him and tell him the truth and he would tolerate nothing but the truth. It gave me the flavor of a Svengali type of approach to the interview."

Ray asked more foundational questions about tape recording his interview with Milke, which said he did "of [his] own volition." Dr. Kassell said Milke became "extremely emotional" when he talked to her about Saldate. Saldate had told her not to cry but "she cried in my office, constantly throughout the time I conducted my interview." Ray also asked what Dr. Kassell thought about Saldate's short, concise questions.

"Yes. Detective Saldate made a point of describing his interview style where he portrays himself as a rather terse individual, rather quiet, where he will talk 10 percent of the time . . . and got the patient or the client to talk 80 percent of the time and perhaps ask another question and then listen the rest of the 10 percent of the time."

Ray asked about "Milke's supposed confession of the events that occurred that night."

"Well, number one, I don't recall having seen *any* confession as to the crime in his supplemental report. I saw a lot of the same information in the supplemental report that was in this report that I read. In trying to give some evaluation to what I was seeing and how I interpreted it, he describes her, Ms. Milke, as becoming very excited and he makes a point of saying that it was not anything other than excitement. I find it difficult to buy that in somebody who has just been informed that she is being accused of murdering her son, that her son has just been shot, killed. In reading his testimony, I got the feeling that he is drawing a picture of a woman who was an actress. She was acting, he felt, in the beginning, her initial experience with him, where she was making noises and crying, but wasn't crying tears. And so that, plus some other factors that progress in the interview where he says that he disbelieved the fact she was really experiencing these emotions, he felt she was acting, she is an actress. Well, if you are a true, natural actress, then how come you suddenly feel the need to unburden yourself? An actress should be an actress that carries through. There are illogical assumptions that he makes. If he will interpret her emotional reaction as anything but excitement, then we have a—I think that she is not acting, that she is actually responding in an appropriate fashion to the news her son has just been killed . . . In addition, Detective Saldate states unequivocally . . . that he came to the interview already with his mind made up that he was going to arrest her and arrest her for complicity in the murder of her son. If you look at that as a starting point and then you look at the rest of the testimony, follow it through, you can see the flavor of what I have described before as a picking out what you want to prove your theory, prove your premise, and reject that which disproves your premise."

"Doctor, if you would assume for a moment that at the time the interview had been commenced, the time was approximately 8:00 o'clock in the evening on December 3rd, and if you assume that the individual had been awake since approximately 10:00 A.M. on December 2nd, with that factor, do you have an opinion concerning what Detective Saldate describes in his report as the conduct and emotional response of Debra Milke?"

"He describes her emotional response, but he rejects it as being true. He rejects it on the basis of the fact he thinks she is play-acting."

Ray asked for an opinion, "to a reasonable degree of medical and psychiatric certainty," whether Debra Milke could understand what her Miranda rights were. Kassell said, "[S]he may have heard what was being said and may have understood to a certain degree what was being said, but I doubt that she really fully comprehended what the Mirandizing was all about."

Ray asked for permission to play the tape recording of Dr. Kassell's interview with Milke "for Mr. Levy's benefit."

Noel Levy said, "I don't need such benefit at this time."

Ray asked for permission to have a duplicate made and "moved it in evidence for the court's consideration."

Judge Hendrix said, "Certainly."

Then she allowed Levy cross-examine Dr. Kassell. What little benefit Ray had just slipped in the record from Dr. Kassell was about to evaporate.

Levy's first question set the tone. "Tell me, Dr. Kassell, are you aware Dr. Kasias has evaluated Debra Milke and found her competent?"

"No, I'm not aware of that."

"You are not aware of that and you are in D-2?"

"Yes."

"Are you aware Dr. Kasias evaluated her and found she was not insane at the time of the crime?"

"No, I'm not."

"Have you been treating Debra Milke?"

"I have been treating her for her symptoms, yes."

"So we have a doctor-patient relationship?"

"Yes."

"And in a doctor-patient relationship under the Hippocratic oath you have an obligation to take and give a great deal of credence to what the patient tells you. Isn't that your obligation?"

"No."

"It's not?"

"No."

"You didn't give very much credence to what she told you?"

"I didn't say that. But that's not my obligation to the Hippocratic oath."

"Is there a certain obligation under a doctor-patient relationship?"

"To understand my patient. If my patient is lying to me, I must understand that. If my patient is telling me the truth, I must understand that, too."

"Have you read all the police reports?"

"No."

"Do you know how many times Debra Milke was interviewed on the Saturday and the Sunday of December 2 and December 3, 1989 preceding the interview by Detective Saldate?"

"No."

Levy spent the next half-hour cross examining Dr. Kassell. He only asked close-ended, yes or no questions designed to elicit answers supporting the prosecution's case. Dr. Kassell admitted that he had not read other interviews given by Milke. He did not understand how Milke responded to other questions from other people. He had no opinion on Milke's guilt or innocence. He understood Milke had gone to college. He knew nothing about her jobs or what she did for a living before December 3, 1989. He did not know what kind of a student she had been.

Levy established on cross-examination that Dr. Kassell did not think that "Detective Saldate was a liar." Or that he did "not put down in his report all the answers of Debra Milke in his interview with her on 12/3 of '89." Dr. Kassell admitted he had interviewed none of Milke's "relatives, sisters, or read any of the reports to the 'degree that Debra Milke is manipulative.'" He said that Milke was sometimes "childlike," but denied having "sympathy" for her. He said he "neither liked her nor disliked her." He had no opinion "on whether she had her son murdered." Ray did not object to any of those questions.

Levy asked, "If she knew, according to her own interview, and it says here, '3:20 P.M. on December 2nd' she knew that her son had been killed by James Styers and had known all along, if she knew that, and she had conspired to have her son killed, do you feel that her responses of a pretense and crying without tears would be inappropriate?"

Perhaps Ray was busy doing something else, but he made no objection to a question that not only misstated the record, it could not possibly be within the expertise of a psychiatrist. Not hearing an objection, Judge Hendrix allowed the following answer by Dr. Kassell:

"That would be inappropriate. Would also be kind of stupid."

"Did you say it would be inappropriate?"

"It would be inappropriate and rather stupid to cry without tears if you are trying to impress somebody that you are really not what you are."

"That's your view, correct?"

"Yes."

"But she could do that, couldn't she?"

"Sure, she could."

Levy was on a roll. He had a witness who was unaware of the damage he was doing, and a lawyer not objecting to that damage. So, he pushed it. "Would it be appropriate that, if she knew she was involved, knew that her son was dead, and when told that fact, she would attempt to make pretenses as though she was surprised about the information? If she conspired to have her son killed, and knew he was dead, and was told that she was under arrest for her son's death[,] wouldn't it be appropriate for her to attempt initially to make pretenses as though she was surprised?"

"Yes."

"Are you suggesting that when Detective Saldate told her to tell the truth as she knew the facts, that she did not tell him the truth?"

"I'm not suggesting that at all."

Levy shifted to high gear with what was now a favorable prosecution witness. He got Dr. Kassell to admit he hadn't read Roger Scott's "confession." Nor had he read the other police reports.

"Now, tell me if there is anything illogical about what I'm going to read to you. 'Approximately one month ago, Debra said that she had contemplated suicide. Debra said the more she thought about it she thought it would not solve her problems with her son. She said that if she committed suicide Mark would have sole custody of Chris and he would definitely grow up like Mark. Because of that, she then spoke to her friend Jim about helping her figure out a way for her child Chris to die. Debra said at first she could not tell Jim she wanted her son Chris killed because it was very hard for her. Finally, she told him it would be better for her son to die than to grow up like her husband, his father. She said Jim agreed with her and that the only agreement they had was he would not tell her the specifics about the killing.' What is illogical about that, in your opinion, Doctor?"

"Nothing."

"Does it contain facts?"

Ray made no objection, and did not remind the judge that these so-called facts came from Saldate, not Milke.

"Yes."

"What about the next paragraph? 'I then asked Debra if she had killed her son because of some insurance she may have had on him and she told me she did not have any life insurance on him, but she believed that her father, who lives in Florence, did. She also believed her father was the beneficiary of that policy. I told Debra it was my understanding that Jim and Roger were to receive a partial payment of the $5000 policy which she had on the child's life. Debra denied having a policy, but said she may have told Jim that her father had a policy and said that may have been Jim and Roger's motivation for the killing, but that it was definitely not hers.' Is that illogical?"

"Not at all."

"You have indicated that you think Detective Saldate is arrogant and borders on paranoia. Did you give him some test?"

"I did not say that the detective is that. I was asked an opinion based upon what I saw here."

"And what you saw there only relates to Detective Saldate, doesn't it?"

"Relates to his testimony here, yes."

"Did you give him any psychological tests?"

"No."

"So you just decided that's your opinion anyway?"

"No. If I decide on opinion . . . I'm entitled to my opinion. I don't think it has to be based upon tests."

"You were asked an opinion about her getting no sleep prior to Saldate's interview. Remember that? And how that might affect her responses?"

"Yes."

"Were you aware that in fact she left for Florence about noon Sunday with her stepmother and when she arrived at Florence she went to sleep and she had been sleeping for quite a period of time when she was awakened around 7:00 P.M. and told that the sheriffs were there to bring her downtown?"

"No, I'm not aware of that."

"So you weren't aware she had a considerable amount of sleep before the interview by Detective Saldate?"

"That's true."

"And you were not aware that she had already experienced several interviews by police detectives? You didn't know that?"

"I vaguely was aware that she had had a number of interviews prior to Detective Saldate's, yes."

"My question is: If a mother conspired to have her son murdered and, further, if she knew already that her son was dead from the previous day, when the murderer called her and told her in such a way that she understood he had been killed, would the fact that Detective

Saldate at the beginning of the interview told her that her son was found dead, would the fact he told her that, with that assumption in mind about her participation and knowledge, would that in any way, that statement to her in any way affect her composure?"

"It depends. If she is carrying forth an illusion, if she is trying to create an illusion, if she is acting the part . . ."

"Dr. Kassell, I specifically told you to assume that she knew this. Did you understand that?"

"I understand that, and I'm trying to answer your question. The question cannot be answered yes or no. . . ."

"Dr. Kassell, based upon what I have heard you testify in court already, you are not claiming Detective Saldate is a liar?"

"No."

"And you are not claiming what he put down in the report didn't actually occur, or isn't what she actually said?"

"That's true."

"If he put down that she made noises as if she were crying but no tears were visible, you don't dispute the accuracy of that, do you?"

"No."

"If he felt that she was feigning a hysterical reaction to the news about her son, do you dispute his conclusion?"

"That's his assumption."

"If she was feigning such, would—and after having been told she was under arrest for her son's death, if she was capable of feigning, would she also be thus aware of her situation?"

"She would. She should."

"And if she is aware of her situation, would she then be aware of what was asked of her and her responses?"

"If she were acting out the part, she should be."

Levy said, "That's all I have, Your Honor."

Kenneth Ray asked a few dozen questions on re-direct, to no effect. Noel Levy asked more questions built on assumptions, to no effect. The court adjourned for the day.

Saldate testified on September 10 and 11, 1990 to support the confession he claimed Milke made. The court reporter's transcript, all 102 pages, reveals a former detective, now a justice court constable, at his prime holding forth and impressing the judge. He testified about his Phoenix Police Department career—hired June 2, 1969, retired July 10, 1990—homicide squad from 1986 until retirement—only "training" was at the police academy in 1969. He received no training in interviewing or interrogating suspects. And he was candid about not complying with a suspect's right to remain silent.

Since Kenneth Ray had asked for the voluntariness hearing, he was the first to question Saldate. He began with the most important topic—Saldate's "style" of interrogation.

"There are occasions that a person may ask for an attorney, I note it in my supplement, I note it in my notes, if that person continues to talk, I will continue to listen. And that has happened . . . if a question does come up in my mind during her conversation; sure, I will ask a question."

Ray spent a good deal of time questioning Saldate but only managed to get him to repeat his version of both the investigation of the other defendants and his opinions about Milke's confession.

Saldate testified about his unique personal trait—he can tell when people are lying. When that happens, he challenges the suspect. Ray asked, "How do you know that they are lying in order to challenge them?"

"Well, several reasons . . . 21 years of police experience . . . 41 years of life experience . . . I listen a lot . . . I use my gut reaction . . . I look directly at the person and expect them to look directly at me . . . we feel each other out . . . I'm honest with the person . . . it's just being straightforward, trying to get the truth . . . and that's what I usually get."

Ray asked Saldate about his "Miranda beliefs." He challenged Saldate. "Sir, as an officer with 20-some-odd years of experience, you know when a suspect invokes his right to remain silent, especially after you have read him his Miranda rights, that you are to break the interview off immediately, aren't you?"

"I don't believe it says in any policy manual that we have in the police department does it tell me I need to stop listening or asking questions. No. I understand that may not be used in court . . . we have different areas of responsibility. Yours is to defend your client. Mine is to see to it that I always obtain the truth . . . That's what I'm after."

The balance of his testimony was an expanded, but not clarifying, conversation about what he claimed Milke said to him on December 3, 1989. He described his personal view. "I consider myself to be intolerant with lies. I'm less tolerant when people tell lies because I have to get the truth. I'm not going to sit there for eight hours and listen to lies."

Judge Hendrix predictably declined to suppress the alleged confession.

16

OPENING STATEMENTS AT TRIAL— SEPTEMBER 12, 1990

*I*N CIVIL LITIGATION, OPENING STATEMENTS are important but not vital. In criminal cases, they are vital for the state because the state must prove guilt beyond any reasonable doubt. The defense has no burden of proof and often limits its case to challenging the prosecution's case. Opening statements are the most overlooked part of criminal litigation. Delivering an effective opening statement requires confidence, talent, and experience. That's why inexperienced lawyers fare so poorly and seasoned advocates sound so convincing. In the Milke case, it was a seasoned prosecutor against an inexperienced defense lawyer. Levy had tried hundreds of cases, including many capital cases. Ray had tried perhaps four or five, none of which were especially challenging, much less one where the death penalty was probable if the jury found guilt.

Noel Levy knew something about opening statements that Kenneth Ray might not have. Verdicts are usually consistent with jurors' initial impressions. If they sense the lawyer is skilled, they equate that to factual accuracy. If they see a lawyer stumble early on, they see it as inexperience, or worse, weak preparation. As with everything else in life, the psychological phenomenon of *primacy* explains why we often believe what we hear first. The experienced lawyer's goal in opening statements is to make that initial impression a lasting one. Lawyers with limited jury trial experience, especially in capital cases, hope to get through it without forgetting something important. An opening statement is neither bad nor good. The test is effectiveness. To be effective in a capital murder trial, the lawyer must deliver the opening statement forcefully, state the facts simply, and communicate directly to each juror.

Court procedural rules demand two things from lawyers in opening statements—they cannot be argumentative and must not include personal opinions. Common sense lawyering means you cannot overstate your case, and you must personalize your client. Each lawyer must have developed a "theory" of the case well before trial. The opening statement is the first, best, and sometimes only chance to present the theory—what are the facts and evidence that dictate a favorable outcome. Failing to articulate that theory inevitably allows opposing counsel to point out the importance of the failure at the end of the trial. The argument is simple—he never had a theory, then or now. That signals a fatal flaw to the jury—the lawyer is merely marking time as the evidence comes in, before committing to a cohesive theory.

Because he represented the "people" of Arizona, and had to prove guilt beyond any reasonable doubt, Noel Levy went first. He spent a few minutes summarizing the grand jury's charges, and explained his burden of proof. Then, while the litigation iron was hot, he jumped directly into his theory.

"What is this conspiracy that the State will prove to you? It is that Debra Milke agreed with James Styers that one of them, or another person would kill her son, Christopher Milke. Debra Milke intended and wanted her son dead and she encouraged James Styers to do it for her, and allowed him to take her child in her car to be killed."

Levy outlined the agreement between Styers and Milke, which was the essence of the conspiracy case. He told them about Styers taking Christopher to see Santa Claus, meeting Roger Scott on the way, and their plan to kill Christopher and pretend he was lost at Metrocenter. He prioritized the sequence of events and talked about specific witnesses that would be called to the stand to prove those facts. The logistical path to the crime scene was laid out, as were the base mechanics of shooting a small boy in the back of the head. He didn't gloss over the murder, but he moved quickly because this was a conspiracy case. Unless Milke conspired with Styers, the details about how Styers killed Christopher were meaningless.

"At 2:45 Styers called Debra Milke. She lived at Styers apartment . . . [he] told her Chris *is* missing, I'm at Metrocenter; there *is* a security guard here next to me. That was the coded meaning as part of the conspiratorial agreement whereby she knew that Christopher Milke, her son, was dead. So, from 2:45 P.M. on, she knew that the boy was dead, that James Styers had done the deed."

Levy wove in related facts—times, places, and small details—before reinforcing the state's conspiracy theory.

"Debra Milke was interviewed about 11:15 P.M. Saturday night by detectives . . . and insisted during the interview that she would not be alone. . . must have her neighbors around her, while she made crying gestures. She described how the boy was dressed in boots, Levi's, and a sweatshirt with a yellow dinosaur. And that was, to the detectives, inappropriate because she knew her son was dead."

In both of these instances, Levy asked the jury to trust him that the evidence would prove that Milke "knew" her son was dead because she took the "coded" phone call at 2:45 P.M. and then misled the detectives about it at 11:15 P.M. that night. In reality, the only witness to testify about either event was Debra Milke, who steadfastly denied knowing her son was dead until Sunday night and misleading detectives about it the prior day. But primacy is vital and Levy knew he had to plant his theory early for it to grow into actual belief.

Levy continued to talk about crime scene details, painting a picture of Styers and Scott's convoluted story about losing the boy at the mall. He brought his star witness, Saldate, into the opening statement narrative by telling the jury he had "obtained information as to Roger Scott." Then Scott, Detective Mills, and Saldate drove out 99th Avenue, just north of Happy Valley Road, where they "found the body of the boy." They found expended ".22 rounds and a live round of .22 Stinger CCI's." He talked about Styers' tennis shoes, and Styers'

.22 revolver, which they "found at Roger Scott's house." And then he connected the CCI Stinger bullets to Milke since she owned the car and let Styers take it to Metrocenter the day of the murder.

Milke's early and casual conversations with officers at her apartment on Saturday night sounded ominous. "She continued to state the scenario of the missing child at Metrocenter and was most anxious to get to Florence, to leave her apartment." Then he got to the heart of his theory.

"When she arrived in Florence, she took a long nap. She was awakened just before 7:50 P.M. . . . by Maureen Sadeik [her stepmother]. Upon being awakened, she was told, 'The Sheriffs want to see you.' She responded, using her words, 'What the fuck do they want.' Then she got up and casually smoked a cigarette, combed her hair, and decided she was ready to go."

Saldate was waiting for her.

"Detective Saldate introduced himself. He told her that her boy was found murdered in the wash. He told her her Miranda rights. She indicated she understood. She agreed to talk to him. And she confessed her involvement in the conspiracy to commit murder, of child abuse, and kidnapping in the context of the elements the State is required to prove. She admitted her involvement of James Styers' call that she got, involvement of Roger Scott, that she understood James Styers was to have killed the child and she wanted the child killed."

However awkward his phrasing was, Levy's narrative about her confession likely struck the jury as something she actually did. He sounded confident. That's as it should be at the opening statement stage, with the defense theory yet a mystery. The elementary simplicity of Levy's version startled the jury. He wanted them to wonder why she would confess if she had *not* done it.

Ramping up the shock value that a confession always has, Levy moved to motive. "Ladies and Gentlemen . . . the State will show as a fact, with regard to her motive and intent, that she never bonded with this boy. Never wanted him. She even said this in her confession. Her hate for her ex-husband, Mark Milke, was greater than her love for this boy."

Levy expanded on his theory. He told them that rather than let the boy live, and be taken by Mark Milke, "she would have him killed. That was to her the only option, as she explained. The child was kept by others, or relatives for up to two months at a time, since the child was born. She cared for the child perhaps only 25 percent of the time."

Letting the confession bombshell mellow in the awful motive of not wanting your own child, he lowered the tempo and talked about Milke's high school, college, and work life, and her current boyfriend, "Ernie Sweat, who at the time, or shortly before, was her lover." She loved and wanted him "very much," according to Levy. But "he was a young professional and wasn't prepared, or ready to be a father to anyone; he was going to break it off. In any event," Levy opined, "he didn't care to have a young child along, and Debra knew this."

Levy offered more motive by telling the jury about Milke's job at John Alden Insurance. As part of the benefits package, Milke applied for and received coverage "on the life of the child, Chris Milke. She indicated [to Saldate] that may have been a motive for James Styers and Roger Scott, to have killed the child, [but] it wasn't *necessarily* her motive."

Levy was categorical with the jury. "She didn't want the child and, as she expressed it, because she didn't want the child to grow up to be like . . . his father, her ex-husband, whom she hated, . . . she arranged to have the child killed by James Styers."

Levy's nutshell version for the jury was straightforward. Milke had motive (she hated her ex-husband more than she loved her child). She had means (Jim Styers would do it for her). And she had opportunity (let Styers and Scott take him to Metrocenter, pretend to lose him, kill him, and come back home).

He spent the next half-hour talking about the legal requirements in a murder and conspiracy case. He talked about child abuse, kidnapping, and the fact that both were "dangerous crimes." Milke was an "accomplice," which necessitated an explanation of the law applied to accomplices of those who actually commit dangerous crimes. He dealt with the murder weapon, the bullets, and the actual killer—James Styers. He closed with a legal whimper:

"Finally, if the State has proven through these facts and this evidence the elements of the four crimes charged—first-degree murder, whether it be premeditated or felony murder[,] conspiracy to commit first-degree murder, child abuse, a dangerous crime against children, and kidnapping, a dangerous crime against children, then I ask you, at the end of that time, as it may be appropriate, to return a verdict of guilty of these charges."

However lacking in oratorical skill, Levy's opening was effective because it presented a straightforward explanation of the crime, tied it to the defendant, and made Milke's confession the centerpiece of his case. To make his theory stick, he had only to make sure the jury saw Saldate as credible, and Milke as guilty.

—

JUDGE HENDRIX ASKED KENNETH RAY whether he wanted to make an opening statement or reserve it until after the state rested its case. He said he would proceed.

"Good afternoon, ladies and gentlemen. My name is Kenneth Ray. I'm an attorney practicing in this city and have the pleasure of representing Debra Jean Milke. As he [Levy] indicated, the critical date in this case is December 2, 1989. That is the day that is of critical importance in determining what transpired on that day, what transpired before that day, the events that occurred over the day of December 2 into December 3, which ultimately culminated in the arrest of my client, as well as two other individuals."

Ray's opening was odd because it began with a platitude, and unnecessarily emphasized the criticality of the day of the murder. It reminded the jury of Milke's arrest the day after the murder, and then wandered off point into a narrative that connected his client with the man everyone in the jury box likely accepted as the actual killer (James Styers). They knew they would not be deciding Styers' guilt. He told the jury how long Milke had been Styers' roommate (two months), how long she had known him (several years), and described Styers' relationship with Milke's father, mother, and several neighbors. His point was that none of these people "had the slightest inkling that James Styers was capable of *such a deed*."

Then Ray tried to distance his client from Styers by reverse logic. "Just as those individuals had no idea that Styers could commit this offense, neither did my client."

Ray talked about Milke's ex-mother-in-law, Ilse Milke. He said that "due to problems that developed, Ms. Milke was required to locate another place to live. So, she turned to the only friend in close proximity she had, and knew, and that was James Styers. Jim said she could reside with him until she got back on her feet, as well as could Christopher."

The case against Styers was open and shut because Scott confessed and because the state had solid forensic evidence from the crime scene to prove Styers was the actual killer. Ray must have known much of that evidence would come in against his client, yet he connected Milke to Styers at the beginning of his statement on her behalf.

Next, he told the jury about Milke's problems with visitation rights with her ex-husband, another man the jury probably would not like. He explained Milke's procurement of an injunction for harassment in city court, "occasions of disagreement" with Mark Milke concerning Christopher, and "other matters." He said Debra "may have disapproved of his [Mark Milke's] background, [but] she nonetheless recognized he had a right to parent that child, to be a part of that child's life, and she permitted ongoing visitations." It may have struck the jury as an apology of sorts.

Ray denied that one of central planks in Levy's theory was his client's hatred of her ex-husband. "While Debra may not have liked him to any great extent, she did not hate him." The jury surely wondered where this was going, since Milke, through her lawyer, was defending both Styers (who killed her son) and Mark Milke (a man no one on the jury would like). "The evidence will indicate that James Styers was disabled, unemployed at the time, and had physical custody of a child of his own at the apartment where they resided; that Debra was working and that she needed to get back on her feet again and he volunteered to look after Christopher while she was working."

Perhaps in response to the negative picture Levy had painted of Milke, Ray used a softer brush. "Debra Milke, as a single mother, did have a social life. Not a flamboyant social life, but nonetheless a social life. She had friends and acquaintances, one of [which was] Ernie, who was the person that she cared a great deal about. There is no suggestion in the evidence that Jim Styers was Debra Milke's boyfriend. There is no suggestion in the evidence that will be presented during the course of this trial that there was anything intimate between Jim Styers and Debra Milke. The evidence will clearly indicate that it was a two-bedroom apartment. She occupied one bedroom; he had the other. She occupied her bedroom with Christopher, her son, and Wendy, Jim Styers' daughter."

Ray seemed unable to be direct. His job in the opening statement was to distance Milke from Styers and establish doubt about the confession. However, when Ray said "there is no suggestion in the evidence" about things that Levy said flat out, Ray failed at the job. He talked almost breezily about the events on Saturday morning up to the time Christopher left the apartment with Styers.

Then, moving to the early afternoon, he told the jury about Styers' phone call telling Debra "her boy was missing at Metrocenter." Levy had told the jury this was a "coded" phone call to let Debra know Christopher was dead. Instead of denying that, Ray was tentative. "The evidence and testimony in this case *will indicate* that Debra became immediately hysterical." Now, instead of saying there was "no suggestion," he said, the evidence "will indicate." Same problem—an obvious lack of confidence in the evidence. Ray did a journeyman's job on the events of the day, most of which would not be contested. The state would focus on connecting her to the crime through Styers and Scott. She didn't have to defend them in her case, but Ray tried to do that job too.

He did a good job of explaining Milke's frantic response to her missing child, saying, "her hysteria, her crying, was not a façade, a ruse, a fabrication; it was genuine, ladies and gentlemen, and that issue, in and of itself permeates this entire case." But he did not say how Milke's emotional response helped her case. If he meant that she was genuinely distraught, which proved she was not complicit in the murder, it likely escaped the jury. He talked about the decision to go to Florence, rather than stay at home beside the phone as the search at Metrocenter carried on. "You are going to have to come to know Debra Milke, indeed in depth, in detail and in depth, and draw upon your own experiences, your own personal events in your life to decide what is, or is not an appropriate emotion."

He insisted that Milke was "bonded—[Christopher] was her pride and joy . . . the child clung to her . . . but yes, to some degree she was a disciplinarian, but only because she loved this child, and wanted this child to grow up happy, and to become a model citizen."

He called the prosecution out. "Mr. Levy ran down a scenario of times and locations and events that occurred . . . But because of innuendo and someone's determination an emotion is, or is not appropriate, and supposition, it was decided that, what a sensational case if you would charge the mother, because she is the one that allowed this child to go with Jim Styers; therefore, she must be rotten as a mother. This is the government's theory. Their theory is, because of that, she should be charged and prosecuted in this case."

After repeating Levy's theory for the jury, just in case they'd forgotten it, he presented the defense theory. "To accept that proposition, ladies and gentlemen, is to ignore common sense and facts. It doesn't really matter in the trial of Debra Milke as to which of the individuals, Roger Scott or James Styers, killed this boy. The evidence that is to be presented in this case will indicate clearly that they are responsible for the death of this boy. But the government will ask you to draw a further conclusion. Because Debra knew Jim Styers, she must have therefore conspired [in Christopher's] death, that because she lived in the same house, that she must have conspired in his death. Point by point by point, the government's position will be held to be wrong, will not be supported by the evidence. The defense will elicit, both on evidence it will present as well as the cross-examination of the government's witnesses."

With this direct challenge, Ray segued into the only risk Milke had in the case—the damning confession Saldate would say she gave. "You ask yourselves now, Well, Mr. Ray there was a confession. You will be asked to evaluate the evidence to determine why it was that anyone went down to Florence in the first place." He got off point on logistics, explaining why Milke went to Florence, and with whom. Eventually he got back to the confession issue.

"As it turns out, Debra was escorted to the Pinal County Sheriff's Office in Florence and placed into a medical office, that medical office being located behind bars, waiting there with two—one or two, maybe more, Phoenix Police Officers who did not commence to speak with her, but were there to carry out their orders as they knew them. Detective Saldate was going to be enroute to conduct an interview of Debra. See, what had been transpiring during this period of time is that the boy had indeed been found. And because of that fact, there was a need to speak further with Debra. Detective Saldate flies down to Florence with an idea in his head. He will testify that he had been instructed by his superior officer, [Sgt.] Ontiveros, to go to Florence and conduct a tape-recorded interview. But he decided in his own mind that he was not going to conduct a tape-recorded interview. He left 620 West Washington, the Phoenix Police Department, without even looking for a tape-recorder. He will tell you he doesn't own one, and he didn't even look for one, after being specifically advised by [Sgt.] Ontiveros as to what he was to do. And as he went to Florence, he formulated in his mind his theory of the case. And his theory included Debra, the person who, to that point, had never been a suspect, never a suspect. And the directive was to conduct the interview, not go and arrest, but to conduct the interview. Enroute, he formulated the idea that it was to arrest. He goes to the Pinal County Sheriff's Office, goes into the jail facility, into the medical office of that facility. As he arrives, Debra is in the company of a friend. Detective Saldate is in the company of Detective Hamrick—well, I shouldn't say Hamrick. It may have been a different officer. But at least another detective. In any event, Detective Saldate asked the friend to leave. The friend complies, goes out and speaks with the other detective. And without a recorder and without a monitor, he enters a room with Debra Milke, a female, closes the door and commences this interview. The defense believes the evidence will show that that was a violation, number one, of direct orders; number two, of protocol and policy. And that is the scenario that develops this, quote, confession. You judge this man's testimony and the evidence that he produces and tells you, which will include that he has a penchant to disregard not only protocol when it comes to interviews and interrogations of people, but also he has a penchant to violate basic, fundamental constitutional rights that we all have, the right to remain silent, the right to counsel. Detective Saldate will tell you that 'As long as they want to talk and keep talking, I will keep talking, it doesn't matter.' He will tell you that it doesn't matter because he is there in quest of the truth, that his quest for the truth, in the past as well as in this case, is not based upon fact, but upon supposition and an innuendo and an idea that this man got in his head. The defense will ask you to consider all of that in determining whether there indeed was ever a confession."

With that, Ray finally established his theory and directly challenged the state's core evidence. "Indeed, was there ever a confession?"

He closed with this: "The defense submits that there should be two verdicts. One says innocent. One should read "innocent," because as she stands before you now, and as she will remain throughout the course of this trial, she is innocent. And after all the evidence and testimony is presented in this case, you will cry out, she is innocent, not just not guilty. Thank you for your time, ladies and gentlemen, and I look forward to the next few weeks with you. Thank you. Thank you, Your Honor, counsel."

However desirable from a defense perspective, there are no "innocent" verdicts in criminal cases. If the prosecution wins, there is a guilty verdict. If the defense prevails, there is an acquittal. And with that, Judge Hendrix called a ten-minute recess. Right on time, she reconvened the jury.

"Mr. Levy, would you call your first witness please?"

He called Detective Armando Saldate, Jr., to the witness stand.

17

TRIAL BY CONFESSION

*I*N RETROSPECT, PERHAPS THE EVIDENTIARY part of the Milke trial should have been labeled *Saldate* v. Milke, rather than the *State of Arizona* v. Milke. This trial, while it took a month to complete, was essentially over on the first day—the day Armando Saldate took the witness stand. He was invincible.

Good prosecutors win on the strength of the case-in-chief, not on the weaknesses of the opponent's case. In criminal cases, the prosecutor often puts his best witness on first, getting the jury's attention immediately, and forcefully presenting the most important facts when the jury is fresh and impressionable. Debra Milke's version of that 30-minute interrogation was not important to the state's case. Only Saldate's version of what she "said" was important. If they believed him, they would not believe her; it was that simple. That's why his version had to reach them first. Her denials would wait their turn. Saldate was not merely the most important state's witness; he was virtually its *only* witness. It had crime scene evidence connecting Scott and Styers. It had circumstantial evidence in family testimony, but Saldate had sandpapered those family witnesses with great care. It had a theory based on police investigation. It had motive based on circumstantial evidence from debatable sources. But save for her confession, there was no other compelling, much less persuasive, evidence that would connect her to a murder she did not physically commit. Her complicity, called a conspiracy by the state, was the essential charge against her. She planned it, the state said, based on what Saldate claims she said. If the jury believed him, Milke was doomed long before she ever opened her mouth on the stand.

Noel Levy was not articulate. His convoluted speech was distracting. Even so, he presented as narrowly focused, always serious, never jocular, and committed to a theory and a motive. He knew the strengths and challenges of direct examination. Direct examination of a high-profile witness demands a clear, logical progression. If each juror listens intently, does not feel the witness is just echoing the lawyer's views, and finds the testimony plausible, then the law of primacy comes into play. What we hear first is often what we believe, even if subsequent testimony is contradictory. Levy's challenge was to cement Saldate's version of the confession in a way that would eventually discredit Milke's denial. To do that, he had to make Saldate the center of attention in the courtroom. He could not risk letting the jury think Saldate was merely a mouthpiece, spouting what the prosecutor wanted. So he posed open-ended questions and kept himself in the background. He stretched, hoping to create a persona for Saldate that would resonate with the jury. If jurors remember one witness as particularly convincing, but do not remember which lawyer conducted that examination, the lawyer will have done his job very well. If the other lawyer does not impeach that witness on cross-examination, he leaves the witness stand with his credibility intact. When that happens, the jury almost always believes that first, credible witness's version of a disputed fact. In *Milke*, the disputed fact was whether the confession actually occurred.

Saldate was on the witness stand all day. Levy methodically walked him through his earlier suppression-hearing testimony, since the jury had not yet heard anything about "the" confession except what he'd told them in his opening statement. Saldate swore that Milke admitted, "Christopher was a difficult child whom she did not want to grow up like his father, a drug and alcohol abuser in trouble with the law." He said she tried to explain things away by recounting "school experiences, saying she was popular with high self-esteem until she met and married Mark," Christopher's father. When she "became pregnant, she considered abortion, but thought it would be too painful. She considered suicide, but did not want Mark to gain custody of Christopher. It would be better," Saldate told the jury, "for Christopher to die." And unflinchingly, Saldate said Milke "expressed her feelings to Styers."

Before getting to her actual admission of guilt, Saldate quoted Milke as saying, "Look, I just didn't want him to grow up like his father. I'm not a crazy person. I'm not an animal. I just didn't want him to grow up like that . . . I'm not a malicious person. I just wanted God to take care of him."

At this point in Saldate's testimony, Levy nudged him toward direct admissions of complicity, setting the stage for the conspiracy charge. According to Saldate, Debra told him she "agreed to have Styers kill Christopher." He told the jury, "She, Scott and Styers discussed the plan several times, and she went with Styers once to kill Christopher but the plan fell through."

According to Saldate, Debra said after that first failed attempt to kill her son, "they planned for Styers *and* Scott to kill Christopher, then go to Metrocenter mall and report him missing." Saldate said he asked "Debra if she dressed her son in special clothes, or gave him a special hug or kiss the morning of his murder. She said she had not because she previously told Christopher he was going to heaven soon, and she would meet him there later." Saldate claimed Debra told him she knew Styers had completed the plan "when he called her from Metrocenter, and that she prayed she would have no more children." Saldate told the jury that after Debra's "confession," she expressed concern that "her family would disown her and think she was crazy." Saldate said she asked him whether he thought she was crazy. "Are you?" he countered. "No, I'm just an emotionally troubled 25-year-old girl who needs help dealing with her problems."

Remarkably, he also told the jury that Debra "always had difficulty discussing her problems 'until now.'" The message was clear. If Debra trusted him, so should the jury. Saldate told the jury he wanted to help her, saying, "[T]here were other options if she no longer wanted custody of her son. But she didn't understand, saying, 'I guess I just made a bad judgment call.'"

—

WHEN SALDATE LEFT THE WITNESS stand, Levy called several background witnesses relative to the crime scene, and several circumstantial witnesses who talked about their various relationships with Milke and what they thought of her. Then, on the first week in October, Levy rested his case. Kenneth Ray called his first witness, Debra Jean Milke, to the stand. She would spend the next five days in the witness box. She categorically denied confessing to Saldate, or anyone else.

After her categorical denial of Saldate's version of their "interview," she said, "Detective Saldate entered the room, told her friend to leave with another officer, and shut the door. He then said her son was murdered and she was under arrest."

She screamed at him, cried and said, "What, what?" Saldate said he would not tolerate her crying, and she asked, "Why are you doing this?" He told her to be quiet, pulled a card out of his pocket, and read her her Miranda rights.

Milke told the jury she recalled "Saldate saying I had the right to remain silent and mentioned the word 'attorney,' but I did not clearly comprehend the Miranda warnings." When Saldate asked if she understood, Debra insisted she had never been arrested and did not understand her rights." Rather than explaining them to her to ensure that she understood them, Saldate changed the subject. He asked "if she wanted the interview recorded." Confused, she said, "No, I need a lawyer." Saldate ignored her and pulled his chair up to hers so they "were sitting face-to-face." She told the jury that Saldate leaned forward "right in front of me" and asked her age. When she said she was 25, he said, "I have a daughter your age, so I understand how you feel."

Judge Hendrix called a break in the testimony to confer with counsel. When Milke returned to the stand, she said, "He then put his hands on my knees and said repeatedly, 'you can trust me, Debbie, I'm your friend, I'm here to help you.'" Then, "[h]e sat back in his chair, and said he would not tolerate this 'type of activity' from me or tolerate 'any lies.' This was my opportunity 'to tell him the truth.'"

"What do you want from me?" she asked. He said, "The truth." Then she yelled, "What do you want from me?," because she still "didn't understand where he was coming from."

Debra told the jury she cried throughout this period and "used a corner of my sweater to wipe my tears, until Saldate gave me some paper towels." Then she just stared "at the floor and was in shock." Saldate asked Debra what she was thinking, and she said she was remembering one night recently when she 'opened up' to Styers about conflicts she and Mark were having over custody and visitation. She told Styers that Mark was constantly harassing her and she had obtained a restraining order, that she wanted to raise Christopher and did not want him to grow up and be like Mark. She was crying and said, "But Jim wouldn't do anything to hurt my son."

Saldate responded by accusing her of "not being truthful." He said he had "an idea already of what happened" and this was her "opportunity" to tell him. Debra became upset at his insinuations and said, "Look, I'm not crazy, I'm not an animal . . . I just didn't want Christopher growing up and being like his father. I don't see anything wrong with that. I wouldn't do anything to hurt anybody."

She tried, albeit ineffectively, to tell the jury about her life, by telling Saldate she was a friendly person who got along with everyone when she was in school. She told Saldate these things because he was arresting her for first-degree murder, and she was trying to explain that she was not capable of that. She had a positive attitude and high self-esteem until she met Mark, who was a drug addict and alcoholic. She said, "I am not sure why I told Detective Saldate these details, but I didn't understand what he wanted, so I just continued recounting my life with Mark and Christopher."

She told the jury she was on birth control when she became pregnant, and "because my parents thought something might be wrong with the baby, I considered abortion, but decided against it." She told them how "Mark was imprisoned shortly after Christopher's birth and that I ultimately divorced him." She said she had allowed Mark visitation, but that he was malicious, and in and out of jail. She said she had been dealing with mixed feelings regarding her ex-husband's ongoing influence on Christopher and was trying "to decide what to do."

At that point in her testimony, she explained that Detective Saldate had asked her how she felt; she said "numb." She was still crying and said, "I'm not a malicious person; God, I just wanted to take care of him." She told the jury that Saldate twisted that into "I just wanted God to take care of him." Saldate asked if she could have let Mark take care of Christopher, and she said she would die before letting him have sole custody and raise her son. She said this "because I did not feel Mark was responsible."

Changing subjects, Ray asked her about other children. She told the jury, "I later looked into having my 'tubes tied' because I was having trouble with birth control and did not want more children as a single parent. The doctors said I was too young." She told Saldate she wondered whether that was something the court could order. She explained, "I don't know exactly why I said this to Detective Saldate." Changing the subject from the crime to her alleged motive for the crime, she said, "Saldate had asked me if I had a life insurance policy on Christopher. I said I thought my father might, but I did not." Debra told the jury she didn't think about the life insurance she selected for her son with her benefits package at work, which she considered part of her health insurance. Ray asked her about Saldate's claim that "Styers and Scott were to receive a $5,000 payment from Christopher's life insurance." She corrected him. "I had no policy on Christopher, but not understanding his question, I said, 'Jim may have heard about my dad's policy. I don't know if that was their motivation, but I wouldn't do something like that.'"

Milke told the jury she was confused when Detective Saldate mentioned Styers, Scott and the life insurance. "I said the only thing I knew was that Styers took Christopher to Metrocenter." Sobbing, she continued recounting the prior day's events for Saldate. She explained how she learned Christopher was missing. After receiving the call from Styers, she said she was in shock and saying, "Oh my God, please find my son, please find my son." She told Saldate she never wanted any more children, and that Christopher was all she wanted. At that point, Debra said she stopped speaking to Saldate and just stared at the floor, crying, for about five minutes. He asked her what she was thinking. She said she was thinking about a recent conversation she had with Christopher in which he brought her a picture from the church he attended with Styers, and asked her about God. She tried to tell Saldate what she had told Christopher. There "was a God and heaven, and a time when people die, and if they are good, they get to go to heaven. He asked when he would get to see God, and I told him Christopher "would not go to heaven to meet God for a long time because he was still a young child."

Ray changed gears, asking about Saldate's questions about giving Christopher a special hug or kiss on the day of his disappearance. She said, "I always gave him a hug and kiss when he left." He also asked if she dressed Christopher "specially" that day, and she said no, that Christopher picked out his own clothes, and she just changed his sweatshirt.

Toward the end of the interrogation, Debra said that she told Saldate she felt her parents would probably disown her because she was being arrested. She said this "in light of the seriousness of the charge and because I had never been in trouble before." She asked Saldate about jail because he said she would have to go. She said, "[C]ouldn't I just go home, can't you take me home?" "[N]o, I was being arrested for first-degree murder." She asked if they would think she was "insane" when she got to jail, and he asked if "I was insane. I told him 'no . . . I just have a real hard time letting go of my emotions, I have a hard time expressing my feelings to people.'"

She categorically denied saying, "I'm just an emotionally troubled 25-year-old girl who needs help dealing with her problems." Debra admitted she and Saldate discussed the possibility of alternative custodial arrangements for Christopher, but said she raised it in response to Saldate's implication that she would have her son killed for insurance money. She said, "If I didn't want my son, then I could give him—I would have given him to my family, my sister or someone else in my family." When she told him that, he said, "Well, I understand that; I guess you just made a bad judgment call." She thought he was implying it was her fault for letting Christopher go with Styers to the mall, and for living with Styers.

In clear language even while sobbing, Milke denied admitting any knowledge of or involvement in, Christopher's death to Detective Saldate. She denied it again for the jury. She denied saying she couldn't talk to anyone, but felt comfortable with Saldate. During the car ride to Phoenix with Saldate, she asked him about bail, but he said he "did not know if this offense was bailable." She asked if he would call her dad when they got to Phoenix, as he said he would do when they were in Florence.

After two days of direct examination and two more of cross-examination, Milke left the witness stand. Both lawyers knew that primacy is a trial lawyer's best friend. Whichever party is fortunate enough to have his story told first is ahead on points. But primacy only lasts until opposing counsel impeaches that first witness on cross-examination. Once discredited, that first witness loses the advantage of primacy; the opponent gains the upper hand of recency. Here, the jury first heard Saldate and undoubtedly saw him as a strong, authoritative witness. On first impression, he did not appear to have a bias, other than that expected of a prosecution witness. On second impression, he was not impeached, nor was his version of the confession effectively challenged on cross-examination. The only opposing witness, Milke herself, was young, hesitant, and sometimes confused. And she had an obvious bias—she was on trial for her life. He was just a cop, doing his job. Since there was no other incriminating evidence, the jury had no choice but to reach their verdict based entirely on which witness seemed most *believable*. The troubled young woman with a clear reason to lie, or the authoritative police man just doing his job?

The prosecution continued to call witnesses to the stand on small, obscure, circumstantial issues. The defense tried to call a substantive witness—Dr. Martin Kassell. The prosecution objected. On October 9, 1990, Levy advised Judge Hendrix's clerk he had a matter to take up with the court. The trial was then in its third week and winding down. That same day, the lawyers would meet in chambers to discuss the court's final instructions to the jury.

"Mr. Levy, do you have a motion you wish to make?"

"Yes, your honor. It is my understanding, because I saw him outside in the hallway, Dr. Kassell is going to testify, presumably first, or second. He says first; Mr. Ray says second. In any event, I thought I had better bring this up out of the hearing of the jury. It is the view of the State that, under evidence Rule 702, that any testimony by Dr. Kassell would go toward things that I would anticipate, such as [that] the supplement by Detective Saldate, is not, in the opinion of Dr. Kassell, a confession. 'I never saw a confession,' is what he suggested when I asked him. It would seem based upon his prior testimony—he was here for the voluntariness [hearing on September 10] . . . I don't believe that under Rule 702 it is necessary for the jury to hear Dr. Kassell with regard to the issue of voluntariness. I don't know that a psychiatrist would aid them in understanding whether her confession was voluntary or not where he is interviewing Debra Milke well after the fact, wasn't there.. . . . Therefore, I don't see, where there is not even an issue here, how he, under Rule 702, is going to aid the jury to determine whether her confession is voluntary."

Evidence Rule 702 controls whether a party may call an expert to elicit an opinion about a trial issue. Here, the issue was whether Milke's confession to Saldate was freely and voluntarily given. That is not a legal issue; it is a factual issue for the jury to resolve. As a preliminary matter, whether any expert may take the witness stand to offer opinions is within the province of the judge. The rule allows expert opinions only if the expert is qualified by training and experience to form the opinion *and* it would be helpful to the jury in resolving the voluntariness dispute. However, an expert's opinion is inadmissible to tell the jury who is lying or who is telling the truth.

Levy opposed expert testimony, arguing to Judge Hendrix, "Well, she was under, that Ms. Milke cried in front of him and they were real tears and she claimed to him that various things which are— the Court, of course, has heard the tape, and it corroborated actually Detective Saldate's factual rendition of what occurred during the confession. And I don't think that we need an expert here. We have no insanity defense, where he is a psychiatrist, to tell the jury in his opinion things about logic and one, two, three, and conclusions and stuff like that with regard to this particular issue of voluntariness. For example, State v. Lindsey suggests that the Court may exercise its discretion when there is a reasonable basis to believe that the jurors will benefit from the use of an expert's opinion that explains recognized principles of social or behavioral sciences. And quite frankly, I don't see where any of the testimony of Dr. Kassell lends itself to their understanding the issue of voluntariness, because that, to me, in my understanding, would be the object issue and is an appropriate instruction later with regard to her confession. And also, *Lindsey* says testimony should only be permitted in those cases where the facts needed to make the ultimate judgment may not be within the common knowledge of the ordinary juror. And here I think it's within the common knowledge of the ordinary juror to determine such an issue."

Predictably, Judge Hendrix ruled for the prosecution, keeping out the only witness the defense had who might have given the jury an alternative view of whether Milke confessed or Saldate made it up.

18

THE PROSECUTION'S CLOSING
ARGUMENT—OCTOBER 10, 1990

OSCAR WILDE NEVER MET A lawyer he liked and famously defamed them all. "Lawyers, they always argue and they always win; the bastards." But Plato, arguably the world's first lawyer, bested him. "Arguments derived from probabilities are idle." In *Milke*, both lawyers could not win and the probabilities were never with Kenneth Ray.

Every lawyer who's ever faced the jury rail in a big case knows the terror of looking into the eyes of an anxious jury—flat, suspicious, skeptical, and unrevealing. All they want to hear from you is what they already think about the case. No matter that the judge has instructed them to keep an open mind until they've heard all the evidence. They *have* heard it all. Begrudgingly, half of the panel looks back at you reluctantly, with condescension. The other half agree with the judge's instruction that lawyers must speak for their clients. The polite ones conceal their impatience to get on with their job—deciding the case and not having to sit through one more lawyer appeal to them with *his* view of the evidence. No one knows the lawyer's feelings of inadequacy, particularly with a life on the line, and credibility the main issue. Final argument is the chronological and psychological culmination of the trial. Trial lawyers with journeyman skills easily meet the chronological tests. It takes a great lawyer to master the psychological challenge.

Judge Hendrix nodded to Noel Levy. "Mr. Levy?"

"May it please the Court, defense counsel, ladies and gentlemen of the jury: I expect to take about 45 minutes. . . ."

He spent the first two minutes repeating what he'd said in his opening statement about burden of proof, reasonable doubt, the four counts against Milke, and identification of the victim before quickly moving away from information, toward persuasion.

"To analyze this case, first of all, what is the keystone of the State's case, really? It's the confession of Debra Milke. Now, with a given of the confession of Debra Milke to Detective Saldate in the early evening hours of December 3, 1989, were the facts Debra Milke shared with Detective Saldate that night in her confession, were they corroborated by the other facts independently investigated by the police and by all of the other testimonial evidence that came in?"

Levy was smart to begin his argument by making the keystone of his case a *given*. Once the jury accepts, as a *given*, that Milke confessed, her fate is psychologically sealed. Juries do not examine evidence psychologically; they are rational observers. They rarely inquire beyond the obvious. Jurors, like almost everyone else on the planet, instinctively accept one of the justice system's most enduring myths— no one confesses to a serious crime unless he is guilty. And there could be no case more consistent with that myth than the murder of a four-year old child. If the murderer also is the child's mother, and her confession is a *given*, then there is little to decide, right? What Levy did for the remainder of his time was cement the given by layering it with Saldate mortar.

"Now, what Debra Milke told Detective Saldate in essence is this: She hated Mark Milke, her husband, so much that she could not stand that her son, Christopher Milke, now age four, would grow up to be like Mark Milke. She described Mark Milke as an alcoholic and a drug abuser and she in effect hated him."

Levy assured the jury they did not have to rely solely on Saldate. They could use, "in deciding this case, your common sense. You do not come to the jury box without your own life's [sic] experiences, and you have some common knowledge, some common sense of what goes on in the world and in your own community."

An appeal to common sense, given a confession, is safe ground to plow in a closing argument. He talked about Christopher, his tender age, his vulnerability, and how he trusted his mother. He re-explained conspiracy law and theory and asked, "Did the [conspiracy] evidence come forth and do they [sic] actually exist?" He said he would "attempt to be somewhat academic," and took the jury on another walk through his conspiracy theory.

"Mark Milke was an alcoholic . . . she had trouble with him . . . take that as a *given* . . . she used birth control because she never wanted to have children, least of all Chris . . . she thought about abortion . . . by 1988, she can't stand Mark . . . she went to Colorado . . . very abusive to the child . . . by now he looks just like his father . . . the child doesn't have a stable home . . . come 1989, she's divorced . . . she meets Ernie Sweat . . . she's in love again . . . he didn't want to be encumbered . . . she dated a lot . . . and then she moved in with James Styers."

Delivered chronologically, and without obvious passion, Levy's low-key style was persuasive, *given* that Milke confessed, and *given* her troubled life. She moved in with Styers, because, "she always moved in with people who would be able to assist her with Christopher, whether it be Susie Stinson, or Dorothy Markwell, or Ilse Milke, there's always someone that's taking care of Christopher while she goes elsewhere." It was by now, in the jury's collective mind, a *given* that Milke was not good at mothering.

Levy ventured toward the understated salaciousness of the evidence, but chose his words carefully. When Milke moved in with Styers, she knew he was married, and had lived with "some other woman and gotten her impregnated and had a child . . . she moved in with a male where the move-out of the other female—Gail was her name—was so rapid that her closet was still filled with Gail's clothes, so much so that she had to use the closet of James Styers as well as use his room for her boxes. A very close relationship in one small apartment with Christopher Milke."

Levy backed off and told the jury about Styers, the "man who did a lot of things for her . . . the testimony is clear, but who occupied her bed? Christopher Milke slept there. Who wanted to get in her bed? James Styers. If Christopher Milke no longer was there, that would leave a vacancy in the bed. Who knows?"

Levy played the judge's role, for just a moment, advising the jury that trial evidence could be "direct or circumstantial . . . you can draw reasonable inferences from the totality of the evidence to reach certain conclusions, should you believe the evidence." He justifiably expected, *given* the confession, *given* the life Milke led, and *given* what Styers wanted, they would infer the conspiracy between Styers and Milke—"kill the child." The conspiracy was the fuse leading to Christopher's murder. The only thing missing was starter fluid. Levy's starter fluid lit up the jury. "Debra Milke decided to move out of Styers' apartment, to a place closer to Ernie Sweat's house."

He got personal with the jury. "She discussed things with Styers. She admitted this to Detective Saldate. She told you this on the stand. What to do with Christopher? Well, by then, she was having difficulty with Ernie Sweat, with whom she supposedly broke off with by the end of November of 1989. She had sent an application for an apartment that was much closer to Ernie Sweat and wasn't near anybody else. And, of course, she had never been in a situation where someone wasn't there to take care of Christopher Milke. Now, while his name was on the application, the situation didn't lend itself that Christopher would necessarily be there. So you can infer from these facts the chilling thought that as early as the first part of November of 1989 became the nucleus and genesis of the idea which was later translated into actuality; she would have her son killed."

It was not a given that the jury bought into this "chilling thought," or Levy's "genesis of an idea." But it is likely they accepted as a given she had confessed to Saldate. So, Levy turned back to the only witness that could support conspiracy to commit murder—Armando Saldate, Jr. If the jury believed him, they had to disbelieve her.

"Now, as she told Detective Saldate, the reason she decided to have her son killed is this: She didn't want him to grow up to be like Mark

Milke. And it isn't that she didn't love the child, it's that God would take care of the child. She would simply have this child's life ended, having prejudged him, have him terminated, and then he would go up to heaven, and God would take care of him, and she would be relieved of the burden. He was becoming more and more and more of a burden to her, and this relationship, because she was not a person, certainly, who wanted to stay home and take care of the child, because there is no evidence that she ever took the child out to any particular things that, in your common sense, you would understand a mother would take their child out to. She went out, and left the child with someone, if not James Styers. She went out with men, she went to bars, she went out; she left Chris. If she ever took Chris, it was to go shopping. So what she is portraying here is a contraction of the possibilities of her options with regard to Christopher Milke because he was interfering with her social life, he was interfering with her ability to try to land Ernie Sweat. And she had James Styers, a willing, compliant, go-along to conceive the plot and the plan. What to do with Christopher Milke? Well, I will have to have him killed. Jim, I just don't want to know how you do it, but there is no other option. I have to have my son killed."

Levy's oratorical skills may have been limited by his use of run-on sentences, repetition, and odd verbs, but what he said likely rang true in the jury box. He was not just repeating the state's evidence, he was repeating what the jury likely took as a *given*—her confession to Saldate. The only way around that given confession would have been evidence, or at least an argument, that the confession was *not* a given. That she had *not* given it. That Saldate made it up.

To reinforce the given, Levy argued Milke's "motivations" on the day of the murder. He reminded the jury of the timing that day. The last time she sees him is as he goes "out the door at 11:00 A.M." There was "no motivation, not even a reasonable inference that James Styers would independently have some desire to kill Christopher . . . there is no evidence . . . the evidence is entirely that Debra Milke wanted to have her son killed."

Levy speculated about Milke's post-killing reality. "Now if the child was dead, then Mark Milke wouldn't come around and bother her, no visitation. If the child was dead, then Ernie Sweat might reconsider whether they might get married, since that child was no longer a consideration, and she could move to that apartment nearer to Ernie Sweat and be closer to him and, for that matter, closer to her work."

Perhaps Levy noticed body movements among jurors signaling they knew speculation when they heard it. He retreated to his "keystone" evidence, but in a way that added more stones. "Now, her confession isn't all that exists here. The confession was fully corroborated by all of the physical evidence, and all of the testimonial evidence. She said she hated Mark Milke. She said she didn't want her child to grow up to be like him. She said that she had these discussions with James Styers. She said that she conspired with him to have her son killed, and knew he would be killed that day, and knew that thereafter James Styers would go to Metro Center, and create the fabrication that the child was missing. She knew if she was called at 2:45 P.M. by James Styers and he said that he was at Metro Center, Sears, as he said it, with the security guard; and Chris was missing, she then knew he was dead from that point on."

He did not even tip-toe into the never-never land of he-said-she-said. He did not want the jury even thinking about the possibility that Saldate might make it all up, that there was *no* confession. He moved on, connecting the physical crime scene evidence to Styers and Scott. He connected the bullets to Milke's car, locked in the glove box until the police opened it. He put the murder graphically in the jury box by talking about Christopher dying in a "fetal position . . . with undigested pizza in his stomach . . . the trip to see Santa Claus. . . ."

Then, Levy backed off the gruesome and toward what might be decisive for his side. Debra Milke's own family—father, stepmother, and stepsister—all made telling revelations about her. Collectively, they offered the jury their view that Milke was not motherly the day her son died. "She was only concerned about James Styers because she knew the child was dead . . . she was concerned that James Styers was in such proximity to the police that he might give it away . . . she didn't bolt out of the house, rush down to Metrocenter, or anything like that . . . she knew the child was dead . . . all of it was just a deception . . . she tells her stepmother and her stepsister 'I know he is dead; I want him cremated and the ashes spread over the back yard of my father'

. . . truly macabre, truly horrifying, except for the fact that she knew he was dead."

Continuing to stoke the confession fire, Levy went back to Saldate. "And finally, when she is talking to Detective Saldate that night, she knew they knew. She didn't ever ask the Pinal County Sheriffs about her son or anything, just calmly went there, went into the room, and waited what she claimed was two hours. Made no problem about it, just waited, waited for the inevitable, which she now had to tell Detective Saldate."

Notwithstanding the fact that there had been no forceful attack on Saldate's credibility, Levy was not a risk taker. He argued credibility, from the state's perspective. "Now, if the two pillars of credibility rest between Detective Saldate and Debra Milke, then you could have a bit of a contest by saying, well, it's only the word of Detective Saldate with regard to the confession since she didn't want it recorded. But, instead, you also have as an additional standard by which you can measure the credibility, corroboration of one witness to the other, because each has some overlapping effect—Sandra Peckinpaugh and Dorothy Markwell. The very things that she enunciated to them about Christopher Milke, non-bonding, not a good mother, hated Mark Milke, could not stand for her son to grow up to be like Mark, could not stand her son, wanted others to take care of him, were all contained in this confession."

What Levy did not mention, nor should he have, was Saldate's role in securing the negative testimony from Sandra Peckinpaugh and Dorothy Markwell. It was not his job to discredit them, or Saldate. He advanced his conspiracy by using Milke's words. When Styers called her on Saturday, "[s]he tells him, 'don't talk to the police, don't tell them nothing, they are assholes.'" When Karen Smith, her stepsister, woke her up on Sunday in Florence to tell her there's a deputy outside who wants to talk to you, "Debra says, what the fuck do they want." And finally, when she talked to Detective Saldate that night, "she knew they knew."

No one can reconstruct the thinking of a jury the day after a trial, much less 24 years later. But Levy's confession argument was most likely easily accepted in the privacy of the jury room.

In retrospect, his next argument was risky. "The very heart of the confession is that she said she contemplated suicide, but that wouldn't do any good because Mark would end up with the child. . . ." The only witness that said she "contemplated suicide" was Saldate. If Saldate's credibility had been effectively challenged, then the *heart* of the confession might have been debated, or at least seen as implausible. Levy argued that the date Milke picked for the murder was no accident. "At precisely the time that she sent her son out with James Styers to be killed, who was missing? Who was not there to do anything? Mark Milke, because he was in Fort Hood, Texas, with his brother. So it was the opportune moment. No interference by Mark Milke. He wouldn't drop in unexpectedly. He wouldn't be there personally to confront her about the situation. So it was a very opportune moment . . . and her exercising her options, as she described them."

He called her "cold and calculating." That was clear, he said, given what she told Saldate. "As she told Detective Saldate when he asked her, Didn't you even give your son a special kiss that day, Well, no, I didn't have to. Didn't you even specially dress him that day? No, he picked out his own clothes. He picked out the triceratops yellow sweatshirt that his grandmother, Maureen Sadeik, made him, and the boots his father bought for him, and she simply sent him out, and without any further concern. . . ."

Levy suggested she made a bad judgment call because that's what Saldate said she said. He explained her comment about low self-esteem as "typical of the rationalization you saw occur. . . ." He outlined her several fabrications. "The application at John Alden [insurance agency], blanking out a whole period of her life." She said she didn't know about the initial denial of the insurance policy, "yet she works for insurance companies." Finally, she admits, "'Well, yes, it was a separate policy and I intentionally bought a policy of $5000 for the child' . . . these kinds of fabrications, though they are small, can also link up with fabrications that are great overlays . . . such as denials by Debra Milke with regard to the confession . . . Well, yes, I said this and I said that, but no, I didn't say that, I didn't say that . . . that's inculpatory . . . the parts that indicated her guilt, her complicity in the conspiracy of the murder of her child."

Levy argued something Milke's *own lawyer* asked as proof. "The most telling statement that Debra Milke stated on direct response to her own attorney's question about whether that report by Detective Saldate, which she had read, was accurate or not, was, 'Well, I agreed with the content, but not the context' . . . the content of that report was her confession of the conspiracy to have her son killed . . . That's far different than the mere context."

Levy stopped arguing and spent the next five minutes summarizing the law of premediation, first-degree murder, conspiracy, liability for a co-conspirator's act, knowledge of the conspiracy, child abuse, kidnapping, and motive.

He closed his argument on something he did *not* have to prove—motive. "Now the state doesn't really have to prove motive. It still applies to a fellow's common sense to note whether there is some motive here. No motive on the part of James Styers. None on the part of Roger Scott. But motive on the part of Debra Milke." He rambled about the ex-husband and child custody, and a possible guardianship, the lack of a mother-child bond. Then he wound down and asked for a guilty verdict, "now that you have been privy to all of the dark, horrible secrets . . . the chilling facts . . . you decide the truth . . . return a guilty verdict on each and every count . . . in the name of justice . . . Thank you, your Honor."

The judge admonished the jury not to discuss the case with anyone, not to form opinions about the facts until such time as she gave the case to them, asked them to "stay healthy," and adjourned to await the arguments of Milke's counsel the next morning.

19

THE DEFENSE'S CLOSING ARGUMENT— OCTOBER 11, 1990

"*Y*our Honor," Kenneth Ray acknowledged as he squared himself in front of the podium. Turning slightly to his left, toward the table closest to the jury box, he nodded and said, "Counsel." Then facing the jury box, he began.

"Good afternoon, ladies and gentlemen. First of all, on behalf of Debra Milke, I and she would like to thank you very much for all your attention you have given to what is now the first one-month anniversary of this trial. It has been a long task. We have appreciated your attention and your patience with all of us, and we just hope it will continue until we reach the final conclusion of this chapter of life."

Some may have wondered about the *chapter of life* reference—was it a Freudian slip? It was just a slip and the jury was, after four weeks, used to the occasional word fractures from Milke's young defense lawyer. The official court transcript confirms he spent the next eight pages, about ten minutes, lecturing the jury on his interpretation of the final jury instructions from Judge Hendrix. He wasted valuable time talking about the nuance in factual assessment, physical evidence, open minds, why arguments by lawyers were not evidence, factual disputes in the evidence, the absence of smoke and mirrors, truths, half-truths, no truths, and memory lapses by witnesses. He meandered his way through how to weigh testimony by law enforcement officers, the legal difference between direct and circumstantial evidence, the reasonable doubt standard, burden of proof, guesses, educated guesses, and the jurors' obligation to find both truth and fact. Then, finally, he argued Milke's case.

"And, of course, in this particular case there is one particular police officer who is, as indicated by Mr. Levy, yesterday, the keystone, the focus in this particular case. The defense would ask you to place the situation on a level playing field in evaluating the testimony that has been given by that individual against all the testimony given by all other witnesses."

Then, inexplicably and without even mentioning Saldate's name, he returned to safe academic form with more explanations about the law and the court's instructions, which, he said, would be "given by the Judge at the end of the case." Levy had used the phrase keystone early in his opening, and now tied it to the confession Saldate claimed to have taken from Milke. But instead of seizing the moment and arguing against the reliability of that confession, Ray retreated to the safety of jury instructions—for another two pages of transcribed text.

His first substantive argument of the day went to a minor issue— whether the state had proven that Christopher was cared for "by others for months, months at a time. Have they done that, ladies and gentlemen?" He continued, in college debate style, picking apart innocuous issues dealing with the time the investigation started, the route to the crime scene from Metrocenter, the medical examiner's scientific determinations on Christopher's actual time of death, whether Debra bonded with Christopher in 1988, Debra's level of emotional distress, the relevance of testimony relating to the month before the murder, the level of hostility in the Sadeik family, the meaning of the word "hate" regarding Debra's ex-husband Mark, whether life is perfect, and Debra's "adamant philosophies, methods and means of raising children."

Ray challenged the government's case on issues entirely beside the point of the keystone issue. He admitted there was no doubt "that

Christopher Milke is dead. There is no doubt how he died, what caused his death. There is doubt as to when he died. There is doubt as to the circumstances leading to his death. And there is an abundance of doubt concerning agreement."

By *agreement*, he meant the legal requirement that conspirators must agree to conspire. One cannot be guilty of conspiracy to commit a crime absent an agreement to conspire. It was a legitimate defense. But the attention span and focus of a jury is a precious thing—hard to hold and easy to squander. Ray spent almost 25 transcript pages before he got to the central issue and the one most likely to be foremost in the minds of the jury. It was not her motive, or lack of it, that would send her to death row; it was her confession.

"The only thing that the government has shown is that Debra lived in Styers' apartment and, therefore, had the opportunity to speak. Now, you say to yourself, 'But, wait minute, Mr. Ray, we have got a confession, we have got a confession here, and that supplies all the missing parts to this case.' The defense begs to differ with that idea."

Calling it an idea and begging to differ with it was a problematic challenge to the most vital piece of evidence in the case. But having labeled it that way, he offered an explanation.

"And the reason is because it goes back to the keystone issue. And that is what occurred at the Pinal County Sheriff's Office on December 2, 1989. What occurred? Detective Saldate gave you an indication as to his background. But again, . . . you are to put him on a level playing field to begin with. And he told you about his method of interrogation and he told you that, specifically referring to page 61 of the transcribed testimony, commencing at line 19, the following question was asked of him. 'Question: And you indicated that you have an obligation not only to the individual that you are addressing in a particular interview or interrogation, but you also have an obligation to the Police Department and their policies and guidelines, as well as the law that applies to such a situation. Didn't you so state yesterday?'"

Ray read several lines of Saldate's testimony. That may have refreshed their memories, but it was hardly an argument challenging Saldate's accuracy or credibility. Saldate agreed on cross-examination he did not strictly follow all of the police department rules regarding interviews or interrogations. But there was no testimony about the consequences of not following the rules. There was no argument about whether Milke confessed, or Saldate made it up. He argued about not using a tape recorder. He argued about a detective who apparently did not care when a person invokes a right to remain silent. He argued about Saldate claiming to take "copious notes," and his "destruction of them, because that was his habit for twenty years on the police force. He always destroyed his notes." He argued about how little sleep Debra had before meeting with Saldate on December 2, 1990. He argued the stress of immediately being told about Christopher's murder, and being informed she was under arrest for it. And when he finally got to the confession, he said, "So then we are left to test the credibility of the final narrative report against the testimony of its author, with the admission in this particular case that many, many things that Debra Milke said did not make it into the final report and many things that she did say were just put in quotations. That's not what is important. We don't have the benefit of the recorder so we can determine what it is, and under what circumstances and context, these statements were made. We are left to rely upon the testimony. We don't have the benefit of the handwritten notes so we can try to determine what the nature and circumstances were, because they were destroyed."

Ray argued against the government's theory concerning credibility, by reminding the jury of the jury instruction they did not yet have. It would tell the jurors to "put the police officer and the Defendant, and all other witnesses on an equal footing. Common sense tells you that [an] officer pits his credibility, 20 years on the Police Department, any time against an accused. Any time. You can go to the bank and bet that all day if you want. But you are not, ladies and gentlemen, given the opportunity, short of listening to this testimony being regurgitated from a report prepared three days after the incident itself, from notes which have been destroyed and from memory, because we don't have the recording, and you are asked to rely on that."

That was a credible, albeit short and late credibility argument. He followed with, "We have an individual who is going to be charged with first-degree murder and we cannot get a tape-recording. We cannot get handwritten notes. Can you think of any crime more serious to be charged with than first-degree murder? And we are going to allow it, to rely strictly upon one's memory of things that are not contained in a report and things which are contained in a report that we cannot test against the notes or the recording. That's pretty serious."

Calling out the confession by describing the scenario as "pretty serious" was not a serious challenge to Saldate's credibility. It was all Ray had, *given* the confession. Ray pressed the point. "Well, if there was a confession that happened, if you confess in moment one, you might as well confess in moment two. Do you have any evidence of a subsequent interview taking place as a recorded situation? No. I mean, if you have already confessed, what the heck, you might as well put it down in a recording, go over the entire interview again. Do we have that? No. How about a signed statement in the hand of the Defendant? She has confessed; she might as well sign a statement. Do we have that? No."

Ray challenged Saldate's methods, his attitude, and his word, but only in closing argument, *not* during cross-examination where it might have made a difference. One of the cardinal rules of jury argument is to focus on the strength of your cross-examination, not on the weakness of the opponent's direct examination. He reminded the jury about the Sandra Peckinpaugh tape, which was not played for the jury, and had not been mentioned by Levy in his argument. Ray told the jury that the tape recorded what Saldate said to Milke's sister. It was "something important about Saldate," he said. It happened "during the interrogation in Florence." But instead of telling the jury what the *something* was, he tried to play the tape for the jury. To his obvious frustration, the sound was weak and scratchy.

Judge Hendrix inserted herself, saying, "It sounds like you need new batteries, Mr. Ray." Ray agreed. She suggested the jury could listen to the tape "when they begin their deliberations." Then Ray tried reading short selections from a transcript of the taped conversation. He told the jury the transcript said there was "noise on tape, couldn't get what was said." Ray tried to fill in the blanks.

"The subject of breasts is being discussed, or a statement being made to Sandra Peckinpaugh that Debra Milke took her blouse, pulled it up to her eyes to wipe tears, but there were no tears, and then he [Saldate] is explaining and talking about breasts."

Whether the jury understood Saldate's claim about Debra Milke showing him her breasts during the interrogation is unknown. Nonetheless, Ray argued the point as a credibility issue. And he gave the jury his client's personal perspective about what happened in Florence.

"Debra Milke, when she testified about the ongoing events of that night, looked you straight in the eye, and the eyes of all those who are present, and she related to the best of her knowledge and recollection the events that happened that night. She wasn't taking notes. There was mention about a recorder. She says, 'No, I don't want a recorder, I want a lawyer.' Is that something unreasonable, ladies and gentlemen, to be charged with first-degree murder and want a lawyer? Being down at the Pinal County Sheriff's Office expecting to hear some news about Christopher, and immediately being told, 'I'm Detective Saldate, your child has been murdered and you are under arrest for murder,' read your rights, in the meantime you are going crazy, what the heck is going on here, what, what. She tried to express to you what was going on some nine-and-a-half, ten months ago, meanwhile trying to absorb all of this, on very little sleep, comprehend that you have the right to remain silent, anything you say can and will be used against you in a court of law, you have the right to an attorney, if you can't afford an attorney one will be appointed for you. All those things. And you are supposed to comprehend that? She at least had the wherewithal to say, 'Wait a minute here, no, I don't want a recording, I want a lawyer.' But in keeping with his custom and habit, he just keeps on talking, eliciting more information and then noting it down on a report, and then later, three days later preparing a report—at least that's when it gets typed—and picking and choosing clauses and phrases of her statement and plugging it in wherever he wants to, throwing the notes away so nobody can cross-check it and compare it for its veracity and then getting on the stand and telling you, 'This is how it happened, ladies and gentlemen.'"

While forceful, Ray's argument did not deny the confession, or the inculpatory statements in it. His argument detailed the circumstances of the confession but he didn't argue the negative—that it was *not* a confession. He reinforced the confession when he said, "Debra Milke did not get on the stand and deny any of this. She did not deny saying [it]. She did not say she didn't talk to the man. What she told you was that certain of the statements that he put down in his report were indeed said, but they were said out of context. The words were picked and chosen as the detective desired, to fit into this story that he had concocted on his way down to Florence in this helicopter ride."

And he argued for an acquittal based on a lack of physical evidence. "[As Saldate] told you, he had no physical evidence to suggest that Debra Milke did anything as he proceeded to Florence. None. Just as he had no physical evidence to suggest that Debra Milke did anything then, neither do they now. There isn't a shred of anything in this pile of material that links Debra Milke to any of these crimes. Not a shred."

Ray spent the rest of his argument on the lack of physical evidence. He had said all he wanted to say about the keystone confession. He wasted time arguing that the murder did not occur the way the police said it occurred, implying there was reasonable doubt about the way it occurred. None of that made any difference. Arguments about crime scene prints, forensic testing of guns and bullets, rocky desert terrain where the body was found, and the inconsistency of witness reports about gunshots in the area on the day of the murder, had nothing to do with the "keystone confession." That evidence did not tie Milke to the crime. The only thing tying her to the crime was her confession. Arguing anything else was a distraction from the one thing that could send her to death row. But he closed strong.

"Ladies and Gentlemen, the defense does not suggest that Debra Milke is an absolute angel, saint. There is no suggestion that she is pristine, lily white. But she is a person, as you can tell from looking at her job applications, who has done a pretty good job in dealing with what she has had to deal with. There is no evidence of this evil monster that she would have to be in order to have anything to do with the death of this child. It is a shame, it is an absolute shame that this child died. There is no doubt about that. And it is a shame that in this day and age, the technology that we have today, that at this point in time, some now ten months after the incident, that we, as a society, and as a people, are no closer to finding out who is responsible for this child's death than we were back in December. That's terrible. Leads have not been followed. Creation of evidence has occurred in order to satisfy what has clearly been a high-profile case, the last hoorah for a retiring detective who then continues in misrepresenting even his private life. Recall the questions and answers concerning information provided to the Department of Elections. Seemingly insignificant, but critical information absent, to which he admitted. Ladies and Gentlemen, in opening statement the defense told you this lady is innocent and that she remains innocent until the government proves her guilty beyond a reasonable doubt. There is an overwhelming amount of reasonable doubt in this case. To list it all again would be nauseating. You have heard the facts, you have heard the evidence, and you have heard the testimony. You are going to draw upon your own common sense and experiences and you are going to put yourselves in the shoes of both the State and the defense in this case and make a determination as to how you would wish to be judged if you were in either position based upon the evidence and testimony that has been presented. Ms. Milke wants to know who killed her son, as she knows she is innocent. Thank you, ladies and gentlemen."

Ray sat down. Judge Hendrix said, "Ladies and Gentlemen, at this time we will take a ten-minute recess. Please remember the admonition." Ten minutes later, Noel Levy gave his rebuttal argument.

20

THE VERDICT, MILKE'S LAST SAY, AND SENTENCING

OEL LEVY, LIKELY SENSING A quick guilty verdict, spent only a few minutes on his rebuttal argument to the jury at 3:30 P.M., on Friday, October 11, 1990. Judge Hendrix gave the jury her final instructions around four o'clock and sent the jurors into the jury room to deliberate. They went home at five, returned the next morning at nine, and at 5:30 P.M. that afternoon, the jury returned to the courtroom. Eric C. Johnson, the jury foreman, carried a sheaf of verdict forms in his hand, gave them to the bailiff, who handed them up to the judge. As always, the jurors wore virtual masks—locked jaws, no eye twinkles, no joviality. They did not look at one another, or anyone in the courtroom, as they marched across the courtroom and stepped up into the jury box. Everyone looked at them but there were no tells— just 12 grim people looking straight ahead. A one-day deliberation is a walk in the park in a capital case. If nothing else, it signaled unanimity, easily reached. The judge read the forms, and with a similarly icy face, handed them to her clerk to read aloud in the official voice all court clerks use when delivering ominous news.

"We, the jury, duly empaneled and sworn in the above entitled action, upon our oaths find the defendant guilty of Murder in the First-Degree and we find this to be a dangerous offense."

Putting that verdict form down on her desk, the clerk lifted the next sheet of lined paper up to reading level, and in her best monotone announced three more guilty verdicts—Conspiracy to Commit Murder—Child Abuse—Kidnapping—all found to be dangerous offenses. The verdicts were unanimous, and delivered in record time. Everyone in the courtroom knew a juror had vacation plans—that's why the verdict was so rushed. The judge allowed it. Justice be damned was the feeling on the defense side of the room, and for many in the pews. They found Milke guilty in less than eight hours of deliberation based on highly debatable evidence, that had taken 17 court days to present. They had listened to 41 witnesses and examined scores of exhibits. It is unlikely any juror knew just how rare their verdicts were. From their side of the box, they had performed their sworn duty. They convicted a mother of murdering her child on the word of a detective whose checkered history had been kept from them by a powerful combination of judge, prosecutor, and police. But they did not know that. All they knew was they'd set a new time record for deliberation solely to honor a juror's vacation needs.

Debra Milke was one of the few Americans tried solely by confession. She testified against herself and no one knew it because the words the jury heard, the ones that convicted her, came out of Armando Saldate's mouth. Two and a half decades would pass before the world would be told how the cop so easily secured what he said was a guilty confession. Absent any direct or forensic evidence, the confession stands as the sole anchor for the murder conviction. This jury unquestionably believed she confessed solely because Saldate said she did. They could not have convicted her because they did not like her, or because they thought she was a bad mother, or even because her lawyer was not as skilled or as experienced as the prosecutor was. The only explanation is the obvious one—they believe the cop over the suspect. And they believed him without knowing how he had earned his reputation as the cop who could get anyone to confess.

Arizona law divides capital cases into two phases—guilt and penalty. Judge Hendrix waited until the jury had "exited" the courtroom before crisply ordering a presentence hearing four weeks later—on November 9, 1990. The penalty phase is burdened by procedural rules and grave decisions. The straightforward part of the process includes rendering judgment on the verdict, setting a date for sentencing, accumulating presentence diagnostic and mental health reports, managing a presentence hearing before the big day—hearing the defendant's "last say," and pronouncing judgment and sentence. In 1990, sentencing in capital cases was strictly a judicial function; no jury input was needed. Presentence reports were required in all cases "in which the court has discretion over the penalty to be imposed." That rule made Milke's penalty subject to Judge Hendrix's *discretion*. Those who followed the Milke case, either in court or through the obsessive media coverage, had little doubt about her discretion—she was not likely to favor the defendant.

The parties exchanged presentence reports. Each party had to notify the court and all other parties of any objections to the content of a report. Importantly, the prosecutor had a special duty—he "must disclose any information in his control, not already disclosed which would tend to reduce the punishment to be imposed." If a prosecutor has exculpatory information, this rule requires its disclosure, even though the guilt phase was complete. Noel Levy had made no such disclosures in the guilt phase, nor did he in the sentencing phase.

The now duly proclaimed *guilty* defendant was "entitled" to be present at any presentencing hearing and "shall" be present at the actual sentencing hearing. In a capital case, the defendant may be present "at both the aggravation and penalty hearings." The last procedural rule of importance in capital cases is the pronouncement of sentence. That was done back then, and now, in open court. The rule says, "The court shall give the defendant an opportunity to speak on her own behalf." Lawyers call it the "last say." It stems from a defendant's constitutional right "of allocution."

Allocution, a word not frequently heard in conversation, has a historic place in law. An allocution is a formal statement made to the judge by a previously found guilty defendant, just prior to sentencing.

In theory, it is mitigation, allowing a defendant to explain why the sentence should be lenient. In practice, it often produces the defendant's "story of innocence." For defense lawyers, preparing one's client for her last say, her allocution to the judge, was often a difficult education and psychological preparation effort. The manual on how to ready a client for her last say in a capital case varies widely, depending on the experience and seasoning of the defense lawyer. At a bare minimum, it should include educating the client so that she articulates a coherent account of her plight, especially viewed in a post-jury verdict environment. It is vital that the defendant understand her place in the justice system, now that the jury has spoken against her.

Milke's trial presented two accounts of her guilt and her life. The jury heard opening statements, testimony, and closing arguments. It chose the story it believed to be true, rendered its verdict, and justice was done—at the guilt phase. That's the *ideal*. But in trial-by-confession cases, it is pure *myth*. In these cases, if the jury believes the officer who took the confession, it accepts it as a *given*, which is exactly what Levy argued in the trial phase. In the penalty phase, the confession would again be treated as a *given*. This time, Levy would argue to Judge Hendrix the *given* confession in juxtaposition to Milke's allocution.

Experienced criminal defense lawyers know allocution matters because it is the only place in the criminal process where every convicted defendant has the chance to speak without the burden of answering questions from either hostile or inexperienced lawyers. Helping a client to speak in the voice of allocution invokes competing approaches. One approach focuses intently on mitigating circumstances. The other humanizes the client. Emphasizing one over the other often depends on how well the defense lawyer knows the judge's underlying personality, history, and tendencies—either toward or away from giving the death penalty. Almost every judge finds death penalty sentences difficult. Both approaches might prove successful. For a tiny minority of judges, who pass out death sentences without personal or professional angst, the choice is risky. Should the lawyer prepare the client to humanize her, or to mitigate her conduct in committing the crime? It is never an easy call. Both approaches can be harmful because either can alienate the judge. One judge might find the humanizing approach deceitful *given* her confession. Another might find the mitigating approach pathetic *given* her confession.

In Arizona, as in most other states, a local probation authority prepares a written report designed to aid the court at the sentencing phase. Judges typically rely on them because they are supposed to be unbiased assessors of the defendant's role in the crime, and response to her conviction of that crime. Typically, the officer will review the relevant portions of the trial record, along with police and medical reports, and interview interested parties. These reports are submitted to the judge after the trial, but before the sentencing hearing. The goal is to give the judge a "neutral" report to supplement the "advocacy" sentencing memoranda filed by the opposing parties. On November 14, 1990, Andrew Lembo, a Deputy Adult Probation Officer for Maricopa County, filed his presentence report. Often, these independent reports are helpful to the judge, who holds the final discretion in capital cases—life or death.

That decision—life imprisonment or death by lethal injection—was made by judges in Arizona until 2002 when the U.S. Supreme Court held that a defendant has the right to have a jury, rather than a judge, decide on the existence of an aggravating factor that makes the defendant eligible for the death penalty. In Ring v. Arizona, the Court held that a death sentence where the necessary aggravating factors are determined by a judge violates a defendant's constitutional right to a trial by jury. It also held that *Ring* was not retroactive. It did not apply to the 1991 Milke sentencing.

Most how-to manuals for defense lawyers in the 1980s and 1990s encouraged them to make sure the probation officer preparing the report hears about all the good things the defendant has done and is doing. It is important that the defense make the presentence report appear as favorable to the defendant as possible. As an abstract proposition, one could always hope that the independent report has a significant impact on the judge's sentencing decision.

Lembo's presentence investigation described the "present offense" based on information taken from "Phoenix Departmental Report #89-179406." Nothing in his report indicated the defendant's view or perspective about the police investigation. And none of it was new to Judge Hendrix. He accurately summarized the grand jury indictment and reported the jury's October 12, 1990 verdict against Milke.

Traditionally, presentence reports begin with the "Defendant's Statement." Lembo's report says, "On the advice of her attorney, the defendant has chosen not to meet with this writer or with any representative of the Adult Probation Department." Under the circumstances, that may have been good advice. Milke's ill-advised meeting with another officer, Saldate, had been disastrous for her.

It is likewise common for probation officers to interview crime victims. Lembo interviewed Mark Milke, Richard Albert Sadeik, Sandra Peckinpaugh, Henry Milke, Ilse Milke, and Robert Hughes. All were Christopher Milke's blood relatives. None offered positive comments about Debra Milke.

Mark Milke, Christopher's father, recounted his difficulties with his ex-wife, whole-heartedly agreed with the jury's guilty verdicts and offered specific incidents of bad mothering on Debra's part. He told Lembo that Debra "should receive the death sentence, or in the alternative a lifetime of isolation in prison."

Richard Sadeik, Christopher's maternal grandfather said, "Christopher had two strikes against him from the start, that being his mother and father." He argued that "his daughter was never meant to be a mother. If given the opportunity to have more children she would probably continue to murder again." He felt she "needed to spend the rest of her life in prison," but that "all the counseling in the world would not help her." He expressed concern, Lembo said, "that the Court may use his daughter as an example for the 'death sentence' which he recommends against, at this juncture." He paid for his grandson's funeral expenses, $1,722.43, and wanted "full restitution."

Milke's sister, Sandra Peckinpaugh, told Lembo she was more "responsible for raising Christopher for the first three years of his life than his mother was." She reported instances of "physical and emotional abuse." She felt that her sister "conspired to kill Christopher to get back at all of us (the family) for some reason." She did not "feel her sister should get the death sentence."

Henry Milke, Christopher's paternal grandfather, believed Milke "most probably suffered a great deal being married to his son, but could not understand why Debra would take that out on his grandson." He "recommended a life sentence and was against the death sentence."

Ilse Milke, Henry's wife and Christopher's paternal grandmother, told Lembo about Debra and Christopher living with her between October of 1988 and August of 1989. She said, "Debra went out a lot and I took care of Christopher." But she said, Debra "did generally bathe and dress Christopher nicely, although her attention seemed to stop there." She also recalled Debra "screaming at Christopher and frequently slapping him in the face for little or no apparent reason." She recommended Debra "be put away for a very long time."

Robert Hughes was Christopher's godfather. He and his wife baby-sat Christopher on a "number of occasions." He said Debra "never seemed to reason with the child—her only form of communication was to holler at him." He saw Debra "spanking Christopher's bare bottom when he was about nine months old." He felt the "defendant should be subjected to the death sentence in this matter."

The family vote was deadlocked—three for the death penalty and three against.

Lembo interviewed people he defined as "interested parties." That list included Noel Levy, Kenneth Ray, Detectives Armando Saldate and Robert Mills, and a social worker from Lamar County, Colorado. Levy was for the death penalty. Ray inexplicably said he had "no particular comments to make at this juncture." One can only imagine what that signaled to the one person the judge might listen to. Saldate told him Milke wanted to be "a single adult without any children." He said she showed no remorse, was extremely selfish, manipulative, and exploited others. But he said he "would like to leave sentencing in this matter up to the Court's complete discretion." Mills felt Milke committed the crime in an "especially heinous and depraved manner and should be subjected to the death sentence." Judy Johnston reported a referral in Colorado in October of 1988 alleging an incident of child neglect about Christopher and his mother. No further action was taken in Colorado, because no arrest was made.

Lembo checked state, county, and FBI records, and contacted Interpol in Germany. She had one arrest in 1984 for possession of marijuana, "which was dismissed." He summarized Debra's social and family history, her educational attainments, her employment records, and her substance abuse and marital information. He evaluated her financial status. Nothing caught his eye, or varied from the picture painted in court. Dr. Garcia-Bunuel said, "[T]here was no evidence of any thought or psychotic disorder."

Based on his investigation and interviews, Lembo made few comments about Milke. She was well provided for and perhaps even "spoiled" as a child. She enjoyed a certain popularity during her school years—she was in National Honor Society and she excelled academically. But, he reported, "[I]t was not until she married Mark and gave birth to Christopher that her life-style changed for the worse." He opined, "[H]er perception that Christopher was simply an obstacle in her life became quite evident to family members. It is felt that this particular mind-set did provide her with the motivation to elicit the services of James Lynn Styers, who eventually put the child to death."

His findings led to his conclusion: "The defendant certainly has demonstrated herself to be a serious risk to the community . . . she has been found guilty of [all her charges] . . . the law is quite specific on providing sentencing ranges for these charges . . . aggravated sentences do appear appropriate. . . ." He recommended "that the defendant be sentenced in accordance with the law on [the murder and conspiracy charges] and be committed to the Department of Corrections for a term greater than the presumptive."

Lembo's report contains a good deal of probation officer code, which judges easily decipher. He did not recommend death on the murder count; he recommended "sentence in accordance with the law." The evasiveness in Lembo's report mirrors the cryptic commentary given by Milke's family. Three family members wanted Milke to get the death "sentence." Three others reportedly were against the death "sentence." No one said Milke should suffer the death "penalty," or be "executed," or even, politely, that she be "put" to death. It's a small distinction, portraying how easy it is to support a death sentence, and yet how queasy people are about recommending or wanting *actual death* by lethal injection in a prison of the government's choosing.

No one, except Judge Hendrix, knows how much she relied on Lembo's report. But its lack of support for the death "sentence" suggests that she exercised her discretion based on other information.

‑‑‑‑

NOEL LEVY CALLED 11 WITNESSES to testify against Milke at her two-day presentence hearing, which began on December 7, 1990. The defense called two—Dr. Garcia-Bunuel and Bill Fowler. The psychiatric staff at the jail treated her for 15 months. Dr. Garcia-Bunuel spoke for the entire staff when he said, "neither the staff nor I found her to be deceptive or manipulative. She was always honest, kind, and never tried to fake her feelings. By the time she went to trial, she had developed a strong faith/belief that she would not be found guilty. In my twenty-one years of dealing with people facing the death penalty or life sentences, I have not seen a reaction like Debra's unless the person was convinced they were innocent. If a person were guilty, he or she would eventually accept the fact they were going to be found guilty, whether they were guilty or not."

A psychiatric report from a jail psychiatrist is standard fare in criminal litigation. But one proclaiming the defendant's innocence is as rare as finding a butterfly at the South Pole. Defense lawyers often consult scientific experts in criminal litigation. Expert opinions are only admissible if they will assist the court, or help the jury understand complex evidence. But the expert must be qualified by knowledge, skill, experience, training, or education. Dr. Garcia-Bunuel was qualified on issues regarding mental competence and mental illness. Guilt or innocence does not inhabit either area. Nonetheless, his opinion should have been helpful to a judge sitting without a jury, because it gave context and perspective to the larger question. The most important witness at the sentencing hearing was Debra Milke; the least important was her lawyer, Kenneth Ray. That's because judges rarely give any weight to what either lawyer says at this stage. Ray went first.

"Your honor, we ask that you spare this woman her life, which will, by the statutory prison sentence that the court must impose, will allow an opportunity for this lady to perhaps, someday, at approximately the age of 62, I think my calculation is correct, that would be the minimum point in her life that she would be eligible for release, and to allow as much appellate review as is possible for the facts and circumstances of this case. Incorporating everything that's been said in the pleadings along with these remarks, your honor, that's all I have."

Judge Hendrix turned to Milke. It was time for her *last say*. For the first time in the case, she framed her life and her new reality differently than what the jury saw. Some observers in court that day said she looked and sounded like a different Debra.

"Ms. Milke, is there anything you wish to say to me on your own behalf?"

Milke stood up and her lawyer moved out of the way so she could approach the podium, notes and a legal pad in hand. She told the judge she'd written it down so "I wouldn't forget anything." Judge Hendrix told her she could read it. Milke squared her shoulders, held tightly to the podium, and looked directly at the judge.

"This is—what I have to say. It is just how I feel and what I have experienced throughout all of this. I want to thank you for the opportunity to allow me to have my final say to the Court before I'm about to be sentenced. Having never been exposed to the legal system before, I must say that experiencing this absolutely is incredible to me. I feel there is more manipulation and game-playing than I have ever seen before, and with something as serious as a capital case, I feel should have been handled with more care and more seriousness. I believe that massive adverse publicity and intrusion of representatives of the news media in my trial, or a trial, can alter or destroy constitutional . . . requirements of impartiality imposed by due process of law . . . [that is] denied to the defendant with the media broadcasting so much. Before I ever went to court I was found guilty by the majority of the public, which left no space for any possible jury to be objective, although they always say they can be objective when in reality they aren't."

Pausing as though deciding how much more to read, she continued, "I'm disappointed that the Court allowed the use of a purported confession against me when there wasn't any evidence to prove this alleged confession. Although Mr. Saldate testified that he follows laws and guidelines, he does not. He didn't follow a direct order from a sergeant to tape-record an interview with me. An officer with over 20 years of experience should also know better than to interview a female suspect in a closed room without a witness. To me, this is only common sense. And with all of the law enforcement around, there was no excuse to not have a witness present. He testified in court that his purpose to contact me was to interview me only. If this interview was done like it should have been done, then an arrest should have been made after a confession. But Mr. Saldate, he had no basis for placing me under arrest as he walked right into the room. He admitted to this in court and arrested me on a gut feeling. I don't deny that this man claims I confessed. However, if this were a true fact, where are these copious notes, as he put it? They have been destroyed. Where is the tape which recorded this confession? Well, there is none. And where is the witness that sat in on the interview? There is none. And where is the document that bears my signature for confessing? There is none. And where is the physical evidence that connected me to this crime? There wasn't any. It's incredible to me that an officer of the law contradicts himself under oath, takes three days to prepare a six-page police supplemental report, claims I confessed with no proof, misconstrues five paragraphs of a four-page report of Ernie Sweat, admits to violating Miranda rights as long as they continue to talk. He does not handcuff me nor search me for weapons after I'm arrested for first-degree murder and guesses at what is true. Can being a police officer that many years have any credibility? This crime was very serious and I feel Mr. Saldate was extremely irresponsible. It is true my Miranda rights were read to me and I was apprised of my Fifth Amendment privilege to have counsel present. However, when I requested such a privilege, he immediately ignored me as if I said nothing. Mr. Saldate moved his chair in front of me, placed his hands on my knees and told me to trust him because he was my friend. To me, this is police misconduct and definitely overreaching.

I'm also disappointed that the Court would not allow any psychiatric and counselor testimony in during my trial. This testimony was not needed for their opinion of my guilt or innocence, but to give the jury the opportunity to know me psychologically. I had this picture painted of me as being an evil person with no remorse and someone who could show no emotion. This is very untrue. First of all, when someone is not guilty of something, then obviously they show no remorse. And second, methods people use in coping or trying to cope are as highly personalized as people themselves. Not every solution is right for everyone. I don't need to be guided by someone else's timetable for what is acceptable.

I'm faced with a dual tragedy here. The loss of my son and being charged for this horrid crime. The feelings that go along with this are too overwhelming and there is no such thing as prioritizing. However, I learned how to separate and set aside my emotion, or the way I feel about these other issues, in order to concentrate wholly on my trial. My emotional being stems back to my childhood and it has always been extremely uncomfortable for me to express emotion in front of people I do not know. And besides, being up on the witness stand in a crowded courtroom when your whole life is exposed is a very intimidating feeling. The jury had no clue as to what I have gone through awaiting trial and even during my trial, and just judging my credibility on the stand for four days was not enough for the jury. I let my inner instincts for self-preservation remain my denominator. We all have them and everyone is different. I'm sorry I didn't put on a show for everyone to see. And the truth is few can understand what I'm feeling unless they, too, have been there. The first sensation every parent has at the news that his child is dead is one of numbness. This numbness stayed with me for weeks and would come in waves, just as my crying and sorrow would come in waves. In reality, I know my son is gone. However, I still have this disbelief about his death because I never got to say goodbye. If I had to face the enormity of my loss for every waking minute, I'm certain it would completely envelope me and consume me and prevent me from ever becoming whole. This is something the jury couldn't know about me without the testimony of my counselors and psychiatrists."

The statement she read was very long. She told Judge Hendrix she should not have allowed Dorothy Markwell to testify as a rebuttal witness. She said she resented the argument by the prosecution that she was "abusive to my son. I was not abusive to him. And if I was, I wonder why no one ever tried to take him away from me or report me to CPS. I want to see medical reports of abuse and papers filed to show attempts of concerned family members wanting to take my son away from me. This is outrageous and I resent it."

Her father and stepfather had testified against her. She told Judge Hendrix she did not want to "go into the issue of my family, because years ago I divorced myself from that family due to their constant hypocrisies. Prior to me getting arrested, my whole family was very supportive of me until they found out I was arrested. Then they all turned against me. And my father [a prison guard] works within the system . . . he believes anything a police officer would say. And I did speak to my father one time before my trial started and he appeared supportive and then—telling me to hang in there and everything, and then two months later I found out he testifies against me. So my family's testimony about me didn't surprise me. I almost expected it.

I truly resent the way the prosecution jumped to conclusions and assumed these to be facts. I did not deceive my son by telling him he was going to see Santa Claus. All I knew was that Jim was going to the mall and Christopher wanted to go to get his picture taken. When they left my apartment, I was under the impression they went straight to the mall. I had absolutely no idea that Jim went elsewhere with Roger. I did not provide the means of transportation to commit a crime. My car was the only one operable because Jim's was broke down. He simply asked to use my car to go to the mall. I was not staying at home to purposely avoid the police. There were police officers at my house throughout the night. I wanted to stay home to answer my phone in case Christopher called, because my voice would be familiar to him. I did not buy an insurance policy for Christopher's life. I have always had Christopher insured since birth, and this insurance was only a benefit from work, available to everyone. I signed up for it 30 days after being employed, which is a requirement.

I never had any intentions on marrying Ernie Sweat. We did date. However, there was no discussion on getting married. This assumption of me wanting to get rid of Christopher in order to marry Ernie is outrageous and absurd. No engagement ring, nor was he given an ultimatum.

The State has known about the contents of my purse since December 1989. I feel it is not my problem that they failed to bring it into evidence during trial. However, I resent the way the State once again assumed the reason for the bullets being in my purse. And since this came out during the aggravation hearing, I feel it's necessary to explain why they were in my purse. The Friday night, December 1st, I came home from work, and Jim got paid that day and wanted to go shopping. I told him I was going to stay home and do laundry. He took Christopher with him Friday night and they were gone for about three hours. I grabbed the laundry basket, which was in Jim's room, and it was full of clothes. And I took the laundry basket, set it down on the couch and started sorting the clothes. And my purse was sitting right next to me on the couch. On the bottom of the laundry basket, out of a pair of jeans, fell these boxes of bullets, and I picked them up. I knew Jim owned a gun, so having seen these bullets didn't surprise me. Rather than getting up to go put them where they belonged, I shoved them in my purse. I continued to sort the clothes. I did the laundry. I forgot all about these bullets being in my purse. And I didn't go anywhere Friday night or Saturday morning. I didn't go anywhere until Sunday when I left Phoenix to go to my father's house. And then I didn't bring my purse with me when the police—the Sheriff told me that the police wanted to question me in the Florence Jail, so my purse was left at my father's house. I had forgotten all about those bullets being in my purse, and they were not put in there for voyeurism [sic] purposes as the State claims. That thought is repulsive.

Which leads me to the audacity of the State bringing in two doctors to testify about me and analyze me without ever speaking one word to me. I feel it is extremely unethical and very unprofessional. I resent being analyzed by strangers who don't have one clue about me whatsoever. My son was my whole life and his safety and welfare was my main concern. This is why my divorce is the way it is.

I was there when he cried. I was there when he fell. I was there when he was sick. And I was there when he asked questions. I'm angry that the prosecution states that I did not bond with my child. This is untrue. My son and I were extremely close and had a great communication. I'm sorry that I subjected him to a life of single parenting, but it was either that or stay in the relationship that was violent and abusive due to drug usage and alcoholism. I didn't want to have my son exposed to that. However, even though I left, I gave Christopher's father every opportunity to have a father-son relationship. I never received child support payments, but money was never an issue. I wasn't on welfare. I maintained employment with a decent job without a college degree, so I could provide for my child. I didn't live with this man and that man and I didn't use drugs. Christopher was in preschool from age two to age four, and very well taken care of by me.

He did spend time with his grandmother and godparents when they asked to see him. Christopher was provided for and then some, when I could afford it. He was never watched by strangers, either. I taught Christopher how to say the ABC's, to know his birthday, his full name, colors, shapes, telephone number, manners, how to dress himself, pick up after himself, etc. I did that, and no one else. I resent being labeled a bad mother who didn't care. I loved my son very much, and I still do. I miss him and will always miss him. I don't pretend to be infallible, because I am not. And no one is and no one ever will be. I did the very best I could in raising my child. I had no experience. He was a happy child and very smart and I miss him so much.

What I must now do is determine how best to handle this tragedy. Most of that handling lies in the approach. At first, surviving is like an infliction, stumbling, picking myself up again until I learn how to handle my grief. To me, it's personal and I choose not to share that with other people. I may appear emotionless, but I'm not. I'm not going to worry about that paralytic, what-will-people-think mentality. Worrying about that kind of thinking is false and trivial and I believe it can dangerously retard my re-entry into society. I will not allow myself to be intimidated by outside judgments at the time, that paralytic, what-will-people-think mentality.

I feel I was wrongfully convicted. I did not participate in this crime and I feel I should be acquitted. I don't deserve to be punished for something I didn't do. The legal system promises justice. I know our system isn't perfect because I'm a perfect example of imperfect, of how imperfect the system is. Injustice is constant and the only thing I can do is fight that injustice and refuse to be seduced into being emotionally immobilized by it. I also refuse to be psychologically defeated by it.

The influential have a separate set of rules. They are not helplessly bound by the authorities. I would ask the Court to please consider allowing me to remain at the Durango Psych Unit awaiting my appeal because of the counseling I receive. Since I have been incarcerated, the staff and officers have become my family and I feel safe and comfortable to express my feelings to them. I understand that at the Department of Corrections there is no therapy or counseling for women. And to not have that counseling would have a tremendous impact on my emotional well-being. My counselor, Rachel, and the rest of the staff at Durango are excellent and I have complete trust in them. Thank you."

Milke sat down.

Judge Hendrix turned to Levy and asked if he had anything to say.

"Yes," he said, first telling the court that Mark Milke also wanted his last say. Levy's last say argued *for* the death penalty and *against* Debra. His was a very personal, highly opinionated view, not so much about what she did, but rather *who* he thought she was.

"Debra Milke not only did not bond to Christopher Milke, but never wanted him and dissociated herself from him throughout all his life . . . Her statement to this court demonstrates that she has a very high level of ability to articulate and communicate; that despite her protestations that she is not able to come before people and express herself, not only did she very carefully, artfully and articulately express herself, casting blame and dispersions upon all but herself, but she had the same opportunity to speak in front of the jury and said many of the same things, which the jury apparently chose to disbelieve."

Levy argued, "The child, Christopher Milke, was in the fall of 1989, becoming an impediment and a restriction on her lifestyle . . . to the point where she decided that he had to be killed . . . it was not a sudden thing . . . it had accumulated over the years . . . she initiated that child's death . . . sent him to his death . . . she prejudged the child and sentenced the child to death. . . ."

Even before her confession, Levy argued, she "knew her son was dead . . . she said so on the drive to Florence . . . I know my son is dead, I'm having him cremated. . . ."

Weaving his star witness into his death penalty argument, Levy said, "When Detective Saldate that evening asked her what happened and she began to lie and he knew by then what the facts were, having been at the site of the murder . . . attempted to fabricate a story to him . . . [but] he said to her I want the truth, I do not want you to lie to me, or I won't listen to you, tell me the truth." Levy gave Saldate credit for creating what he called a "unique window and probably the only time where she was, because of this guilt and foreknowledge that she had been caught and detected, finally confessed. And did confess."

Levy made clear why he felt so strongly about her guilt. "Because Detective demanded the truth and she told him the truth, she now condemns him . . . because she did tell the truth but thereafter attempted to deny her involvement, and then shift blame to anyone she could, and now including James Styers, who at one time she suggested specifically could not do anything to her son."

Levy was an eloquent spokesman for the death penalty. His argument revealed how he *felt*, how the State *felt*, and what it was that makes the death penalty the only *appropriate* penalty. "Since Debra Milke sentenced her son to death and since the death penalty is the only appropriate retribution for what she has done, because this case is indeed above the norm, where a mother would send her only begotten child out to be murdered, the State *feels* that the death penalty is applicable." The death penalty was *appropriate*, he said, because, "[i]t is so aberrant to the human species that a mother would send her only begotten child to be killed simply because he was a burden to her and it would free her for her own lifestyle."

In his last say, Levy noted that it was "a great burden to ask the court to impose the death sentence. It is not done lightly . . . but the state feels after due consideration that there is no other appropriate form of punishment . . . Whatever the court may do, the tragedy cannot be undone. Christopher Milke is gone and gone forever. The bell tolls for us. Society requests through its laws, and its Legislature, and the laws they enact, and the judgment of the courts of the land, including appellate courts, and the United States Supreme Court, that in certain cases, the death penalty is available. And this is it."

As he moved away from the podium, Levy asked the court to allow "Mark Milke, the father of the child, to briefly address the court as a victim."

Mark Milke began, "My heart is pretty—there's too many conflicting messages between my mind and heart, and I would rather read from my notes."

Judge Hendrix said, "Certainly."

"Debra," he said, "appears to be the type of person who the person she is seeking a relationship with wants. For example, children or no children, the type of music, and social activities. She will do anything to obtain someone, or something that she wants. Through trickery, deception and manipulation, she usually gets what she wants."

Mark Milke continued reading to the court and covering events from 1983 involving Debra's roommate and a trip to a bar called the Library to celebrate the departure of her mother to Germany. She "strutted around the pool table and said she'd do anything to obtain me." He related stories about "harmless, humorless little lies she told." He said she knew how to figure out a person's weakness and use it against them. That ability, he said, "earned her the title of a trouble-shooter for me." He denied calling her a "baby killer." He said she was "madly in love with me," but "she was pregnant before we became married." Her mother came to visit and there was a "verbal war and some slapping. Debbie miscarried right there at that time and I saw what would have been my firstborn child go down the toilet."

From Mark Milke's perspective, "Debbie blamed her problems and trouble she would get into on me, her dysfunctions. She was depressed and very humble when I agreed to take her back. It only lasted until New Year's Eve, 1985 . . . life had become hell on earth for me, and Chris as well, if I wasn't around to take her abuse . . . I wanted to quit drinking and start fresh, she did everything in her power to keep me from it. She feared the loss of control that alcohol gave her over me. She couldn't face the music, that the party was over. I had become a machine to her. Take abuse, take care of Christopher, both mother and father roles. I worked to buy her things."

He claimed that Debbie "allowed me to have Chris under the condition that I live with Denise Peckinpaugh, then Sandy Sadeik, and take over those roles for her and her illegitimate son, as well, Jason Sadeik . . . Hell hath no fury like two women scorned, working together. It's like a competitive game for that family. The player with the most destroyed lives at the end is the winner."

There was no video in the courtroom that day, so there is no record of Mark Milke's show for the court, or his movement in the courtroom. But it seems plausible to assume that he looked at Debra Milke when he said, "Congratulations, Debbie. I think you are the victor. The more stronger the opponent, the more points. Christopher was far more points than I."

He told Judge Hendrix, "Debbie has two personalities. The positive is who and what she appears to be, but it doesn't take long for her true self to come out. Hence, as time goes on, and the jobs get shorter termed and the relationships grow lesser lasting, the only attribute she has left is Christopher. But it's too much for Debbie to handle that he has a false image of her and has all my attributes with none of hers or her family. She can't keep the family's and her own secrets and lives hidden. She acts them out."

Mark Milke was understandably critical of the Phoenix police. "Unlike the Phoenix Police, I had done an investigation of truth before acting on hearsay, as she had done with me in the past." He did not explain his investigation, or its outcome. It's unclear whether he meant an investigation into the murder, or some unrelated event. He told the court he got out of prison in January of 1989, but would "not live under the same roof as her or have an intimate relationship with her until May when I would give her one last chance at peace and happiness." He said by October of 1989, two months before the murder he "came to a decision, and didn't budge. I wouldn't allow her to use Chris as a tool anymore on my side from anyone or godparents to get her desires."

He closed his statement to the court with, "She aborted her four-year old child to obtain Ernie Sweat. She has tasted my blood over the years and she is constantly going for more."

When Mark Milke left the podium, Judge Hendrix asked the lawyers whether there "are any other victims present who would like to make statements to the court." Apparently hearing none, she asked, "Is there any legal cause why sentence should not now be pronounced?"

Ray said, "No, your honor."

The judge gathered the papers on her bench saying, "With no legal cause appearing, based on the evidence introduced at trial, the evidence received at the sentencing hearing and arguments of counsel, the Court hereby renders this special verdict. Mr. Ray, Ms. Milke, I have about 16 pages to read. Why don't you have a seat."

Her reading took some time, but the essence was in her first sentence. " . . . although the evidence demonstrates the defendant was not the person who fired the gun and inflicted the mortal wound, the evidence is clear and the court concludes beyond a reasonable doubt that the defendant contemplated and anticipated and intended with premeditation that Christopher Milke be killed and that the defendant Debra Milke is responsible for his death."

The remainder of the court's recitation of verdict was standard legal process, citing the appropriate state statutes, referring to aggravating and mitigating circumstances, and a summary of what the court considered probative evidence supporting the jury's verdict and her sentence. Much of her in-court recitation went to the statutory elements of aggravating and mitigating circumstances. Then came her conclusion: "Considering the nature of the person and the nature of the crimes and the nature of the mitigating circumstances, I find that, no matter how much weight I try to give to the mitigating circumstances, they are not sufficient to call for leniency. It is the judgment of this court that the defendant shall be sentenced to, on Count 1, to death."

She imposed lengthy prison terms for each of the other three counts and made them concurrent only because "the imposition of a consecutive sentence would be constitutionally infirm." She gave the defendant credit for "412 days of presentence incarceration," imposed a fine of "$400 to the Victims Compensation Fund," and ordered her clerk to "file a notice of appeal on behalf of the defendant, immediately." With that she said, "[W]e stand at recess."

On January 18, 1991, Judge Hendrix filed the formal pronouncement of the death sentence. The Arizona Supreme Court affirmed her decision on May 6, 1993. Milke's post-conviction proceedings were finalized on December 16, 1997 when the Arizona Supreme Court denied Milke's petition to review Judge Hendrix's original sentencing decision or her denial of post-conviction relief. Three days later, on December 19, 1997, the Arizona Supreme Court issued the formal Warrant of Execution:

It is ORDERED that, Thursday, the 29th day of January, 1998, be and the same is hereby fixed as the time when the judgment and sentence of death pronounced upon the appellant, Debra Jean Milke, by the Superior Court of Maricopa County, State of Arizona, shall be executed by administering to Debra Jean Milke an intravenous injection of a substance or substances in a legal quality sufficient to cause death, except that the choice of either lethal injection or lethal gas. It is FURTHER ORDERED that the Clerk of this Court forthwith prepare and certify under his hand and the seal of this court a full, true and correct copy of this order to the Director of the Department of Corrections and the Superintendent of the State Prison at Florence Arizona, and the same shall be sufficient authority to them for the execution of Appellant, Debra Jean Milke, as commanded by the judgment and sentence of death pronounced against Debra Jean Milke by the Superior Court of Maricopa County, State of Arizona, on the 18th Day of January, 1991.

—

THE ARIZONA SUPREME COURT STAYED Milke's death warrant several times. This seemingly spared her the grim task of choosing death by legal injection or lethal gas. Even death penalty advocates would understand the numbness that envelopes a person living subject to a formal "warrant of execution" from December 19, 1997 until March 13, 2013. During that time, Milke lived, as one reporter put it, "in a twelve-foot square box on a one-woman death row."

21

THE DEATH PENALTY IN ARIZONA
AND AMERICA

*T*HERE ARE MANY WORDS FOR it: death penalty, death sentence, death by lethal injection. The legal world calls it capital punishment, from the Latin, *capitalis*, literally—"of the head." World history buffs tell us beheading was the most frequent mode of dispatch. It never caught on in America. Apparently, our first legal execution by hanging was in the state of Mississippi, which hung a white man in 1818 for "stealing a Negro." Hangings and firing squads were the preferred mode until the 1930s when electrocution caught on. That lasted until the mid-1950s when we switched to the gas chamber, which lost favor in the early 2000s to lethal injection.

The Eighth Amendment to the Constitution applies to the states through the Fourteenth Amendment's "cruel and unusual" punishments prohibition. To date, no Supreme Court majority has interpreted that phrase to prohibit all forms of capital punishment in all circumstances.

Meanwhile, capital punishment penalizes those convicted of certain classes of crimes, in certain states, by killing them. Arizona is one of those states. Over the millennia, most societies practiced it. But most of the developed world had abolished the death penalty by 2003, except for the United States and a handful of other outliers.

Two Supreme Court cases serve as judicial bookends for the constitutionality of capital punishment in America—Furman v. Georgia and Ring v. Arizona. In 1972, *Furman* nullified all death sentences imposed without statutory guidelines. In 2002, Ring v. Arizona held that because Arizona's enumerated aggravating factors operate as "the functional equivalent of an element of a greater offense," the Sixth Amendment requires that they be found by a jury. Justice Ginsburg wrote, "The result was that the right to trial by jury guaranteed by the Sixth Amendment would be 'senselessly diminished' if it encompassed the fact-finding necessary to increase a defendant's sentence by two years, but not the fact-finding necessary to put him to death."

Taken together, both cases suggest that states could nullify capital punishment by statute, but that would require incumbent legislators to vote to end what pluralities still seem to want. Voting to end capital punishment is not a predictable outcome in 2015. While complex moral and empirical questions are associated with it, the 1993 *Milke* state court decision relied on the answer to the constitutional question *as of the date* she was sentenced, three years earlier. Milke challenged the Arizona death penalty procedure on constitutional grounds because Judge Hendrix's sentencing discretion was not "adequately channeled." Judge Hendrix found three statutory factors against Milke: (1) she was an adult and Christopher was under the age of 15; (2) the murder was committed in expectation of pecuniary gain; and (3) it was committed in an especially heinous and depraved manner. The Arizona Supreme Court accepted the trial court findings, on independent review, and upheld the constitutionality of Arizona's capital punishment statutes.

There are many questions about the efficacy of capital punishment in the United States; the "why" question paramount among them. Federalism is part of the answer. Under our constitution, the power of the federal government is limited in imposing laws on the several states. Politics is an even larger part of the answer, given the interplay between state politics and federal law. And there is the role of the U.S. Supreme Court in interpreting the Constitution. One result of America's emphasis on federalism and local autonomy is that the United States is not one single place when it comes to the death penalty. The law and practice of capital punishment varies from state to state and region to region. Below the Mason-Dixon line, 13 states actively practice capital punishment; Arizona and California are the westernmost outliers.

The *Embassy of the United States of America* released a worldwide article written by David Garland in 2013 to explain to the rest of the world "why" we still practice capital punishment. Nineteen states and the District of Columbia have no death penalty, having repealed their capital punishment laws sometime between 1846—when Michigan became the first state to abolish capital punishment—and the last few years, when New York, New Jersey, Illinois, New Mexico, Connecticut, Maryland, and recently Nebraska ended the practice.

An additional 18 states (and the federal government) have death penalty laws but rarely use them. States such as Kansas and New Hampshire are "death penalty states" in name only, since they have not executed anyone in many decades. Other states, such as California and Pennsylvania, sentence many murderers to death but rarely execute them; these states have hundreds of inmates whose existence is an oxymoron—they *live on death row*. Another 13 states—11 in the South—have capital punishment laws that result in death sentences being imposed and executions being routinely carried out. Texas and Oklahoma top most lists. Mr. Garland's worldwide press release indicates executions are comparatively rare and take place only after many years of legal "contestation." The average time between sentence and execution is 14 years.

Beyond the federal government's response, there are politically grounded reasons why 13 states still execute prisoners. That necessitates a discussion about *who* controls death penalty availability in those states. The urban myth is that the judiciary and the legislative branches control the *who* decision, i.e., the men and women who make the threshold decision regarding death or life. At a surface level, state law allows the death penalty in those 13 states. However, that is somewhat beside the point. In every state that allows the death penalty, there is a prosecutor in each county or parish that controls the charging decision. It is a classic local law–local power dogma. Prosecutors are elected to office in every death-penalty available state. They have the *sole discretion*, accountable to no other authority except the voters in the next primary election, to pursue death or a prison term against every murder suspect in their respective jurisdictions. The initial charging decision is *entirely* discretional. Prosecutors have the unfettered right to declare one murder a capital case, and another a prison case. Depending on one's perspective, the decision is a political perquisite, or an occupational hazard. Either way, the decision avoids moral or religious underpinnings.

Prosecutorial discretion is a deeply embedded political reality in this country. Elected prosecutors will not disregard the political preferences of their voters. Short election cycles, vigorously contested primary elections, weak or disarrayed political parties, and campaign finance practices combine to make it difficult for elected prosecutors to stray very far from the political will of their constituents.

Death sentences are the exception, not the rule. The 2010 data confirm that out of 14,000 homicides, only 114 resulted in death sentences. Governors will commute or appeals courts will overturn 50 percent of them. But until a Supreme Court majority interprets the Eighth Amendment's prohibition of cruel and unusual punishment to extend to all capital punishment via the Fourteenth Amendment, nothing will change. Elected prosecutors in individual counties will continue to control the *who* question. Elected state legislators will control the *whether* question. Suspects, mostly of color, and with less than stellar counsel, will suffer the outcome.

22

MILKE'S APPELLATE BRIEF TO THE ARIZONA SUPREME COURT

*D*EPUTY PUBLIC DEFENDER JAMES H. Kemper wrote Milke's opening appellate brief to the Arizona Supreme Court in 1992. He posed six arguments, four of which centered on judicial errors made by Judge Hendrix. Two others posed constitutional issues *vis-à-vis* Milke's death sentence. None had anything to do with the two central questions that might have made a difference at the trial level—Saldate's history of confession misconduct, and the prosecutor's failure to produce exculpatory evidence. The brief was strikingly silent on whether Debra Milke was innocent of the crime, or even whether she confessed to it.

The six arguments, in order of perceived importance, are:

1. The trial court erroneously struck, for cause, potential juror Pete Moquino.
2. The trial court's instruction to the jury on motive was erroneous.
3. The record does not support a finding that the murder of Christopher Milke was especially heinous or depraved; if it does then this aggravating factor is unconstitutionally vague.

4. The trial court erroneously failed to find grief as a mitigating factor.
5. Milke was denied her right, under the Fourteenth Amendment to the United States Constitution, to equal protection of the law when she was denied a jury trial on aggravating factors in a capital case while defendants in non-capital cases have juries to determine aggravating factors.
6. The Arizona death penalty statute violates the Eighth Amendment because it does not sufficiently channel the sentencer's discretion.

Curiously, Mr. Kemper only asked for relief from the appellate court on his first two arguments: "Based upon Argument 1 or 2, Debra Milke asks that her convictions be reversed and that she be given a new trial." Typically, appellate lawyers do not leave it up to the appellate court to figure out what to do if they agree with the other four arguments made. Substantively, Mr. Kemper started his brief with what should have been a compelling fact for the Arizona Supreme Court to think about in resolving this appeal. Debra Jean Milke "is the only woman in Arizona on death row and the only woman in Arizona sentenced to die in the gas chamber since prior to the second world war."

ARGUMENT 1—ERROR STRIKING A JUROR FOR CAUSE

As was the custom, the judge queried potential jurors first. Judge Hendrix made the following statement to the entire panel: "Ladies and gentlemen, on the jury questionnaire that you were given earlier today, I indicated that the defendant in this case has been charged with first-degree murder, kidnapping, and child abuse. And one of the other questions on the questionnaire asked you whether or not you had an opinion about the death penalty. Is there anyone here who feels they would rather not sit as a juror on this case because there is a possibility that the death penalty could be imposed?"

A juror named Pete Moquino raised his hand, and said, "Yes."

"Would it make a difference if I told you that the jurors did not determine punishment; even in a capital case that decision is left to the judge?"

Mr. Moquino answered, "I don't think I'd want to have anything to do with it. I don't believe in capital punishment."

Judge Hendrix said, "All right. Thank you, sir. Anyone else? Is there anyone here who is so opposed to capital punishment that you could not sit and listen to the evidence, listen to the law and make your determination solely on the evidence and the law without considering the facts as to what the punishment might be? Is there anyone here who is so opposed to the death penalty, regardless of what you really thought the evidence showed? Is there anyone here that has any feelings against the death penalty that might interfere with your ability to reach an impartial decision?"

Apparently, no other hands were raised, because Judge Hendrix said, "Thank you. Counsel, any additional questions?" There were none for her, but both lawyers asked the panel numerous questions designed to help them guess whose side individual jurors might favor. At the end of the jury selection process, the judge asked whether either lawyer wished to strike any juror "for cause." The only basis for striking a juror "for cause" is a legal inability of the juror to be fair and impartial. Noel Levy exercised a strike for cause on Mr. Moquino, without articulating any particular basis or reason for the strike. Instead of ruling on Levy's request, Judge Hendrix took the matter into her own hands: "The Court excuses Mr. Moquino for cause." But curiously, she then added, "[T]he court does not *need* to excuse Mr. Moquino for cause." The record was clear; Judge Hendrix struck Moquino. The record also makes clear that the only possible "cause" for striking him was "his opposition to the death penalty." There was nothing on the record to suggest that he could not be "a fair and impartial juror," or that he could not "decide the case on the merits of the evidence." All of those vital legal elements were cut short by the judge's interruption of the process and her takeover of the issue when the prosecutor moved to strike Moquino for cause. It would prove to be a typical reaction of the judge to important legal issues.

Kemper's brief cited the Arizona cases on the issue, all of which held the correct legal test that should have been applied was an inquiry, by the court or counsel, on whether Moquino held "a bias that would have prevented [him] from performing [his] duty." If a trial judge strikes a juror for "cause" arising out of a death penalty opinion, the appellate court must determine whether the strike is "fairly supported by the record considered as a whole."

Like all the other potential jurors, Moquino had responded in writing to a pretrial questionnaire. He said he had no opinion on Milke's "guilt or innocence." He said he had no personal or family experiences that would have impaired his "ability to serve as a juror."

ARGUMENT 2—JUDICIAL ERROR INSTRUCTING THE JURY ON MOTIVE

Kemper's second argument complained there was no jury instruction "on motive." Normally, appellate lawyers do not object to legal errors by the trial judge unless the trial lawyer made a timely objection to the judge during trial. Failure to object at trial is a waiver on appeal. However, in this case, Mr. Kemper explained that Kenneth Ray's failure to object "may constitute ineffective assistance." That's legal jargon for a separate appellate claim based on the ineffective assistance of counsel—a constitutional violation of the Sixth Amendment's right to counsel. Mr. Kemper said, "[T]his failure to object . . . as well as other failures in this record . . . cannot be made for the first time on appeal." He cited cases to support this position.

Arizona, like most states, has a rule of criminal procedure that governs post-conviction proceedings in a "direct appeal" to the state's court of last resort. The Arizona Supreme Court had earlier clarified that it would not reverse a conviction in a criminal case on "ineffective assistance of counsel grounds on direct appeal, absent a separate evidentiary hearing concerning counsel's actions or inactions . . . only where that court may clearly determine from the record that the ineffective assistance claim is meritless will it elect to consider the issue on direct appeal." For this reason, Mr. Kemper told the court in footnote number 1 of his brief that "no waiver of any sort is intended by Milke's failure to raise ineffectiveness claims in this appeal." This would later come back to haunt Milke when Judge Hendrix became the post-conviction review judge and flatly refused to conduct the "evidentiary hearing" that was vital under the criminal procedural rule and the clear holding of the Arizona Supreme Court that it would not consider ineffectiveness claims "absent a *separate* evidentiary hearing."

In criminal litigation, the appellate lawyer's job differs greatly from the trial lawyer's job. In an opening appellate brief, the writer presents "significant arguments, supported by authority." Failing to argue a claim constitutes abandonment and waiver of that claim. That is why Mr. Kemper was so emphatic in his footnote about *not* waiving anything. It also explains why he asserted the argument about "motive." Neither side requested a jury instruction on motive. However, the judge created her own "amalgamated document," which she called "jury instructions." One sentence read, "[I]t is not necessary for the State to establish a motive for the defendant to commit the crime." This sentence conveyed to the jury the base notion that the prosecution need not prove motive. Kenneth Ray agreed, stating "that's clearly the law," but offered no additional language to clarify the defendant's position. So, all the jury knew about "motive" was that the state did not have to establish the "defendant's motive to commit the crime." This benefited the prosecutor and the judge's view of the evidence, but offered no counterbalance for the defendant. Kemper argued on appeal this was "fundamental error."

In Arizona, a *fair* trial is a *fundamental liberty* secured by the United States and Arizona Constitutions. Embedded in the phrase is the guarantee that the jury determine guilt or innocence based solely on the evidence admitted. Error is fundamental when it reaches the "foundation of the case or takes from the defendant a right substantial to her defense. Existing case law in 1990 confirmed the litmus test—it is an error of such dimensions that it cannot be said it is possible for a defendant to have had a fair trial."

Kemper cited a 1983 Arizona Supreme Court case that had reversed a trial court criminal conviction for giving "the very same one sentence instruction we are talking about here." The thesis was simple. The state need not prove motive, but motive or lack of it is a circumstance that may be considered in determining guilt or innocence. Milke's problem was three-fold. Her lawyer did not ask for an instruction clarifying that the jury could consider lack of motive. The judge did not include anything remotely benefiting the defendant in her amalgamated statement. And the jury did not know that the lack of motive was a defense they could consider. The judge's failure to give a proper motive instruction had "the potential to mislead the jury into thinking that lack of motive had no significance at all."

Kemper also argued the factual predicates used by Levy at trial. "At various points the prosecution's theory seems to be that Milke's motive to kill her little boy was so she could be unencumbered, and thus be more attractive to her career-minded boyfriend, Ernie Sweat. At other points, the prosecution's theory is that Milke had the boy killed so that he would not grow up to be like his drunken, drug using, prison bound father, Mark Milke. Yet at other times, the state's theory is that Milke had the boy murdered so she could collect a $5000 insurance policy on his life."

All was to no avail since the jury was "not told it could even consider lack of motive as a defense. It must therefore have thought the lack of motive was of no significance at all," Kemper argued.

ARGUMENT 3—NO FINDING THAT CHRISTOPHER'S MURDER WAS ESPECIALLY HEINOUS OR DEPRAVED

The legally charged phrase "heinous or depraved" focuses on the killer's state of mind at the time of the killing. What is heinous to one citizen might not be to another. Jurors might disagree on how heinous you have to be to commit first-degree murder. Arizona courts developed a list of essential elements of "heinousness": (1) relishing of the murder by the defendant; (2) the infliction of gratuitous violence on the victim beyond that necessary to kill; (3) mutilation of the victim's body; (4) the senselessness of the crime; (5) helplessness of the victim; and (6) depravity. At the end of the trial, Judge Hendrix made a specific finding on this issue, making it "especially heinous and depraved."

The fact that a mother would plan and instigate and cause the death of her son is shocking and repugnant to all social mores and values, takes this case out of the "norm" of first-degree murders, and evidences depravity. The court finds that the state has proven, beyond a reasonable doubt, that the murder was committed in especially heinous and depraved manner.

Having correctly stated the law and the court's role in advancing the heinous and depraved theory, Kemper argued the record does not support the conclusion of heinousness or depravity. The actual killer's words and actions were absent from this record. There was no record of anything said by Milke to indicate she "relished Christopher's death." The state's theory that she carried cartridges in her purse as a "trophy of the killing" was unproven. The court found there was no support in the record that Milke had inflicted gratuitous violence. Likewise, there was no evidence of mutilation. There was a finding by Judge Hendrix that the crime was "senseless," but here the only goal, as postulated by the state, *was* the death of the child.

Kemper took special note of "the only other death penalty case in Arizona where a defendant was convicted of killing his own child, a child almost the exact age of Christopher. In State v. Stanley, the child was also shot to death by a bullet to the head. The child was killed by his father, after he shot and killed the boy's mother. There the child was killed 'for no reason other than to eliminate her [the boy's mother] as a witness.'" Kemper argued that Judge Hendrix had relied on "the mother/child relationship to find depravity." That, he said, was not permitted under Arizona law.

ARGUMENT 4—JUDGE HENDRIX ERRONEOUSLY FAILED TO FIND GRIEF AS A MITIGATING FACTOR

During the penalty phase, four weeks after the jury found her guilty, Milke argued that she *was* grief stricken and this *was* a mitigating factor in her favor. Judge Hendrix had issued a confusing order on the subject of grief. "Testimony had been presented that the defendant has experienced grief. However, no one has been able to state whether the grieving is for the loss of a son, or is for the loss of freedom. On

December 3, 1989, the defendant demonstrated little grief concerning the death of her son." Saldate doubted Milke's grief and Judge Hendrix apparently believed him.

To come to the opposite conclusion, Judge Hendrix had to disagree with three jail officials, each of whom had worked with Milke between her arrest and her trial. She did not believe Rachel Roth, a counselor who visited Milke in jail pending trial. Roth had daily contact with Milke for 13 months while awaiting trial. She concluded that Milke was "devastated by the loss of her child." She assessed Milke was having "grief reaction" and said, "I don't believe her grief reaction was due to her being in jail."

Judge Hendrix also apparently disbelieved Dr. Leonardo Garcia-Bunuel, a psychiatrist with 35 years of experience, who served as director of the Psychiatric Treatment Program at the jail. He had diagnosed Milke as "suffering from grief exactly a year before his testimony." Last, Judge Hendrix also apparently disbelieved the testimony of Dr. Martin Kassell, the jail psychiatrist who had spent the most time with Milke. His testimony was recorded as an offer of proof to the court, but kept out of the jury's hearing by Judge Hendrix. He too diagnosed her as suffering from grief, and did not attribute her grief to the "loss of freedom" as did Judge Hendrix in denying it as a mitigating factor in the sentencing phase.

The judge's defining remark in her order claimed that Milke demonstrated "little grief on December 3" was true only in the most "hyper-technical sense of strictly separating Sunday December 3rd the day Milke went to Florence, from Saturday, December 2nd, the day the child went to Metrocenter and was reported missing."

Kemper said, "If one regards this time period as a single day, which is only fair since Milke was awake all night, amid the many people who milled around, while the search for the missing boy went on, then there is ample evidence of her immediate grief upon learning the boy was lost." He described three trial witnesses, John Ciulla, Karen Ciulla, and Patrick Murphy, who described her as "really upset, hysterical, crying real tears, and [showing] a genuine emotional state." Altogether, six witnesses established beyond "any doubt that she suffered from genuine and profound grief."

ARGUMENT 5—DENIAL OF A JURY TRIAL ON AGGRAVATING FACTORS

Kemper's theory that the Constitution guaranteed a jury trial to determine aggravating factors was postulated as an "equal protection issue." He argued that Arizona "grants a jury trial, by rule and by state constitution in all *but* capital cases." Other courts, namely the U.S. Court of Appeals for the Ninth Circuit, had held that an "irrational and unfair distinction made by a state court in the application of state law violates the equal protection clause of the Fourteenth Amendment." He noted that although the Arizona Supreme Court had "never articulated its reasons for the distinction between capital and non-capital cases . . . that may make a difference in equal protection analysis." Equal protection prohibits "*de facto* as well as explicit unequal and arbitrary treatment." He argued, "[T]he lack of any rational explanation for this distinction renders this capital sentencing scheme unconstitutional."

ARGUMENT 6—THE ARIZONA DEATH PENALTY STATUTE VIOLATES THE EIGHTH AMENDMENT

In 1972, in the famous case of Furman v. Georgia, the U.S. Supreme Court, for the first time, struck down the death penalty under the "cruel and unusual punishment" clause of the Eighth Amendment. It did so because Georgia had no guidelines or limits on its discretion to assess the death penalty. Justice William O. Douglas, writing for a 5 to 4 majority of the Court, concluded that death was disproportionately applied to the poor and socially disadvantaged, which virtually equated the Eighth Amendment to equal protection values.

As applied in Arizona, that meant that state death-sentencing procedures had to provide a "meaningful basis for distinguishing the few cases in which the death penalty is imposed from the many cases in which it was not." Kemper argued that the state had to establish "rational criteria that narrowed the decision maker's judgment as to whether the circumstances of a particular case met the threshold."

Arizona's legislative response to Furman v. Georgia was to establish "aggravating circumstances" that would "genuinely narrow the class of persons eligible for the death penalty, and reasonably impose a more severe sentence on the defendant compared to others found guilty of murder." Kemper said Arizona's aggravating circumstances were "exceptionally broad . . . establishing an aggravating circumstance in almost every case . . . on the order of 90% or more." Accordingly, "there is no meaningful proportionality review that would allow this court to narrow the class of death-eligible cases at the appellate stage of the process." He stressed that "in fact, the [only] limits are the prosecutor's discretion, and the state's frequent inability to present detailed proof of what happened during the actual killing." The net is cast so wide, he said, "that it no longer complies with the Eighth Amendment."

What Kemper did not argue was the fly in any defense lawyer's ointment. Once an elected prosecutor seeks the death penalty, trial courts are bound. There can be no relief except via the Fourteenth Amendment and the Supreme Court of the United States.

23

THE STATE'S ANSWERING BRIEF IN THE ARIZONA SUPREME COURT

ANDALL M. HOWE, ASSISTANT ATTORNEY General, Criminal Appeals Section, wrote the answering brief for the state of Arizona in the Milke case. He answered the six questions in Milke's brief, and offered three new questions of his own, by cross-appealing. His 71-page brief included a 41-page "Statement of the Case," which restated Milke's factual statement from a prosecutor's perspective. His brief in opposition is a fine example of "did/did not" in lawyerlike *One/Two/Three/Four/Five/Six* formatting.

One, there was no error in Judge Hendrix's striking of a juror when the juror was "opposed to the death penalty and would not be impartial." *Two*, there was no judicial error in providing the jurors with an incomplete instruction on motive because Milke "waived this claim and it did not prejudice her." *Three*, Judge Hendrix did not commit error by finding Milke committed the murder in an "especially heinous and depraved manner, when a mother's murder of her own small child is above the norm of first-degree murders." *Four*, Judge Hendrix correctly rejected "grief" as a mitigating circumstance because "the record does not support that circumstance." *Five*, the Arizona death penalty statute does not violate Milke's equal protection rights because she was "treated the same as non-capital defendants regarding aggravating and mitigating circumstances, and a rational basis exists for treating capital defendants differently from non-capital defendants." *Six*, the Arizona death penalty statute does not violate the Eighth Amendment by failing to narrow the class of murderers eligible for the death penalty because "the murder statute and the death penalty statute restrict the death penalty to a select class of murderers."

In each of the six arguments, Howe stayed as far away as possible from Saldate's credibility, or the prosecutor's failure to provide exculpatory evidence. This was entirely understandable since only Judge Hendrix and the trial prosecutor knew what evidence the state provided to her for her in-camera review of Saldate's personnel file. And neither Kenneth Ray nor James Kemper had suggested any *Brady* violation in the lower court record.

Milke's appellate lawyer had identified four errors by Judge Hendrix in his appeal on her behalf. Now, in its answering brief, the state's appellate lawyer identified three additional judicial errors as the basis for its cross-appeal. Accordingly, the Arizona Supreme Court would review seven errors by Judge Hendrix. It would ultimately turn out that Judge Hendrix committed scores of other reversible errors, all of which would eventually find their way to the Ninth Circuit Court of Appeals. But for the moment, the Arizona Supreme Court would only address the seven asserted by the opposing sides.

In the first of Howe's cross claims, he argued that Judge Hendrix had "improperly refused to consider the confessions made by James Styers and Roger Scott at Milke's sentencing hearing." He took the position that they were "admissible under the rules of evidence and did not violate the Sixth Amendment's confrontation clause."

Second, he argued that Judge Hendrix imposed an "illegal sentence" on Milke's child abuse conviction by "failing to order her to serve that sentence consecutive to her sentences for first-degree murder, conspiracy to commit first-degree murder, and kidnapping." His reasoning was that "the dangerous crimes against children statute requires the sentence to be consecutive to her other sentences."

Third, he argued that Judge Hendrix imposed another "illegal" sentence of "life imprisonment [sic] *with* possibility of release for 25 years" on Milke's conspiracy convictions. He reasoned, "[T]he murder statute requires that she serve life *without* possibility of release for 35 years."

Once both sides had briefed all the issues they thought worthy of direct review, the court heard oral arguments and rendered its decision on December 21, 1993.

24

THE ARIZONA SUPREME COURT'S DECISION

State v. Milke, 177 Ariz. 118, 865 P.2d 779 (1993)

Statement of the Case

Defendant, Debra Jean Milke, was convicted by a jury of first-degree murder, conspiracy to commit first-degree murder, kidnapping, and child abuse. The victim of each of these crimes was her four-year-old son, Christopher. Defendant was sentenced to death for the murder of her son and to terms of imprisonment on the other counts. Appeal to this court is automatic on the death sentence[,] *see* Ariz. R. Crim. P. 31.2(B)[,] and defendant timely appealed the other convictions and sentences. We have jurisdiction pursuant to Ariz. Const. art. 6, § 5(3) and A.R.S. §§ 13-4031, 13-4033, 13-4035. The state has filed a cross-appeal. We have jurisdiction of the cross-appeal pursuant to A.R.S. § 13-4032(5). Milke's co-defendants, James Styers and Roger Scott, were convicted in separate trials and have also appealed. Although the three cases were consolidated for oral argument, we resolve each by separate opinion.

Arizona's court of last resort, the Arizona Supreme Court, is a co-equal branch of state government. Co-equal does not mean "the same." The executive and legislative branches are political entities and behave accordingly—their members are in the public eye, at the podium, and almost always running for office. The Arizona Supreme Court is nearly the opposite. Its members are apolitical, rarely seen in public, and do not run for or seek elected office. It is a cloistered institution. The justices only communicate with the people of Arizona through written opinions. Its opinions are the only way we can know the justices, or how they resolve the most important legal disputes in the state. If an opinion does its job—to explain the actual decision—then we feel all is well and justice was served.

The prosecution—representing crime victims—and the defendants charged with committing crimes are the first readers of judicial opinions. They read opinions to see who won or lost. Everyone else in the justice system reads judicial opinions for fairness and correctness. If the court's opinion is confusing, or seems false or unjust, then a sense of unfairness shrouds the opinion like a gauze over the defendant's coffin or a fog over the state's prosecutorial sword. At the policy level, the court's words must be well chosen, its use of language skillful and clear, or else we all suffer, to one degree or another. To preserve our faith in justice, the court must write well.

State supreme court opinions, unlike trial court minute entries or dispositive orders, are polished, spartan offerings stressing logic and precedent. They are often turgid and unreadable, and full of string citations that serve largely to interrupt cognitive grasp. In the second half of the twentieth century, supreme court opinions gave rise to legal realism with obvious efforts to write elaborate legal doctrines with layered sets of tests, standards, and balances. Finally, they are pragmatic, resolving only what must be answered now and deferring what can be put off to a future case.

The Milke opinion succeeds at many levels, but only if one knows what is missing from the opinion. It arrives at a logically defensible result because it answered the narrow questions posed in the written briefs. It did not address the pivotal questions that could explain what happened in the lower court. There is nothing in the opinion about Saldate's credibility, nothing about the state's failure to produce exculpatory information that would have changed the outcome, and no challenge to the most important factual question: Did Milke confess or did Saldate make it up? All of that would have to wait for a higher court, empowered to answer new questions posed by new counsel.

Judicial opinions are formally structured such that the holding of the court is paramount. A "holding" is a statement of law that is necessary to resolve the legal problem in the case. "Dictum" is a gratuitous statement of opinion in a decision, unnecessary to the result in the case. A "finding" is a factual resolution courts make to support or explain decisions made.

The court *held* that Milke waived any objection to the excusal of a venireperson for cause both by failing to object and by expressly approving the panel. It was not improper to excuse the juror based on his views about the death penalty. The court *found* that the incomplete motive instruction to the jury was not fundamental error. The court *held* that Milke should not have been convicted of a separate child abuse offense based upon the premeditated murder of her child. The court *found* that the death sentence was proper, even though Milke "was not personally the trigger-person and even though the aggravating circumstance of pecuniary gain was inapplicable, because the crime was especially heinous and depraved, the victim was under the age of 15, and the mitigating circumstances were *de minimis.*" Based on these findings and holdings, the Arizona Supreme Court vacated part of Judge Hendrix's judgment and affirmed other parts. It vacated Milke's conviction for child abuse, and affirmed her convictions for murder, conspiracy, and kidnapping. It affirmed the death penalty on the murder count, although it vacated the trial court's finding of pecuniary gain as a statutory aggravating factor, and affirmed the other sentences.

Milke waived any objection to the juror's excusal by the judge "both by failing to object at the time of the excusal . . . and by expressly approving the panel at the conclusion of *voir dire*." Even if she had not waived this issue, the excusal was proper because "excusing jurors is committed to the sound discretion of the trial court." Absent clear and prejudicial abuse of that discretion, "its determination will not be disturbed on appeal," the court said. It is not improper to excuse a juror whose views about the death penalty "would prevent or substantially impair the performance of his duties as a juror in accordance with his instructions and his oath."

Milke's second ground for appeal was Judge Hendrix's incomplete jury instruction on motive. "Absent a finding of fundamental error, failure to raise an issue at trial . . . waives the right to raise the issue on appeal." "Therefore," the court said, Milke must "establish that the motive instruction constituted fundamental error." That required Milke to establish that the incomplete jury instruction was an "error of such dimensions that it cannot be said it is possible for a defendant to have had a fair trial." Whether the incomplete instruction rises to the level of fundamental error necessitates an evaluation "in light of the totality of the circumstances." The state contends there was no fundamental error because any prejudice defendant suffered by the incomplete instruction was cured by the closing arguments of defense counsel. Under the facts, "we agree with the state. Both the prosecution and Milke's lawyers argued this issue to the jury at the close of the case. Each side discussed motive and lack of motive several times. Indeed, defense counsel's closing argument focused on refuting every motive offered by the state and attempting to show they were illogical. The arguments eliminated the possibility . . . that the jury might be misled into thinking that motive or lack of motive is insignificant. The jury was not misled as to the significance of motive or lack of motive, nor was the defendant prevented from arguing lack of motive at closing. Certainly, we cannot say that the instruction here made it impossible for defendant to receive a fair trial; thus there was no fundamental error."

The court discounted Milke's arguments regarding the death penalty. Milke contended that "Arizona death penalty procedure is unconstitutional because the jury does not determine the existence of aggravating factors and because the judge's sentencing discretion is not adequately channeled." The Ninth Circuit had dismissed the same Fourteenth Amendment challenge to the fact that the judge determines the existence of aggravating factors in a case in 1992. In 1990, the U.S. Supreme Court forcefully rejected a similar challenge in the context of the Sixth Amendment: "Any argument that the Constitution requires that a jury impose the sentence of death or make the findings prerequisite to imposition of such a sentence has been soundly rejected by prior decisions of this Court. The Constitution does not require that a jury find the aggravating circumstances supporting a death sentence. We reject defendant's claim."

Milke also argued the sentencer's discretion is not adequately channeled under Arizona death penalty procedure. But the court had rejected that claim in 1988 and would not change its collective mind for Milke in 1993. "The jury found defendant guilty of conspiracy to murder her son, as well as of the completed crime of premeditated murder pursuant to that conspiracy. These findings are amply supported by the evidence, and provide an adequate basis upon which to find defendant death eligible, although she was not personally the trigger-person."

Milke's lawyers devoted considerable space in their brief to the legally complex issue of "aggravating factors." The Arizona Supreme Court noted and discussed three statutory aggravating factors: (1) defendant was an adult and the victim was under age 15; (2) the murder was committed in expectation of pecuniary gain; and (3) the murder was committed in an especially heinous and depraved manner. However, Milke "only challenged the finding that the killing was especially heinous and depraved. However, in conducting our independent review of the death sentence, we necessarily examine all aggravating factors to determine whether they properly apply."

The court offered a studied assessment of the factor challenged by Milke. "In determining whether a crime is especially heinous or depraved, we examine the mental state and attitude of the perpetrator as reflected in his words and actions." The court cataloged specific findings that could lead to a finding of heinousness or depravity. These factors include "relishing of the murder by the killer; infliction of gratuitous violence on the victim; needless mutilation of the victim; senselessness of the crime; and helplessness of the victim . . . In addition to these five factors, we have also held that killing a person to eliminate a witness to a crime may be considered evidence of depravity."

Judge Hendrix had found that the victim was helpless and the killing was senseless. The trial court also noted that the special parental relationship supported a finding of depravity, and that the "finding of depravity, at least in part, was based upon the age of the victim."

Milke contends that because the state argued that the murder of her child was her ultimate goal, the killing was not senseless because it was necessary to accomplish her purported goal. "Killing her own son so that he would not grow up to be like his father, or killing him so she could be free from parental burdens is, indeed, senseless. Christopher's father wanted to increase his visitation and custody rights, and Milke's parents, Christopher's grandparents, were willing to take care of Christopher on a full-time basis. This crime most certainly was senseless in that it was unnecessary for Debra Milke to *kill* her son to free herself from the responsibility of being a single mother or to prevent the boy from growing up like his father."

The court also rejected Milke's claim about "helplessness." The court said, "Most assuredly, four-year-old Christopher was a helpless victim. He was delivered into the hands of his killers by the person upon whom he should have been able to rely for protection and compassion—his mother. He had no control over what his mother had planned for him. His mother knew that Christopher trusted Styers."

Next, the court took up Milke's claim that the trial court improperly relied upon the parent/child relationship to support its finding of depravity. Milke contended that to do so unconstitutionally broadens the term "especially cruel, heinous, or depraved." That necessitated a determination "whether the trial court properly applied [a] constitutionally narrow interpretation of the heinous/depraved factor. The trial court's findings of helplessness and senselessness are correct. The parent/child relationship also supports the finding of heinous and depraved. We believe the record supports the findings of heinous or depraved conduct in the case before us. Defendant senselessly killed a helpless victim, and as reprehensible as this may be, also violated the special parental relationship." "As the trial court noted . . . [the victim] was a child under parental control and capable of manipulation by the Defendant. We hold that the use of the parent/child relationship by the trial court in this case is permissible. . . ." Finally, "[defendant argues], even if this court agrees that the victim was helpless and the killing senseless, additional aggravation is necessary to support the especially heinous and depraved factor. Although the language of several cases would seem to belie defendant's argument, it is unnecessary to resolve it because the additional factor of the parent/child relationship is present here. A mother's conspiracy to murder her own four-year-old child and the resultant premeditated murder of that child is the ultimate perversion of the parent/child relationship. The crime in this case can be described without reservation as 'hatefully or shockingly evil' and 'marked by debasement, corruption, perversion or deterioration.'" The parent/child relationship is a circumstance "that separates this crime from the *norm* of first-degree murders. The use of that relationship in partial support of a finding of heinousness and depravity . . . is constitutionally permissible."

Pecuniary gain is a commonly considered factor in death penalty cases. Judge Hendrix found that the murder was committed in the expectation of pecuniary gain. In making this finding, the trial court accepted the prosecution's theory that Milke had a life insurance policy insuring the life of Christopher Milke. The Arizona Supreme Court correctly noted that "the mere existence of the policy does not prove, beyond a reasonable doubt, that the murder was committed for the money—that the money was the reason the child was killed. The State argues the insurance money was the impetus for the murder. In the opening statement, closing argument and during the course of the trial the State has advanced other theories and motives for the murder . . . The State produced evidence of the Defendant's wish that the child were dead before the life insurance came into existence."

At this point in its opinion, the Arizona Supreme Court used Milke's own testimony to affirm her conviction. "The only evidence presented linking the death to the procurement of life insurance proceeds has come from the defendant's testimony. In her statement to Det. Saldate, Ms. Milke denied having a life insurance policy insuring her son. At trial, Ms. Milke testified she did not know she was purchasing life insurance on her son as part of her employment benefits package—that she thought the life insurance was an automatic part of the benefits package. She later testified she has always maintained life insurance on Christopher, ever since he was born, using the rationale 'since I was fully insured I thought he should be.' Were it not for these inconsistent statements and initial denial as to the existence of the policy, the trial judge would not have been able to find that the defendant committed the offense in expectation of the receipt of anything of pecuniary value. But taking all of the evidence as a whole, it is clear, and the state has proven, beyond a reasonable doubt, that *a* motivating factor for the murder, although not the only reason for the murder, was the proceeds from the life insurance policy."

"From Milke's inconsistent statements, the trial court infers that one of her motives for killing her son was to collect the $5000 life insurance proceeds, and that the statements were an attempt to conceal this motive. In our independent reweighing of the evidence, however, we conclude that it is equally plausible that the inconsistent statements were Milke's attempt to divert suspicion from her. Believing that the police suspected insurance money to be a motive, she may have felt that she could deflect suspicion by denying knowledge of the insurance. One inference is as believable as the other is. Because conflicting inferences can be drawn from the evidence on pecuniary gain, we conclude that the state did *not* establish this factor beyond a reasonable doubt."

Turning to the victim's age as a relevant aggravating factor, the court noted that Milke had not challenged this factor, nor is it subject to challenge. "Milke was 25 years old at the time of the offense, and her son, Christopher, was only four years old. Although evidence of Christopher's age was also used, in part, to establish that the crime was especially heinous and depraved, the trial court properly weighed the victim's age only once."

As was its obligation under the independent review doctrine, the court examined the mitigating circumstances. "Defendant offered the following non-statutory mitigating factors: defendant's grief, alleged legitimate question concerning guilt, lack of a prior felony record, potential for rehabilitation, defendant's deprived childhood, defendant's employment history, defendant's conduct while incarcerated and during trial, her risk of future criminal conduct, and gender. The trial court found that no statutory mitigating circumstances were present and that only three of the non-statutory circumstances were entitled to any weight: no prior felony record, employment history, and conduct while incarcerated. In determining the appropriate sentence, the trial court concluded, 'considering the nature of the person and the nature of the crimes, the nature and extent of the aggravating circumstances and the nature and extent of the mitigating circumstances, I find that the mitigating circumstances are not sufficient to call for leniency.'"

Milke argued the trial court erroneously failed to consider her grief as non-statutory mitigation. But the supreme court said,

She bears the burden of proving mitigating circumstances by a preponderance of the evidence. She relied on testimony from her prison counselor, two prison psychiatrists, and three neighbors to establish her grief. The state rebutted with testimony from two psychiatrists who had not personally examined Milke. There was trial testimony of several witnesses who saw defendant on December 2 and 3, 1989. The mental health experts disagreed on whether defendant's grief was a reaction to her loss of freedom or losing her son. The witnesses, who observed defendant's conduct on December 2 and 3, 1989, also gave conflicting accounts. Although she apparently was upset and nervous, she did not behave like a mother concerned for her son's welfare. She appeared to be overly concerned with Styers' welfare and with what would happen to her.

The trial court's special verdict stated:

Testimony has been presented that the Defendant has experienced grief. However, no one has been able to state whether the grieving is for the loss of a son or is for the loss of freedom.

On December 3, 1989[,] the defendant demonstrated little grief concerning the death of her son.

Whatever the proper role of grief may be because of one's own acts, our independent review of the conflicting evidence leads us to agree with the trial court that defendant's grief has not been shown to be a mitigating factor. When mitigation evidence is conflicting and involves considerations of credibility, we give great deference to the trial court's conclusions.

In death penalty cases, this court independently reviews aggravating and mitigating circumstances to determine whether the death penalty was properly imposed. In this case, we have concluded that the trial court correctly found two statutory aggravating circumstances; namely, the age of the victim and the especially heinous or depraved nature of the murder. Defendant is therefore to receive the death penalty unless there are mitigating circumstances sufficiently substantial to call for leniency. The trial court found no statutory mitigating circumstances. Based upon our independent review of the entire record, we agree with that conclusion. The trial court considered all of the items offered as non-statutory mitigating circumstances and concluded that only three amounted to mitigation. Those three were no prior record, employment history, and conduct while incarcerated. Based upon our independent review of the record, we agree with the trial court's finding that the other items offered as non-statutory mitigation were not shown by a preponderance of the evidence to be mitigating. Regarding the remaining three items, the trial court found them to be insufficient to warrant reduction of the death penalty and we agree. We agree with all of the trial court's findings and weighings save one: in our independent review, we conclude that the state did not prove beyond a reasonable doubt that this defendant committed the crime for pecuniary gain.

Recently, this court engaged in an extensive discussion of the proper procedure to be employed when this court sets aside one, but not all, of the statutory aggravating circumstances. The advantages and disadvantages of reweighing versus remand are fully set forth in State v. Bible. We believe the instant case falls within the narrow class of cases where it is appropriate for this court to itself reweigh rather than to remand. There is no new evidence to be received and no evidence was improperly excluded at the sentencing hearing. The mitigation evidence is, at best, *de minimis*. Although one statutory aggravating circumstance was set aside, there is certainly nothing in the evidence concerning that topic that constitutes mitigation.

Given the facts of this case, the presence of two separate statutory aggravating circumstances and the *de minimis* nature of the mitigation, it is inconceivable that the removal of the pecuniary gain factor would lead to any different result in the trial court. Our review satisfies us that the mitigation is wholly insufficient to reduce to life even given the absence of the pecuniary gain factor. As we stated in *Bible*, there is "simply nothing to weigh or balance." Thus, as in *Bible*, "we are able to affirm the imposition of the death sentence even though we have found that one of the three aggravating circumstances was inapplicable."

Having unanimously ruled against Milke, the supreme court turned to the prosecutor's cross claims. They suffered the same fate Milke's had—denial across the board.

The first cross claim said Judge Hendrix erred in disallowing co-defendant Roger Scott's confession in evidence against Milke. The prosecution's theory was that Scott's confession proved Milke "procured the commission of the offense by promising payment from the insurance proceeds." Judge Hendrix had based her trial court ruling on the confrontation clause in the Constitution. But the state argued that the Sixth Amendment did not apply to sentencing proceedings. No, the supreme court said. "Because we are affirming the murder conviction and death sentence, this issue in the state's cross-appeal is moot. Nevertheless, the state urges us to address this issue notwithstanding its mootness because (1) it is a recurring problem in homicide cases, particularly capital cases; (2) the Arizona Court of Appeals has allegedly misconstrued the applicability of the confrontation clause to hearsay exceptions in some cases; and (3) resolution now will stream-line future litigation in this case should a federal court reverse the sentence and remand for resentencing. Although sympathetic to the state's desire to have the issue resolved, we must also recognize that, in resolving an important and difficult issue of law, the prudent approach is to decide it in a case in which it is *necessary* to decide it and in which all of the permanent members of this court are participating, if pos-sible. Therefore, we decline the invitation to consider this moot issue."

The state's second cross claim went to a concurrent sentence for child abuse. The state claims the sentence for child abuse is illegal because Judge Hendrix had "failed to order that the sentence be con-secutive to the murder, conspiracy, and kidnapping sentences." But the supreme court demurred because "[t]he child abuse conviction is being reversed for reasons stated in the companion case of [State of Arizona v. Styers]. Therefore, sentencing on the child abuse conviction is moot."

The state's third cross claim urged a longer sentence on Milke's conviction under the conspiracy statute. "The state argues that defen-dant should have received, on the conspiracy count, life without pos-sibility of release for 35, rather than 25, years because Christopher, the victim, was under age 15. This is the sentence defendant would have received for the murder of Christopher had she been spared the death sentence. It argues that the statute is ambiguous and its lan-guage is contrary to the legislature's intent to punish more severely those criminals whose victims are under age 15. The legislature is the proper forum to which the state should make its policy argument that potential child victims of first-degree murder conspiracies deserve more protection."

The state next argues: "[T]he legislature intended to punish per-sons convicted of conspiracy pursuant to a *specified scheme* by which conspiracy would be subject to the same sentence as the offense that is the object of the conspiracy. This theory advanced by the state could cause a death sentence when the object of the conspiracy is first-degree murder, even if the murder was never carried out. Defendant was con-victed of conspiracy to commit first-degree murder. First-degree murder is a class 1 felony. The statutory language is precise, unambiguous, and leaves no room for interpretation. The sentence imposed by the trial court on the conspiracy count was proper. We have searched the record for fundamental error. Under that search, we vacate the conviction for child abuse. We affirm the convictions for murder, conspiracy, and kidnapping. Although we vacate the trial court's finding of pecuniary gain as a statutory aggravating factor, we nevertheless affirm the death penalty on the murder count. We affirm the other sentences."

The trial judge and the prosecution welcomed this opinion. Milke's new legal team essentially ignored it when they filed her *habeas corpus* petition in the federal court system in 1997. As is always the case, the state court outcome is never final if appeals legally can be made to other higher courts, or post-conviction reviews in lower courts. State supreme court opinions are transient explanations based on limited information, or questions. Milke's lawyers advanced her defense *downward*, invoking the error-ridden state post-conviction review process with Judge Hendrix, and *upward*, invoking federal *habeas corpus* review process with Judge Broomfield. There is no little irony in the fact that Judge Broomfield was himself once a Maricopa County Superior Court Judge, serving as presiding judge while Judge Hendrix was on the criminal bench.

25

JAMES STYERS' APPEAL TO THE ARIZONA SUPREME COURT—1993

*T*HE ARIZONA SUPREME COURT WROTE a précis summarizing Styers' role in the lives of Debra Jean Milke and her son, Christopher Conan Milke, as the lead to its 14-page opinion on his case. It gives context to the otherwise stark reality of Styers' short legal history.

> His jury in Maricopa County Superior found him guilty of first-degree murder, conspiracy to commit first-degree murder, child abuse and kidnapping. His judge, the Hon. Peter T. D'Angelo, sentenced him to death on the murder count and to terms of imprisonment on the other counts.

The court recounted the basic factual crime story, the police investigation, and how the three defendants related to one another. John M. Antieau, Styers' appellant counsel, posed 12 issues to the court, only one of which resonated in his favor: whether there was sufficient evidence to support defendant's conviction for child abuse.

Six errors went to sentencing issues, one raised an erroneous jury instruction, and five challenged the sufficiency of the evidence to support the jury's verdict. Under long-established legal principles in Arizona, challenges alleging insufficiency of evidence are usually unsuccessful. But if the evidence cannot support the conviction, the charge *must* be dismissed. Arizona courts consider the evidence of defendant's guilt in the light most favorable to supporting the verdict. An acquittal is only appropriate where there is *no* substantial evidence to warrant a conviction. "Substantiality" is the primary test on appeal, i.e., a reasoned analysis of the quality of the evidence. It must be more than "a mere scintilla." In criminal litigation, the proof must "be such that reasonable persons could accept as adequate and sufficient to support a conclusion of defendant's guilt beyond a reasonable doubt."

Styers won on a narrow, almost irrelevant issue. The court held the evidence was insufficient to support the conviction of child abuse. It was not a "win" because he lost on all other appealable issues and the child abuse win did not change his death sentence. Judge Hendrix had instructed the jury that child abuse required proof beyond a reasonable doubt that defendant, "acting intentionally or knowingly and under circumstances likely to cause death or serious physical injury, caused a child to suffer physical injury or abuse." The court noted that the only evidence of serious physical injury were the gunshot wounds in Christopher's head. The state had conceded that point. Christopher had an abrasion on his lip. The medical examiner testified this could have occurred from falling after being shot.

The court clarified what many might think is a technical abstraction. "Although there is ample evidence that defendant committed the act that caused Chris' death (shooting the child in the head), we conclude that his separate child abuse conviction cannot stand on the facts of this case. Putting aside for a moment any considerations of double jeopardy, or double punishment, this question is, in the first instance, one of legislative intent: Did the legislature intend for the child abuse statute to apply to all murders where the victim is a child? We conclude that it did not."

Under Arizona law, a person commits first-degree murder if he intentionally or knowingly causes the death of another with premeditation, or causes a death during the commission of, or in furtherance of, an enumerated predicate felony offense, such as child abuse. The court said, "If a defendant cannot be convicted for an intentional aggravated assault that necessarily occurs when there is a premeditated murder, it logically follows that he also cannot be convicted for an intentional child abuse that necessarily occurs when there is a premeditated murder of a child victim."

The court was sensitive to how the general public might see this result. "We therefore set aside the conviction for child abuse. The jury was instructed on both premeditated murder, and felony murder. In the felony murder instruction, the jury was told that either kidnapping or child abuse could serve as a predicate felony. In view of the jury's finding of premeditation, we find the instruction on child abuse as a predicate felony to be harmless surplusage. We emphasize that nothing in this opinion should be read as suggesting that child abuse may not still be a predicate felony for felony murder. If a person intentionally *injures* a child, he is guilty of child abuse . . . if that injury results in the death of the child it becomes a first-degree *felony* murder." Although felony murder is first-degree murder, it is arrived at differently than premeditated murder. The first-degree murder statute, "not the child abuse statute, applies when a person intentionally *kills* a child victim."

The court was also mindful of how the legislature might view this decision. "Nor does our holding frustrate the legislature's goal of punishing more harshly those criminals who prey on children. A defendant guilty of premeditated murder of a child is subject to harsher punishment for murder, though he is not subject to separate punishment for child abuse." The legislature had already passed statutes that increased the punishment when the murder victim is a child. "For the foregoing reasons, we agree with defendant's contention that his child abuse conviction must be reversed."

The court denied Styers' claim of insufficient evidence on the kidnapping conviction. Styers argued there was no evidence he had *restrained* Christopher, a necessary element of kidnapping. "Restrain" means to restrict a person's movements without consent, without legal authority, and in a manner that interferes substantially with such person's liberty, by either moving such person from one place to another or by confining such person. Case law defines "restraint" as an act without consent if it is accomplished by: "(a) Physical force, intimidation, or *deception*; or (b) Any means including acquiescence of the victim if the victim is a child less than eighteen years old . . . and the victim's lawful custodian has not acquiesced in the movement or confinement."

The court analyzed Styers' claims sequentially, and brought Debra Milke into its assessment of Jim Styers' guilt. "Taking the last element first, defendant interfered with Christopher's liberty by moving him from his apartment to various drugstores, a pizza restaurant, and finally to a desert wash in northwest Phoenix. Turning to the element of consent, it cannot be based on the boy's acquiescence because he was a minor. His mother consented and, indeed, *conspired with defendant to take her son to the desert to be killed*. This consent, however, could not confer legal authority on the defendant. Clearly, defendant had no other legal authority from any source. Finally, restraint without consent can be accomplished by deception. Although Christopher went along willingly, he was deceived into going by being told that he was going to see Santa Claus at the mall, and he went into the wash in the desert under the pretext of looking for snakes. Lastly, [the state statute] could not confer consent on defendant by reason of [the] mother's acquiescence. There is ample evidence that defendant restrained the victim within the meaning of the kidnapping statute."

One other aspect of Styers' appeal brought Debra Milke into the equation. Styers' lawyer had appealed regarding the trial court's jury instruction on "persuading false testimony." The jury had been told that if they found "the defendant attempted to persuade a witness to testify falsely, or tried to fabricate evidence to be produced at trial, such attempt may be considered by you as a circumstance tending to show a consciousness of guilt. However, such attempt is not sufficient to prove guilt, and its weight and significance, if any, are matters for your determination." The Arizona Supreme court upheld the instruction. "The weight to be given to the evidence was up to the jury, as the instruction expressly told them. The state introduced letters written by defendant to Debra Milke while the two were incarcerated . . . The court found no error in giving the instruction."

Next, the court addressed Styers' challenge of his consecutive sentence for kidnapping. One aspect of this issue relates to Milke. Separate acts constituted the offenses of conspiracy and kidnapping. "Although the conspiracy continued while the kidnapping was being accomplished, it started before the acts that constitute the restraint. Here, although the conspiracy continued beyond the actual killing, the crime of conspiracy was complete even before the kidnapping began. The kidnapping occurred on the morning of December 2, when Christopher was taken by defendant and Scott and moved from place to place with the intent to kill him. Defendant, Milke, and Scott *could have conspired* to murder Christopher without committing or even contemplating a kidnapping. We conclude that making the kidnapping sentence consecutive to the conspiracy sentence does not violate the double punishment statute."

The court recounted the trial evidence against Styers. "Defendant owned the tennis shoes found in the parking lot near the Sears store and which had a tread pattern similar to the partial prints found in the wash near the body. Defendant purchased two .22 caliber weapons shortly before the murder, one of which was found in Scott's apartment, and could have fired the bullets found in the victim's head. Defendant possessed bullets like those found along the road near the wash. Defendant participated in the two-day charade at Metrocenter where he told police that Christopher had disappeared from a restroom. During that time, he did not, for several hours, even mention Scott's name, or that Scott had been with defendant and Christopher that day. Defendant now claims that Scott killed Christopher; yet defendant participated in the phantom search with the police without mentioning Scott. The jury's finding of conspiracy and premeditated murder satisfies *Enmund*. The trial court's finding merely confirms it."

The highly contested issue of pecuniary gain, on Styers' part, was decided in his favor. In the process of making that finding, the court talked about Milke. This issue arose from Styers' knowledge of a $5000 life insurance policy on Christopher. The court said, "We agree with defendant's assertion that this factor was *not* established beyond a reasonable doubt. The evidence showed that defendant was having financial troubles. Several letters to defendant from various creditors regarding bounced checks were admitted at trial. There is also testimony from defendant's neighbor that defendant told him that his checking account was 'in the hole.' Defendant's car was broken and needed repair work. Defendant knew of and discussed with Milke the $5000 life insurance policy on Christopher, payable to Milke."

However, the court said, "This evidence is insufficient to establish beyond a reasonable doubt *either that Milke agreed to pay defendant any of the proceeds to help her carry out her plan to kill Christopher,* or that defendant killed for pecuniary gain. Milke and defendant were in contact several times during the police investigation, and each was concerned about how the other was holding up. Milke was especially concerned about why the police were detaining defendant. The evidence demonstrated that Milke's behavior during the police investigation showed more concern over defendant than the location of her son. There was also evidence that Milke had attempted to transfer responsibility for Christopher to several other people throughout Christopher's short life. The evidence demonstrated that Milke cared very much for a man who clearly was not interested in continuing a relationship with a woman who had a small child. In short, there was ample evidence that Milke had a desire and a motive to want her son killed; however, *this does not establish that Milke had a financial* motive to have her son killed, much less an agreement to share the insurance proceeds with defendant."

Just as Milke had done, Styers challenged the "especially heinous and depraved" finding at the trial court level. In his case, Judge D'Angelo made a specific finding that Christopher's murder "was committed in an especially heinous or depraved manner." Both heinousness and depravity focus on the mental state and attitude of the defendant. Responding to Styers' challenge necessitated a connection between Milke and Styers. "We have discussed these factors and the rules applicable thereto at length in co-defendant Milke's case, also being filed today. The discussion is equally applicable here."

IN ALL DEATH PENALTY LITIGATION, the state supreme court independently reviews the evidence. In this context, independent means that the justices search the entire trial record for error that might not have been noted by the parties in their opposing briefs. Independent review mandates a careful assessment of aggravating and mitigating circumstances to determine whether the death penalty was properly imposed in the lower court.

In *Styers*, the court said, "We have excluded from our consideration pecuniary gain, having found the evidence does not prove that factor beyond a reasonable doubt. We have considered all of the proffered mitigation and, like the trial court, find it is not sufficiently substantial to warrant leniency. Although we have set aside one aggravating circumstance, a remand is unnecessary for the same reasons we have discussed in greater detail in co-defendant Milke's case, also filed today."

With that, the court turned to the state's cross appeal related to the admissibility of Milke and Scott's confessions at Styers' sentencing and a technical application of how Styers should have been sentenced on his conspiracy count.

On the first issue, the court, without saying so, resorted to an ancient common law writ affectionately known by old lawyers as "demurrer." It is a useful device for situations when, even if the party's allegations and challenges are true, and well founded in law, the party is not entitled to succeed. Today, demurrer is obsolete. But here is how it worked in the state's cross claim. The state posited that Judge D'Angelo improperly refused to consider at defendant's presentence hearing the confessions of co-defendants Milke and Scott. The trial court found that the confrontation clause of the Sixth Amendment and an Arizona statute precluded the use of the confessions. "Because we are affirming the sentences, we decline to reach this issue for the same reasons we declined to reach it in State v. Milke, also filed today." Those "same reasons" can be summed up in one word—mootness. Courts avoid mootness like politicians avoid clarity.

Finally, the court dealt with Styers' conspiracy sentence. Judge D'Angelo had given him a life sentence without possibility of release for 25 years on the conspiracy count. But the state thought that too light by 10 years. It contended the minimum term without release should have been 35 years. "We today rejected this same argument in State v. Milke. Defendant's sentence for conspiracy is therefore affirmed. We have searched the record for fundamental error and find none, except that discussed in this opinion. We vacate defendant's conviction and sentence for child abuse and affirm the convictions and sentences for murder, conspiracy, and kidnapping."

The outcome in *Styers* was predictable, but the court's pairing of *Styers* with *Milke* was less so. There is an obvious connection between them based on the conspiracy so vigorously advanced by the state against both defendants. Beyond that, the two cases took different paths through the lower court system. Styers, even though he denied it at his trial, was almost certainly the "trigger man." And there was a good deal of forensic and circumstantial evidence to support his convictions. He did not confess. Saldate was the case agent on his case, just as he was on Milke's.

However, Milke's appellate path was a road paved *entirely* by Armando Saldate. There was no forensic evidence against her. The only circumstantial evidence came from witnesses that Saldate manipulated. So, in every conceivable way, Milke's convictions and sentences were the sole product of Saldate's testimony against her. But in affirming Styers' convictions and sentences, the court often referred to Milke's case—her testimony, her outcome, and her relationship with Styers, which began as an accommodation but ended, if one believes Saldate, as a conspiracy to murder. That connection, Saldate's "word," was never developed in either case because Saldate did not need that—he only needed Milke's "confession." Without that, she would never have been convicted of anything. And if her conviction were to be overturned, then much of the Arizona Supreme Court's opinion about Styers is moot. Even so, Styers would likely have been convicted of first-degree murder. His conspiracy charge was icing on a trigger man's cake.

26

ROGER SCOTT AND THE ARIZONA SUPREME COURT

*T*HE COURT'S OPINION IN ROGER Scott's case began with a point of order: "Because defendant challenges both the sufficiency of the evidence and the voluntariness of his statements to police, we set forth the facts in detail." The essential facts relating to the crime and the involvement of Scott's co-defendants, Milke and Styers, as reported in the companion opinions, were repeated in this opinion. In addition, the following facts unique to Scott were stated. There is repetition, but the court's focus on Styers and Scott was unquestionably colored by its *simultaneous* rulings in the Milke case. Both cases—Styers' and Scott's—raise the possibility of renewed appellate action if the case against Milke ultimately collapses.

About a week before the murder, Styers told Scott "he and Milke planned to kill Christopher." According to Scott, Styers asked him to help. According to Scott, Milke told him "twice in the week before the murder she wanted her son killed—she had to get away from the child—she wasn't cut out to be a mother." The Arizona Supreme Court's opinion assumes the accuracy of triple hearsay in resolving

Scott's appeal: "Milke wanted Styers and Scott to take care of it. Milke had a $5000 life insurance policy on her son as part of her employee benefits package. Styers and Milke offered to pay defendant $250 from the insurance proceeds if he would drive the car. Scott told police he and Styers had attempted to kill Christopher at least once in the week before the murder." Given Saldate's role in shaping the testimony, or admissions of both Scott and Milke, it is possible that none of this happened.

In its opinion, the court repeated the factual predicates from both the Milke opinion and the Styers opinion, both of which were simultaneously briefed, argued the same day, written by the same justice, and released the same day. All three opinions consistently use Saldate's version of Milke's role in the case.

Besides his challenges to the sufficiency of the evidence and the voluntariness of his confession, Scott attacked the death penalty on constitutional grounds. He lost on all three challenges. Good appellate lawyers list their challenges in the order of the ones they think are most likely to prevail. The first of his seven challenges went to his confession to Saldate on December 3, 1989.

Scott's position was that he was "in custody" before he was read his Miranda rights, and the confession he made after they read his Miranda warnings to him resulted from improper and coercive police conduct (deprivation of food, sleep, and medication). He said Detective Saldate told him that if he didn't tell him the truth, "police would be sent to question his mother." The state's position was that while Scott was in custody *until* he made incriminating statements to Saldate, he was never deprived "of any items and was always free to obtain the items himself." Besides, the state argued, his claims about "deprivation of sleep, food, or medication did not affect the voluntariness of the statements." Saldate's statement that he would send police to speak with Scott's mother was not improper, and did not affect his confession.

Because the only statements challenged were made "after defendant was given his *Miranda* warnings," the Arizona Supreme Court focused only upon the separate voluntariness issue. Under Arizona law, confessions are presumed to be involuntary, and the state must prove by a preponderance of the evidence that the confession was voluntary. But, absent clear and manifest error, the trial court's ruling regarding the voluntariness of a confession is never disturbed on appeal. "In reviewing the trial court's ruling, we consider the totality of the circumstances. In determining whether the confession was voluntary, the critical inquiry 'is whether police conduct constituted overreaching.'"

The court reviewed the record, noting, "When police officers arrived at defendant's residence at 2:15 A.M., defendant voluntarily agreed to accompany them to the police station. He was transported in an unmarked and uncaged police car, and was not handcuffed. The officer who took defendant's first statement at the station, in which he related the 'Phil' story, testified that, at that point, defendant could leave; he was not considered a suspect. The police, however, did not tell defendant he was *not* under arrest. At 4:18 A.M. defendant gave a taped statement in which he again told the 'Phil' story. At 11:00 A.M., after defendant had been with the police for several hours, Detective Mills interviewed him. Mills testified that defendant did not appear 'overly tired,' and that he was alert and aware of the situation. Mills knew that defendant was taking prescription medication; however, defendant never requested any medication."

Based on these facts, the court said, "Nothing suggests that any lack of medication had an adverse effect on defendant. In fact, the taped statement indicates that defendant received his medication that afternoon, though Detective Mills did not remember him taking it. Throughout the investigation, defendant was provided with soft drinks and cigarettes upon request. Thus, it is reasonable to assume that had defendant asked to sleep, eat, or take his medication, the police would have responded similarly and provided these things. Detective Mills bought both himself and defendant dinner before defendant made the taped confession. Indeed, in his taped confession, defendant stated that the police had 'been pretty nice' to him. There is no indication that the police should have known, absent a request, that defendant was in need of anything. Despite the fact that defendant had been at the police station for nearly 14 hours before he made any incriminating statements, there is no evidence to suggest overreaching or misconduct by the police. The trial court was justified in finding that Saldate used no improper influence. Saldate did nothing improper when he suggested that police would be sent to defendant's residence to talk to his mother. Defendant waived his *Miranda* rights, and answered questions for two hours before Saldate mentioned sending police to speak to defendant's mother. Saldate was being honest with defendant when he said that police would verify his story by questioning his mother. There was no promise that police would not speak to defendant's mother if he confessed. We cannot say that defendant's statements were the result of anything but his own compulsion to tell the truth. We also affirm the trial court's finding that defendant voluntarily and knowingly waived his *Miranda* rights when read by Saldate, and later by Mills. Police did not threaten or intimidate defendant into waiving his rights. In fact, he had been volunteering the 'Phil' story for several hours, and continued with the story for two hours after he was given his *Miranda* warnings. There is also no evidence that defendant exhibited objective signs of distress, confusion, or incomprehension, before he was read his *Miranda* rights. The trial court's finding of voluntariness is fully supported by the record."

SCOTT CHALLENGED ARIZONA'S DEATH PENALTY statutes and his death sentence on all of the same grounds that Milke and Styers had used in their separate appeals. The same panel of justices heard all three cases, at the same time, and issued opinions in all three cases on the same day. It said Scott's challenges were the same as those in Milke and Styers' cases; it denied Scott's challenges for the same reasons.

27

PROSECUTORIAL MISCONDUCT AND IMPEACHMENT: BRADY AND GIGLIO VIOLATIONS

*V*IOLENT CRIME—ESPECIALLY CHILD MURDER—IS ALWAYS vigorously prosecuted in America. Prosecutors who handle those cases perform a vital public service. But they must be equally vigilant that excessive zeal does not violate a defendant's rights. A child-murder trial should not be, but often is, only about the victim. It should also be about the defendant. When prosecutors fail to follow the law, courts cannot balance the needs of the community with the defendant's constitutional right to a fair trial.

Under the landmark case of Brady v. Maryland, prosecutors are constitutionally obligated to disclose "evidence favorable to the accused . . . that is material to guilt, or to punishment." This prosecutorial duty is grounded in the Fourteenth Amendment, which instructs that states shall not "deprive any person of life, liberty, or property without due process of law." The *Brady* doctrine ensures that criminal trials are fair and that a miscarriage of justice does not occur. Placing the burden on prosecutors to voluntarily disclose exculpatory or favorable information to the defense illustrates the special role played by the American prosecutor. In America, we trust our prosecutors to turn over evidence to the defense because we believe their interest is not merely to win the case, but that justice should be done.

Prosecutors have not only a legal duty to turn over exculpatory evidence to the defense, they also have a broader ethical duty to "make timely disclosure to the defense of all information known to the prosecutor that tends to negate the guilt of the accused or mitigates the offense. . . ." From an ethical perspective, prosecutors have the special responsibility of a minister of justice, rather than that of an advocate. This entails an obligation to see that the defendant is accorded procedural justice and that guilt is decided upon the basis of sufficient evidence. Precisely how far the prosecutor must go in this direction is debatable. A knowing disregard of ethical obligations or a systematic abuse of prosecutorial discretion can constitute a substantive violation such that the prosecutor can be disbarred. Disbarring a lawyer requires clear and convincing evidence of conduct that is prejudicial to the administration of justice. Which, some say, is the trap door in the floor of prosecutorial misconduct.

On the legal side, a *Brady* claim of professional misconduct only requires proof by a preponderance of the evidence that (1) the evidence is favorable to the accused, because it is exculpatory, or because it is impeaching; (2) that evidence was suppressed by the state, either willfully or inadvertently; and (3) that the defendant was prejudiced. Favorable evidence is not limited to just exculpatory evidence; it extends to information that impeaches a prosecution witness.

The best-known case on impeachment evidence is Giglio v. United States. There the government's case depended almost entirely on one witness, yet the prosecution failed to inform the defense that the witness testified in exchange for a promise from the government that he would not be prosecuted. The court held that the prosecutor had to disclose that fact because it "went to the witness's credibility and the jury was entitled to know of it." The similarities between *Giglio* and

Milke are striking, "because if the prosecution is in a unique position to obtain information known to other agents of the government, it may not be excused from disclosing what it does not know, but could have learned." The prosecutor's obligation under *Brady* is not excused by the defense lawyer's failure to exercise diligence regarding suppressed evidence.

28

1995: POST-CONVICTION RELIEF

$\mathcal{U}$NDER ARIZONA LAW, ANY PERSON convicted of a criminal offense is entitled to have the conviction reviewed by a trial court judge *after* the appellate court has resolved any direct appeals. The grounds for post-conviction relief included Milke's precise situation: "Newly discovered material facts probably exist and such facts would have changed the verdict or sentence." Rule 32.1 of the Arizona Rules of Criminal Procedure mandates that such "*newly discovered* facts were discovered *after* the trial and the defendant exercised due diligence in securing the newly discovered facts." The rule also encompasses relief based on incompetency of counsel. The 1992 amendment to the post-conviction rule specifically covered impeachment, albeit warning that it would have to be "of a type which would probably have changed the verdict at trial." However, "where newly-discovered impeachment evidence substantially undermines testimony which was of critical significance at trial, the court should evaluate whether relief should be granted on the grounds that the evidence probably would have changed the result."

Debra Milke's first real break was the appointment of Anders Rosenquist as her post-conviction lawyer in 1995. Prior to this she had not been represented by a lawyer nearly as talented or as disciplined as Rosenquist. He had 25 years of solid trial and appellate work behind him, was board certified by the Arizona Bar Association as a specialist in criminal law, and had the right mix of intellect and investigative focus to take her case to a new level. His work set the stage that eventually led to her *habeas corpus* petition at the United States Court of Appeals for the Ninth Circuit. He filed Milke's original PCR petition in Maricopa County Superior Court on October 30, 1995, and amended it on November 1, 1995. Simultaneously, he also moved to disqualify Judge Hendrix. She denied his motion to disqualify on November 2, 1995, without a hearing.

Rosenquist detailed the factual basis for his motion in a sworn affidavit. He informed the court he intended to call her, Judge Hendrix, as a *witness* at the post-conviction evidentiary hearing. He based this position on his investigation of Milke's case, in which "[i]ssues have been raised that call into question the potential bias of the trial judge." He said he would question her, presumably under oath, about her "rulings regarding Detective Saldate's records, and the underlying reasons for her severe limitation on the scope of his cross-examination." This was the first shot over the state's bow that had shielded Saldate from public exposure. Rosenquist noted in his motion that the trial lawyer, Kenneth Ray, had "alleged that the trial court was biased against Milke."

Rosenquist intended to question Judge Hendrix about her "state of mind as it pertains to the application of her discretion in several areas of this case . . . pacing of the trial . . . juror selection and recusal . . . [and] interactions that may have occurred off the record." He clarified that he intended to press Judge Hendrix's *abuse of her discretion* in deciding trial issues against Milke.

He also brought Kenneth Ray's competence into question. "Further, allegations about the competence of trial counsel must be fully probed. The issues of the trial judge's bias and trial counsel's professional response to her rulings are relevant to the issue of his effectiveness in representing Milke." He intended, he said, "to question [Judge Hendrix] about her experiences with counsel both before *and subsequent* to this case." It is virtually unheard of in criminal case litigation for an appellate lawyer to "question" the trial judge about anything, much less her "experiences with the defense counsel." But

Rosenquist pressed the point. "The issue of the trial court's ability to fairly and properly mete out the [death] sentence in this case is also at issue. Though the court is expected to set aside her personal views in sentencing petitioner, I must . . . examine her personal feelings about the death penalty as well as her prior experience in meting out that particular punishment."

And with that factual predicate, delivered in a legal time bomb, Rosenquist offered an alternative to the spectacle that would have ensued if he were to "examine" Judge Cheryl Hendrix about her about her bias against the defendant, her death penalty views, and her interactions with the defense lawyer, during and after the trial. This case, he said, "[m]ust be transferred from Judge Hendrix to another Maricopa County Superior Court Judge in accordance with [the Arizona Rules of Criminal Procedure and] and the Fifth, Sixth, Eighth, and Fourteenth Amendments to the United States Constitution."

He gave several examples of potential bias, but threw his strongest punch first. "The trial court reviewed the personnel records of Detective Saldate *in camera* and limited the scope of Petitioner's discovery of those records." Those records most likely contained damning impeachment evidence that would have severely damaged Saldate's credibility. Judge Hendrix's review was *in camera*, meaning literally, "in the chamber, privately." This phrase when used by lawyers or judges describes the environment in which some judges review records relevant to a case. By design, the practice excludes public and press knowledge about what the judge saw or learned *in camera*, that is, in private. It is the mirror opposite of trial in open court, where all parties and witnesses testify in a public courtroom, and the lawyers publicly present their arguments to the judge and the jury. Had Judge Hendrix shared with defense counsel whatever Levy gave her *in camera* it is likely, if not probable, that Saldate would have been impeached at trial. That would likely have changed the outcome, since there was no other substantive evidence against Milke. Unfortunately, Judge Hendrix exercised her judicial discretion in favor of shielding Saldate from the possibility of impeachment by not disclosing whatever was in those *in camera* files. That was the bias Rosenquist was trying to uncover in the post-conviction review phase.

Rosenquist cited additional examples of potential bias: ". . . decisions regarding expenditures for experts, the selection and recusal of jurors, the pacing of the trial, and the court's reasoning." He informed the court that Mr. Ray "has acknowledged that his representation was ineffective, but holds that the trial court's biased rulings [were] responsible *for his* ineffectiveness." That is not surprising, given his remarkably short tenure as a lawyer before accepting a high-profile murder case. The Arizona Supreme Court licensed Ray on October 24, 1984, just five years before he became Milke's lawyer. He had only tried a handful of cases, none of which were complicated.

Rosenquist argued for Judge Hendrix's disqualification because the questions about trial and sentencing bias made her "continued governance over the resolution of these issues an appearance of impropriety that mandates her disqualification . . . By its very nature, she is incapable of making an objective inquiry [into her own bias]." He cited a well-known case, State v. Carver: "The right to a fair trial is the foundation of our criminal justice system." That right, he said, includes having a judge who "is completely impartial, [and] free of bias or prejudice. Bias or prejudice means a hostile feeling, ill will, undue friendship, or favoritism towards one of the litigants." Rosenquist's plan included a detailed explanation of how and why Judge Hendrix protected Saldate, and why she gave the state an advantage by not forcing it to produce impeachment evidence that might have buried the alleged confession.

He cited In re Haddad, a case routinely cited for the proposition that the public is entitled to "confidence in the impartiality of its judiciary." He cited the Arizona Code of Judicial Conduct for its own standard: "An independent and honorable judiciary is indispensable to justice in our society." That code contains a poignant reminder of Milke's treatment at her trial. "Deference to the judgments and rulings of courts depends upon public confidence in the integrity and independence of judges . . . violation of this code diminishes public confidence and thereby does injury to the system of government under law."

His plea for a new judge to hear Milke's post-conviction review connected the dots between the death penalty and judicial bias. Noting that "[d]eath penalty cases are subjected to more particular and exacting scrutiny by the press and public than are other criminal cases," he made the central point in her case. The death penalty plays a large role "because of the public's perception [as to] whether our justice system is biased." The due process clause guaranteed by the Fourteenth Amendment requires judicial disqualification when necessary to avoid the "appearance of impropriety." The question of Judge Hendrix's actual bias or impropriety can never be answered. But the question of her "appearance" of impropriety could be resolved if she either recused herself, or another judge either granted or denied Rosenquist's motion. Neither happened.

On March 20, 1996, Judge Hendrix predictably ruled on the motion to disqualify her. And she did something she rarely did—she issued a written order detailing her reasons for denying the motion. In her own defense, she said, "The affidavit of Anders Rosenquist accompanies the motion. However, the affidavit says nothing about what Mr. Rosenquist or any other person has discovered in the ten days preceding the filing of the motion, that demonstrates bias, prejudice, or the inability of the petitioner to have a fair consideration of her petition. . . What the affidavit does state is the desire of petitioner's counsel to have the trial judge explain and clarify her actions, discover the reason for rulings that were made, question the trial judge as to her experiences with counsel, and to examine the judge's personal feelings about the death penalty . . . the affidavit alleges no facts, which if taken as true, would entitle the petitioner to a change of judge . . . The defendant is not entitled to *voir dire* the trial judge."

The Latin phrase, *voir dire*, meaning literally, "to speak the truth," is ironic in this setting. What Milke wanted was the truth about what was in Saldate's file and the truth about Saldate's claim that she confessed. Judge Hendrix denied Milke the chance to prove that truth at trial and again by dismissing, without a hearing, her post-conviction relief motion.

To help Milke in her search for truth, Rosenquist tracked down a psychiatrist, Dr. Kevin Zuerlein, as part of Milke's post-conviction review process. Dr. Zuerlein had played a very important role in the Milke case one year *before* Christopher was murdered. In December of 1988, Milke took Christopher to the Maricopa County hospital because she noticed a red, slightly swollen area on the front of his neck. The first doctor to examine Christopher was Dr. Kay Miller. She took a brief medical history from the boy's mother, who told her she was sure it had not been there earlier in the day. There was no trauma or evidence of bug bite. She also said that the swelling had increased since their arrival at the hospital. Dr. Miller asked about the boy's appetite; a slight decrease, Debra said, but no fever, chills, vomiting, or diarrhea. Dr. Miller noted in Christopher's chart that the area was slightly tender to palpation.

Dr. Zuerlein was a psychiatric resident at the hospital, working with Dr. Miller on a pediatric rotation, the morning Milke brought Christopher to the hospital. He assisted in taking the basic medical history and making notes in the medical chart. Those notes confirm the acute and difficult circumstances surrounding Christopher's condition in 1988. He was admitted to the hospital on December 4 and discharged, following surgery, on December 22, 1988. His past medical history, as reported by his mother, confirmed his birth weight at six pounds 12 ounces. He was a full term baby, delivered in good health, following an uncomplicated pregnancy. There had been a failure to progress, resulting in delivery by cesarean section. No neonatal problems were noted in his birth chart. He presented as "age appropriate," although his mother noted her son was a "picky eater." The only incident noted on the admission chart was that his babysitter had strep throat. Debra said she and Christopher were living with the boy's father and paternal grandmother. The babysitter was the primary caretaker during the day, while Debra worked.

Christopher's physical examination was unremarkable—"Well nourished, well developed Caucasian male in no acute distress with an obvious anterior neck mass . . . a supple 7 x 8 cm firm, nonfluctuant mass . . . chest clear to auscultation . . . heart regular rate and rhythm without murmur . . . alert and responsive . . . motor and sensory grossly intact . . . CT scan revealed large soft tissue mass in the left side of the neck, probably in the large thyroid. . . ."

The doctors recommended surgery because the mass consolidated in the anterior neck. They felt he needed incision and drainage, which they successfully performed 15 days later, on December 19, 1988. A second wound incision followed on December 21 and he was discharged on December 22 with a final diagnosis—suppurative thyroiditis with abscess.

Seven years later, as part of Debra Milke's post-conviction review process, Rosenquist asked Dr. Zuerlein to give a sworn affidavit regarding his observations of both Christopher and his mother during the boy's 19-day hospital stay. Rosenquist knew that Dr. Zuerlein, as a psychiatric resident assigned to the pediatric unit, was in a unique position to comment on the mother/child relationship, from both a pediatric and a psychiatric perspective. He reviewed Christopher's medical chart to refresh his memory, but also said he had "an independent recollection of him and his mother because I was the intern assigned to Christopher's case."

Dr. Zuerlein "interacted with Christopher and his mother several times a day during the 19 days he was hospitalized." His interaction "with them" and his training as a psychiatrist gave him the ability to form definite conclusions.

Christopher was well mannered and displayed the usual age appropriate developmental milestones. During his hospitalization, his mother, Debra Milke, was very concerned about him. She sought treatment within days of noticing a change in his physical condition. She was often at his bedside. She interacted well with the hospital staff.

Debra appeared to be well bonded to Christopher, and Christopher appeared to be well bonded with his mother. There were no abnormalities noted in Christopher and his mother's relationship.

Compared to many other families whose children were being treated at the Medical Center, and seen by me, Debra's presence and concern for Christopher were above average. Debra did not display an increased nervousness during any of the questioning involving the history and relationship of her and her child. She was genuinely concerned for her child. She was cooperative, helpful, informative, and pleasant, throughout Christopher's stay in the hospital.

Christopher showed no signs of failure to progress at a normal rate; he appeared to be growing both physically and mentally at a normal rate. He showed no signs of physical or mental abuse.

Judge Hendrix presumably read Dr. Zuerlein's affidavit, but did not mention it in her written order denying Milke any post-conviction relief. The state responded to the amended petition for post-conviction review in March 1996. With the motion to disqualify out of the way, both sides waited for Judge Hendrix to schedule an evidentiary hearing so they could ferret out, in open court, the scores of new issues raised by Milke. But that never happened. On November 18, 1996, Judge Hendrix issued a 55-page order summarily dismissing the petition, *without* giving Milke an evidentiary hearing of any kind. That order included a specific finding by Judge Hendrix: "The court finds that the amended petition for post-conviction relief does not raise any factual issues. The petitioner would be entitled to an evidentiary hearing if a colorable claim, a claim which if true might have changed the outcome had been presented. The court is unable to find any colorable claim. The court is unable to find any merit in any of the issues raised by the defendant. The court finds further proceedings would not serve any useful purpose. It is ordered dismissing the amended petition."

The order is a line-by-line rejection of the errors noted in the trial record. While it served the state well at the time, that record was relied on by Milke in her 1998, 2002, 2006, and 2008 federal *habeas corpus* petitions. Those petitions include 26 specific errors, omissions, and misjudgments by Judge Hendrix, each of which she categorically rejected without an evidentiary hearing into the merits of any of them. The following list, prepared by Lori Voepel, Milke's appellate counsel, and cited in the official trial transcript, evidences Judge Hendrix's shortcomings in the Milke case.

At the PCR level, Anders Rosenquist challenged Saldate's interrogation tactics and presented significant additional evidence of Saldate's history and pattern of overreaching and unprofessional conduct including interrogating impaired and injured suspects, violating suspects' Miranda Rights, lying to the grand jury, corrupting and misusing line-up identifications, and fabricating confessions. He presented 18 different cases of Saldate misconduct. Hendrix paid no attention to them.

Debra's post-conviction counsel argued that when combined with an evaluation of the facts of Debra's case, Saldate's history and pattern of misconduct and untruthfulness support the position she has consistently maintained—that she never *confessed* to Saldate. He asserted that Saldate's pattern/history should be considered in assessing the reliability of his assertions, and that had Debra's jury been provided with this information, it would have given far less weight to Saldate's testimony. Post-conviction counsel also attached affidavits from three longtime law enforcement officers who evaluated testimony regarding Saldate's interrogation and opined that Debra's *confession* was unreliable.

Judge Hendrix summarily denied Debra's claims, finding that "If the [confession] had been improperly admitted, the Supreme Court would have addressed the issue ... since the Supreme Court reviews the entire record for any and all fundamental error."

She disregarded evidence of Saldate's misconduct in the eighteen other cases, finding it inadmissible under Arizona evidence rules.

She rejected the officers' affidavits, construing them as expert opinions that Saldate "was a liar."

She also stated she "knows of no law requiring an interrogator to be fair and impartial" and focused her analysis on whether Debra's statements were voluntary.

Calling interrogation techniques a "necessary part of law enforcement," she held that an interrogation "only becomes improper if there are implied promises or improper influence."

She found "no indication the defendant was mentally impaired or hysterical to the point of being unable to comprehend what was being said to her and no indication of any implied promise or improper influence."

She also found that the extent to which Debra may have felt intimidated or coerced to make a statement to Saldate was a jury question.

Incredibly, the judge also called Debra's version of events "substantially the same" as Saldate's report. She said the only significant difference between their versions "is when and how [Debra] requested an attorney." Referencing her own suppression hearing, she stated, "the trial court made the factual determination that the defendant did not ask for an attorney at the beginning of the interview."

Judge Hendrix also rejected the argument that Saldate's destruction of his notes was improper, calling this a meritless argument often made by defense attorneys.

Yet, she determined that Debra's statements to Saldate were not an unequivocal confession of "yes, I did it," and she considered Debra's "most inculpatory statement to be that she did not want her son to grow up to be like his father," adding, "Reasonable minds could differ as to the interpretations to be given to the statements and the conclusions that could be reached. The jury made the determination of the reliability of the statements and the conclusions to be reached after considering the statements."

The judge's overall ruling improperly defers to her own decisions in the suppression hearing and the jury's verdict. One of the most egregious errors is her finding that the reliability of the alleged confession was solely a jury question. This is clearly contrary to established federal law because it is the court's obligation to exclude a *confession* once its unreliability becomes apparent.

Judge Hendrix found that no law requires an interrogator to be fair and impartial. In her view, a confession only becomes improper if there are implied promises given or improper influence used, contrary to federal law." But Rosenquist argued that certain interrogation techniques, either in isolation or as applied to the unique characteristics of a particular suspect are so offensive to a civilized system of justice that they must be condemned. The techniques employed by Saldate reflect an "ends over means" mentality, which offends our system of justice. His pattern shows he is unconcerned with a suspect's mental or physical state during interrogation, willing to lie to the grand jury and court to obtain warrants, indictments and convictions, and willing to ignore Miranda assertions. To ensure he receives the benefit of any doubt, he chooses not to tape record or otherwise independently document what occurs in the interrogation room. Here, besides ignoring his supervisor's directive to record and Debra's assertion of Miranda, Saldate interrogated Debra without a witness, failed to have her sign a statement and destroyed any contemporaneous notes. Judge Hendrix's ruling is also contrary to established federal law because it focuses exclusively on voluntariness. Both the voluntariness and reliability of a purported confession must be evaluated in determining admissibility.

Significant evidence indicates Saldate twisted and fabricated portions of Debra's alleged confession, undermining its reliability. Numerous inconsistencies taint Saldate's testimony, police reports, interviews and other statements.

These include his Grand Jury testimony that Debra supposedly formed the idea to have Chris killed one month prior to the killing, which is *nowhere else* in the record.

In his report, Saldate claimed he told Debra that both Scott and Styers had implicated her. He acknowledged this was false during his pretrial interview. He also said in his interview he had checked this assertion against his notes. Yet at trial, Saldate said he destroyed his notes immediately after preparing his report.

One of the most bizarre discrepancies is Saldate's accusation during an interview of Debra's sister that Debra "flashed her breasts" during the interrogation in attempting to "manipulate" him. Saldate also claimed in a newspaper interview that during the investigation, Debra tried "to get me in her stable of guys who would do things for her." Yet, Saldate failed to mention either of these very unusual "facts" in his written reports or pretrial interview, and he testified that nothing "unusual" occurred during his interrogation that was not contained in his report. The assertion makes no sense in light of what Debra wore that day—a t-shirt tucked into jeans with a sweater. When viewed with Saldate's history, such discrepancies seriously call into question Saldate's ability to objectively interpret and convey information regarding Debra's statements and non-verbal behaviors and undermines the reliability of the *confession*.

One of Judge Hendrix's objectively unreasonable factual determinations is that Debra's version of the interrogation was substantially the same as that in Saldate's report. According to Debra, Saldate twisted certain statements she made in a way that made them appear inculpatory, and he completely invented others to make them "fit" his theory of the case. Nothing in Debra's explanation even implies she participated in the murder of her son. Rather, it details the lengths she went to protect and care for him, albeit in a somewhat disconnected fashion likely resulting from lack of sleep and trauma over learning of Christopher's death. In contrast, Saldate's version is highly inculpatory and paints Debra as an extraordinarily selfish mother who would rather have her young child killed than grow up like his father. Although there are certain similarities, a comparison of Saldate and Debra's testimony highlights the objective unreasonableness of the judge's determination that their versions are essentially the same.

The judge's determination (at trial and in PCR proceedings) that evidence regarding Saldate's history was inadmissible is also contrary to established federal law. The State's principal evidence against Debra was her purported *confession* and Saldate's opinion that he obtained the "truth" because he "knows" when suspects are lying. The State touted Saldate's experience, training and background in conducting interrogations to establish the very foundation for his opinion testimony that he could "know" that Debra was lying when she denied wrongdoing, and telling the "truth" when she finally *confessed* during Saldate's interrogation.

Debra's counsel was entitled to cross-examine Saldate concerning his character for truthfulness or untruthfulness. The judge shut the door Saldate opened when he established his credentials to support his opinions about Debra's truthfulness and confession. Debra was entitled to explore other cases involving Saldate's tainted confessions and to present opinion or reputation evidence to refute the State's claims about Saldate's history and experience. Such evidence was also admissible to show Saldate's state of mind, motive, opportunity and intent. Such evidence was also admissible to show Saldate's habit and routine practices during interrogations, to prove that Saldate acted in conformity during Debra's interrogation.

Saldate's other cases were all litigated within the same timeframe as Debra's or within the preceding seven years. His actions are also "sufficiently similar" to those alleged here[: a]n egregious pattern of conduct designed to elicit alleged confessions and inculpatory statements regardless of their truth or falsity. Saldate interrogated suspects based on a premise they were guilty. He did not cease interrogating until the suspect proved him "right," and "bolstered" statements if the suspect did not. These are the very claims made by Debra.

Judge Hendrix's finding that Saldate's "other cases evidence" was inadmissible is clearly contrary to established federal law, especially where Debra's capital conviction turned entirely on the issue of credibility, and the evidence at trial consisted of opposing stories by Debra and Saldate. Failing to admit this evidence violated Debra's fundamental right to due process and a fair trial.

A review of the evidence at each stage of Debra's proceedings illustrates the objective unreasonableness of Judge Hendrix's finding that evidence of Saldate's history is cumulative. When combined with an evaluation of the facts of Debra's case, Saldate's history and pattern supports the position she has consistently maintained—that her alleged *confession* never occurred. Had the jury been provided with this crucial information regarding Saldate's pattern of conduct, it would no doubt have given far less, if any, credence to the purported confession.

The last two paragraphs of the judge's order strikingly reveal the objective unreasonableness of her findings and highlight what is wrong with this conviction. After conceding this is not an "unequivocal confession," she identifies Debra's most inculpatory statement as her comment that "she did not want her son to grow up to be like his father." Even though Debra explained what she was trying to convey, Judge Hendrix basically said, "oh well, reasonable minds can differ as to the meaning of these statements, and the jury decided what the statements meant." It is frightening to think that a person's life can hinge on a jury's interpretation of such an innocuous statement, especially when viewed in the context Debra claims she made it.

Perhaps the most revealing finding was the judge's final paragraph. Notwithstanding the inflammatory adjectives used to describe Det. Saldate and his conduct (overzealous, rampant overreaching, abusive interrogation techniques, coercive interrogative methods, manipulation of evidence, lying under oath, spurious practices, and oppressive and unprofessional interrogation tactics), the jury heard his version of the interview, and they heard the defendant's version of the interview. The jury decided the case. Obviously, the judge felt more compelled to protect Saldate's reputation than to ensure Debra received a fair trial. Her language further illustrates this entire case hinged on who the judge and jury believed in this "swearing contest"—the 21-year veteran police detective and recently elected constable, or the single mother charged with the first-degree murder of her 4-year-old child. Debra stood no chance absent some additional way for the jury to assess the credibility of these witnesses. Unfortunately, the judge kept the additional evidence from the jury, leaving them to decide the case on the word of these two witnesses and character evidence about Debra from other witnesses tainted by Saldate.

If for no other reason, the 26-point itemized list is important because it proves Rosenquist's basic thesis. A judge must not only make correct and supportable rulings in a case, she must also *not appear* to have acted improperly. Because it was a death penalty case, Milke had a constitutional right to bring those errors to the attention of an impartial judge. At the least, she had a right to an evidentiary hearing before a partial one. By denying Milke a hearing, and by denying her own bias, Judge Hendrix may have stacked time on Milke's prison stay. Had she recused herself, or granted an evidentiary hearing, Milke might have won relief at the PCR level. That would assume that, on reflection, three years after the high-profile trial stress, she could objectively assess claims of judicial error.

Because Milke's trial and state court appellate counsel did not present the evidence, or make the arguments that Rosenquist did, the last clear chance Milke had for that evidence to reach an impartial court was her post-conviction review in 1996. But that review was as illusory as the confession Saldate claimed he took from her in 1989. Judge Hendrix's summary denial of post-conviction relief sent two clear messages to Milke. First, she could not secure post-conviction relief without a hearing before an impartial judge. Second, she could stand convicted of murder and be given the death penalty based on a confession she never gave. That was Milke's reality when she turned to the federal courts for relief in 1998.

29

HABEAS CORPUS—HOCUS POCUS

*H*OCUS POCUS—A NOUN USED TO portray meaningless talk or activity. It often draws attention away from and disguises what is actually happening. It seems apt for the ancient common law writ of *habeas corpus*. Often called the "Great Writ," *habeas corpus* is historically rooted in section 39 of the Magna Carta. In medieval times, the writ compelled common folk, as well as some landed gentry, to appear in court to give testimony. That made it a useful remedy against the Crown. In the United States, it became part of our common law. After the War of Independence, most colonies guaranteed it. The U.S. Constitution forbade its suspension, "unless in cases of Rebellion or Invasion, as Public Safety may require it."

Today, the writ orders the person responsible for the detention of a prisoner to produce her quickly in court, so a judge may decide the lawfulness of the detention. Here is where hocus pocus comes in. Neither federal law, nor state *habeas corpus* statutes attempt to define just what constitutes an "unlawful detention." Conservative politicians see it as a mere procedural device allowing a judge to look into the matter. Progressives hope it provides a remedy for discrimination and wrongful conviction at every level. Legal scholars see it as substantive policy. As Justice William Brennan said in a famous 1963 case, "[*habeas corpus*] is inextricably intertwined with the growth of fundamental rights of personal liberty . . . its root principle is that in a civilized society, government must always be accountable to the judiciary for a man's imprisonment . . . if the imprisonment cannot be shown to conform with the fundamental requirements of law, the individual is entitled to his immediate release."

Hocus pocus seeps back into *habeas corpus* when state courts resent granting *habeas corpus* writs for *state* prisoners by *federal* judges. However, granting habeas relief is an intended consequence of the Fourteenth Amendment's guarantee to state defendants of the right to a fair hearing. Over time, that became a broad predicate for granting the writ. But state courts often see it as an improper denial of deference to fact and guilt findings by local authority. Some state authorities, particularly elected prosecutors, see federal writs of *habeas corpus* as a mere reexamination by a federal judges of an issue already settled in a state court. State attorneys general often see federal *habeas corpus* as a side show designed to thwart their efforts to imprison guilty defendants. Hocus pocus.

There are always politics at play at the intersection of capital punishment and judicial review. It is at that precise intersection where legislative activity extends the U.S. Supreme Court's discretionary review of capital punishment cases, while curtailing the jurisdiction of lower federal courts in the same arena. The 1996 Antiterrorism and Effective Death Penalty Act (ADEPA) was Congress's codification of several Supreme Court decisions restricting federal *habeas corpus* review. The intended effect was to diminish the role of lower federal judges, by limiting their power to review state court decisions in death penalty cases. Seeing lower federal court review in death penalty cases as hocus pocus, ADEPA advocates ignore the wisdom in the Constitution's guarantee of the independence of the federal courts from partisan politics. The grand irony is that partisan politics are the ultimate hocus pocus, while *habeas corpus* is due process at its core.

ADEPA establishes *deferential* standards of review for state-court factual findings and legal conclusions. It mandates that state court factual findings are "presumptively correct and may be rebutted only by 'clear and convincing evidence.'" And if the federal claim was adjudicated on the merits in a state court, federal judges can only grant relief if the defendant: (1) establishes that the state court decision "was contrary to, or involved an objectively unreasonable application of, clearly established Federal law, as determined by the Supreme Court of the United States," or (2) "was based on an unreasonable determination of the facts in light of the evidence presented in the State court proceeding."

Ultimately, ADEPA forces lower court judges to defer to state court judges even in cases where they find specific instances of unconstitutional acts that denied due process to the habeas petitioner. The historic concept of judicial independence becomes hocus pocus and the partisan political goal becomes a rule of law, in a fashion. There will be no need for such hocus pocus when all legislators and all judges adhere to the same political view of judicial review in death penalty cases. That may be a long time coming.

30

DEBRA MILKE'S ODYSSEY ON THE FEDERAL HABEAS CORPUS TRAIL— 1998 TO 2010

*O*DYSSEY IS DEFINED AS A long "wandering" usually marked by many changes of fortune. The notion of "wandering" is remarkably apt for Debra Milke's odyssey, even though Homer did not have her in mind when he recounted Odysseus' long wanderings. Anders Rosenquist filed Milke's original petition for a writ of *habeas corpus* and a stay of execution on January 13, 1998 in the United States District Court for the District of Arizona. The court record in her case (Debra Jean Milke v. Terry Stewart et al., Docket Number CV-98-0060-PHX-RCB) confirms the uphill climb that took fifteen years and seven months (January 1998 to July 2013). The docket does not document the changes in fortune. However, putting it plainly, Milke's fortune went up while Saldate's went down. Milke's presumption of innocence gained traction and Saldate's presumption of fabrication began to emerge, all resulting from the fateful 30 minutes they spent together on December 3, 1989.

Jess Lorona, John Edward Charland, and Elizabeth Hurley assisted Anders Rosenquist at various points in Milke's *habeas corpus* pathway. Rosenquist was lead attorney until April 23, 2001, when Lori Voepel and Mike Kimerer took over as lead attorneys. Steve Drizin and Amy Lynn Nguyen were Milke's co-counsel on some of the briefing.

Jim Nielsen and Julie Done represented Terry Stewart, the Director of the Arizona Department of Corrections (the respondent in the initial habeas filings). Randall Mack Howe represented the warden of the Perryville State Complex where Milke was imprisoned. Angela Lynn Polizzi from the ACLU of Arizona and Larry A. Hammond of Osborn Maledon, PA filed an *amicus* brief, with the assistance of Pamela Kirkpatrick Sutherland and Rudolph J. Gerber.

Rosenquist asserted nine claims on Milke's behalf in the original petition: (1) The overreaching tactics of Phoenix Police Detective Armando Saldate deprived Debra Milke of her constitutional rights against self-incrimination, and to due process, a fair trial, and a just sentencing determination. (2) Repeated instances of prosecutorial misconduct denied Debra Milke due process, a fair trial, and reliable sentencing determination. (3) The errors of the trial court in the conduct of Debra's trial and sentencing infringed upon her right to due process, a fair trial, and a just sentencing process. (4) Defense counsel was so deficient in his representation of Debra Milke during her trial and sentencing as to deny her constitutional right to effective assistance of counsel. (5) Debra Milke was denied her constitutional right to a representative jury. (6) The trial court's denial of petitioner's motion to acquit, her imposition of the death penalty, and the Arizona Supreme Court's affirmance of Debra Milke's convictions and death sentence violated her constitutional rights. (7) The aggregate of errors in petitioner's trial, sentencing, and appeal violated her constitutional rights. (8) Debra Milke was denied her rights by the Arizona Supreme Court's failure to determine whether her sentence was proportionate to sentences handed down in other cases. (9) Debra Milke was denied her constitutional right to effective assistance of counsel on direct appeal.

In a subsequent pleading, Rosenquist made an additional argument on Milke's behalf. "In upholding her death sentence on the basis that the 'senselessness' and 'shockingly evil' nature of her offense made it 'heinous . . . or depraved,' the Arizona Supreme Court violated the Eighth and Fourteenth Amendments by relying on constitutionally insufficient narrowing constructions of a facially vague statutory aggravating circumstance."

Good lawyers always start important briefs with their strongest arguments. Rosenquist did that when he opened with Saldate's "overreaching tactics." Rosenquist's second argument focused on Noel Levy's "repeated instances of prosecutorial misconduct." Then, he articulated Judge Hendrix's "trial court and sentencing errors." His fourth argument was about Kenneth Ray's "deficient representation." His remaining arguments went to jury selection problems, trial court judgmental errors, James Kemper's ineffective assistance of counsel on the direct appeal to the Arizona Supreme Court, and five claims about Milke's death sentence.

On July 2, 2000, the federal court granted review of some of the claims. In April 2001, Judge Broomfield issued a discovery order granting Milke's request to secure "any and all Phoenix Police Dept. regulations, policies, and procedures in effect from 1988 through 1992 concerning the interrogation of suspects, and for an *in camera* review, all evaluations of Detective Armando Saldate by the Phoenix Police Department, and all documents evidencing investigations of or disciplinary actions taken or contemplated against Saldate by the Phoenix Police Department." In February 2002, Judge Broomfield ordered respondent's counsel to "inquire of the Custodian of Records for the Phoenix Police Department and the Internal Affairs Department whether every document subject to this court's order has been provided to him and respondent's counsel shall file a notice to this court and shall submit those documents ex parte and under seal for in camera inspection by this court."

On November 28, 2006, Judge Broomfield denied Milke's petition for a writ of *habeas corpus*, and entered judgment for respondents and against Milke. Milke's lawyers appealed the denial to the United States Court of Appeals for the Ninth Circuit.

In their Ninth Circuit brief, Milke's new lawyers, Lori Voepel and Mike Kimerer, expanded on the positions taken by Anders Rosenquist in his 1995 PCR, and his 2002 habeas petition. Neither Judge Hendrix at the state level, nor Judge Broomfield at the federal level conducted an evidentiary hearing on the claims. But by this time, the national epidemic of false, coerced, and fabricated confessions was well known in the legal community. Legal scholars such as Professor Thomas P. Sullivan called out prosecutors and trial judges in provocative law review articles. Sullivan's 2006 article ("The Time Has Come for Law Enforcement Recordings of Custodial Interviews") invigorated civil rights advocates across the country. By mid-year 2007, several states had adopted rules mandating electronic recording of interrogations and confessions as the price of admissibility in court. Milke's case drew the attention of two very talented lawyers—Daniel Pochoda and Larry Hammond of the ACLU. They authored and filed an *amicus* brief on Milke's behalf with the Ninth Circuit. Both were experienced constitutional litigators. Both were adjunct faculty at good law schools and Hammond had led the American Judicature Society's national effort to ensure criminal defendants' right to a fair court process. Neither thought Milke got a fair trial.

Their statement of interest in the *amicus* brief began by noting that they had read all of the briefs in the district court and the briefs in the Ninth Circuit. The ACLU's interest, they said, "involves the constitutional arguments regarding the admissibility of uncorroborated and unrecorded confessions . . . moreover this is a case in which a woman's life is at stake . . . the U.S. Supreme Court has recognized the 'truly awesome responsibility' associated with death penalty cases."

Milke's brief articulated the constitutional issues directly affecting her case, her conviction, and her life. The ACLU's *amicus* brief stated the issues quite differently. "Does the secretive and coercive nature of jailhouse confessions result in violations of a suspect's fundamental rights? Have courts and legislatures correctly recognized that the failure to require a contemporaneous recording of a confession effectively eliminates the ability to safeguard a suspect's fundamental rights? Should the intentional failure to record the confession of Debra Milke despite the problematic nature of the interrogation techniques and her state of mind, and of the police officer, result in a finding of inadmissibility?"

Hammond and Pochoda premised their argument on what Noel Levy had called a "given" at the trial level—the alleged confession. The *amicus* brief brought that claim full circle. Levy's insistence that the confession was a "given" convinced both judge and jury that the confession was a *fait accompli*—already decided, leaving them with no option but to accept. *Amici* counsel argued that "a confession is one of the most powerful pieces of evidence that can be introduced at trial. All the more reason to call into question the practices by which confessions are elicited. Confessions obtained through unrecorded interrogations are 'inherently untrustworthy and their use by the state violated defendant's right to a fair trial.'" They argued, "[L]egions of psychological studies and analysis of interrogation room practices since Miranda v. Arizona prove that the Miranda warnings have not succeeded in alleviating the secrecy surrounding a custodial interrogation." They noted that evidence "from police manuals and reported cases show[s] that unrecorded police interrogations result in Fifth Amendment violations of both the right to counsel and the privilege against self-incrimination."

Their central point was that Saldate's techniques "make her alleged confession highly suspect. No objective record of the interrogation exists. This is precisely because the same interrogator failed to electronically record the event even after being instructed to do so by his superior." They cited the Illinois experience. "Out of 45 wrongful convictions for murder discovered in Illinois since 1945, 15 or 33 percent involved a false confession by the defendant, or the fabrication of such confessions by authorities." The "swearing match" that often takes place between defendants and police over whether a confession was made is highly untrustworthy. Milke lost her swearing match to Saldate because the jury did not know Saldate's history and had no reason to doubt his credibility. As in many other cases, "the officer's testimony is often erroneously held to satisfy the due process voluntariness test."

They argued against the "rubber stamping of police testimony," by arguing Alaska's position. Alaska excludes statements made by defendants based solely on the officer's failure to electronically record them. That policy position is premised on the fact that "human memory is often faulty. It is not because a police officer is more dishonest than the rest of us . . . we demand an objective recordation of the critical events . . . because we are entitled to assume he is no less human, no less inclined to reconstruct and interpret past events in a light most favorable to himself—that we should not permit him to be a 'judge of his own cause.'"

Hammond and Pochoda challenged the Ninth Circuit by detailing the positions of courts and legislatures that had already recognized that the "failure to require a contemporaneous recording of a confession effectively eliminates the ability of a defendant to demonstrate improper police practices." This, they said, "nullifies the ban against involuntary coerced confessions."

Reminding the court of the precise function of a judicial proceeding (to determine where the truth lies), they presented numerous examples of confessions obtained through coercion and intimidation as inherently untrustworthy because they "obfuscate rather than illuminate the truth." Recording allows the court access to a custodial interrogation. It lifts the veil of secrecy in the interrogation room. There is no need, then, to fill the "gap of knowledge." They cited data confirming that, as of 2007, 238 cities and counties had instituted some form of mandatory recording of custodial interrogations.

In the instant case, they said, "Detective Saldate's failure to record resulted in nullifying the reviewing court to adequately assess the multiple violations of Milke's constitutionally protected rights. That knowing failure is a shining example of bad faith." They argued the ample evidence demonstrating his purposeful avoidance of recording so "he alone would be the 'record' of events at trial."

The sad fact of the 1990 trial is that the jury had no way of knowing the arguments presented by the *amici* brief, any more than they knew Saldate's long history of confession misconduct. The negative won—they believed Saldate over Milke. The Ninth Circuit could right that wrong, thanks in part to Hammond and Pochoda's brief.

On September 28, 2009, the Ninth Circuit entered its order, saying, "A complete review of the record discloses no evidence supporting a finding that Milke voluntarily, knowingly and intelligently waived her rights under Miranda v. Arizona. Under these circumstances, an evidentiary hearing in federal court is required. We therefore remand with instructions to conduct a limited hearing on the sole issue of whether the petitioner validly waived her Miranda rights; respondent shall have the burden of proof. The district court must conduct the hearing and render its findings within 60 days of this order."

Judge Broomfield set the hearing for November 16, 2009. He also issued a Writ of Habeas Corpus Ad Testificandum to bring Debra Milke to the U.S. courthouse on that date. The 2009 hearing was canceled and rescheduled several times, but was finally conducted before Judge Broomfield on January 11 and 12, 2010.

31

DR. RICHARD LEO'S CASE REVIEW— DID MILKE CONFESS TO SALDATE?

A UNIQUE CULTURAL PERSPECTIVE IN AMERICA colors everyone's thinking about confessions. A confession is something we keep secret. Something we tell only in strict confidence and then only to our closest friends. But the culture of the legal system is different. In law, confessions always have consequences, because they reveal wrongdoing. A religious confession is a ritual by which the person acknowledges thoughts or actions considered sinful or morally wrong within the confines of a particular sect or faith. As a practical matter, the term includes admissions that are neither legally nor religiously significant. However defined, confessions are almost always private, dark things, not shared with strangers, especially if that stranger is likely to harm you once he learns the secret you just confessed.

Debra Milke would only have confessed to Armando Saldate if you assume two things: that he was no stranger and her confession was truthful. No mother makes up a confession about killing her child. And at the deepest possible level, absent torture, no guilty person makes a murder confession to a stranger, especially a policer officer, in under 30 minutes.

Except for Armando Saldate, Noel Levy, and perhaps Judge Cheryl Hendrix, the vast majority of individuals that have studied this case do not believe she confessed. Many who have not studied the case think her innocent, and therefore believe that she would not have confessed. There may be tens of thousands of people, both here and abroad, who are *for* her. In social media, people accept her innocence as a given, knowing Saldate's history of confession misconduct, and the way he claims she confessed. They know instinctively that she's innocent in much the same way that Saldate so quickly knew she was guilty. But setting guilt or innocence aside just for the moment, one thing is almost indisputable—she was wrongfully convicted because the jury did not know about Saldate's history of confession misconduct.

From either an intellectual or an emotional perspective, her removal from death row is more important than the abstract question of whether she confessed. And except for some of his colleagues, most people now believe that Saldate made it up to make his case. That is why the focus turned from "did she do it" to "did she say she did it."

In the philosophical sense that no one ever really "knows" anything, the public will never know to an absolute certainty *whether* she confessed to Saldate. But as a scientific proposition, it is possible to evaluate the environmental, social, intellectual, personal, and motivational realities surrounding her 30-minute interaction with Saldate on the night of December 3, 1989. In that well-defined area of social science and legal abstraction, strong, almost irrefutable conclusions are easily drawn. By whatever measure, the end result is the same—there was no confession.

Dr. Richard Leo is the only individual who intellectually dissected the *entire* case in order to express an informed, scientific, rational opinion about *whether* she confessed. This dissection had not been done by any of the lawyers, judges, or other parties to any of the three cases (Milke, Scott, and Styers) up to this point in time. The state objected to even allowing his testimony. But when that objection failed, the prosecutor cross-examined him at deposition. Then, the state decided *not* to call an opposing expert. Dr. Leo gave his conclusions under oath to the opposing sides of the legal case, and to the federal judge charged with reassessing the legal validity of the judicial process that sent Milke to death row. Leo wrote two reports. Both are testament to the interaction of social science and law. Both give credence to the widely accepted civilian view—there was no confession. His point-by-point review of the *he said/she said* swearing contest was a Herculean effort. And he approached the problem from a direction no one else had even thought about, much less attempted. Instead of trying to evaluate whether she *gave* a confession, Leo assessed whether Saldate *took* one. That fundamentally different approach gives his assessment unique credibility.

His conclusions, for the first time in the legal case, provide deep insight into Saldate's motives in the swearing contest. He did what the jury might have done, had they known what he knew. Leo began with an objective, analytical assessment of Saldate's claim, rather than with Milke's denial. That social science perspective, tested by well-established legal principles, produced ten discrete predicates for disbelieving Saldate's claim.

1. SALDATE PRESUMED HER GUILT FROM THE START

Police officers are trained only to arrest and interrogate suspects whom they "believe" to be guilty. Anyone else is merely interviewed. No one believes that he *interviewed* Milke into spontaneously admitting killing her child. By his own testimony, and giving modest credence to the "paraphrased account" he wrote four days later, he knew before going to Florence he would arrest her. By his own account, he arrested her before reading her rights to her and before telling her that he was there "to get the truth." This is textbook material on how cops interact in custodial interrogation settings with suspects they believe to be guilty. She was a classic "suspect"; he would countenance "no lies from her."

Dr. Leo called it "telling" that Saldate told Debra she "was not telling the truth" even before she denied committing the crime, and before he had any basis for assuming truth or falsity. He was careful not to ask open-ended questions, or non-threatening questions. He cut off her denials and pressured her.

2. His Failure to Record Her Was Vital to His Success in Breaking the Case

His intentional failure to record her meant that no one, other than the two of them, could ever know with complete certainty what transpired during the interrogation. As Dr. Leo put it, "his failure to record is tantamount to destroying the evidentiary record of the most significant piece of information in the case." This act on his part had insurmountable consequences at the trial level. No one could examine a tape or transcript to see if the confession was extracted by coercive and untrustworthy means. His direct violation of his supervisor's order to record the confession would be forgiven *only if* he claimed that she confessed. And he could always say that his style was not to record— thus establishing consistency, albeit illegal consistency.

3. Saldate Excused Not Recording What She Said by Claiming She Refused Permission

The plausibility of this claim scarcely survives its repetition. Dr. Leo felt it "severely undermines his credibility. He took control, not her. He told her to be quiet and calm down while he informed her of her Miranda rights. No one could imagine such a commanding authority figure suddenly becoming so accommodating when asking for permission to tape." Dr. Leo doubts Saldate asked her at all. "It is far more probable that, instead, Detective Saldate simply made up this statement in order to justify the failure to follow orders, his inexplicable failure to bring a tape-recorder with him, and his failure to record the interrogation." In short, Dr. Leo believed Saldate's failure to record was intentional, not a mere oversight, or the result of not having a recorder with him.

Asking for permission to record is contrary to good police practice. In the 800 interrogation cases Dr. Leo evaluated before taking on Milke's case, he could not recall a single case where an interrogator asked a suspect for permission to record. More often than not, interrogators record *without* telling the suspect. It was, Dr. Leo said, "curious that Saldate states on the final sentence of his report that it was not recorded because she denied permission." This is especially curious considering that "he did not make such disclaimers regarding his other reports when interrogating Roger Scott, Mark Milke, Chris Landry, or Sandra Peckinpaugh." And last, Saldate acknowledged in other documents that it is "simply not his practice to tape record interviews or interrogations."

4. SALDATE'S BEHAVIOR CASTS DOUBT ON HIS CREDIBILITY

The manner in which Saldate says he elicited her Miranda waiver "is troubling, if not illegal." That there is no writing to confirm it, that she says she was bullied into waiving her Miranda rights, and that he destroyed his contemporaneous notes are all suspicious, "especially in light of the other circumstances surrounding the case." They suggest that Saldate may well have psychologically coerced her into answering his questions. That, and his destruction of the notes, hid his illegal behavior and diverted suspicion from himself to her. It is "highly unprofessional for police detectives to destroy their notes. And he also failed to write out or have her sign a confession statement. He also waited three days before writing his version of what happened. This is 'an extraordinary lapse of professionalism,' especially in a capital murder case such as this in which there is no physical evidence corroborating the alleged confession." All of this violated Phoenix Police Department policy.

5. WHAT HE SAID SHE SAID IS SIMPLY IMPLAUSIBLE

Saldate's assertion that he "did not use any interrogation techniques is very hard to believe." Police detectives are taught to use specific techniques on criminal suspects. Everyone "in the police business knows that suspects do not give spontaneous, unprompted, free-wheeling narratives to serious crimes such as murder." His account "simply does not wash." It takes a lot of pressure to get an individual to confess to murder. Interrogation, by design, involves accusation, confrontation, the overcoming of denials and objections, and using inducements and appeals to motivate the suspect to comply. Interrogators use a wide range of psychological techniques to influence, pressure, and manipulate suspects into confessing. "Here it is almost certainly the case that Detective Saldate is confusing what really did occur during the Milke interrogation with what he would like to believe occurred *ex post facto*."

6. WIDE INCONGRUITY BETWEEN WHAT HAPPENED AND IN HOW HE SUPPOSEDLY QUESTIONED HER

Some police interrogators "like to think that a suspect experiences some kind of moral or cathartic relief after confession to them." This almost never occurs and precious few suspects report feeling better after confessing to a police detective. Leo's report says, "It is very unlikely that Milke actually told Saldate that she felt better or suddenly unburdened, or as if she had a load taken off her shoulders after confessing to him." She did not regard him as "a friend." She did not feel "comfortable" with him. She knew she was "under arrest and going to jail."

"It is almost certainly the case that [she] did not ask if she could get probation for life after confessing to murder or ask if she could have her tubes tied in exchange for probation for life." Dr. Leo called this "bizarre." It also defies credulity to believe that someone would first confess to murder and then say that "she finally found someone to whom she could speak her mind—Saldate's assertion here borders on the ludicrous." The only possibility, Dr. Leo said, is that Saldate's self-serving statements seek to cast the interrogation in the "highly simplistic and idealized way he would like to have us believe this interrogation occurred." Debra's purported assertions, according to him, "fly in the face of all reason, logic and experience. [Saldate] said that she experienced almost instantaneous bonding with and moral catharsis from [him] (as if speaking to a priest) because he was so uncommonly straightforward with her." She felt rewarded by the half-hour she spent with him because she "had found a friend in Detective Saldate."

7. Her Body Language

In his written report, deposition, and testimony, Saldate "too often treats his gut hunches, speculations, and intuitions as if they are established facts, rather than hypotheses to be tested against the evidence." He claims she "feigned grief when told of her son's death." She "pretended to cry but no tears were coming out." He inferred that her actions were clear evidence of her "disingenuousness and guilt." But it was nothing more than his presumption of her guilt. Suspects react to the stress of accusation. Even if she had been crying or acting hysterical, this is not, Dr. Leo said, "a reliable indicator of guilt or deception." Saldate treated his perceptions of her body language as "evidence." But it was only his bias against her, his poor training, and his inability to objectively investigate the case.

8. Saldate's Demonstrable Investigative Bias

The most salient fact in the entire case, according to Dr. Leo, is "that there is no evidence other than his word, that Debra Milke confessed to the capital murder of her only child and that as a result, she now awaits execution." By presuming her guilt from the beginning, that is, from Scott's reluctant suggestion in the car on the way to the murder scene, Saldate "set out to confirm this belief by getting a confession from her. His rush to judgment and investigative bias explains how he could interpret her body language and behavior during interrogation in such self-serving, if utterly impossible ways." Saldate gave an "equally implausible scenario of how and why Ms. Milke confessed . . . virtually spontaneously in a largely uninterrupted narrative format." He went so far as to say Milke felt "relieved" by telling him and that he was a "friend to whom he could unburden herself." Astoundingly, her confession to Saldate would "allow her to regain her self-esteem."

Social science uses established methodologies to contrast and compare what appears to be consistent behavioral patterns. Saldate failed to record or otherwise preserve his "interview" with Milke, and subsequently destroyed his notes about it. But he faithfully recorded his interview with Milke's sister, Sandra Peckinpaugh. "This interview demonstrates two key facts with respect to Detective Saldate's bias against Ms. Milke. First, it reveals that Detective Saldate is attempting to persuade and influence Ms. Peckinpaugh's perceptions of Ms. Milke's guilt rather than merely soliciting information from her as if his role is to be an advocate rather than an investigator. Detective Saldate's role here is contrary to any expectations of objectivity and contemporary standards of professional police investigation. Second, Detective Saldate's investigative bias can also be demonstrated by the discrepancies between his portrayal of what was said during his interview and what the transcript of the recorded interview reveals was actually said."

9. DETECTIVE SALDATE'S PROFESSIONAL MISCONDUCT HISTORY

Leo found "especially troubling" Saldate's long pattern of both alleged and proven misconduct in criminal cases involving disputed interrogations and confessions. Leo reviewed Saldate's entire record—all 18 cases submitted by Milke's lawyers in federal court. He found that Saldate had "repeatedly either been accused of or shown to violate suspect's Miranda rights . . . repeatedly exploited vulnerable suspects' Miranda rights . . . repeatedly rushed to judgment and manipulated information . . . construed evidence in order to build a case rather than objectively and dispassionately investigating and assembling facts." Those cases "cast considerable doubt on Detective Saldate's credibility, integrity and professionalism. So too, does Detective Saldate's disciplinary record with the Phoenix Police Department."

Leo was "dismayed to learn that Detective Saldate once pursued sexual favors from a female motorist in exchange for not arresting her on a traffic warrant and then lied to a supervisor about this act of corruption." The record confirms that Saldate took and failed a polygraph test on this issue. The Phoenix Police Department's internal affairs group interrogated him after he failed the polygraph. He admitted pursing sexual favors "leading the Phoenix Police Department to question his honesty, competency and overall reliability."

18. Saldate's Misconduct with Witnesses in the Milke Case

After reading all of the police reports, the trial testimony, and the related case against Roger Scott, Leo connected the dots from Saldate's misconduct with Milke to his misconduct with other witnesses. Looking at the statements that Saldate elicited from Roger Scott "to inculpate" Milke, Leo said they were "inherently unreliable." The statements cannot reasonably be construed to "corroborate Milke's alleged, but undocumented confession. By his own admission, Detective Saldate used coercive interrogation techniques to elicit [those] statements from Mr. Scott."

Leo cited four coercive interrogation techniques used by Saldate to extract inculpatory comments from Scott: (1) Scott was detained for 18 hours, (2) not given food or water or medication for 11 hours, (3) left alone for long periods during interrogation, and (4) threatened by Saldate that he would go to his sick mother's apartment and interrogate *her*. These coercive techniques, Leo said, "could easily have caused a person of normal intelligence and hardiness to make false statements to please his interrogator." The risk of coerced false statements, in Roger Scott's case, was "heightened by his weak personality and history of psychological problems." Leo had reviewed Dr. Donald Tatro's August 2, 1990 report on Roger Scott, and Scott's Pre-Sentence Investigation Report. He quoted from Dr. Tatro's report. "Mr. Scott is a Vietnam veteran with a history of psychological problems [and] has a passive dependent personality. He is by his nature, highly suggestible, submissive and compliant." Scott was known to "agree to sign anything they put before him, even if he did not comprehend it, or it was not the truth, just to please them and avoid conflict." All those factors, Dr. Leo opined, "bear out Dr. Tatro's diagnosis." Scott was a personality "at marked risk for making false statements in response to minimal police pressure, let alone the kinds of interrogative pressures that Detective Saldate brought to bear here. It is perhaps not surprising that over the course of eighteen hours, Scott changes his story five times, and at times appears to give confused, illogical, disjointed, inconsistent statements."

Scott "may have been" an accessory to, or aider and abettor of, the murder of Christopher Milke. But his "interrogator-induced statements about Ms. Milke in this crime appear to be inherently unreliable . . . and do not serve as corroboration for her undocumented, unsigned, and disputed confession." Conversely, the weight of the evidence Dr. Leo reviewed suggests that Scott's statement that Milke "orchestrated the murder of her child is not accurate." The combination of all these risk factors strongly raises the possibility that "the ultimate miscarriage of justice may have occurred here: the wrongful conviction of a factually innocent person who awaits execution."

Leo earned two doctorate degrees from prestigious universities (a Ph.D. and a J.D.). He held, at the time he wrote his initial report, two academic appointments at the University of California Irvine. He was an Associate Professor of Criminology, Law and Society and an Associate Professor of Psychology and Social Behavior. In customary academic fashion, he wrote a formal conclusion to his report. "Although it is not possible, based on the materials I have reviewed, to conclude with 100% certainty that Ms. Milke's confession *was fabricated*, it is my professional opinion that Detective Saldate's account of the interrogation and alleged confession is too untrustworthy to support a conviction (especially a capital conviction) and that he *may very well have fabricated* or coerced a false or non-existent confession from Debra Milke. In the hundreds of cases I have studied, I have never seen a convection rest on nothing more than a disputed, undocumented and unsigned confession."

Seven years later, on January 6, 2009, Dr. Leo wrote an addendum to his original report. He updated his 43-page single-spaced curriculum vitae, confirming his tenured position as of 2001. By this time, Dr. Leo had been consulted in many more cases (several thousand by his own count), and had authored many more peer-reviewed academic articles on interrogation and confession law. The Harvard

University Press published his master work in 2008: *Police Interrogation and American Justice.* It is widely considered the most comprehensive and most highly praised book on the core subject underlying Milke's alleged confession. By 2009, he had become the preeminent American scholar on police interrogation policy and procedure. Appellate courts, including the United States Supreme Court, often cited his book and other writings. The reason for the new report was his reading of ten important documents, which had not yet been written during his initial 2002 evaluation of the case. These included the pleadings filed in the then pending Ninth Circuit appeal, Paul Huebl's May 23, 2002 affidavit, and most importantly, Armando Saldate's December 21, 2009 sworn deposition.

In his new report, Dr. Leo clarified statements in his earlier report about the Miranda waiver issue and noted new information on the waiver issue from Saldate's 2009 deposition. Saldate admitted in that deposition that "it wasn't his practice . . . to expressly ask for a written or oral Miranda waiver." Even so, Dr. Leo said, "it is very uncommon for police interrogators not to memorialize or corroborate the suspect's waiver in any form." Accordingly, Saldate's lapse was "extraordinary because in the typical case where a suspect gives a waiver . . . there is no dispute about the facts . . . because the police created a record of what occurred and there is no dispute about whether there was a confession. None of this is true here because Saldate failed to record anything, any alleged waiver, *or* the alleged confession."

Commenting on Saldate's 2009 deposition, Dr. Leo continued, "Detective Saldate also indicated that although he knows he is supposed to stop 'interrogating' a suspect who invokes her Miranda rights, he will continue having a conversation with the suspect and include in his report any statements made by the suspect after invocation, even if they can't be used in court except for impeachment. He also claims he always notes when a person asserts her rights."

Dr. Leo compared the 2009 sworn testimony by Saldate with the 18 cases he had earlier reviewed. Those cases reveal that "what Saldate claims is not always true." And because Detective Saldate presumed Milke's guilt, "he appears to have experienced what cognitive psychologists call *confirmation bias*—the tendency to select only information from one's environment that confirms our pre-existing beliefs and discount or ignore evidence at odds with pre-existing beliefs."

Dr. Leo offered three new observations to supplement his initial report.

> First, because he failed to memorialize the interrogation, there is no evidence that he ever elicited a Miranda waiver from her. Indeed, Ms. Milke states both that she told Detective Saldate that she did not understand her rights and that she wanted an attorney. If either one of these statements is true, and especially if both are true, then Ms. Milke did not waive her rights, but [rather] invoked them.
>
> Second, Detective Saldate never states in any of his testimony that he elicited a waiver from Milke . . . what he describes is the practice of eliciting a so-called implicit waiver . . . but it is extraordinarily uncommon for police interrogators to fail to document an implicit waiver . . . it will not stand up in court because an unmemorialized police recollection will not meet the State's "heavy burden" to demonstrate a knowing and voluntary waiver.
>
> Finally, it is possible that Detective Saldate . . . was so cognitively biased that he mistakenly interpreted Ms. Milke's response as a waiver in his zeal to build a case against her . . . however it is my professional opinion that it is far more likely that he knowingly failed to elicit a waiver.

Dr. Leo's academic opinions are factual and supported by both experience and research as a social scientist and law professor. They are compelling because they are disinterested, objective, and professionally presented. But there is another perspective that may not be as academic or as detached. A large number of lawyers, former judges, law professors, and students reviewed the same data that Dr. Leo did. Their opinions, while not uniform, provide context to the larger question presented in this chapter—did she confess or not? One way to answer that question is to compare Saldate's motives with Milke's motives. Dr. Leo did not make such a comparison because there is no existing sociological research on point. That begs the question of non-experts, i.e., the lawyers, former judges, law professors, students, and authors. What *motivated* Saldate to say she confessed and her to deny it? That calls for a comparison of egos.

EGO

Ego is a motive. It often explains why people do one thing and say another. Ego is that part of all of us that presents as personality, separates itself from the outside world, and separates us from the cosmos. It was vital to survival in an evolutionary sense and is manifested mostly by delusion. It is an interesting way to examine which combatant to the swearing contest would have been motivated by ego to fabricate something.

Saldate's ego—his reputation for getting a confession where most other officers fail, his need for peer recognition, and his record of misconduct with female suspects—all suggest that ego drove him to make up Milke's confession.

Milke's ego—her somewhat distanced view of motherhood, her failed marriage, her use of Styers without romantic involvement with him, and her record of reasonably good care of her son—all suggest that she did not confess to Saldate.

PSYCHIC VALUE

Psychic value motivates people in less visible ways. It is the intangible benefit above and beyond the utilitarian value that people get from what they do, or how they do it. Police officers, while well paid, are also compensated in psychic value. They "serve" the public interest and are proud of it. They fight crime at personal risk to themselves. And when they solve a crime, while their pay check stays the same as if they had not found the culprit, they are rewarded within the police fraternity and beyond by recognition, respect, and an enhanced feeling of self-worth. Sometimes, the psychic value of police work comes in gratifying psychological and emotional needs. For some, but not most, police officers, it comes in the form of power and prestige. By reputation, Armando Saldate was a man driven at least as much by psychic value as he was by his paycheck. The psychic value of securing a confession in under 30 minutes in a murder case cannot be undervalued in assessing Saldate's claim.

Debra Milke had emotional, personal, and self-worth challenges as evidenced by her relationships with men, her reactions to being a young mother with little outside support, and her need to find a more satisfying life than what she had in the fall of 1989. There was nothing in her history, character, outlook, or attitude that remotely suggested she might be complicit in her son's murder or that she would confess to anything so vile and heinous that it made most people ill just to think about it. She could get no psychic value from confessing, but a great deal from denying she did.

Saldate's need for psychic value is consistent with the fabrication theory of the Milke confession. He needed to live up to his reputation. He was beginning the retirement process when he got the call that Sunday morning to "step in" to the Milke investigation almost solely because of his "get the confession" reputation. He would not make more money by extracting one more confession from an unlikely murderer, but he would go out in a blaze of glory if he got it.

Milke's need for psychic value was likewise high but entirely contradicts the theory that she confessed complicity in Christopher's murder. Such a confession would only degrade her in the eyes of her few friends, and destroy family ties in short order. She wanted more freedom, but a confession would guarantee the opposite. She loved her son even though child care was often troublesome. But confessing to his murder was no solution to that problem. Perhaps most importantly, Milke secured enormous psychic value from Christopher. A four-year old child loves his mother unconditionally. She had that even if the rest of the world did not know it. She felt enormous grief over his loss and the jail psychiatrist confirmed that, even if Judge Hendrix refused to allow the jury to hear about it. She was never close to Roger Scott and the likelihood of her trusting him to do anything was nil. She used Jim Styers, but did not want a romantic relationship with him. Confessing

complicity with either man in Christopher's murder entirely contradicts
the psychic value she received daily from Christopher's life. And the
aftermath of hiding her complicity, assuming *arguendo* that she did,
would have been the most emotionally fraught form of negative psychic
value.

MOTIVE IN THE ABSTRACT

Investigators and interrogators always look for motive in every murder case. In the Christopher Milke murder, the police spent untold
hours evaluating and investigating all three suspects' motive to kill.
They eventually settled on a financial motive for Roger Scott, a mixed
financial-romantic motive for James Styers, and a troubled-mother
motive for Debra Milke. While those motives are debatable for the
murder itself, no one studied, much less opined about, motive regarding Milke's confession.

Motive often explains why one person confesses to a crime and
another does not. Guilty people are sometimes motivated by guilt
to confess their guilt. Innocent people are sometimes motivated to
confess by fear, or the hopelessness of the interrogation chamber.
Troubled, overwrought, weak-willed, or weak-minded people sometimes confess because it mirrors how they approach everything else
in life. Vulnerable populations are prone to false confessions—drunk,
demented, psychotic, seriously mentally ill, young, old, easily fooled,
or easily confused people confess. And they do it all the time. Police,
social scientists, lawyers, judges, and law professors know that. Legislators ignore it. Some prosecutors cover it up. Vulnerable people are
easy pickings when facing motivated interrogators who come into the
interrogation chamber convinced of the suspect's guilt. But Milke did
not fit any of these general classifications, other than being already
guilty in the eyes of her personal interrogator. In her case, there is
no clear, easy motive that might explain why she so quickly and so
effortlessly confessed. The only rational explanation is that she did *not*
confess. People who do not confess have no motive. More often than
not, they are victims of fabricated confessions.

Motive, in its rawest form, is not determinative in assessing the larger two-fold question here—did she confess or not. But it is helpful in assessing why he would *say* she confessed when she *insists* she did not. He profits in every way by saying she did, even if she didn't. Proving the negative is always hard, especially when your opponent has prosecutorial and judicial protection. He had little to lose by saying she confessed because the only defense weapon was impeachment. And he had every reason to believe that the prosecutor and the judge would prevent that. The impeachment evidence was deftly hid from the jury by the double barrel of prosecutor and judge. Together, but not as co-conspirators, one of them shelved the impeachment evidence and the other rubber-stamped it.

Even so, on close examination, motive does not entirely explain Milke's denial that she confessed. Innocence explains her denial. Had the police, the county attorney's office, or the judge given her the presumption of innocence, her impeachment evidence would almost surely have seen the light of day.

She was motivated to deny confessing because she denied complicity in the death of her child. Saldate was motivated to say she confessed because he believed in his own reputation and in the infallibility of his judgment about guilty suspects. He knew guilty people when he saw them. In her case, he *knew* she was guilty long before he met her in that small room in Florence where he says he got her to confess in 30 minutes flat. If you give her the constitutional presumption of innocence, she *knew* she was innocent.

Timing

In addition to ego, psychic value, and motive, there is one more circumstance that strongly indicates Milke did not confess—timing. The detectives began their investigation in the late afternoon of December 2, 1989 as a "missing person" case. Within 24 hours, they had a capital murder case. In that short span, they found Christopher's body, arrested two likely killers, and solved the case. But still, they only had one shot at cementing an iron-clad case of conspiracy to murder—Debra Milke. Timing explains why Saldate took a helicopter to Florence, something he dreaded. Timing explains why he pressured her when he walked into the room and why he would not allow her to cry or "lie." Timing explains why the police tried hard to keep the news about finding Christopher's body a secret from the press. Timing explains why other detectives were on standby—to inform the grandparents of Christopher's death—pending the one shot they had at getting her to confess. Timing explains why they needed to buttress the physical crime scene evidence—Scott's statements about Milke were weak, second-hand, and likely to crumble once everyone lawyered up. Timing explains why Styers implicated Scott, but not Milke. And finally, timing explains why they could not simply arrest Milke without first interrogating her. The conspiracy case could not stand without her confession. But with it, the case against the actual killers was a walk in the legal park.

32

ROGER SCOTT'S HABEAS CORPUS PETITION— 1998 TO 2013

Roger Scott's lawyers labored mightily on his behalf from his final post-conviction loss in the state court system in 1998, to October 7, 2013, when the United States Supreme Court denied his final petition for a writ of *certiorari*. It ended his tortuous tour of the federal court system to avoid his death sentence. From his sentencing in 1990 to this final federal court order, Scott never challenged the sufficiency of the evidence to support his conviction; he only challenged his death sentence. It was due, he argued, to the ineffective assistance of counsel at the state court level. The Supreme Court's denial of *certiorari* made him *death-eligible*. Thirty-two states permit capital punishment, as does the federal civilian and military legal systems. The Eighth Amendment limits the death penalty to aggravated murders committed by mentally competent adults.

On August 1, 2012, the Ninth Circuit Court of Appeals issued Scott's penultimate opinion, subject only to discretionary review by the U.S. Supreme Court. Chief Judge Kozinski wrote the panel's *per curiam* opinion, which affirmed the district court's denial of *habeas corpus* relief. The six-page opinion, couched in formal and straightforward language, carries a tone of reluctance, as though the panel had uttered a silent judicial sigh with its affirmance. The court-prepared précis bears repeating here.

> The prisoner had presented several pieces of evidence to the district court which he contended his counsel was ineffective for not presenting at his original sentencing hearing. He presented evidence that he had suffered four head injuries, and that these injuries affected his mental functions at the time of the murder. At trial, his counsel's theory of defense was that the prisoner was an unwitting "dupe" with a personality disorder that made him easily manipulated by his co-conspirators. Because the evidence provided through the prisoner's confession demonstrated he did not act in an impulsive way and that in fact he helped carefully to plan the murder, evidence of a brain injury would not have helped his defense. Therefore, the prisoner was not prejudiced by his counsel's decision not to investigate the prisoner's head injuries further and the court did not need to decide whether that decision constituted deficient performance.

The nexus between Scott's head injuries, which may have made him "brain-injured," and his death penalty is elusive. The Supreme Court's clear position on death-eligibility limits the ultimate sentence to "mentally competent adults." In his brief, Michael L. Burke, Scott's appellate lawyer, noted that his client's trial lawyer, Roland Steinle, "did not present any evidence about the head injuries Scott had suffered prior to the crime."

At his federal evidentiary hearing in 2005, Scott's lawyers presented new evidence concerning his brain damage and contended his counsel was ineffective for not presenting it earlier. This evidence included reports and testimony from two new defense witnesses: neurologist Thomas Hyde and neuropsychologist Tora Brawley. Dr. Hyde found that Scott "has multiple neurological deficits that within a reasonable degree of medical certainty" existed during the crime in 1989. In particular, Hyde found evidence of: (1) frontal lobe dysfunction;

(2) chronic cerebellum damage, most likely secondary to alcohol abuse; and (3) a history of seizures consistent with brain dysfunction, either from closed head injury, chronic alcohol abuse, or both. Besides his examination of Scott, Dr. Hyde reviewed medical records that preexisted the crime and that "could have been easily obtained by Scott's trial counsel, Roland Steinle, had he attempted to do so."

The lower court record included CT scans performed on Scott in 1987 and 1988, *before* Christopher's murder. Both revealed atrophy of Scott's brain that "was unusual for a person his age. Scott had told Steinle he had suffered 'brain shrinkage' because of numerous head injuries, including a bicycle accident in the seventh grade with a car, two motorcycle accidents, and a car accident—all of which rendered Scott unconscious." He did not get a CT scan *after* the murder in 1989, which may have provided the elusive nexus. That proved dispositive 24 years later, when nexus, and *cause and effect*, became legally significant.

Dr. Hyde opined that Scott's neurological deficits "would have had a significant impact on his behavior. He observed that "particularly the cognitive deficits, the frontal lobe dysfunction would affect his judgment, reasoning, problem solving, behavior under stress, [and] his decision making."

Dr. Brawley and a forensic psychiatrist working at his direction concluded, "Scott has an IQ of 88, which falls in the low-average range. The testing also revealed deficits in Scott's executive decision making and frontal lobe functioning." Dr. Brawley observed, "[P]atients with frontal lobe dysfunction often exhibit poor judgment, difficult problem solving due to an inability to explore options (decreased cognitive flexibility), poor sequencing ability, and problems fully comprehending consequences of behavior."

Dr. Harry Tamm, a neurologist, and Dr. James Seward, a neuropsychologist, were the state's medical experts. They did not dispute the findings of Drs. Hyde and Brawley as to Scott's current condition. However, they disagreed "as to whether the neurological and neuropsychological deficits from which Scott suffers were present in 1989, when he committed the crimes."

District Court Judge P.G. Rosenblatt, following a post-hearing briefing, denied habeas relief to Scott. The court held Steinle's failure to investigate the evidence of Scott's brain injuries was *not* ineffective assistance of counsel. It offered a homily as well—even if his lawyer was ineffective, Scott was not prejudiced by it. The Ninth Circuit turned to the federal standard of review for an answer to the conundrum. Where the state court had not decided on the merits, the district court reviews the merits *de novo*, Latin, meaning "from the new." When an appellate court hears a case *de novo*, it decides issues without reference to the legal conclusions or assumptions made by the lower court. Appeals courts hearing cases *de novo* refer to the trial court's record to determine the facts. Once done, they rule on the evidence and matters of law without giving deference to that lower court's findings.

The Ninth Circuit Court of Appeals gave no deference to the lower court: "Although the claims were presented to the state postconviction court, that court dismissed the claims on purely procedural grounds. We held that dismissal was erroneous."

Federal courts, in 2012, followed the *Strickland* standard, announced in a famous U.S. case, Strickland v. Washington. Under *Strickland*, counsel is ineffective if "representation fell below an objective standard of reasonableness" and "there is a reasonable probability that, but for counsel's unprofessional errors, the result of the proceeding would have been different." In resolving death-sentence appeals, courts assess prejudice by "[comparing] the evidence that actually was presented . . . with evidence that might have been presented had counsel acted differently." That process presents an opportunity on appeal to determine whether "absent the errors, the sentencer . . . would have concluded that the balance of aggravating and mitigating circumstances did not warrant death."

A new standard of review arises in federal litigation. Appellate courts review a district court's legal holdings *de novo* and its factual findings for *abuse of discretion* to see if those findings are "illogical, implausible, or without support in inferences that may be drawn from the facts in the record." As every fisherman knows, there is a point where the worm turns. And it turned here, against Roger Scott. The Ninth Circuit analyzed the performance of Scott's trial lawyer, Roger Steinle, at trial in 1990.

Steinle's trial theory was that "Scott was an unwitting dupe with a personality disorder that made him easily manipulated by Styers and Debra Milke. Because the evidence provided through Scott's confession demonstrated he did *not* act in an impulsive way and that in fact he helped carefully to plan the murder, evidence of a brain injury would not have helped his defense." The Ninth Circuit found "Scott was not prejudiced by Steinle's decision not to investigate Scott's head injuries further and we need not decide in this case whether that decision constituted deficient performance." As proof of this, the court noted the district court's remand, during which Scott was "allowed to present the new evidence of his head injuries that he had wanted to present to the state court." After considering this evidence, the district court concluded, "Petitioner has not met his burden of proving that he was prejudiced by Steinle's performance at sentencing . . . Assuming evidence existed at the time to support a finding that Petitioner suffered from [cognitive] defects, Petitioner has not established that a mitigation case based on that evidence would have been more persuasive than the theory Steinle did present at sentencing."

There was also the matter of Scott's confession. It revealed "he was an active participant in the planning, preparation, execution, and cover-up of the crime, and that he was able to appreciate the wrongful nature of his crime. Scott gave a taped interview to Detective Mills, detailing the events leading up to, resulting in, and attempting to cover up the murder of Christopher . . . The new evidence that Scott had brain damage does not explain his actions in this case and is insufficient to overcome their egregious nature: helping plan the murder; recommending that there was too much traffic in one place to commit the murder and that they should relocate to a more remote area; negotiating over his fee for participating in the murder; and attempting to cover up the murder by hiding Styers's shoes and the murder weapon and by going along with Styers's story that Christopher had disappeared at the mall. We cannot say that Scott was prejudiced by Steinle's tactical decision. Even considering the totality of mitigation evidence that Scott introduced at the district court on remand— evidence of his head injuries, brain shrinkage, and seizures; evidence that the State once offered him a plea bargain to testify against Styers and Debra Milke; and evidence that the victim's father, Mark Milke, thought the trial court should show Scott leniency—we cannot say it would have made any difference in the outcome. Scott was not prejudiced by Steinle's failure to present it at sentencing."

With that, the Ninth Circuit affirmed Judge Rosenblatt's denial of *habeas corpus* relief.

33

JAMES STYERS' HABEAS CORPUS PETITION— 1998 TO 2013

*J*AMES LYNN STYERS FILED HIS original petition for a writ of *habeas corpus* in the United States District Court for the District of Arizona, in 1998. His new appellate lawyer, Treasure Lynn Van Dreumel, amended the petition on September 3, 1999, raising nine claims for relief. Judge Earl H. Carroll found four claims were "procedurally barred" and one "lacked merit." Then he found that the remaining claims were properly exhausted and therefore not subject to review on the merits. Following a lengthy briefing schedule, Judge Carroll addressed the four surviving claims, found them lacking, and decided that Styers was not entitled to any habeas relief.

In a 24-page, carefully drawn opinion, Judge Carroll addressed all five claims, cited solid authority against each position, and declined to grant Styers relief. Styers changed counsel. His new lawyers, Cary Sandman and Amy Beth Krauss, appealed Judge Carroll's order to the U.S. Court of Appeals for the Ninth Circuit. That court granted relief on one count on October 23, 2008. The Ninth Circuit's "overview" of the appeal was narrow. The court accepted as factual that Styers "shot and killed the four-year old son of the woman with whom he and his daughter shared an apartment." They were mindful of his claim that his lawyer was ineffective, but found no merit in the particulars of that claim. But the court expanded Styers' certificate of appealability to include his claims that the state supreme court "failed to adequately narrow a facially vague aggravating factor and failed to fulfill its constitutional obligation to reweigh all aggravating and mitigating factors after striking one of the aggravating factors."

The three-judge panel, Chief Judge Alex Kozinski, and Circuit Judges Jerome Ferris and Carlos T. Bea, found Styers did not "demonstrate that his trial attorney would have likely prevailed on a request to strike the jury panel." However, the court said, "In applying a nexus test to conclude that the inmate's post-traumatic stress disorder did not qualify as mitigating evidence, the state supreme court appeared to have imposed a test directly contrary to the constitutional requirement that all relevant mitigating evidence be considered by the sentencing body." The Ninth Circuit vacated the district court's judgment and remanded to the district court with instructions to grant the writ regarding the inmate's sentence "unless the state, within a reasonable period of time, either corrects the constitutional error in the inmate's death sentence, or vacates the sentence and imposes a lesser sentence consistent with law."

The Arizona Supreme Court took a second look at the trial record, based on the Ninth Circuit's mandate. On July 1, 2011, it affirmed Styers' death sentence. On this second direct review, the court considered Styers' PTSD as a mitigating circumstance. In evaluating whether Styers established he had PTSD and was affected by it at the time of the murder, the court came to an unfavorable conclusion. "Ultimately, we must decide whether the evidence of Styers' PTSD alters our earlier determination that the mitigating evidence presented in this case is not sufficient to warrant leniency in light of the aggravating factors." It found Styers presented no evidence that his PTSD affected his conduct during the crime. Based on that finding, the court held that "Styers' PTSD, in combination with all other mitigating evidence presented at Styers' mitigation hearing and previously considered by this Court, is not sufficient to warrant leniency in light of the aggravating factors proven in this case."

When he lost in 2011 at the Arizona Supreme Court, Styers' lead counsel, Amy B. Krauss, refiled the case in the U.S. District Court for the District of Arizona by way of a motion to enter judgment granting a writ of *habeas corpus*. The new filing was assigned to Judge James Teilborg. Judge Teilborg wrote a six-page opinion denying the motion. He said, "On remand, the district court did not vacate Petitioner's sentence. Rather, the court indicated that a writ of *habeas corpus* (releasing Petitioner from his sentence) would be granted, "unless the State of Arizona . . . initiates proceedings either to correct the constitutional error in [Styers'] death sentence or to vacate the sentence and impose a lesser sentence consistent with the law . . . On this record, it is clear the Arizona Supreme Court considered all of Petitioner's mitigating evidence in conducting its reweighing. Thus, the state court satisfied its constitutional obligations."

In his final effort to secure federal *habeas corpus* relief, Styers sought a second *habeas corpus* writ on October 30, 2012, asserting eight grounds for relief.

—

JUDGE TEILBORG'S ANALYSIS WAS CLEAR and cogent. "Thus, where there is a new judgment intervening between the two *habeas* petitions, the latter petition challenging the new judgment is not second or successive. Styers' brief characterizes his death sentence as *new* (in light of the independent review undertaken by the Arizona Supreme Court in response to the district court's conditional writ) and suggests that a second *habeas* petition challenging the 'new death sentence' is not successive. Further, the petition asserts that Petitioner's death sentence was 'vacated' by the conditional writ. In making these assertions, Petitioner misapprehends the nature of the relief provided during his first *habeas* proceeding."

Courts communicate to lawyers in jargon, which may be incomprehensible to the lay public. Judge Teilborg's opinion references "ripe claims not previously raised" and "unripe claims not previously raised." Before judges trouble themselves with positions taken by either side, they first test "ripeness" for judicial resolution. The underlying rationale of the ripeness doctrine is to prevent courts from becoming entangled in disagreements that are abstract, rather than real. Ripeness requires a court to evaluate both whether the issues are fit for judicial determination and the hardship to the parties of not permitting the case to be heard. There are two "threshold criteria" to determine if a claim is ripe. The first has its underpinnings in the case or controversy clause of Article III of the Constitution, since courts can hear only actual "cases or controversies." Judicial prudence is a flexible doctrine, permitting an exception to the rule that courts must exercise jurisdiction if it exists. Constitutional ripeness is a limit on the power of the courts, while prudential ripeness means, in lay terms, never mind—we will take this issue up at a later time, and no constitutional rights will be thwarted by the delay.

The procedural morass created by the Arizona Supreme Court's second direct review of Styers' case now became something of a legal conundrum. Styers' second petition for habeas relief would likely become moot if he prevailed on appeal from Judge Teilborg's order in his original habeas proceeding denying his motion to grant an unconditional writ. That was because the vast majority of the issues remaining in the second petition were identical to ones Styers raised in his motion for an unconditional writ releasing him from his capital sentence. At this procedural point in time, Judge Teilborg had already granted a Certificate of Appealability to the Ninth Circuit on whether Styers was entitled to a new sentencing proceeding before a jury. That appeal remained pending. A decision by the Ninth Circuit would likely will be dispositive, mooting the entire petition. So, Judge Teilborg found "that the interests of justice and judicial economy are best served by staying these proceedings pending a decision by the Ninth Circuit."

34

DEBRA MILKE'S OPENING BRIEF IN THE NINTH CIRCUIT— DECEMBER 11, 2007

*A*N APPELLATE BRIEF FILED IN any court is momentous, but when you finally reach the United States Court of Appeals, it signals the end of a long, mind-numbing writing and research project. Traditionally, appellate briefs are bland, straightforward recitations of fact, law, theory, and remedy. Most lack a distinctive voice. But Lori Voepel's brief was on behalf of a woman imprisoned for 17 years and facing the death penalty. That made the task as daunting as dredging up a buried anchor 5000 feet below the surface of the Arctic Ocean. Finding a narrative voice in a death penalty case is a challenge few lawyers even attempt. Voepel's narrative voice vaulted over the usual mishmash of appellate phrasing; she stated her client's case bluntly.

"In December 1989, the State charged Debra Milke and co-defendants James Styers and Roger Scott with first-degree murder, conspiracy to commit murder, child abuse, and kidnapping relating to the death of Debra's four-year old son, Christopher. In separate trials, the State sought the death penalty against all three defendants. Prior to trial, Judge Cheryl Hendrix held a suppression hearing regarding Debra's 'alleged' confession to police detective Armando Saldate. Trial counsel did not call Debra to testify, and the judge ruled her confession admissible. On October 12, 1990, a jury found Debra guilty on all counts."

By honing down the opening narrative to just five sentences containing a scant 95 words, Voepel framed the issue so that, if accepted, Milke would at least stand a chance. The contrast between Voepel's brief at the federal level and Jim Kemper's brief at the Arizona Supreme Court level in 1991 is stark. Voepel opened with the ill-fated suppression hearing before Judge Hendrix and Milke's "alleged" confession to Saldate. Kemper opened with Milke's death sentence. Voepel attacked the only evidence against Milke—a confession she fittingly labelled as "alleged." Kemper attacked the death sentence on constitutional grounds but did not mention the core issue—did Debra Milke confess to Armando Saldate?

Voepel knew the Ninth Circuit judges would review the record. They would see, without her help, why Milke was so easily convicted and denied relief on direct appeal to the state supreme court—she confessed. Her confession was not challenged at trial, although her lawyer had engaged the jury in an academic debate about what her words meant. Her suppression hearing was perfunctory because the prosecutor presented the confession as a "given." It worked on the judge and it worked on the jury. Once the jury accepted it that way, the only argument was *why* she confessed, not *whether* she did. Voepel's Ninth Circuit brief advanced the *whether* question in 137 pages of carefully articulated fact, law, and argument.

Whether she confessed became a two-pronged argument. Did her alleged confession meet Miranda standards? And even if it did, what did she confess to? She noted that the District Court of Arizona had granted leave to file two *amicus curiae* briefs on the confession issue—one by Steve Drizin from Northwestern University's Center on Wrongful Convictions and the other by Larry Hammond and former appellate judge Rudy Gerber on behalf of the ACLU. And she asked them to pay attention to the "26 exhibits from the lower court record regarding the unreliability of Saldate's interrogation techniques and the purported confession."

She emphasized that Judge Broomfield, after granting leave to file *amicus* briefs and to expand the record by allowing those 26 additional exhibits, summarily denied habeas relief, without granting an evidentiary hearing to flesh out the depth of exactly how unreliable the alleged confession was. She carefully noted in her brief the unusual event whereby a district court issued a *sua sponte* (on its own motion) Certificate of Appealability. What made it unusual was the inexplicable absence of any certification of the claims regarding Kenneth Ray and James Kemper's failures to challenge the admissibility of the alleged confession at all.

Voepel began her argument with her strongest point. "By the time he arrived [in Florence, Arizona], Saldate had already concluded that Debra had conspired with Scott and Styers to have Christopher murdered." Saldate had admitted in post-trial interviews that he based his belief about her guilt "solely upon a few words by Scott." Instead of ignoring the alleged confession, as had been done at the state level appeal, Voepel hit the issue as hard as she could. "Every action the 21-year police veteran took from that point forward was designed to support his belief." While claiming she had confessed to participating in the murder, without the benefit of a witness, audio tape, or video tape to memorialize the interrogation, Saldate rode in the back seat of a police car to Phoenix with her for the next hour without "handcuffing her." He never asked her to sign a statement, and several days later destroyed his notes and wrote a "paraphrased account" of the alleged confession. In less than five pages, Voepel summarized the now infamous 30-minute interrogation—"Nothing corroborates Saldate's account of Debra's purported confession." If the court, after reviewing the record and all opposing arguments, accepted the utter lack of corroboration in a case where the confession was also unrecorded and unwitnessed, then Milke had a chance.

Voepel posed her factual thesis to the court in plain language. "Saldate twisted and took [Milke's] statements out of context, gave them a different meaning than intended, and completely fabricated [a confession]. Unfortunately, because of Saldate's failure to record, document, or have the interrogation witnessed, no one can prove with certainty what occurred. Given his long tenure as a police officer and confidence in his ability to sway a jury, Saldate knew he would receive the benefit of any doubt."

This argument advanced two hopeful premises. First, that the federal court would accept the issue as framed (no one can prove with certainty what occurred). Second, lacking certainty, the trial court convictions and sentences were not proven beyond a reasonable doubt. If both premises were accepted, a remand for retrial was the only remedy.

And finally, she argued the obvious: "No physical evidence implicates Debra. The state never even claimed she was present at the murder scene. Nor did either co-defendant testify against her. Jim Styers adamantly insists Debra had nothing to do with the murder. Although Roger Scott vaguely implicated Debra after repeated coercive interrogation by Saldate, he refused to testify against her even for a plea agreement to save his own life." In turning down a very favorable plea bargain, Scott said, on the record, that "he would say what his attorney wanted him to say, but his testimony would not be what he felt was the truth."

Coup de grâce is a phrase often used to describe a death blow to end the suffering of a severely wounded person. Voepel's coup de grâce in her brief argued for ending civilized society's over-reliance on confession testimony. "Defense counsel was precluded from asking about Saldate's interrogation history and from calling any experts to assist the jury in evaluating Saldate's tactics and the reliability of the purported confession. If we as a civilized society have learned anything in recent years, it is that 'confession' evidence is inherently unreliable." She connected the abject failure of the trial judge, the ineffectiveness of the defense lawyer, the prosecutor's failure to reveal known exculpatory information, to Saldate's overzealousness. Voepel connected all the dots. The appellate court could see, in one brief, how the jury so easily accepted Saldate's word over Milke's. All that was left was to deal with was whether Milke confessed.

35

OYEZ, OYEZ, THE UNITED STATES COURT OF APPEALS FOR THE NINTH CIRCUIT IS NOW IN SESSION— AUGUST 28, 2008

HE RICHARD H. CHAMBERS U.S. Court of Appeals building in Pasadena, California is an imposing building just east of old downtown Pasadena. Built as a hotel, and remodeled five times between 1882 and 1991, it went from guest rooms to hospital rooms. Its most recent makeover, in 1981, turned it into a modern set of courtrooms. Formerly known as the Vista del Arroyo, and listed on the National Register of Historic Places, the federal government's General Services Administration (GSA) began design work to restore the building as the southern seat of the Ninth Circuit Court of Appeals. In 1995, the building was renamed to honor Judge Richard H. Chambers, one of America's most articulate federal judges. The main appellate courtroom, once called the Spanish Room, is opulent, richly detailed, and grilled with ornamental cast iron. The elevator lobby and west foyer feature original decorative elevator doors and glazed-tile risers on the staircase. The deceptively kind rose-covered pergola and the brightly colored paintings are striking to lawyers coming to work there for the first time.

On August 20, 2008, two Phoenix lawyers, Lori Voepel and Kent Cattani, entered the pit, arranged their briefing notes on opposite sides of the carved podium, and waited. At the stroke of 10 o'clock in the morning, the well-dressed bailiff made the historic call, "*Oyez, Oyez,* all rise—the United States Court of Appeals for the Ninth Circuit is now in session." Everyone rose from his or her seat like synchronized swimmers. Lawyers at the ready, clerks and staff with poised pens and yellow legal tablets, and well-dressed observers in the polished oak pews, stood at parade rest. Three black-robed judges entered and took the middle three seats on the nine-seat raised bench. Once seated, everyone else took a breath and found their places. Judge Alex Kozinski, the Chief Judge of the Ninth Circuit, took the middle seat, with Circuit Judge Jerome Farris settled on one side and Circuit Judge Carlos T. Bea on the other. They took only seconds to settle themselves and open their briefing books. The clerk called the case, by caption and docket. Judge Kozinski acknowledged Ms. Lori Voepel as counsel for the Petitioner Debra Milke, and Mr. Kent Cattani as counsel for the State of Arizona, Respondent. He did not waste time announcing they were here to engage in an oral argument about a death row inmate's petition for *habeas corpus* denied her by three lower courts, or that it had taken 20 years to reach this august point in capital crime litigation. Everyone already knew that.

Oral arguments are widely misunderstood by lawyers and citizens. Most think the movie version is real—lawyers standing before the judges making eloquent arguments for absent clients. In the movie version, judges only occasionally interrupt, and even then, they do so politely and ask few questions. Screenwriters love creating dialogues with silver-tongued actors playing the role of lawyer on big screens. At the Ninth Circuit, while the room is glamorous, the interchange between bench and podium is a verbal sparring match. It is spontaneous, not spell-checked, full of unnecessary "thats," and dulled by the passive voice. Unlike formal written briefs, the actors (judges and lawyers) use contractions and jargon. In real life, especially before senior appellate judges like Kozinski, Farris, and Bea, there is no argument. With high-end lawyers like Voepel and Cattani, appearing before three of the best appellate judges on any circuit court, the Q & A is non-stop. It is an intellectual Gatling gun, firing terse questions which ricochet in tightly drawn answers. Those answers come back up at the bench as though they were lacrosse balls snared in leather pouches. There is much firing down at the advocates, followed by equally focused hurling back up at the bench, respectfully but in self-defense. In this and all other high-end arguments, the game is in knowing the record. The judges have read the written briefs and bench memos written by their top-ranked young law clerks. The lawyers have spent weeks poring over the record, memorizing facts, and making lists that can instantly be accessed. No one needs an "argument." What all *three* sides want is an engaged discussion ferreting out all of the gray areas and identifying those few legal positions and factual disputes that will carry, or sink, the case.

Judge Kozinski nodded down at Lori Voepel, who stood at the ready before the bench, watching the two small lights on the podium—one white, signaling OK to start—one red, signaling stop, now.

"Good morning. May it please the court. I'm Lori Voepel, counsel for Debra Milke, the appellant in this case. With me this morning is Michael Kimerer. I am going to focus this morning on the interrogation confession issue. I'm also prepared if the Court has questions on the sentencing issue. If the Court has questions regarding the ineffective assistance claim, Mr. Kimerer would like to address those. And I'd like to reserve five minutes for rebuttal."

The court engaged Voepel for a few minutes about Mr. Kimerer's role at oral argument. Once settled, Voepel began anew, "Debra Milke was condemned to death solely on the basis of the uncorroborated testimony. . . ."

Judge Farris interrupted, "You started off in an interesting way. 'She was condemned to death.' Why do you say that?"

"Your honor, she was sentenced to die."

"All right."

"On very . . ."

Judge Farris probed, "I think accurately you would say she was sentenced to death, isn't that the accurate statement of what happened to her?"

"Yes."

"Because I don't want to use your dime on that point. I was just surprised because if you're gonna make an argument that's gonna be other than on this record, we're gonna have some difficulty with it."

Like every good lawyer snapped by a wide-awake judge, Voepel said the exactly right thing: "I agree, your honor."

"All right," Judge Farris said, indicating with a nod of his head they were now back on track. Everyone knew that *condemned to die* was Hollywood-speak, whereas *sentenced to die* was consistent with the lower court record, which controlled everything in appellate litigation. There are few things more frightening to an appellate lawyer than a judge who knows the record better than you do. This argument would prove the point, to both Voepel and Cattani.

The strictest clock in the country runs appellate arguments. You get exactly 30 minutes to make your case. When the red light goes on, you stop, mid-sentence. Voepel used a small part of "her dime" to get back in the good graces of the panel.

"It is on the record. She was sentenced to die solely on the basis of an uncorroborated confession."

Not so fast, Judge Farris implied, as he interrupted her flow, again. "And isn't that a conclusion that somebody can reach? But [one] that not everybody would reach?"

"That it is uncorroborated? In this case?"

"No, you said solely."

"Yes, your honor. No, I don't believe so. Other than character evidence? Detective Saldate is . . ."

Judge Farris explained his point. "What about statements of her relatives?"

"They have absolutely no personal information relating to this process. . . ."

Judge Farris was not to be denied his point. "No, but when you say, solely, don't worry. We're gonna hear it and we've reviewed the record. When you give us these editorial slants, it makes it a little difficult to get to the heart of the matter. And I hope you're gonna get to the heart of the matter."

"I'm going to get to the heart of the matter, your honor."

"Thank you."

"Other than character evidence, the only direct evidence . . ."

The heart of the matter would have to wait. Judge Bea entered the fray. "You say character evidence. As I understand, character evidence is circumstantial evidence of acts committed by a person that show a trait of character to show action on the time involved consistent with that character. That wasn't exactly what the testimony by the relatives and friends and officers were, what you call 'lack of corroboration.' The evidence was evidence of an intent or state of mind, of dislike for her child, and a wish to be away from her child. That evidence seems to me very probative on the issue of premeditation."

"Your honor . . ."

Judge Bea: "And this is a first-degree murder case."

"This is a first-degree murder case, your honor. Unfortunately, as I set forth in the briefs . . . Ms. Milke's father and sister were both heavily influenced . . . by Detective Saldate prior to trial."

Judge Bea probed. "They were heavily influenced? Is there anything in the record which shows that he strong armed them before they took the stand?"

Voepel turned the question into a positive for her side. "Your honor, what it shows, first of all, as to Sandra Peckinpaugh, Debra's sister, the record does show that he heavily influenced her in her interview. She actually tape-recorded that when Detective Saldate came. And it shows throughout the course of that interview Detective Saldate, through a combination of untruths and through influencing Sandra and working with what he knew to be a pretty strong sibling rivalry with Debra , he manipulated her throughout that interview."

Voepel offered the court other examples of Saldate's manipulation of Milke's sister. She quoted from Sandy Peckinpaugh's interview with post-conviction counsel Anders Rosenquist, three years after the trial.

Judge Kozinski, perhaps sensing the validity of the point, or perhaps just wanting to get the arguments back on point, interrupted. "I don't know how any of this helps your client . . . This may not have been what we'd hope and expect of the police to do but the evidence of the sister came before the jury . . . the jury heard it and as Judge Bea has suggested that evidence was not character evidence, it was corroborative. But perhaps not strongly corroborative but it's corroborative in the sense that it showed dislike for, or dissatisfaction with her status as a mother. Now how they got there is the stuff of cross-examination. And just saying gee, it's unfair . . . I don't know see where that helps your client any. What is the constitutional hook here?"

The interchange with Judge Kozinski went on for a minute or two. The transcript deals with many issues besides whether Milke confessed to Saldate. Those were ultimately unsuccessful. But the back and forth between Saldate and Milke got everyone's attention.

Voepel: "Our position is that overall, the admission of the uncorroborated confession together with the admission of the other evidence regarding Debra's performance as the mother, and the ineffective assistance . . ."

Judge Kozinski, interrupted, "See, you're aiming too far and too high. I mean all you really have to say is the confession came in improperly. And it was highly damaging. It doesn't have to be the only thing. It doesn't have to be right."

Voepel got the Chief Judge's drift. "I understand your Honor."

"And you know, if you manage to knock out the confession, then it's a different ball game."

Likely hoping Judge Kozinski was foreshadowing the panel's decision—a new ball game—Voepel said, "Right."

Did she get the hint? Judge Kozinski laid a little sauce on the possibility. "And I think you're fighting for too much by saying, well, there was nothing else. Even [if] there were other things, if you were to manage to knock out the confession[,] you would obviously have saved your client. And this is what we need to get on to."

"Okay."

"This is why, you know, rather than fighting these sort of side battles about whether there was anything else, I mean."

Voepel got more than just the hint. "When I say 'solely[,]' I apologize. What I'm really talking about is that the confession is uncorroborated. . . ."

Judge Kozinski did not want to hear any more argument about whether the confession was uncorroborated. He explained his colleague's position. "What Judge Farris said is really a very fine observation and it's something that counsel, I don't mean to lecture, but sometimes you lose credibility by overstating. You don't need to overstate here. Obviously, the confession was very important. And it doesn't have had to have been the sole thing that convicted, or anything else. It's obviously something that if improperly admitted would change this landscape. That's all you need, really need to say."

"I do agree with that, your honor, and again, I, just to clarify what I'm really saying is that there is no physical evidence linking her and . . ."

Judge Kozinski's tone went up a notch. "You know, we really have read the briefs and the record. We really do know what came in [evidence.] And I can't speak for my colleagues but it seems to me if you manage to knock out the confession, to me, the case would look very different. So, that's all we really need, all right? So why don't you just go to that issue, please?"

Voepel went straight to the point Judge Kozinski asked for. "Thank you. First of all, Detective Saldate, as you are aware, interrogated Debra in a room alone. No witness. No tape recording. Didn't have her sign any statement. She has denied confessing. . . ."

Judge Kozinski finally had Voepel where he and his colleagues wanted her to be—at the pinch-point in the whole case. He interrupted her and asked, "Was there any Miranda card?"

The civilian observers in the courtroom that morning might not have appreciated the significance of this question. A "Miranda card" is a shirt-pocket-sized card containing the basic Miranda warnings with a space for the suspect to confirm he or she understood and waived those constitutional rights. It is virtually unheard of in American appellate jurisprudence for a confession to be upheld unless the suspect knowingly waived those rights, in writing, often right there on the card. In other settings, the "card" is a more formal written document. In virtually all cases where an appellate court upholds the admission of a confession in evidence, the record contains an actual record of either explicit or implicit waiver—hence the "Miranda card" exchange at this oral argument.

Voepel gave the wrong answer. "Yes, your honor, there, she claims that she . . ."

Judge Kozinski pounced. "No! Was there a Miranda card that she signed?"

"Oh, no, your honor. She did not sign a waiver."

"In twenty-two years of doing this, or twenty-three, I've never seen a case where there hasn't been a signed Miranda warning."

"Exactly," Voepel said. "And our position is that the . . . the state court's finding that Debra waived her Miranda rights is objectively unreasonable because it really is just a credibility determination that was not, first of all, not based on any corroboration. She [Judge Hendrix] just heard Debra. And she heard Detective Saldate and chose to believe Detective Saldate."

But "exactly" was not the point Judge Kozinski was making. "But that's normally enough. If you have two witnesses. I mean, we do this all the time. He said, she said, right. You know, we're in a room together. He propositioned me . . . let's say this was a civil case, sexual harassment, let's say, for example. There was just two of us. He propositioned me. I slapped him, I got fired, right?"

Now, Voepel reverted to form. "That's different, your honor, from a situation involving an interrogation where the credibility issue centers on what an interrogating officer is saying happened alone with a witness . . . in incommunicado interrogation. This court has held that."

"How is that constitutionally different?"

Voepel gave him a long answer, talked about an important case (Taylor v. Maddox) and made the point that this detective (Saldate) created the conditions by which Milke could not corroborate what happened in that room. That's why, she argued, "The State is held to a higher burden of proof in proving waiver of Miranda."

Judge Bea asked whether Dr. Kassell, Milke's psychiatrist at the time of trial, testified that Milke told him she had been Mirandized. When Voepel confirmed that point, Judge Bea remarked there was "no question about Miranda" if she admitted she had been given the warnings. Voepel dealt with that series of questions by arguing they were not claiming he had not given her Miranda warnings, only that she had not waived her Miranda rights. She asserted her right to an attorney, but Saldate did not listen to her.

Judge Bea said, "There we go. Now we're getting the real claim. Your claim is that it is [an] unreasonable finding of fact for the trial court to have found that Saldate did not hear because she did not say that she wanted an attorney until the end of the interrogation."

"That's correct, your honor."

"Why do you say that that is an unreasonable finding of fact given the fact that Saldate so testified? And the court, the trial court on two occasions—once on the suppression hearing and once on the post-conviction relief hearing—made a finding that there was no request for an attorney either before or after the interview began?"

Voepel did not correct Judge Bea's error: there was no post-conviction relief hearing—Judge Hendrix had refused to grant Milke an evidentiary hearing at that point. She answered the question. "First of all, your honor, it's an unreasonable determination because the very admission, or the very statement by Debra that the state court relies on in saying that she refused to be recorded is also the same statement where Debra claims that she asserted her right to an attorney."

Judge Bea reminded her that the Taylor v. Maddox case was "was written by Judge Kozinski. It's almost as good as the Supreme Court."

Voepel jumped on that one. "Yes, your honor, it is."

The reporter's transcript and the audio of the argument confirm a bit of laughter in the courtroom, proving that humor can advance oral argument, sometimes.

Judge Kozinski came to the rescue. "Can I walk you back a step or two from where you followed Judge Bea?"

"On the waiver? Yes, your honor."

"Well you, and again I'm trying to just recite accurately what . . . Judge Bea asked you about her statement to the psychiatrist, that she had been Mirandized. Now, there are two steps in applying Miranda. I'm not trying to put words in your mouth or suggest anything. I'm just trying to make sure what it is you're conceding and what it is you're not conceding. The one step is the officer says you have the right to remain silent and all of those things that we all . . . [know] about."

Voepel: "She concedes that."

"The next step is that she waives it."

"There's a step before that. And that is whether she comprehended it. . . . And there is evidence that she indicated that she did not fully comprehend that . . . Dr. Kassel confirmed that in his interview with her. Because of her state; she had gone thirty hours without sleep. . . ."

"Okay. And did the state court make findings on the comprehension?"

"She did."

"It did make findings?"

"Yes."

"How about the question of waiver."

"And on the waiver."

"But you're not conceding comprehension?"

"No, your honor we are not. Not full comprehension."

Judge Kozinski got more laughs when he responded, "Do any of us have full comprehension?"

Voepel acknowledged the obvious. "Some more than others."

The discussion moved from corroboration of the confession to waiver of Miranda rights. Judge Kozinski put a battery of questions to Voepel. They ultimately agreed that Milke never waived her rights to silence, or an attorney, and that the record below did not support a finding to the contrary. The judge held to his earlier point about the absence of a Miranda card from Saldate and made a new one: Saldate secured no waiver and opposing counsel was "not going to pull a rabbit out of the hat" on the waiver issue. Judge Bea asked whether Saldate gave Milke a "free choice to discuss, admit, or deny, or refuse to answer questions." Voepel said there was no free choice. Then they debated an earlier answer by Voepel saying there was no "finding" on the waiver issue. Now she agreed there was a finding, but there "was no evidence to support it." Judge Farris joined the discussion asking for specific language "in the record" that was used by Milke to request counsel. He told Voepel his reading of the record failed to disclose specific language.

AT THIS POINT, JUDGE KOZINSKI noted that Voepel was "kind of short, and probably wanted to save some time for rebuttal."

"I would, your honor."

"But I do have a question which you might want to answer now. You might want to think about this answer now. You might want to think about and answer when you come for rebuttal. In your reply brief, you raise for the first time a *Brady* claim . . . having to do with the failure of the State to provide the disciplinary records . . . now I can't find where *Brady* has been raised before that. Do you have a viable *Brady* claim here?"

Voepel answered vaguely, mentioning "discovery motions . . . trying to get those [disciplinary records] from the beginning from the trial and through the post-conviction proceedings . . . *Brady* and other cases relying on *Brady* that there is a right to this impeachment information."

Judge Kozinski wanted direct answers. "Well, let's start with the trial. Was *Brady* raised, cited as part of the request for the materials? Yes? I don't know?"

"I don't know . . . I believe it was in the discovery motions . . . I know that it was in post-conviction proceedings in the motion for discovery."

"Was it raised on direct appeal?"

"No, your honor. Nothing relating to the interrogation or confession was raised on direct appeal. We had an ineffective assistance claim."

"And was it raised in the post-conviction motion?"

"Yes, your honor."

"And *Brady* was cited?"

"That's correct, your honor."

Judge Cheryl Hendrix was the trial judge in 1989 and also served as the post-conviction judge in 1996. Judge Kozinski said, "I've read the judge's ruling and she doesn't cite *Brady* at all. She makes no reference to *Brady*. I haven't actually looked at your brief, but are you telling me if I look at the post-conviction brief in the trial court, I'll find the citation to *Brady*?"

"Your honor, not in the post, I believe that it is in the discovery. There were separate discovery motions that were filed by post-conviction counsel in support of post-conviction discovery. And those were also filed in *habeas* proceedings."

"And then there was an appeal of the denial of the post-conviction motion?"

"That's correct, your honor. That's correct."

"Was *Brady* cited to the state appellate court?"

"I'm not sure on that, your honor. I cannot recall if it was."

"Was *Brady* cited to the district court?"

"Your honor, I know that we cited cases that do rely on *Brady* but I don't know if we specifically cited *Brady*. We argued that she had a right to that impeachment. . . ."

Judge Kozinski was keying in on a fundamental aspect of appellate law. As a general proposition, issues not raised in the lower courts could not be raised for the first time on appeal. Kozinski was pointed in saying, "See, what I'm trying to figure out is, do you have a *Brady* claim here before us now? Is there . . . a Constitutional claim properly before us raising *Brady* or *Brady*-like claims . . . the State's refusal to present exculpatory impeachment evidence?"

"Your honor, I do believe that there is. However, I am not sure that other than the discovery motions, that the *Brady* argument was made and all the way through in other ones."

Judge Kozinski asked about the disciplinary files that the district court "ordered up."

"The district court, interestingly, went through and listed all of these other 18 cases in which Saldate had engaged in different forms of alleged misconduct involving five confessions that were suppressed, two or three remands to the grand jury for misrepresentations to the grand jury and tainting line-ups. And specifically went through and listed all of those and indicating that there is a basis for looking at his disciplinary record and that the trial court and/or the post-conviction court should have ordered an *in camera* review of his disciplinary records and release of anything that related to veracity. That's what the district court did, in ordering that disclosure, that discovery. Finally."

Judge Kozinski asked, perhaps incredulously, "But then ruled against you on the merits?"

"That's correct, your honor."

Judge Kozinski said he was "trying to understand whether the district court believed it had a *Brady*-type claim."

Voepel said those were litigated, "before we got involved in the case." Judge Kozinski wanted to know if it was now a certified question. Voepel said it was not, but the question was "before the court."

Judge Kozinski: "Is it as simple as this? To establish overreaching tactics, you have to believe Debra and disbelieve Saldate. And the disciplinary record helps you disbelieve Saldate?"

"Yes, your honor. This all came down to a swearing contest . . . a 'he-said, she-said' . . . we're saying that not only is it not reliable what he said, but because it was not corroborated . . . she was also unable to challenge his credibility through this other evidence."

"I see. So what you're saying is if you'd had this evidence and the state had provided it and should have, you could have impeached him at the suppression hearing and the judge might have disbelieved him?"

Voepel. "And at trial."

Judge Kozinski said, "You know, you're making things more complicated for yourself. You're not listening to the question. You're not listening to the question. You really need to listen. So what you're saying is the reason it's part of the suppression claim is because if you'd had this evidence, the suppression motion would have come out differently because you could have impeached him? That's how it's tied in?"

"That's correct, your honor."

"Okay," Judge Kozinski concluded, "Well, we've used up your time. We'll hear from the State."

Voepel said, "Thank you," and took her seat, no doubt much relieved.

—

THE LAWYER FOR THE STATE of Arizona approached the podium, quickly organized his argument book, and turned to the waiting bench. "May it please the court, my name is Kent Cattani. I represent respondents in this matter. . . ."

Judge Kozinski cut Cattani off in the middle of his second sentence. He honed in on what he thought was the dispositive issue before the court. "Was there a Miranda card here? Was there a signed Miranda waiver?"

Cattani, a highly respected appellate lawyer, knew better than to equivocate. "I'm not aware of there being a signed Miranda card."

With what sounded vaguely like a sigh of relief on the audio tape, Judge Kozinski said, "You know, I have never seen a case where there has been no signed Miranda waiver. Is this [common] practice in Arizona?"

"I'm not sure, your honor."

"Have you ever seen a case like this?"

"I'm not sure that I've seen the issue. I haven't . . ."

"Do you ever recollect seeing a case where there hasn't been a signed Miranda waiver? I mean, I don't know any place in the civilized world in the last 30 years where people, where a state has found a waiver of Constitutional rights without a signed waiver."

"I've never seen the issue raised on appeal in my sixteen years."

There was a long exchange of questions and answers regarding Milke's alleged waiver of her Miranda rights.

Cattani: "The only evidence I'm aware of is simply evidence that's implicit in what transpired."

Judge Kozinski: "Why isn't that the end of the case for you? Why isn't that the end of the case? Insufficient evidence. There is no evidence at all that she waived. Sure, there's evidence that he told her this. But we require more. The Supreme Court requires more. The Supreme Court requires a knowing and intelligent waiver. I don't see any evidence of that. I don't even see Saldate saying, yes, she said she waived. Yes, I said I don't want a lawyer. Yes, I'm ready to talk. He doesn't say anything like that."

"All I recall of what Detective Saldate said . . ."

Judge Kozinski was specific. "I don't want your memory. Go look at the transcript and point out to me anything that you find that supports the finding of waiver, please."

Cattani looked through his black three-ring binder. "Detective Saldate testified that she stated that she understood her rights. She nodded and then she affirmatively said . . ."

"Do you understand the difference between saying I understand my rights and I give up my rights? There are lots of things I understand, that I don't give up. Do you understand the difference?"

"Yes. And that's . . ."

"Where does he say she said I understand my rights, I give up my rights? Where is that evidence in the record?"

"I don't know that it is in the record as specific . . ."

"Why don't you lose in that case? Why isn't that simply a finding that's unsupported by evidence and therefore falls for lack of support? Why don't you, you know, spend the last, next twenty-six and one-half minutes explaining to me how we can possibly sustain that finding?"

"Well, the judge made that finding. It was not challenged at the time she made it in the trial court at the suppression hearing. And then it was . . ."

"I'm sorry, is this a waiver argument? You're saying she waived her challenge to the finding? Is that where you're going?"

"Well, I think she did by not making any objection at that point and then by not raising it on direct appeal. This issue was never raised."

"Wasn't this raised on the post-conviction hearing and considered by the state court on the merits?"

"It was raised in the post-conviction proceeding. The only issue that was raised was her suggestion that she had said she requested an attorney. I don't recall her saying I never affirmatively waived my rights. The focus of both at the suppression hearing and in the PCR was, I asked for an attorney."

Judge Kozinski let the answer settle a few moments. Then, he summed up. "Okay, so let me just make sure I understand where we stand. You more or less concede you don't have anything to support the finding."

"Yes."

"So now you're off on waiver. You're saying so all this stuff she never raises is the first time you've heard the argument there was nothing to support the waiver. You're surprised? Is that your position on behalf of the State of Arizona?"

"She did, the position is she did not raise it on direct appeal, and that was the argument about why the claim is precluded. It should have been raised on direct appeal. Nothing was challenged on direct appeal relating to the suppression hearing."

"But you don't disagree with the general proposition that even though something in Arizona is not raised on direct appeal, it can be raised in post-conviction hearings and if the state courts do not unequivocally find there was a waiver by failing to raise it on direct appeal and they actually go to the merits of the claim. I'm not talking about this case. This is a general proposition, then the waiver is waived, essentially. The state courts will have addressed it on the merits and it's properly then considered in federal court. You don't quarrel with that proposition?"

"Well, what I quarrel with is what's raised in the brief that the . . ."

"Why don't you answer my question? And then we can go on to what you want to talk about."

"Okay."

"So just answer, do you remember my question?"

"Relating to whether there's a waiver, an express waiver on the part of Debra Milke?"

"No. You know, I don't know why counsel don't listen to these questions. I mean, you think we just sort of ask them to hear ourselves talk? The question, you don't quarrel with the proposition that even though a matter is not raised on direct appeal, it can be raised on *habeas* and if the state courts choose to consider it on the merits, then the matter is properly presented and the waiver is waived. I'm not talking about this case. Just as a general proposition, you don't quarrel with that?"

"I agree the state court can reach the merits."

"And if the state court in this case did reach the merits on *habeas*, then whatever happened on direct appeal would be wiped out?"

"No, not necessarily. If the state court is also free to find the, find preclusion and then alternatively address the merits. And I think that's what happened here."

"Fair enough. We won't walk through that line."

The court engaged Cattani in a discussion about the post-conviction review process in Arizona. It ultimately yielded no points for the state's position.

Cattani answered Judge Kozinski with a long and focused argument: "I certainly would agree that it would be better to have recorded confessions and that's certainly the advice we give repeatedly—to record all confessions. I don't disagree with that. But I'm not aware of any Supreme Court authority that says you have to throw it out if it's not recorded. And I think it's important to note that when you go through Ms. Milke's testimony at trial, she really doesn't dispute anything about the facts and circumstances of the interview other than the 'I asked for an attorney.' Beyond that, there's nothing. There's really nothing that suggests her will was overborne by some overreaching tactics. So, to the extent there's some concern that something went on in this room, I don't think that concern is well-founded because Ms. Milke herself testified at trial and raised nothing about the circumstances of the interrogation. Her real argument is he misinterpreted 'what I said,' or he lied about what I said. And that's simply a credibility issue that was before the jury. The jury heard her testimony. They heard Detective Saldate's testimony. And in fact, I think it helped to a certain extent that Ms. Milke was able to say Detective Saldate's supervisor told him to record this interview and he didn't. The jurors heard that. That came out during Detective Saldate's testimony. They were aware of the circumstances of the interview."

Judge Kozinski listened patiently and then went back to the core issue before the Ninth Circuit: "They were not aware of his prior misconduct."

Cattani had an answer for that. "Well, it's not admissible in Arizona under Rule 608. It does not come in under Rule 404(b). Other acts don't come in."

Judge Kozinski countered, "It doesn't matter. It's Constitutionally required. The Sixth Amendment trumps rules of evidence. This is what the Supreme Court has told us. So the fact that rules of evidence happen not to allow this is of really of no consequence at all. This is the kind of impeachment evidence that the state must allow."

Cattani, respectful as always, disagreed. "I disagree with the type of evidence. In fact, Detective Saldate's personnel records showed that he'd been commended for his performance. The rules of evidence are designed to avoid having to go through a mini-trial of every case [in which] a detective has testified in the past. The detective acknowledged that he had questioned people after they had asked for an attorney. He said I understand it won't be admissible at trial. I view my job as being different. I'm there to get information. But he testified that in each instance, he would write down that the person had invoked their rights. I think that came up, I think it's the *Running Eagle* case. Came up in the suppression hearing. And he specifically testified, 'yeah, I noted that and then I kept talking to him, I understand that.' So I think it does, it does come down to a swearing contest. Ms. Milke suggests repeatedly in the brief that she doesn't stand a chance in a swearing contest with a police officer. I would submit that that's illogical. This is a single mother without a criminal history who's working to support herself and her child. There really isn't a built-in bias. Usually we [have] someone who has a criminal record who is gonna be on the stand against a uniform, or against a police officer. That's certainly not the case here. There's nothing that would create this imbalance where she would automatically lose a swearing contest with a police officer."

Judge Kozinski. "On that point, Mr. Cattani, what is the narrow issue before us?"

"The issue here is whether her confession was voluntary and knowing. And, whether his overreaching tactics led her to confess . . . That's all I have, your honor."

—

WITH THAT, JUDGE KOZINSKI TURNED back to Milke's counsel. "Okay, we'll give you a couple more minutes for rebuttal." The rebuttal was taken up by more questions from the bench. Then, conforming to longstanding protocol, Judge Kozinski, rising from the center chair, said, "Case is argued, this stands submitted. We'll take a short break before the next . . ."

The federal appellate courts in America are extraordinarily productive at processing the massive volume of appeals in civil and criminal cases. But they do their job at a glacial pace that frustrates litigants,
especially death row prisoners. The "case-submitted" phase for Debra
Milke's habeas petition started on August 20, 2008 and came to life
again on September 28, 2009. The court could not plug the holes in
the record related to Saldate's claim that he Mirandized Milke. The
specific hole that troubled the Ninth Circuit panel was the "waiver"
issue that took so much time at oral argument. The court's formal
order reads:

> A complete review of the record discloses no evidence sup-
> porting a finding that petitioner voluntarily, knowingly and
> intelligently waived her rights under Miranda v. Arizona,
> 384 U.S. 436, 444-45 (1966). See 28 U.S.C. § 2254(d)-(e).
> Under these circumstances, an evidentiary hearing in federal
> court is required. See Frantz v. Hazey, 533 F.3d 724, 745 (9th
> Cir. 2008) (*en banc*). We therefore remand with instructions
> to conduct a limited hearing on the sole issue of whether peti-
> tioner validly waived her Miranda rights; respondent shall
> have the burden of proof. The district court must conduct the
> hearing and render its findings within 60 days of this order.

What made this order legally significant was what it did *not* say—
it was silent on the *Brady* issue. That signaled that the court was ready
to rule on that aspect of the case, but uncertain about the waiver issue.
Both sides likely took the court's direction regarding urgency as somewhat ominous. Directing the lower court to conduct an "immediate"
evidentiary hearing sends a message. District court judges are very
busy and work calendars are full every day, all the time, and certainly
for the ensuing 60 days after September 28. Something was up, and
it undoubtedly got the attention of the legal teams on both side of the
Brady issue.

36

UNITED STATES DISTRICT COURT FOR THE DISTRICT OF ARIZONA, THE HONORABLE ROBERT C. BROOMFIELD, PRESIDING— JANUARY 11, 2010

*J*UDGE BROOMFIELD'S SPACIOUS COURTROOM IN the Sandra Day O'Connor Federal Court Complex seemed crowded that morning, January 22, 2010. Michael Kimerer, Amy Nguyen, and Lori Voepel sat with their client, Petitioner Debra Milke, at the table closest to the jury box. There was no jury that morning. Judges, not juries, resolve evidentiary hearings on habeas petitions. Two U.S. Marshals sat behind the petitioner's table. On the other side of the courtroom, Kent Cattani and Julie Ann Done, from the Arizona Attorney General's office, waited to present the state's case. Doug Irish represented the victim, Christopher Milke, who would have been 26 years old in

2010. Irish was lead counsel for the Arizona Crime Victims Legal Assistance office in Phoenix. The lawyers were there to put questions to Debra Milke, again. The federal marshals were there to make sure Milke did not escape. Judge Broomfield's courtroom clerk picked up her phone, said something inaudible, and put the phone down. In less than half a minute, Judge Robert Broomfield came in from the almost invisible wood-paneled door on the right side of the bench.

The courtroom came to attention as everyone rose for the judge. "Please be seated," he said.

Lori Voepel remained standing while everyone else in the courtroom took his or her seat. "Your Honor," she said, looking first at Debra Milke, and then at the bench, "Our next witness will be Debra Milke."

Judge Broomfield looked at the defendant but addressed the U.S. Marshal standing closest to her. "Any reason we shouldn't remove the shackles?"

"No, your honor."

"Go ahead," Judge Broomfield, said.

The clerk looked at Milke and said, "Please remain standing and raise your right hand." Milke did so, listened to the clerk's incantation, and swore to tell the truth. Judge Broomfield said, "Thank you. Please be seated and please speak into the microphone."

"Okay."

Voepel waited until her client was settled in the witness box. "Okay, Debra. Can you please state your full name for the record?"

"Debra Milke."

"Okay. And how old are you, Debra?"

"Forty-five."

"And how old were you at the time of the murder of your son?"

"Twenty-five."

Voepel carefully led her client through a series of preliminary questions about where, when, and how Milke first learned Christopher was missing. She covered the Saturday afternoon telephone conversation with Jim Styers on December 2, 1989. Milke told Judge Broomfield that Styers asked her whether Christopher called; she said no. Styers said Christopher is missing. Milke became hysterical, called her father in Florence, and Crimestop in Phoenix. She stayed at home to "wait by the phone," and had several conversations, by telephone, and in person with Phoenix police officers. "They came to my house about 9:00 that night and stayed with me."

Voepel asked, "What were you feeling during this time? What kind of feelings were you having? What kind of thoughts were going through your mind?"

"I was very distraught, crying on and off, and worried about Christopher, wondering where he could be and with whom . . . And I felt distressed and just agonizing fear. Christopher had never disappeared before and I was just sick with worry. I didn't know. I just started thinking of the worst possible things, that maybe a child molester had taken him, or some desperate childless woman. I didn't know."

Milke spoke directly to the judge, something she had not done in 1990 in Judge Hendrix's court. She said she had eaten nothing since Friday night. During the night, she had a rum and coke.

Milke explained that her friend, Carmen, made it for her in a large tumbler and that early Sunday morning her stepmother gave her a Valium pill. It didn't help. She could not sleep. Her stepmother and father were her only relatives in Arizona then. Her mother lived in Germany and her sister in Wyoming. The detectives, named House and Davis, asked her lots of questions about Jim Styers, including whether he had a gun. She told them he did, showed them where it was, and gave it to them. About noon or 1:00 P.M. on Sunday, her stepmother and stepsister took her to Florence to be with her dad. It'd been about 20 hours since Christopher disappeared and they thought she should be with her dad, a state prison guard. She stayed with them for several hours. Then, a sheriff's deputy came to the house and said a detective from Phoenix was coming down to Florence. He wanted to talk to her. So, a friend of her dad's drove her to the sheriff's office to wait for the police officer from Phoenix. They waited about two hours.

Voepel moved the questioning to what happened at the sheriff's office in Florence. Milke said a deputy escorted her to a medical office and told her to wait there for a police officer from Phoenix. "It wasn't very big, but it wasn't very small . . . off to the left was an examining table . . . there was a desk against the wall and there was a chair next to the desk against the wall. And there was a chair in front of the desk . . . on another wall, there were like shelves or a bookcase. And then on the right-hand side, there was a little room that looked like a storage room . . . I guess it had medical supplies in it . . . there was a phone on the desk."

Detective Saldate came in around eight o'clock, two hours after she was told to sit and wait for him. Milke told Judge Broomfield, "He walked into the room and he asked, 'Which one of you is Debra?' And I raised my hand. And then he looked at Jan and asked her to step out . . . she stepped out and he shut the door."

"Now, what did Saldate do at that point? Did he then come and sit down or . . ."

"He took the chair that Jan was in, which was still in front of the desk, he had a notepad. And he put it on the desk and sat down. And he started writing something . . . I asked him, 'Have you heard anything about my son?' But he ignored me."

"And you were still seated, correct, in the chair that was up against the wall?"

"Yes."

"I asked him, 'Have you heard anything about my son,' [and] he just ignored me. And he was writing something on the paper. And then he just looked at me. And he said, 'We found your son. He was murdered and you're under arrest.'

"I screamed out, 'What? What?' And then I just started crying uncontrollably. And he said, 'I'm not going to tolerate your crying' . . . and he pulled a card out of his pocket. . . .

"I couldn't believe what he had just said to me. It just shocked me . . . then he got this card out of his pocket and he started reading these rights. And I moaned, 'Why are you doing this?'

"And he told me to be quiet."

"Were you quiet at that point?"

"No, I was crying."

"Did you hear what he was saying?"

"I was in such shock, and shock because of the horror that my son was dead, and disbelief of being accused of his murder. And so when he was reading these off this card. I could hear him speaking. And I heard the word 'attorney' a few times."

"When he finished reading your rights, did he ask you anything?"

"He said 'do you understand your rights?' And I said, 'No. I've never been in trouble before. I've never been arrested. I never had my rights read to me before.'"

Milke said Saldate did not show her the rights card, did not repeat the warnings, but asked her if she wanted him to record the interview. She said, "No. I need a lawyer."

Voepel asked Milke to explain needing a lawyer and not understanding her rights. Milke explained, "I didn't understand why he was reading me my rights. That's why I asked him, 'Why are you doing this?'" Milke was repetitive. "He just ignored me . . . I was trying to defend myself . . . Every time I tried to tell him, 'I wouldn't do anything like that. I don't know anything about Christopher's murder . . . I wasn't involved in it . . .' Every time I tried to tell him that . . . I'm not a bad person. I wouldn't do anything to hurt anybody, and especially to my own child . . . It just didn't seem good enough. So I felt like I just had to defend myself."

Voepel took pains to paint a physical picture for the judge and asked why Milke explained "parts of her life" to Saldate.

"Well, he was in my face . . . and he was badgering me . . . 'I'm not going to tolerate any lies. I'm here to get the truth' . . . He was just saying this in my face . . . And so then I didn't know what he wanted to hear from me . . . So I told him . . . I went into my past a little bit and told him that in high school I was a nearly straight-A student . . . I got along with everybody . . . I'm not a bad person . . . I didn't understand . . . He was making an accusation against me that was so vile . . . I had to defend myself."

Milke was clear. She never told Detective Saldate she had anything to do with the murder of her son. She did not confess to him, or make any statements about anything indicating a conspiracy to have Christopher murdered.

Through short questions and narrative answers, Voepel established that during the 30-minute interview, Saldate never offered to get an attorney for her, or let her use the phone to call one. He just took her out of the room and put her into a highway patrol car with another officer as the driver. Saldate sat in the back seat with her on the drive to Phoenix. She asked him to take her home. She was never searched. She asked him to call her dad. He agreed. She was confused about why he said he was taking her to jail. That is why she asked him, "If I'm going to jail, then can I get bailed out?"

"Where did you go to when you first got to Phoenix?"

"The main police station downtown . . . I don't know where it's at . . . he got me a Pepsi . . . then they took me to the Madison Street Jail. . . ."

"At some point did you learn that Saldate and the police were saying that you had confessed to the murder of your son?"

"[Yes,] it was when I was at the receiving area at the Madison jail. A private investigative reporter asked to speak to me. And so I agreed. And then when we were talking . . . I was very astounded to hear him ask me about me wanting Christopher dead. And then he said, 'The police are saying that you confessed.' And I was very shocked and confused. And I said, 'No, I didn't do that.'"

Voepel asked Milke several questions to lay a foundation for the March 6, 1990 tape-recorded interview between herself and Dr. Kassell, the Maricopa County Jail psychiatrist. The court allowed her to play the tape in open court. At the ending of the tape recording, Voepel continued her questioning of Milke.

"Okay, Debra. As we just heard, do you recall telling Dr. Kassell that you told Saldate you didn't understand your rights?"

"Yes, I do."

"And you said Detective Saldate did not bring a recorder with him, or offer to get one, is that right?"

"I did not see one, no."

"And at the end of the interrogation, did Detective Saldate ever offer to have you write a statement of what you told him?"

"No.

"And did he ever, at any point after that, ask you if you would allow him to re-interview you on tape? Did he offer that?"

"No."

"Did he ever give you an opportunity to speak with an attorney?"

"No."

Lori Voepel retreated to the Petitioner's table and Julie Done took the podium.

"Good afternoon, Ms. Milke," she said.

"Good afternoon."

"My name is Julie Done, from the Attorney General's office. We've never spoken before, have we?"

"No."

"Have you spoken to anyone at our office recently?"

"No."

"Or ever?"

"No."

"Thank you. You just testified that you told Detective Saldate after he started reading you your Miranda rights, you said, 'Why are you reading me these rights?' Is that correct?"

"No, I didn't say that. I said, 'Why are you doing this?'"

"And so you did not just testify, 'Why are you reading me these rights?'"

"No. Are you asking me when he—that night on December 3rd?"

"I'm asking you what you just testified here in court."

"I said, 'Why are you doing this?'"

"So you're saying now that you did not testify, 'Why are you reading me my rights?'"

"No, I said, 'Why are you doing this?' I said that twice. I said while he was reading me my rights I asked him the second time, 'Why are you doing this?'"

This exchange is illustrative of how some lawyers cross-examine a witness to gain control rather than to inquire. That's accepted mojo in cross-examination, but it rarely affects how the judge evaluates witnesses. They know that most witnesses are not sensitive to the nuance of establishing control over a witness by drilling down to small points of difference. Ms. Done switched one gear down and asked why Milke asked Saldate questions.

"Because he accused me. He arrested me and he was accusing me. I didn't understand why he was doing that. I hadn't committed a crime. I had nothing to do with Christopher's disappearance and murder. So, I didn't understand why he was reading me my rights."

Rather than accept that answer, Done pressed Milke.

"So you understood that he was reading you those rights because you'd been arrested and that's why he was reading them to you?"

"Yes."

"So you actually do understand something about your Miranda rights, correct?"

"At that time on December 3 when he was reading me my rights, I was in shock. He just told me my son had been found murdered."

This line of cross went on for several pages of transcript.

Done shifted gears again to ask about an incident a year before the murder when Debra and her ex-husband, Mark, "were living with someone named Earl." Milke recalled the incident. Done asked, "You testified at trial that 20 police officers rushed your house looking for drugs."

"Yes."

"And you testified that you spoke to the police on that occasion?"

"Yes."

"So you had spoken to the police before?"

"Yes."

"And had contact with the police?"

"Yes."

"And you knew what Miranda rights were?"

"Yes."

As if that were a dispositive issue, Done returned to the case at hand and asked about Milke's interview with the private investigative reporter at the Madison Avenue Jail while she was waiting to be processed into the system. Milke repeated what she'd said on direct exam and Done shifted to a different topic. She asked Milke to confirm her "earlier testimony" that she felt "threatened" by Saldate in the medical office in Florence.

"No. I didn't say 'threatened.' I said he was badgering me."

"He was badgering you?"

"Yes."

"So you didn't feel threatened by him?"

"No. I mean, I was backed up against the wall in the chair and he was in my face. And he was just badgering me, demanding the truth, and telling me over and over, 'I'm not going to tolerate any lies.'"

"Did you have any bad feelings toward Detective Saldate at all?"

"No."

"So did you think he was your friend?"

"No."

"Did you think you could confide in him?"

"No."

"But you actually did confide in him during the interview, correct, with some kind of personal issues?"

"I did, but I was trying to defend myself. And, you know, in my mental anguish, I was . . . by detailing some personal things, I thought maybe he would understand how much I loved Christopher."

"So it was a defense mechanism."

"Yes."

"So you didn't actually feel comfortable confiding in him?"

"No."

"And yet you asked him to call your father for you, correct?"

"Well, on the way to Phoenix, yes."

"Why did you ask him to call your father if you didn't feel like you could confide in him?"

"He was in control of everything. And we're going back to the Phoenix police station, so I just . . ."

The interplay between witness and lawyer was not working well, so Done asked about "shock."

"So in this state of shock though, you *now* remember exactly what happened during that interview?"

"Exactly. I remember Mr. Saldate saying repeatedly, 'I'm not here to tolerate any lies. I'm here to get the truth. This is your opportunity to tell the truth.' I mean these are things that were repeated over and over and over."

"But you quite vividly remember some of the things that you stated to him in your interview, correct, even though you were in shock? Is that correct? Is that what you're testifying to now, that you vividly remember this interview, but you were in shock?"

Milke repeated her earlier testimony that she was in shock. To impeach that thesis, Done used a flank attack. "You were, in fact, a pretty good student in high school, correct?"

"Yes."

"What was your GPA in high school?"

"I think it was a 3.9."

"Okay. And you were also a member of the Spanish Honor Society?"

"Yes."

"And then also a club called DECA?"

"Uh-huh, yes."

"And did you have to do anything specific to get into . . . was it a club actually or a membership or . . ."

"No. It was just some school thing where you got a credit for the class and a credit for working a job."

"So you would consider yourself pretty intelligent then, correct?"

"I wouldn't say intelligent, but smart, yes."

"With a 3.9 GPA, I think most people would strive for that, correct? So you vividly remember being read your Miranda rights and you asked for an attorney, but you're now claiming that you don't understand your rights or you didn't understand your rights, correct? Is that your testimony?"

"I am saying that I did not understand why he was reading them to me . . . He asked me, 'Do you understand?' This was all so fast. Had just received shocking news and then on top of that he's arresting me for it. So he reads the rights. I hear words. I hear him speaking. I heard the word 'attorney' a few times. And then he . . . after he was finished, he said, 'Do you understand your rights?' And I said, no, I've never been in trouble before. I've never been arrested. I've never had . . ."

"But then when he asked you if you wanted the interview recorded, according to your testimony, you're saying, 'No, I wanted a lawyer,' correct?"

"Yes."

"So you understood your rights enough to ask for an attorney, correct?"

"Yes."

That line of cross seemed to work well for Done, so she move to Saldate's failure to record the interview despite his supervisor's direct order to make sure it was recorded.

"You've never denied that you told Detective Saldate that you didn't want it recorded, correct?"

"I've never denied it?"

"Uh-huh. You've always said, 'Yes, when he asked me if I wanted the interview recorded, I said no.' You're also testifying that you said, 'I want a lawyer,' afterwards. But you've always maintained that you told him, 'No, I didn't want it recorded.' Correct?"

"I said, 'No, I need a lawyer.' I said that in one sentence."

"Uh-huh. But you've never said later, 'I said, No, I do want this recorded,' correct?"

"No."

"Okay. So, when he asked you, 'Do you want this recorded?' . . . you said, 'No.' If Detective Saldate testified that you had told him, no, you didn't want it recorded, that wouldn't be an incorrect statement, correct?"

"Yes."

"And do you understand what it means, your right to remain silent, right?"

"I understand that, yes."

The cross-examination went on a good deal longer, but neither lawyer nor witness scored major hits. Done tried hard to get Milke to say she talked willingly, even after she fully understood her constitutional rights. Milke tried hard to say Saldate badgered her into telling him about her personal life. Done closed on a high point for the prosecution.

"Ms. Milke, do you understand what it means to be under oath in court?"

"Yes."

"Have you ever lied in court before?"

"One time."

"And when was that?"

"It was during . . . I don't remember the date, but there was an incident where Mark became violent and I called the police and they arrested him and took him to jail. And it was a domestic violence case. And I was . . . after he got out of jail and had to go to court, he asked me or he told me, I don't know which, but to say that none of that stuff happened."

"And why did you agree to lie in court?"

"Because Mark scared me."

"So if you're scared for your own health, then you'll lie in court?"

"At that time, Mark scared me and so I just . . . it was just say that it didn't happen."

"If I could just have a moment, your Honor."

Judge Broomfield. "You may."

"Your Honor, I have no other questions."

Judge Broomfield thanked Ms. Done and turned to Lori Voepel. "Redirect, Ms. Voepel?"

Voepel took Milke back over the connection between her arrest and reading her Miranda rights. Then she asked what the right to remain silent meant to her. Milke said she never "clearly comprehended the difference between what he read to her from the little card and what he told her about her rights. She said she did not comprehend any of it because "[h]e'd just told me my son had been found murdered and that I'm under arrest for it. I was just shocked."

Voepel returned to one of the most frequent realities in custodial interrogation, whether suspects really understand what the right to remain silent means.

"Did you at least understand that you needed to talk to an attorney?"

"Yes."

"You said you'd heard the word 'attorney' over and over again?"

"Yes."

"Did you, when you asked for an attorney and he ignored you, did you understand? Did you fully understand that you didn't have to continue talking to him?"

"I didn't know that I could stop talking to him."

"Do you know that now? Do you know that if you assert your right to an attorney that you do not have to continue talking to an interrogator?"

"I know that now. But when I ask for a lawyer and I'm ignored, how am I supposed to know that I'm allowed to be silent?"

Voepel asked Milke's opinion about Saldate. Surprisingly, Done did not object. "Did he seem to believe anything that you were telling him?"

"No."

"Now, the assistant AG also asked you if you felt threatened when you were in that room with Detective Saldate. What did you mean by that? Did you mean physically threatened?"

"Physically."

"Did you feel psychologically threatened?"

"Yes, yes."

"Why and how?"

"Because he was badgering me."

"Okay."

"He was in my face and he was just demanding the truth. And I was trying to tell him that I wasn't involved in Christopher's murder. I wouldn't do anything like that."

Turning to face Judge Broomfield, Milke said, "Your Honor, you know, I was trying to—I'm not a malicious person. I was just trying to tell him that, but it just didn't seem good enough."

"And you said he was a physically imposing man?"

"He was a large, imposing man, and he was in my face."

"Did you feel vulnerable during that time?"

"Yes, I did."

"Tired?"

"Very."

"And in shock."

"And in shock."

"Thank you. I have nothing further, Debra."

Judge Broomfield: "You may step down."

Milke: "Thank you. Do I just leave this here?"

Judge Broomfield: "You can leave it there."

37

DR. RICHARD LEO IN THE UNITED STATES DISTRICT COURT FOR THE DISTRICT OF ARIZONA— JANUARY 12, 2010

*T*HE NEXT WITNESS, DR. RICHARD Leo, was one of America's most highly respected experts on custodial interrogation. As a noted law professor and highly acclaimed sociologist, Leo knew more about the dynamics and risks of both interrogator and suspect than almost anyone else in the criminal justice system. And he was no stranger to courtrooms.

Judge Broomfield: "You may call your next witness."

Mike Kimerer, Milke's lead counsel, rose and took the podium. "Your Honor, Petitioner Debra Milke calls Professor Richard Leo."

The court clerk waited as Leo made his way from the pews, through the swinging gate into the pit of the courtroom, past the lawyers' notebook-cluttered tables to the slightly raised staff area in front of the bench. She read him the oath, and directed him to take the witness box to the right of the judge. "Please have a seat there. Speak into the microphone."

Kimerer asked the court clerk to give Dr. Leo Exhibits 5, 6, and 7. Leo accepted them, arrayed them on the shelf in front of him, and nodded at Kimerer at the podium. Over the next 15 minutes, Kimerer credentialed Leo as an expert witness. The underlying thesis for the admission of expert witness testimony in court is whether it will assist the trier of fact to understand the evidence. Here, Judge Broomfield knew the constitutional parameters regarding a suspect's Fifth Amendment rights, and the law governing the admissibility of confessions in federal courts. But like most good judges, he knew little about the psychology, pressure, tactics, and human dynamics that often dictate what happens in custodial interrogation settings. Guilty people often avoid admissions of guilt and innocent people often confess to guilt. The unique human dynamics that control the setting and communication in custodial settings often dictate both ends of the confession spectrum.

Over a 20-minute period, Leo responded to Kimerer's direct examination. Together they painted a word picture of Leo's expertise for Judge Broomfield. Leo explained his day job—professor of law at the University of San Francisco. And he covered some of his related activities—professor of criminology and psychology and sociology at the University of California Irvine, and the University of Colorado Boulder. He had spent most of his professional life studying the broad area of interrogation and interrogation practices. That had been his research focus for 20 years, having studied, researched, and written about the science, practice, and misuse of custodial interrogation since the 1990s.

Kimerer spent a bit of time establishing Leo's bona fides in the field by walking him through his curriculum vitae for the benefit of the court. Leo earned undergraduate and graduate degrees in psychology, sociology, law, and criminology. He held both J.D. and Ph.D. degrees from prestigious universities. When asked what criminology was, he answered, "Well, it's in a specialized inter-disciplinary law and social science program that goes by the name of jurisprudence and social policy. But it allows you to study legal institutions from a specialized training in a particular social science or social sciences. And in my case I specialized in criminology and social psychology and sociology as they apply to the study of law in legal institutions."

Kimerer asked about the process of earning a Ph.D. in this field. Dr. Leo explained, "When you get a Ph.D. you have to take classes and exams and you get specialized in general fields so that you're competent to teach and understand the principles and methods in those fields. And in my case, those would be the fields of criminology, social psychology, sociology and law. But very few people who go on to be researchers, whether at universities or not, are generalists. And so you carve out a specialized niche in terms of your research specialization. So what I just described is my academic specialization but my research specialization, the topics on which I've done my research have been police interrogation and investigation, the psychology and practices, Miranda requirements and how Miranda plays out in practice, false confessions and wrongful convictions. Those are the areas that I've focused my research on."

Leo told Judge Broomfield he had been an expert witness in 186 cases. He'd written numerous books on the subject, as well as 23 academic articles documenting his research in custodial interrogation by police officers of suspects. He had given lectures and presented programs all over America; he trained police officers; his entire academic life had been spent on the issues before the court in the Milke case. His most recent book, *Police Interrogation and American Justice*, was published by the Harvard University Press and was widely accepted as the leading text in the country. After carefully establishing his credentials for the record, Kimerer shifted to Milke's case. Leo explained that he had been studying her case since 2002. A Phoenix lawyer, Anders Rosenquist, initially engaged him as a consultant and expert witness for the federal court habeas process.

He read the entire trial and appellate record, then wrote a report for Mr. Rosenquist, which Judge Broomfield admitted in evidence as Exhibit 5. The first five pages is a documented list of the trial and appellate record. Kimerer asked Leo to confirm for the court that the record he reviewed included the sworn testimony of both Saldate and Milke at the pretrial hearings, the trial, and all of the interrogation reports.

"Correct. Everything that was memorialized, yes."

"Now late last year, were you again asked to review the Milke case?"

"Yes."

"And who asked you to do that?"

"Lori Voepel."

"And did you go back and review your old report, along with new material?"

"Yes."

"I now ask you to look at Exhibit number 6; what is this?"

"This is an addendum to the 2002 report dated January 6, 2009 with additional analysis and opinions."

"Were you asked by Ms. Voepel . . . to focus more on the issue of waiver in this case? And is waiver a concept or something that is studied in your area of expertise?"

Leo told the judge that waiver of Miranda rights was within his area of expertise, and for the next quarter-hour explained, from his academic perspective, how waiver plays into his evaluation of the Milke interrogation.

"Well, prior to any custodial interrogation beginning, of course, there has to be not only the reading of the Miranda rights . . . but also a knowing and voluntary waiver [of those rights]. And so what I'm interested in [in] my research is police practices. How they structure interrogations, what they do . . . how they give Miranda warnings, and how they elicit waivers. A waiver, either implicit or explicit, would be required for a custodial interrogation barring a public safety exception situation to go forward. And so police receive training on eliciting and documenting waivers so that their statements, if they elicit statements, won't be suppressed on Miranda violation grounds. Broadly that fits into research on interrogation and confession because that's a very substantial part of the process from a legal perspective and from a kind of organizational rules and compliance perspective."

"And in your area of expertise on interrogations and waiver, do you look into the reliability of waivers and the reliability of interrogations as they're done?"

"Yeah, . . . reliability is often used to refer to the confessions if you get confessions and whether they're reliable. The reliability, so to speak, of waivers and interrogations would really have to do I think with documentation showing what occurred during the interrogation and documentation showing that there was a proper reading of the rights and a proper waiver elicited."

Leo said he had reviewed the Ninth Circuit opinions mandating this hearing. That review necessitated modifications to his initial opinion that he'd given to Mr. Rosenquist. Leo explained how the focus of his prior report differed from the focus of this report. It was broader because he had "much more material to review." He corrected three parts of the first report. The first was the "manner in which Detective Saldate claimed that he elicited Ms. Milke's waiver." He found that "troubling, if not illegal." Next, he corrected his first report because Saldate never said explicitly that Milke had waived her Miranda rights. Saldate implied that Milke had waived her rights but never said that explicitly. Milke's position at trial was that Saldate had bullied her into waiving her rights. But Leo found that troubling because there was no evidence she had waived them. There was no need to determine whether Saldate bullied her into something that the state had not proved. That pivotal point was Leo's second change to his first report. Third, Leo corrected his original report regarding Saldate's claim that he asked Milke for permission to record the interrogation. The issue really was, Leo said, Milke's interpretation of the question about tape recording her interrogation. He believes, based on her testimony, that when she answered Saldate's question about tape recording, she said no, meaning that she wanted an attorney, not "no," she didn't want a recording.

Leo's explanation of the difference between implicit and explicit waivers was entirely consistent with Ninth Circuit case law:

"Typically, an explicit waiver involves reading a suspect the fourfold Miranda rights, usually from a card. And then at the end of those fourfold rights saying, 'Do you understand these rights?' And then, the person says 'Yes.' 'Having these rights in mind, do you wish to speak to me, or do you wish to waive these rights and speak to me?' And then the suspect would say 'Yes,' so they've explicitly waived through those two questions the four Miranda rights that they were read. That would be an explicit waiver. An implicit waiver is when the interrogator reads the fourfold rights, or if they're going by memory, tells the suspect the fourfold rights and either continues interrogating after that, or asks them, 'Do you understand these rights?' The person says 'yes,' but doesn't ask them having these rights in mind, do you wish to speak to me. But the interrogator presumably infers from context that the person is actually waiving their rights without asking the second of the two follow-up questions, having these rights in mind, do you wish to talk to me."

"And based upon your review of the facts in this case and your knowledge about police practices, did you see in this case whether there was an explicit waiver?"

"No, there's no explicit waiver in this case, no."

"And why is that?"

"Because Detective Saldate doesn't say that he asked a second question, 'Having these rights in mind, do you wish to speak to me.' He never says he got an explicit waiver. Even if he had said that, there's no record of it, of course. So what he's saying is that he . . . or what he's implying is that what he took was an implicit waiver."

Kimerer pressed the point by asking whether Saldate secured an "implicit waiver."

"Well, one could infer that. I'm not sure he ever used the word 'implicit' waiver in the documents I reviewed. But if there was a waiver in Saldate's account, it would have to be an implicit, not an explicit waiver. Assuming there even was a waiver."

From that inference, Kimerer inserted a new equation into the analysis. Detective Saldate said in his deposition it wasn't his practice at the time to expressly ask for a written or oral Miranda waiver. From that premise, Kimerer asked, "Was that generally the practice of police interrogators based upon all your review and research at that time?"

"No, the general practice of police is to get documented waivers, whether they're implicit or explicit. As I mentioned in this report, the 1979 Supreme Court case of North Carolina v. Butler opened the door to implicit waivers. Prior to that, the standard practice was to get explicit waivers. After that, either explicit or implicit waivers, both oral and documented through some sort of recording became more common. I think this is still the primary way today—get written form acknowledging the reading of the rights at the very least."

"Why is it important to secure a written acknowledgment of waiver of one's rights?"

"In my opinion, it's a huge problem in this case. I think it's extraordinary . . . because usually the police are very good about memorializing, creating a written record that they read those rights and at the very least have a suspect initial that they were read those rights, or sign and/or signed at the bottom. So the absence of a record, the failure to memorialize, means we get a swearing contest where one side says one thing, the other side says another. There's no objective record to adjudicate what really occurred. There's the burden. The reason this is important in police work and the reason I think it is rare to find the absence of any memorialization is because police are trained in the law of Miranda and police know they have to do things to maximize the likelihood that the confession will be admitted and not suppressed. The burden is on the State to demonstrate knowing and voluntary waiver." Kimerer asked whether that was the standard when Saldate claimed Milke waived her rights and confessed to him.

"Correct. The standard has always been to memorialize waivers."

The direct examination of Professor Leo went on for several hours. Kimerer gave Judge Broomfield a comprehensive understanding of the substantive opinions Leo had drawn from the materials he read, all of which were marked as exhibits at the hearing. Leo had a great deal to say based on Saldate's own reports and testimony over the 20 years that had elapsed between the date he said he took Milke's confession (December 3, 1989) and the most recent date he gave testimony about that confession (January 10, 2013).

On "recording interrogations," Leo said, "Detective Saldate's actions in the Debra Milke interrogation were not isolated. They are clearly part of a pattern and practice. In his testimony, Detective Saldate indicated that he does not record interrogations. Detective Saldate also indicated that although he knows he is supposed to stop interrogating a suspect who invokes his or her Miranda rights, he will continue having a conversation with the suspect and include in his report any statements made by the suspect after invocation, even if they can't be used in court except as impeachment. He also claims he always notes when a person asserts his or her rights. Of course, in the absence of a record of what occurred during a disputed interrogation, it is difficult to verify whether what Detective Saldate is saying is truthful. However, a close look at 18 of Detective Saldate's other cases reveals that what Detective Saldate claims is not always true. In those cases, sometimes Detective Saldate noted that the suspect waived his or her Miranda rights and Detective Saldate acknowledges that when a suspect invokes their Miranda rights he does not stop talking to them and thus does not adhere to *Edwards'* clear rule that police must scrupulously honor any invocation of the Miranda right to counsel by immediately ceasing all interrogation. And again, Detective Saldate appears to be in violation of Phoenix Police Department procedures in these cases—both for failing to document everything, as the procedures require, as well as for failing to consult a legal advisor before speaking to a suspect who has invoked his or her Miranda rights, as the Phoenix Police Department's procedures also require."

Regarding "how" Saldate interviewed Milke, he said, "It is clear from Detective Saldate's behavior and statements prior to and during the interrogation of Ms. Milke that he rushed to judgment and presumed her guilt from the start. Police interrogators in America are trained that they should only interrogate suspects whose guilt they are certain of. The goal of the (guilt presumptive) interrogation is not necessarily to get the truth, but to elicit incriminating statements from the suspect. Because Detective Saldate presumed Ms. Milke's guilt, he appears to have experienced what cognitive psychologists have called 'confirmation bias'—the tendency to select only information from one's environment that confirms our pre-existing beliefs and discount, or ignore evidence [that] is at odds with our pre-existing beliefs. That explains how Saldate interpreted Ms. Milke's behaviors in response to his interrogation questions and statements."

Leo pointed to an example of Saldate's confirmation bias. "He asserted that Ms. Milke's ambiguous body language and how she experienced the news of her son's death somehow constituted evidence of her guilt. Even if he accurately described her body language, it does not support his inferences about her guilt. It may also be possible that because of his confirmation bias going into the interrogation that Detective Saldate mistakenly interpreted Ms. Milke's response to his reading of her Miranda rights as a waiver of those rights even if she did not, in fact, waive those rights. In light of Detective Saldate's pattern and practice of interrogation misconduct in other cases, his extraordinary failure to memorialize any aspect of his interrogation of Ms. Milke, or her alleged confession, and his many implausible assertions about what occurred during her interrogation, I think it is more likely that he knowingly failed to elicit a waiver from Ms. Milke."

Kimerer asked Leo to give Judge Broomfield an assessment of whether there was evidence of confirmation bias in this record. Leo said, "Well, in my opinion, there is evidence of confirmation bias. There are things that Detective Saldate says in his report . . . I don't think there's anything in the record that contradicts this, is that he went into that interrogation believing that Debra Milke was guilty and his goal was to get a confession and not looking for exculpatory evidence. He was not even heavily evaluating the hypothesis of innocence, hypothesis of guilt, where will the evidence take me. It was a theory-driven interrogation. He says things in his police report that bear this out and I think he was looking for things that would confirm his own bias, his presumption of guilt at that moment of interrogation . . . interrogations are guilt presumptive and their goal typically is to get a confession. The idea being that prior to the interrogation, you've done a thorough investigation and that investigation is where there's no room for confirmation bias."

Kimerer asked about the difference between interviewing and interrogating.

"If Detective Saldate were to say this is an interview, I'd say no, this is an interrogation. And confirmation bias is always a problem because if you are wrong, you've made a judgment that the person is guilty and you're only concerned with evidence that supports your theory in building a case against them, and if the person's innocent, you're going to ignore the evidence of innocence."

"In this case, as you are aware, the only information that Detective Saldate had when he went to talk to Debra Milke was a statement by Roger Scott while driving to the scene of the crime that Debra Milke was implicated without any details or a great deal of facts."

"Correct."

"When a detective conducts a normal interrogation where he has substantial belief that the person is guilty, generally the best practice is to have evidence of that, pretty strong evidence of that, right?"

"Yeah, something substantial. The idea is that the leading training manual says thoroughly investigate before you interrogate. This is one of their mantras. The idea being that you don't go into a fishing expedition. You don't go on gut hunches. You really want to have a solid, you know, done your homework prior to doing the interrogation where you're going to try to get a confession."

"Now are there areas in some of the other interviews that Detective Saldate did with witnesses in the case that would demonstrate this particular type of confirmation bias?"

"When I did the original review, I reviewed . . . hundreds of thousands of pages. I didn't review all the documents for that this time but my recollection is that there were people in this investigation whom Saldate interviewed, some of whom were on tape for part or all of their interview, unlike his interrogation of Ms. Milke, where he summarized in reports things that they said that they disputed or he mischaracterized and always in ways that were most unfavorable to Ms. Milke. Always in ways that cast her in the most possible negative light, made her look as bad as possible, described the worst possible motives to her. That would be an illustration of confirmation bias."

Leo closed his direct examination in language rarely used in court by experts. He said, "This is strikingly bad interrogation practice . . . this is extraordinary in the context of a capital case, where you have all these other things, that weren't memorialized, the alleged disputed confession, the interrogation, I think this is shocking. Shockingly bad police practice."

"Would it have actually been to the benefit of the State to have memorialized what happened in that *one on one* interrogation setting?"

"What strikes social scientists, who study interrogation, is that if police do Miranda right, even when there are allegations of impropriety during the interrogation, the confession is almost always admitted [in evidence] . . . The most important thing is whether the Miranda procedures were properly followed . . . it's easy to document—that makes it in the State's interest."

Kimerer closed with dramatic flair. "So, based on your review of everything in this particular case, is it your conclusion that this was not a 'reliable' interrogation?"

"Well, yeah, there's no objective record of the interrogation. And, so if you want 'reliable' interrogation, then yes, there's no way of knowing exactly what occurred."

"And there's no evidence . . . based upon the record in this case of any type of waiver?"

"Correct. There's no evidence of a waiver . . . implicit or explicit."

"I have no other questions. Thank you."

⁓

Ms. JULIE DONE INFORMED THE court her cross-examination would "take at least an hour." The court ordered a lunch break. When court reconvened in the afternoon, Julie Done took the podium. "Good afternoon. Do you prefer Professor Leo or Dr. Leo?"

"Whatever you prefer is fine."

"All right, my name is Julie Done. Do you recall that we spoke last week?"

Ms. Done and the head of the Attorney General's appellate division, Kent Cattani, had conducted a telephonic recorded interview with Dr. Leo on January 9, 2010, as part of the court's established pre-hearing discovery practice. She had the 67-page transcript of that interview with her. It was obvious from her open-court questions she had carefully prepared for this cross-examination. Contrary to movies about lawyers, cross-examination is not part of the information-gathering process. She already had "information"; what she wanted now was agreement with her view of the case. This was the time to discredit the witness and minimize the impact of his direct examination by Mr. Kimerer.

She elicited admissions from Dr. Leo designed to minimize his credentials by establishing that he had "never practiced law . . . never taken a bar examination . . . was never certified as a law enforcement officer . . . had not practiced as a clinical psychologist . . . was not a psychiatrist . . . but had testified as an expert in court 186 or 187 times, but only twice for the state." She wasted a little time going over those two occasions—once at a trial in San Diego, California, and the other in a suppression hearing. Dr. Leo explained that the "Tuey" case involved three false confessions in a murder case and that the prosecution wanted him to "educate the judge about the psychology of confessions and why people make false and involuntary confessions" to police officers. He said the case did not involve testimony about Mr. Tuey.

Ms. Done spent some of her time covering neutral ground about the circumstances surrounding waiver of Miranda rights. The Q & A involved explicit and implicit waivers, as a general proposition, and to a lesser extent, situations in which some suspects claim a lack of understanding about Miranda rights. She asked him a few questions about the two reports he had written in the Milke case. When asked whether this case was essentially different from the other cases he had worked on, Leo said this was a "post-conviction case, and that most of his cases were pre-conviction cases." The difference, he said, was in the "volume of documents available in post-conviction cases." He admitted not interviewing Milke or Saldate, explaining that the only reason to interview a suspect or a police interrogator officer would be to "reconstruct" the record, but because this is a post-conviction case, he had the transcripts of their testimony about "what occurred during the interrogation." He noted that their "contemporaneous accounts of what occurred many years ago, . . . given the decay of memory, should be more accurate than what they would say today."

Done allowed Leo to expound on the methodology of gathering data in social science. Following his general explanation, she confirmed that he had not been present at the December 3, 1989 "interview" of Milke by Saldate. He admitted he could not "certify what was said in the interview." And he could not "certify" whether Milke "invoked her right to an attorney or stated that she did not want the interview recorded." But he could, he said, "analyze both accounts and make inferences or give personal opinions" about both issues. He clarified that he could not "testify about the factual record of any unrecorded interrogation." That answer became a pattern in the cross-examination—Ms. Done would call what happened an "interview" and Leo consistently called it an "interrogation." Leo often referred to the interaction as a "swearing contest." He explained that because the interrogation was not recorded, "you have a situation where you are going to get this swearing contest, this competition of credibility, where literally the trier of fact has to choose who's telling the truth—who do they *think* is telling the truth, not *adjudicate* a record that will tell them."

When asked whether something was going on "in the situation" that would have affected Ms. Milke's capability to understand her rights, Leo said, "Her account is that, you know, she's told her son is dead. And she's been accused of being the person who murdered her son. And she's immediately placed under arrest. I can imagine someone easily being in such a state of shock and so overwhelmed that even if they had the intellectual capacity to understand or comprehend, in that moment, they were so overwhelmed with shock or confusion or disorientation that they didn't fully understand the words that were being read to them."

His point was even more striking because it came in during cross-examination. "When you have a swearing contest, then all observers have to make inferences about what occurred. And these become credibility contests, that's typically why they're called swearing contests, before a jury. Obviously, an expert who's trying to evaluate the [different] accounts will have more information on which to make that judgment. Not just who *appears* to be telling the truth, but knowledge of police practices, training, things that happen that make one account seem more likely, or fit with existing research and therefore be more plausible than the other."

Done tried a more oblique approach to Leo's abstract concept of credibility. He told her the connotation of credibility includes subtleties such as body language, ability to speak, education, analyzing the "fit and logic" of what both parties are saying, "in relation to what we know about how the world works." He said most judges were good at determining credibility but that "anybody who knows more about how interrogation works would be in a better position to judge how the accounts match what we know from police training and the social science research on police."

In their earlier telephone interview, Done had engaged Leo in an exchange about something Saldate had said in his testimony—he had talked about his interview style, which was to "talk about ten percent at the beginning, then listen eighty percent of the time, and then talk again about ten percent of the time." She asked Dr. Leo whether that was a "plausible interview style."

"Well, it's a plausible *interview* style. It's not a plausible *interrogation* style. There's a difference between the two. Interviewing you're supposed to do most of the listening. And interviewing is supposed to be open-ended. You are not supposed to do that in interrogation, which is accuse, cut denials, confront somebody with facts that you believe establish[] their guilt, and get them to start denying and then start admitting."

"And after your review of the police report in this case and all the information that you have reviewed, would you call the interview between Detective Saldate and Ms. Milke an interview or an interrogation?"

"I would call it an interrogation for a number of reasons. He places her under arrest. He reads her the Miranda rights. He is the police. If you don't have to give Miranda, you don't because there is no need to and it gets in the way of police objectives . . . And he used interrogation techniques . . . to me it is very clear that this was an interrogation as police use the term in their training materials and in their culture."

Done changed gears, now challenging Leo. "Do you believe it is possible for *any* suspect to fully understand their Miranda rights?"

"The issue of understanding . . . there is comprehension, the ability to comprehend, and then there's understanding in the moment. Clinical psychology is better at telling us whether you have the intellectual capacity to comprehend, but not whether you understood in the moment . . . I do think it's possible to understand your Miranda rights because it's really understanding three things. One, what you say can be used against you in a court of law—which is a form of notice. Two, that you can stop the interrogation, terminate it at *any* time. Three, that you get counsel, and you get counsel *now* if you want. So, anybody who understood those three things in the way I've just said them, would *understand* their Miranda rights."

Pausing, Leo added, "[N]either an innocent nor guilty party is likely to appreciate the full significance of the Miranda warnings."

Ms. Done apparently agreed. "[N]o one can ever fully appreciate them."

Leo took her admission one step further. He explained that the research studies on whether suspects *understand* Miranda warnings "perplexes law professors and social scientists because most people waive their rights." From that premise, he explained how interrogation is actually a process, not just an event. "At the point where police officers give suspects their Miranda rights, they are in rapport with the suspect. They build rapport slowly. The interrogation seems non-threatening at this point. Non-accusatorial. But when things heat up, people tend not to remember, or fully appreciate what they've been told earlier, about quitting at any time, and the right to remain silent. People never think, even if they understood their Miranda rights in the beginning, in the moment, that they could invoke those rights later. They do not think they can stop it."

Leo admitted there was nothing in the Phoenix Police Department's procedures that required Saldate to get Milke to sign a Miranda rights card. But Leo offered the notion that their procedures included general statements about documenting things that are "relevant to constitutional rights and legal disputes about constitutional rights."

Ms. Done spent the bulk of her cross-examination time on Miranda rights and waiver issues. That was because in his report, Dr. Leo said, "The manner in which Detective Saldate states he elicited Ms. Milke's Miranda waiver is troubling, if not illegal." In response to her questions, he explained, "I mean it's illegal in the sense that it's a violation of the Constitution when someone says, 'I want an attorney' to steamroll over them and do the interrogation."

Ms. Done changed tack. "In fact, your reports are based solely on the notion that Ms. Milke's testimony is accurate and Detective Saldate's is not. Correct?"

"No, that doesn't fully capture what my reports are based on. I analyzed all the materials. All of the detective's accounts and what I know about police interrogation practices, the research, all of it. It just does not wash in so many ways. It strains credulity . . . I don't know if Ms. Milke's account of what happened is the true account and not Detective Saldate's. Take a step back from all of this. Social scientists would say you could never get a fully true account when there's no [written or recorded] account because people have incomplete memories. What I'm saying is that Detective Saldate's account is highly implausible, contradicts known research, sometimes does not make sense, is self-serving in many ways, and sometimes is just plainly absurd . . . I'm not saying what she said is true, because I don't know. I'm only analyzing these two accounts."

Ms. Done closed her cross-examination with this question:

"Dr. Leo, are you aware of any case law that says an unrecorded confession is not admissible simply because the defendant disputes what the detective said?"

"There are certain states now that require recording, absent exigent circumstances . . . there the confession would not be admissible . . . There are 13 states that require recording either by statute or by state supreme court decision . . . Arizona does not require recording."

      ~

MIKE KIMERER RETURNED TO THE podium for a few re-direct examination questions. He covered a specific Phoenix Police Department procedure in effect in 1989 that required all officers to "document everything said by a suspect."

Leo agreed. "The whole situation was controlled by Detective Saldate from the minute he walked into that room." And, he walked in there "with the concept in his mind that she was guilty because he placed her under arrest." He told her he would "not let her minimize her involvement."

Dr. Leo agreed that it would be a very rare case in which there was no independent memorialization of a Miranda waiver. There was no *independent* memorialization in the Milke case.

Kimerer hammered the memorialization point. "So there's absolutely nothing as far as memorialization goes in this case?"

"Correct. It all boils down to Saldate's word."

The record before Judge Broomfield included copies of two very lengthy reports. Judge Broomfield, a focused, smart judge who was attentive to details, had read them. The first, dated April 19, 2002, was also focused, detail-rich, and voluminous. It identifies 54 police reports; Saldate's interviews on May 30 and June 26, 1990; all of the trial transcript; all of the grand jury transcripts and indictments, given on May 30, 1990; the affidavits of all of the prosecution's trial witnesses; all of Roger Scott's statements to police; and all of the testimony and statements by James Styers. It also included Saldate's 1973 suspension from the Phoenix PD and many Phoenix Police Department procedures regarding arrest and interrogation of suspects. His report documents his experience in the field at three levels: First, extensive research and analysis of over 800 cases involving police interrogations and suspect confessions. Second, consultation on over 300 cases involving disputed interrogations and confessions. Third, testimony before state, federal, and military courts on 66 separate matters. With that foundation, Kimerer asked, "Have you ever seen in any of the cases you've looked at, studied, analyzed, researched, that had all of the circumstances there are in this case *and* someone found there was a waiver?"

Leo paused, apparently gathering his thoughts before answering that pivotal question. "No, I have never seen a case like this . . . What makes this case extraordinary is that it's not just a dispute about the waiver and the invocation, it's also a dispute about whether there *even was* a confession. I've never seen a case where the stakes are so high, there were so many levels of dispute, and the record was so poorly established that everything turned on one person's word."

38

DEBRA MILKE'S LAST STAND: UNITED STATES DISTRICT COURT FOR THE DISTRICT OF ARIZONA— JANUARY 29, 2010

*D*EBRA MILKE FINALLY HAD WHAT she wanted most—an evidentiary hearing in federal court. The Ninth Circuit had carefully instructed Judge Broomfield to conduct "a limited evidentiary hearing on the *sole* issue of whether Milke *validly waived* her Miranda rights." Judge Broomfield, one of the most highly respected federal judges in Arizona, did exactly as instructed; he limited her evidentiary hearing as narrowly as he could. He did not revisit the underlying issue of whether Milke was entitled to habeas relief. At the conclusion of the evidentiary hearing, Judge Broomfield made five narrow *factual* findings:

1. Saldate advised Petitioner of her *Miranda* rights and asked her if she understood them. In doing so, Saldate followed Phoenix police procedures. He read, verbatim, the *Miranda* advisory, which listed four rights and one follow-up question. He documented Petitioner's statements in his contemporaneous, handwritten notes and then in his supplemental report.

2. Petitioner acknowledged that she understood her rights, first by nodding affirmatively and then, when asked to supply a verbal answer, by stating yes. There was no evidence that Petitioner was incapable of comprehending her rights, and only her self-serving testimony suggested that she did not understand them when they were recited by Saldate. Petitioner was 25 years old at the time of the interrogation. She was employed at an insurance agency. In high school, she achieved a 3.9 GPA. She had had prior encounters with the police and the court system.

3. Petitioner did not invoke her right to counsel or her right to remain silent. There is no contention that she invoked her right to remain silent. As described below, the Court's determination that Petitioner did not invoke her right to an attorney is based on the Court's assessment of the relative credibility of Petitioner and Saldate and their versions of the interrogation.

4. The circumstances of the subsequent interrogation support a finding that Petitioner waived her *Miranda* rights. Petitioner chose not to have the interrogation recorded. She exhibited no unwillingness to answer questions or provide information. She did not remain silent or ask to terminate the interview. Instead, Petitioner spoke freely about a range of topics, seeking to explain and justify her actions. According to her own testimony, which was consistent with Saldate's, Petitioner dominated the conversation with her attempts to explain and defend herself.

5. Petitioner's testimony at the evidentiary hearing before this Court was inconsistent and self-serving. She stated that Saldate 'badgered' her and was 'in her face' throughout the 30-minute interrogation. However, she acknowledged that she did most

of the talking during the interrogation, providing Saldate with a variety of information and confiding details about her personal life and background. During the period when Saldate was allegedly badgering Petitioner and in her face, he was listening to her story and taking notes."

Understanding these factual findings requires an awareness of the calculus underlying factual findings in a federal court—the *standard of review*. Legal standards of review vary widely. Essentially, the standard of review defines how deferential a higher court must be in reviewing what a lower court did. Sometimes, a low standard of review is appropriate. If so, a lower court decision or finding could be overturned if there was mere error, a mistake, or a disagreement. In other cases, a high standard of review is called for. If so, deference is given to the decision under review; the decision will stand even if the reviewing court might have decided differently; that is sometimes called an "obvious error" standard. To complicate matters, a standard of review may be set by someone other than the reviewing judge. That happens when a statute, rule, or precedent defines a particular standard of review. The most well-known review standard is the one controlling the level of deference the judiciary gives to Congress when ruling on the constitutionality of legislation.

Judge Broomfield recognized the complexity surrounding which standard applied in the unique situation created by the Ninth Circuit's order. "Given the posture of the case and the directive from the Court of Appeals, it appears that this court is being instructed to make its findings based on an independent review of the evidence, without regard to the state court's rulings. In doing so, the court must assess the witnesses' relative credibility and the plausibility of their conflicting accounts."

From that perspective, Judge Broomfield did exactly what the Ninth Circuit told him to do. After assessing and evaluating the testimonial evidence at the hearing, he rejected Milke's "contention that as a matter of law Respondents cannot prove under the preponderance of the evidence standard, the existence of a valid Miranda waiver based on the conflicting testimony of Saldate and Petitioner."

To arrive at this position, Judge Broomfield noted there was no *express* waiver, written or oral. He reviewed the evidence to determine whether a valid *implied* waiver could found. Each of his five findings accepted the state's version of the interrogation and the state's legal position that a suspect can *impliedly* waive her Miranda rights.

In his first finding, Judge Broomfield accepted Saldate's word that he had advised Milke of her rights. In the second finding, he noted Milke had acknowledged that she understood her rights, and there was no evidence suggesting she was incapable of understanding them "when recited by Saldate." The third finding accepts, as a given, that Milke did not invoke her right to remain silent. The fourth finding accepts the state's argument that Milke "choose not to have the interrogation recorded." And the fifth finding goes to the heart of every testimonial conflict—Judge Broomfield simply did not believe Debra Milke. He thought her "inconsistent and self-serving." She claimed Saldate "badgered" her and was "in her face," she but acknowledged that "she did most of the talking." Judge Broomfield said, "During the period when Saldate was allegedly badgering Petitioner and in her face, he was listening to her story and taking notes."

Milke's lack of credibility with Judge Broomfield contrasted with his easy acceptance of Saldate's version. "By contrast, the credibility of Saldate's testimony is supported by several factors. As already noted, there are many similarities in the two accounts. The key differences pertain to the details of the interrogation which are incriminating or detrimental to Petitioner's claim of a Miranda violation. In addition, the details Saldate provided with respect to the content of the interrogation lends credibility to his testimony that Petitioner did not request an attorney."

But Judge Broomfield did not just believe Saldate's version, he found truth in something *no* previous judge had noted. "Saldate did not report that Petitioner gave a straight-forward confession of guilt as to her role in her son's murder, as he could have done if he was fabricating his account of the interrogation. Instead, he reported that Petitioner offered a series of justifications for her conduct and attempted to portray herself in a positive light. It is simply not plausible that Saldate concocted this information, particularly since much of it was corroborated by Petitioner's version of the interrogation. The credibility of this aspect of Saldate's account supports a conclusion that he also accurately reported Petitioner's failure to request an attorney."

Judge Broomfield's written order gave no credence to Saldate's long history of confession misconduct. It studiously avoided any discussion or consideration of the state's failure to provide *Brady* or *Giglio* impeachment evidence. The written order gave scant reference to the testimony given in his courtroom. It rejected Milke's version, accepted Saldate's version, and concluded there was an "implied waiver of Miranda rights." In pop culture language, Judge Broomfield kicked the judicial can back up to the Ninth Circuit.

39

ROUND TWO: ORAL ARGUMENTS BEFORE THE NINTH CIRCUIT— NOVEMBER 10, 2010

THE JAMES R. BROWNING U.S. Court of Appeals at 95 Seventh Street in San Francisco is majestic. Its architectural beauty almost pales in the light of the terror it instills in lawyers who arrive, notebook in hand, to present an oral argument before this court sitting at the second highest level of American appeals courts. Built as a U.S. courthouse and post office at the turn of the twentieth century, it was intended to reflect the affluence and increasing importance of the United States as a world power. The architect, James Knox Taylor, selected a design influenced by Italian Renaissance architecture with magnificent Beaux Arts grandeur. In the twenty-first century, it is a showcase for magnificent arguments by skilled appellate lawyers to some of America's most intellectually gifted appellate judges.

To get to the courtroom, lawyers walk through lobbies and hallways ornamented with enclosed pediments, balustrades, and rows of arched windows. The beautiful bronze entry lanterns are replicas of torch-holders in Florence, Italy. The third floor houses one of the most ornate courtrooms in America. Originally called the Great Hall, it presents an overpowering image of the pinnacle of our justice system: white marble walls, Doric columns, and a vaulted ceiling beautifully ribbed with gold-trimmed plaster ornamentation. Details include the labyrinth-patterned ceiling, cork walls, and gilded plaster eagles.

Lori Voepel had argued against Assistant Attorney General Kent Cattani in what is now known as Round One in the Milke Ninth Circuit arguments. This time, Round Two, Assistant Attorney General Julie Done was appearing for the new director of the Arizona Department of Corrections. Her primary assignment was to represent the state's prison wardens in federal habeas cases. She was well versed in habeas law and process, with a keen awareness of how the ancient Latin writ applied to her client. In English, *habeas corpus* means, "you may have the body." Her client, Charles L. Ryan, was the individual under Arizona law responsible for its prison population. Debra Milke was one of its most highly guarded inmates—one of two women on death row in 2010. Milke's writ of *habeas corpus*, issued by the federal district court in Phoenix, commanded, in a figurative sense, Ryan to produce Milke before the court. In theory, his job as warden was limited to housing prisoners lawfully detained. *Habeas corpus* ensures that a prisoner will be released from unlawful detention—that is, detention lacking sufficient cause or evidence. Milke's lawyers argued that her detention was unlawful for several reasons, including the state's failure to produce exculpatory evidence regarding Saldate's disciplinary history and his failure to comply with the Miranda doctrine. While habeas relief originated in the English legal system, its role in the American criminal justice system is the most important legal instrument safeguarding individual freedom against arbitrary state action. The legal premise is simple—does Director Ryan have the requisite authority to keep Milke in custody given her claims of a *Brady* violation and a Miranda violation? Today, the Ninth Circuit would question both lawyers on the second prong—failing to comply with Miranda.

After the *Oyez, Oyez* call to order, and after Judges Kozinski, Farris, and Bea took their seats on the bench, Milke's counsel addressed the court.

"Good morning, I'm Lori Voepel, counsel for Debra Milke, the petitioner in this case. With me seated at the counsel table is my co-counsel Michael Kimerer. As we stated in the supplemental briefing following the evidentiary hearing held in this case, we believe the District Court Judge's waiver finding is clearly erroneous and an abuse of discretion for three reasons primarily. First of all that the State's evidence at the evidentiary hearing was materially no different from that which was presented in state court. And on the basis of the evidence presented in state court this court found that there was no evidence of waiver. Second, the District Court failed to apply the appropriate law regarding waiver and did not consider critical facts including critical impeachment evidence that was presented regarding the detective in this case. And third, the other cases involving implied waiver in which there were findings of implied waiver cited by the District Court, and by the State, all had some form of either an objective record, corroboration through multiple officers, or undisputed facts as to what happened actually during the interrogation."

Judge Bea, apologizing for the interruption, posed the first question. "Would you excuse me please? Would you repeat your first point?"

"The first point is that . . . the evidence that was presented at the evidentiary hearing on remand [before Judge Broomfield] was [not] materially different [from that presented at the last oral argument] . . . In other words there was no smoking gun. . . ."

Judge Kozinski disagreed. "But we have more law. We have the Supreme Court's case in Berghuis versus Thompkins."

"Yes we do, Your Honor."

Judge Kozinski: "It was arguable last time we heard the case that you needed an explicit waiver. But *Berghuis* makes it quite clear and arguably is a pull-back from *Miranda*. Here you explicitly say certainly the sentencing is a pull-back from *Miranda*. And that's a very difficult case for you."

"Your Honor, I think it's clearly distinct. First of all, we disagree that an explicit waiver was required. We think it's pretty clear that under the *Butler* case that an implied waiver is acceptable, that you don't have to have an explicit waiver. However . . . *Thompkins* . . . dealt with assertions of the right to remain silent . . . the Supreme Court held that you can't just be silent in order to assert your right to remain silent. You have to affirmatively, unambiguously assert the right to remain silent. In other words, the Supreme Court applied the *Davis* standard that there must be an unequivocal assertion of the right to counsel to the context of the right to silence."

Judge Kozinski: "But that's the situation here because the District Court did not believe your client when she claims that she asserted her right to remain silent. In fact, we know she didn't. We know that she admitted that she talked. She did most of the talking . . . [the] interview lasted half an hour . . . There are two parts to *Thompkins*. It was their assertion of the right to remain silent. And what the Supreme Court said is you have to affirmatively assert the right in order to stop the interview altogether."

"That's correct."

"If you don't affirmatively assert it then the police can keep asking you questions."

"That's correct, your Honor."

Judges Kozinski and Farris asked Voepel several additional questions about Miranda waivers. They narrowed the issue to whether implicit waivers were acceptable under the *Thompkins* doctrine recently announced by the U.S. Supreme Court. Voepel recited the correct doctrine and moved to her second point.

"My second point is that the [District] Court, contrary to *Miranda*, contrary to this Court's decision and guidance in *Taylor*, treated this like an ordinary credibility contest. He did not view Saldate's testimony with suspicion, which is required when a police officer creates isolated conditions of interrogation that make it impossible for a suspect to show other than his or her own word [about] what happened in that room."

Judge Bea: "What's your citation for the increased suspicion with which the Judge [must evaluate] Saldate's testimony?"

"*Miranda*. On page 475, . . . the entire reason that the State has the burden of proof, the burden to . . . affirmatively show a waiver is that the State is responsible, the police are responsible for creating the isolated circumstances of interrogation and has the only means of making available corroborated evidence of warnings given, and whether a waiver or invocation occurred . . . In fact that's the entire premise of *Miranda* in all of the cases going forward from there. And then, this Court's position in *Taylor*, this Court was faced not with an identical situation, but a very similar situation in that although there were two officers for part of the time when he said that he requested a lawyer and/or his parent, he was alone in a room with one officer who claimed that he didn't invoke [his constitutional rights.] And this Court said that you must, you can't treat this as an ordinary credibility determination. You have a police officer who has created isolated circumstances and you can't view it just as some kind of ordinary credibility determination."

Judge Farris: "Do you think that the youthfulness of the accused had any bearing on the holding of the court?"

"I think it had some bearing, yes your Honor."

"We don't have that situation here though do we?"

"Yes. She was 25, that's true . . . We did show [on] the record that she hadn't had any sleep or very little sleep for two days and no food."

"But that wouldn't be inconsistent with a mother who arranged a murder of her child . . . Any mother who had done that would not have slept hopefully, would not have slept unless she had a mighty cold heart. So that doesn't, it doesn't give the implication that you would hope . . . does it?"

"Your Honor, I think that what I'm trying to say is that [in] this Court, even setting aside the fact [of] the youthfulness or the differences in the particular suspects in this case, *Taylor* makes clear that you cannot treat a one-on-one interrogation and swearing contest between a police officer and a suspect . . . of what happens in an interrogation room where there is no corroboration, there is no recording, there is nothing but the word of those two people. That's an uneven playing field. That is a situation where the police officer has the opportunity to make corroboration available. . . ."

Judge Kozinski: "Are you talking about Taylor v. Maddox?"

"Yes your Honor . . . I think it's in line with *Miranda*."

Judge Kozinski delivered a short lecture differentiating Taylor v. Maddox from Miranda v. Arizona. Then he moved to what he saw as the lower court's review of the evidence in the Milke case.

"Here, the District Judge takes additional testimony, and clearly finds the policeman more credible. And you jump around between the waiver of the right to counsel and the waiver of the right to Miranda warnings, but you have an explicit finding by the District Judge that your client didn't invoke the right to an attorney. So, you don't get any help from that. I don't see how we can reverse that finding."

"Your Honor, I think, and we set [that] forth in the briefs: The District Court's finding that police officer Saldate was more credible not only treated this . . . as an ordinary credibility determination, but he also ignored all of the impeachment evidence that we provided in the form of other cases . . . Numerous other cases—not only showing that Detective Saldate ignored Miranda warnings and acknowledged that he would continue interrogating, but also showing that he repeatedly misrepresented evidence to grand jurors under oath, he tainted line-ups, and he had this disciplinary history which we believe showed a part of a pattern where the police department specifically said that he lied, that he was dishonest until he failed a polygraph."

Judge Bea: "That evidence of other acts by officer Saldate comes in as habit testimony?"

"Yes, your Honor."

"And not as 404(a) character evidence?"

"That's correct, Your Honor. It's habit and it's impeachment evidence that shows a pattern by this detective . . . he disregarded Miranda rights . . . in fact it was his belief that he didn't even have to stop interrogating."

"Do we have any cases that say that policemen's conduct in other cases is habit testimony rather than 404(a) [character] testimony and not allowed?"

"Your Honor, if I can have a moment . . . we actually briefed that in the original briefs . . . the parties stipulated to admit that evidence at the evidentiary hearing. All of that was allowed, and there was no argument that [it] wasn't relevant. Because it all went directly to his credibility as an officer, and to the fact that he did not honor Miranda invocations. And he acknowledges that."

Judge Bea: "What was wrong with the Judge's disdain of that evidence?"

"He doesn't even mention the other cases in his order. There's no indication that he considers it. . . ."

"He heard it?"

"Yes, your Honor. He heard it. There were questions asked about it. The exhibits were highlighted at the hearing. And, it wasn't the first time the Judge had seen it. These were all excerpts of the record that had previously been presented. . . ."

Judge Kozinski: "Let's say we were to reverse and believe her when she said what she said. Was that the sufficient invocation of her right to counsel? I mean what he asked her is do you want a tape recorder. And she says, 'No, I need a lawyer.'"

Voepel tried to answer. "No, I want . . ."

Judge Kozinski interrupted. "Is that an invocation of her right to counsel even if we believe that that's what she said?"

"Yes, your Honor. I want a lawyer. Because he had just read her Miranda rights. And said, do you understand them."

Judge Kozinski: "I thought she said, no I need a lawyer."

Voepel: "No, I need a lawyer. I apologize."

Judge Kozinski: "Quite different to say I need a lawyer than to say I want a lawyer. Want a lawyer is a request for something."

"The cases are pretty clear . . . I don't think there's even been an argument that if she said that, that wouldn't be an unequivocal invocation. Saying I need a lawyer . . . I want a lawyer . . . I won't continue without a lawyer. Those are all considered unequivocal invocations."

Judge Kozinski: "Certainly, I won't continue without a lawyer would be. I want a lawyer is a little closer, but probably would be. Because that's a request. 'I need a lawyer' doesn't sound to me like a request. Really, when said in a response to do you want this tape recorded? The question is [whether] she's invoking her right to counsel."

"Yes, I think under the cases, stating, 'I need a lawyer' . . . that comes right after he reads her rights . . . he says do you understand your rights and do you want this tape recorded, she says, 'no, I need a lawyer.' There hasn't even been a question, at least raised in this case, that is not somehow equivocal."

Judge Kozinski: "She's doesn't separately invoke her right to silence. That's correct, but the invocation . . ."

"That's because the invocation of the right to counsel subsumes a request . . . that you want the interrogation to cease."

Judge Kozinski: "Right but there has been no invocation of the right to counsel . . . And but for this business about the lawyer, you really can't argue with District Court in saying that she waived her right to counsel by talking. I mean she talked a lot more than Thompkins. Thompkins answered a few questions, I mean, she yakked and yakked."

"That's true. She testified your, Honor, that when Saldate ignored her request stating that she needed a lawyer . . . he ignored her . . . she didn't understand that she could stop talking. She had never been arrested before. She had never been in trouble with the law before. She didn't fully understand . . . there was testimony . . . expert testimony that she didn't fully comprehend it. She heard . . ."

Judge Kozinski: "Well, but the District Court found that she was intelligent, that she spoke English, that she had had . . . some college education. . . ."

"No your Honor. She had no college."

Judge Kozinski: "Yeah, high school she did . . . She had a 3.9 average in high school. She was working for an insurance company . . . she understood the warnings, I mean. . . ."

Voepel: "There was testimony at the voluntariness hearing, that we reintroduced at the [district court] evidentiary hearing, that the only medical psychological opinion in this case came from Dr. Kassell, a jail psychiatrist who had evaluated Debra and who opined: it was uncontested, opined at the voluntariness hearing that Debra, while she might have heard certain words including 'attorney' and 'silence,' that she did not, because of her state of mind, first being hit with finding out that her son was dead and then being accused of his murder, especially in a situation where she hadn't had hardly any sleep, like two hours of sleep for three days, and virtually no food that she didn't fully understand."

Judge Kozinski: "He's not a mind reader. This is his opinion."

"That's correct. But that was uncontroverted, your Honor. There was no controverting evidence to that."

Judge Farris: "Don't you get into some problem though when you tell us what this, what that, and what the other, when we know that if this had been audiotaped these questions wouldn't be there? We'd just play the tape and we'd know. So, you get a catch-22 situation. You say, no I don't want a tape. But, I need a lawyer. So, then you continue to answer the questions, and it's pretty clear she went well beyond any questioning of her. She just talked to the officer. She wasn't coerced into giving certain answers to certain questions. She just talked. Isn't that what the record shows?"

"She did talk, but even Detective Saldate indicates that he was six to twelve inches from her face. He was continuing to say, whenever she would say anything that he did not feel comported with the truth, he'd say 'I will not tolerate your lies. I will tolerate only the truth.' He continued saying that throughout. And Debra testified that she felt badgered by him and that she felt that she had no choice but to continue talking and to try to defend herself and to come up with, try to find out, and respond to what she thought he wanted to hear. And, the *Shatzer* case makes it very clear that where there is an assertion of the right to counsel, the police officer can't do that."

Judge Kozinski: "She said she understood. I mean he asked her whether she understood her rights. She nodded and he says no I need a verbal answer from you. And she said yes."

"That's Detective Saldate's version. She disputes that, your Honor."

"Oh, I know but we have findings from District Court."

"That's correct, your Honor but we have a . . ."

"We can't sort of be redoing the evidentiary hearing here. The District Court found certain things . . . one of the things he found is that she said 'yes.' Did she dispute that? Did she dispute that she said yes?"

"Yes, your Honor. She said 'no, I've never been in trouble before and I don't understand my rights.' She disputes that."

"I asked you a different question. Did she dispute?"

"Excuse me?"

"That she said yes."

"That she understood?"

"Listen to what I'm saying."

"I am, your Honor, I apologize."

"Did she dispute that she answered yes to his question as to whether she understood . . . Where does she dispute that?"

"That is at the evidentiary hearing transcript page 141."

Judge Kozinski: "141?"

"Yes."

"Never mind, I have it right here. And what words are you reading? What line?"

"She's always contested that, your Honor."

"Well I'm asking you where?"

"I apologize . . . 142, your Honor . . . This is line seven . . . 'So when he finished reading your rights did he ask you anything? Answer: he said do you understand your rights, and I said no. I've never been in trouble before. I've never been arrested. I never had my rights read to me before. And did he repeat the rights? No. Redo them again? No. Or offer to say, or say do you want me to reread those rights to you again. No. Did [he] show you a rights card? No. Have you read it yourself? No. What happened next? Do you want this interview recorded and I looked at him and I said no, I need a lawyer.'"

Judge Kozinski: "Do you see this as a dispute of his statement that she said, 'yes I understand?'"

"Yes, your Honor. We believe she didn't fully comprehend or understand her rights and that she didn't waive them. That she invoked . . . it's both. I only have about a minute left. If I could save that for rebuttal? Your Honor."

Judge Kozinski: "Okay. Thank you. We'll hear from the Warden."

~

"GOOD MORNING, YOUR HONORS. JULIE Done representing Respondent Dora Schiro in this matter. I just wanted to start out by pointing out that yes we believe the *Thompkins* case, the recent *Thompkins* case, makes clear that a waiver of Miranda rights does not need to be express." The court was patient with Done and allowed her to lecture them about the case law for several minutes. Then, Judge Kozinski interrupted. "The District Court didn't spend much time on Detective Saldate's poor disciplinary record. It was a single mention that he'd been disciplined, but it really didn't have to do with . . . the District Court just said he'd been disciplined. But in fact, Saldate had a long record of sort of ignoring Miranda and the policy of sort—of pushing on asking questions in violation of Miranda. The District Court doesn't seem to have given that much weight."

"But they do talk about the *Running Eagle* case and . . ."

Judge Bea: "Who's they?"

"The District Court, I'm sorry. He talks about the *Running Eagle* case and the *King* case in his ruling. We did agree to admit that evidence at the District Court. We decided it would be fair for the District Court to have all the evidence that Ms. Milke has asserted all along that would have changed the decision . . . We stipulated to have all that evidence introduced. But the District Court weighed it and found that despite that, he found Saldate credible. One of the reasons was that we argued in our briefs . . . that even if Saldate did have a method or a practice of continuing the interrogation after someone had invoked their right to counsel, he also did have a practice or a habit of noting that in his report. And in both the *Running Eagle* and the *King* case, he noted that the defendants had asked for counsel. So our argument is if they're going to rely on that as habit of his misconduct going past when someone invokes their right to counsel, he also had the habit of noting that in his supplemental. . . ."

Judge Farris: "But then you have to if you say he had the habit, you'd have to show he did it invariably in every case, and in this record we can't see that. Can we?"

"No but what I'm arguing is its more gain . . ."

"So when you talk about habit, you're talking . . . two events. That's twice. I think the records shows twice when he said he noted. Isn't my recollection accurate?"

"Yes."

Judge Farris: "The one thing that the record shows, and nobody has hammered it, but the supervisor told the detective to audiotape this interview. Now he might have done it for any number of reasons . . . we aren't going to try to guess his motive. But one of the reasons might be because somebody can raise a question about who said what, and because of past history, you audiotape it and we'll know. He didn't bring equipment with him to audiotape it. Now, he says he could have borrowed it after he arrived. Let's say we have to accept that since nobody has refuted it. But if he had done what his supervisor told him he would have had the audiotape set up and her statement, 'no I don't want audiotape' would have been on the audiotape. It would have cut off at that point hopefully or if he continued we would have . . . heard it but here he didn't. And he didn't do it. Now does that, is that significant?"

Julie Done: "Well, and if I'm understanding what you're saying, you're saying if he had started recording right away and . . ."

Judge Farris: "Absolutely."

"He asked her."

Judge Farris: "If he had done what his supervisor said, 'audiotape this interview,' and he had the equipment set up, and would have been starting the audiotape, when he asked her, 'do you want me to audiotape,' that question would have been on the audiotape record. And, her answer would have been there, and then he would have shut it down. We don't have that. Is that significant?"

Julie Done: "Well that's assuming also that she would have said anything to him with the audiotape running. She might not have responded to him knowing that it was going to be."

Judge Farris: "Well we can always speculate, but we've got a case here with a record. The record creates some problems for both sides actually. But the problem it creates for your side, I think, is that we're down to a swearing contest and we've got a person who admits that he goes forward even after the request that you say he said he had a habit of recording it when they made the request, but the record affirmatively shows that he didn't have a habit. That on two occasions he did record. Now, I'm assuming that to do it twice doesn't make it a habit if we have evidence that there are times when you didn't do it. Now am I assuming too much?"

Done: "No. No. But I guess we're asserting that he did testify at the voluntariness hearing and then also again at the evidentiary hearing. But, if she had invoked her right to counsel he would have noted it in his case."

Judge Farris: "And if he had had the audiotape as his supervisor told him, we would have seen what happened leading up to his turning off the audiotape. You say she might not have said anything, but we would have seen that too. I mean the audiotape would show her silence."

"I didn't mean silence."

Judge Farris: "So we'd have had it. Now does that pose a problem? We have a death penalty case and you . . . we can't fill in the facts, can we? We have to take the record as we see it."

"Yes and that's why we believe that the evidentiary hearing at the District Court was so important. That's why we allowed all that evidence in."

"It may have been so important. But we asked for specific questions and the District Court gave what I assume are the best answers the District Court could give. In your view, do those answers clarify the question that's before us?"

"Whether or not she waived her Miranda rights?"

"Yes."

"Yes. I believe essentially based on the credibility determinations that the District Court made."

Judge Kozinski: "There's really no other evidence connecting her to the crime. Her confession is really key. And all we have . . . is Detective Saldate's statement. He destroys his notes, so if he has something in there that says she invoked her right to counsel in the handwritten notes, that was destroyed. He doesn't tape record. And he gives a materially different version of what happened in his testimony than what Petitioner gives. It all hinges on these reconstructions that we, and the jury, and the District Court, and the Superior Court had to make based on the imperfect process of evaluating credibility. Whereas, if he had followed his instructions as Judge Farris has pointed out to you a couple of times, if he'd just done what his supervisor said to do, we wouldn't be there. We'd have a tape. We wouldn't have to guess about it. We could all listen to the tape and see what exactly she said. And what exactly he said. The entire problem is created by Saldate deciding to be a law unto himself. So, like that Detective Callahan, right?"

Done: "I'm sorry, Detective Callahan?"

Judge Kozinski: "Yeah, you know, from the Dirty Harry movies?"

"Okay. Sorry, I didn't get that."

"We're in San Francisco so it's a little evoked."

Done: "I used to know that. A wild, wild west."

Judge Kozinski: "I mean, that's really the heart of it isn't it? That if he had just gotten a tape recorder and this was 1989 . . . You know, we had cassette tape recorders . . . even in the '60s . . . So, yeah, getting a tape recorder was not difficult in 1989."

Judge Bea: "No."

Judge Kozinski nodded at Julie Done. She was out of time.

"Thank you," she said, and moved away from the podium.

Lori Voepel returned for her rebuttal argument. Judge Kozinski said, "You have a minute or so left for rebuttal. Minute and a half, make it two minutes."

"Thank you, Judge. It's our position that, as the Court noted there is no objective record here because Detective Saldate did not record this interrogation. His testimony was and the evidence was that he never recorded interrogations. And it's our position that regardless of what she said . . ."

Judge Kozinski: "Well it's unfortunate and we've all commented on the fact it's unfortunate. He should have and he's a bad guy, and probably should have been disciplined for it, rather than commended. But the fact remains she [sic] didn't record it. So, we are left with the usual situation that we have because most facts are not recorded in real life. And we have to rely on witnesses and recollections and credibility and all those things. And in this case, you had two hearings. One in state court, one in District Court, and a highly respected District Judge went through a lengthy hearing and entered a lengthy order and explained his reasons for why he believed the officer and he didn't believe your client . . . You and I know if any of us was sitting as district judges we might, or might not reach the same conclusion. But we weren't there. Aren't we bound by the District Court's findings?"

"No, your Honor. The reason that you're not bound is that the District Court ignored evidence impeaching Saldate's credibility and showing . . ."

Judge Kozinski: "So, when you say ignored, that's a very strong term."

"It is very strong, your Honor. The only thing he did . . ."

"All we can say is he doesn't mention all the evidence that he presented in his order. It doesn't mean he ignored it. He could well have taken into account; probably did take into account. He just didn't put it down on paper. Does that mean he ignored it?"

"Yes, your Honor, I think it [does]. First of all, if I can just very briefly review the reasons he gave. He said that Saldate was more credible because his report didn't reflect a straightforward confession of guilt. That's not true. We urge you to look at the police report. He gives a very straightforward confession of guilt that he attributes to her. Number two. He says that most of what she said he said was corroborated by Debra. That's not true. About half of what he said, including her invocation of the right to counsel, and including all of the inculpatory statements that say 'I decided Chris should die' and 'I talked to Styers about it and he did it and I knew that he did it,' are completely disputed by Debra. Number three. He said, well he had a practice of noting in his reports when somebody invoked . . . he didn't do that here. As we said, he only did that twice in *Running Eagle* and *King*. *King* he ended up apparently forgetting that he did that because he testified there was no invocation. He never did that in the other cases and he never did it when somebody invoked their right to counsel. . . ."

Judge Bea: "There's something you haven't mentioned. The Court made a specific finding that the demeanor of your client did not inspire confidence in her credibility. That her responses appeared rehearsed and formulated to support her legal arguments. That is a basic concept upon which we affirm credibility findings. Demeanor testimony. Was he wrong on that?"

"Yes your Honor. And the reason that he is wrong . . ."

"Why was he wrong? Where in the record is there some evidence, which shows that that determination has no basis in the record?"

"Because he makes inconsistent findings with respect to her. He says she didn't detail her version of events in one paragraph and [in] the very next one, he says that she did. Number two. He says that her responses appeared rehearsed and recently formulated to support her legal arguments. Yet the District Court says that her testimony mirrored what she gave in state court at trial. How could she recently formulate those, when it mirrored her testimony at trial . . . [which was] long before these arguments?"

Judge Bea: "It doesn't say recently. It says rehearsed and formulated. It could have been formulated for the first hearing."

"Your Honor. She didn't know what the legal arguments would be in her case. She has maintained her position of what happened in that interrogation since day one. Since she talked to the investigative reporter at jail. Since she talked to Dr. Kassell in that tape-recorded interview three months after her arrest. Long before trial, your Honor, and long before the legal arguments were formulated in this case. With all due respect, we really feel that the District Court Judge felt that there needed to be a continued ongoing deference to the state court Judge. He incorporated many of [Judge Hendrix's] errors in his findings, including saying that she didn't really dispute it; that this wasn't a straightforward confession; Saldate could have done a better job of making this up. Look at his report. That is just not an accurate finding. We really feel that he felt that the court, and this Court included, should continue to defer to the state court Judge . . . he made findings consistent with hers."

Judge Bea: "For an inaccurate finding to be affirmed it has to be an abuse of discretion to be reversed."

"And for all the reasons that we set forth including . . . including the fact that, I think you do need to take into account all of the other implied waiver cases. Not one of them is a case like this where it's 'he said, she said.' There is no objective recording, there's no other officer, the facts are disputed including on issues as important as whether she invoked."

Judge Farris: "When the case comes to us, though, the facts are not disputed, they're in cement, and in cement this time, what I think you're asking us to do is to retry the case, aren't you?"

"No, your Honor. I think that you need to look at the reasons that the District Court Judge gave for his findings. The fact that he didn't apply the presumption against waiver. The fact that he treated this as an ordinary credibility contest. And you need to look at the facts and circumstances of this case relative to the facts and circumstances of other cases finding implied waiver and see that this is the exact same error. . . ."

Judge Kozinski: "You are over your time. Case is argued will stand submitted. We are adjourned."

40

THE NINTH CIRCUIT REVERSES—
MARCH 14, 2013

AMERICA'S FEDERAL APPELLATE BENCH IS a court of last resort for many reasons. It terminates litigation, settles the law, and rarely changes its collective mind. But unlike any other civic institution, it is a creature of the inherent constraints embedded in appellate decision making. Contrary to popular belief, appellate courts rely to a considerable degree on the lawyers and judges responsible for the case *before* oral argument. Appellate lawyers get the first bite because they frame the issues and pose the essential questions on appeal. But appellate judges get to cross-examine the lawyers at oral argument and they always get the last word. They often defer, sometimes unwillingly, to issues within the sound discretion of the lower court. Unlike trial judges, appellate judges do not issue minute entries or make oral pronouncements from the bench. Appellate decisions are painstakingly wrought, carefully edited, written opinions. Those opinions are open to the world for view and never subject to copyright or other literary protections. An appellate panel's most demanding task is persuading a majority to join in any proposed decision. Federal appellate judges are lawyers who have demonstrated intellectual brilliance and have a lifetime of experience in the law. By careful design, the structure and makeup of appellate courts always discourages aberrant decision making. Viewed from an international perspective, America's appellate system is the most comprehensive and deliberate "second chance" in the world.

Debra Milke's lawyers, Michael Kimerer and Lori Voepel, filed their opening brief with the Ninth Circuit on December 7, 2007. Both sides filed additional briefs. A three-judge panel of the Ninth Circuit heard oral arguments November 3, 2010. Chief Judge Alex Kozinski, joined by Circuit Judges Jerome Farris and Carlos T. Bea, rendered a final opinion on March 14, 2013. The unanimous order reverses the lower court's denial of Milke's petition for a writ of *habeas corpus*.

The first paragraph in the Ninth Circuit opinion connects the dots between police misconduct and judicial error to present a clear picture of the manifest injustice documented in the court record.

In 1990, a jury convicted Debra Milke of murdering her four-year-old son, Christopher. The judge sentenced her to death. The trial was, essentially, a swearing contest between Milke and Phoenix Police Detective Armando Saldate, Jr. Saldate testified that Milke, twenty-five at the time, had confessed when he interviewed her shortly after the murder; Milke protested her innocence and denied confessing. There were no other witnesses or direct evidence linking Milke to the crime. The judge and jury believed Saldate, but they didn't know about Saldate's long history of lying under oath and other misconduct. The state knew about this misconduct but didn't disclose it, despite the requirements of Brady v. Maryland, 373 U.S. 83, 87, 83 S. Ct. 1194, 10 L. Ed. 2d 215 (1963), and Giglio v. United States, 405 U.S. 150, 153-55, 92 S. Ct. 763, 31 L. Ed. 2d 104 (1972). Some of the misconduct wasn't disclosed until the case came to federal court, and even today, some evidence relevant to Saldate's credibility hasn't been produced, perhaps because it's been destroyed. In the balance hangs the life of Milke, who has been on Arizona's death row for twenty-two years.

On the last page of the unanimous opinion, the court rebalanced Milke's life. "Milke is entitled to habeas relief. We therefore reverse the decision of the district court and remand with instructions to grant a conditional writ of habeas corpus setting aside her convictions and sentences."

Appellate opinions are rarely this blunt. But this case demanded an unvarnished look at manifest injustice. Detective Saldate proximately caused Milke's conviction and death sentence. Without him, there was no case. He was the Phoenix Police Department's "case agent," the self-appointed interrogator-in-chief, and the Maricopa County Attorney's Office's front-row charging witness in court. But he is not the only person whose hand kept Debra Milke on death row for 23 years. Other individuals, some unknowingly, stamped their approval on and participated in what the Ninth Circuit branded as "the State of Arizona's unconstitutional silence."

Besides examining the trial court process, the Ninth Circuit shredded Milke's illusory post-conviction review, nominally provided by Maricopa County Superior Court Judge Cheryl Hendrix. That decision, the Ninth Circuit said, "resulted in a decision by a state post-conviction court that was contrary to clearly established Supreme Court law . . . the state post-conviction court so misread the evidence documenting the state's *Brady* violations that its decision was based on an unreasonable determination of the facts."

Judge Hendrix served as both trial court judge in 1990 and sentencing judge in 1991. She was also the post-conviction judge in 1996. Her legal errors and factual misunderstandings mirrored Saldate's view that the ends justify the means. The Ninth Circuit decried the fact that Saldate's misconduct was not timely disclosed, and that the state of Arizona remained unconstitutionally silent. Both charges went to Judge Hendrix's handling of the case. She may not have had all of the damning evidence about Saldate on her bench, but she did not push prosecutor Noel Levy to produce anything more than what he and the police department's lawyer gave her, in private, out of the presence of the defense lawyer.

Arguably, the most important question before the Ninth Circuit was the extent, rather than the existence, of Judge Hendrix's prejudice. The court probed Saldate's testimony and the state's failure to disclose his pretrial misconduct in other cases. The legal test for what constitutes prejudice in a setting like this is whether there is a reasonable probability of a different jury result on either guilt or penalty. As a matter of law, prejudice exists when the government's evidentiary suppression undermines confidence in the outcome of the trial. It is on this precise point that the Ninth Circuit made its most forceful statement. Noting that Milke's *alleged* confession, as reported by Saldate, was the only direct evidence linking Milke to the crime, the court stated what Judge Hendrix, Noel Levy, and Saldate had ignored. This confession "was only as good as Saldate's word." Saldate is the only one who "claims to have heard Milke confess." No one recorded what he or she said to one another. There is no written statement, or any other evidence, that Milke confessed. The Ninth Circuit's reasoning is the real story about what happened to Debra Milke.

> It's hard to imagine anything more relevant to the jury's—or the judge's—determination whether to believe Saldate than evidence that Saldate lied under oath and trampled the constitutional rights of suspects in discharging his official duties. If even a single juror had found Saldate untrustworthy based on the documentation that he habitually lied under oath or that he took advantage of women he had in his power, there would have been at least a hung jury. Likewise, if this evidence had been disclosed, it may well have led the judge to order a new trial, enter judgment notwithstanding the verdict or, at least, impose a sentence less than death. The prosecution did its best to impugn Milke's credibility. It wasn't entitled, at the same time, to hide the evidence that undermined Saldate's credibility.

The Ninth Circuit's opinion is now the "law of the case." That hoary old legal phrase means that an appellate court's determination on a question of law cannot be second-guessed or ignored by the lower court on remand. Judge Mroz, the remand judge, must conduct the retrial in accordance with the legal findings enunciated in the appellate court's opinion. She and the litigants are *bound* by the specific points of law enunciated in the opinion. She will foster no relitigation of issues settled by the Ninth Circuit.

Because Milke had always denied involvement in the murder, Saldate's trial court evidence concerning the alleged confession he claimed he extracted from her was especially vexing for the defense at her first trial. Milke's account of her forced meeting with Saldate differed "substantially from Saldate's." At her 1990 trial, Milke testified she told Saldate she didn't understand the Miranda warnings. When Saldate asked if she wanted the interrogation taped, she said, "No, I need a lawyer." According to Milke, Saldate ignored her request, put his hands on her knees, and proceeded with the interrogation. Then, she said, he "embellished and twisted [her] statements to make it sound like she had confessed."

Saldate also skipped the basic step of having Milke sign a Miranda waiver. Not even Saldate's interview notes made it into court. Saldate testified he destroyed them after writing his official report three days after the interrogation."

Our constitution guarantees every defendant a fair trial. The most essential element of fairness is the prosecution's obligation to turn over exculpatory evidence. This means that "Arizona had to disclose to Milke all material evidence that could exculpate her, including evidence that could impeach the only substantive witness the state called to the stand. Reliable evidence of a law enforcement officer's misconduct in unrelated cases is admissible to impeach that officer's credibility, particularly where credibility is the central issue and the evidence comprises opposing stories presented by the defendant and government agents." Judge Hendrix had mangled those basic legal concepts twice (first at the 1991 trial and later at the 1996 post-conviction review). But those core concepts saved Milke on appeal.

What proved insurmountable for the prosecution at the Ninth Circuit was its intentional or inadvertent failure to disclose Saldate's "long history of lies and misconduct." The court's appendix to its opinion documents Saldate's flagrant abuse of suspects:

This history includes a five-day suspension for taking "liberties" with a female motorist and then lying about it to his supervisors; four court cases where judges tossed out confessions or indictments because Saldate lied under oath; and four cases where judges suppressed confessions or vacated convictions because Saldate had violated the Fifth Amendment or the Fourth Amendment in the course of interrogations. And it is far from clear that this reflects a full account of Saldate's misconduct as a police officer. All of this information should have been disclosed to Milke and the jury, but the state remained unconstitutionally silent.

Chief Judge Alex Kozinski's opinion took special note of the consequences of Saldate's claim that Milke confessed. ". . . Saldate claims Milke opened up to him about the most intimate details of her life. He testified that, in just thirty minutes, Milke knowingly waived her rights to silence and counsel, reminisced about her high school years when she was 'in love with life,' feigned tears, calmed down, narrated her failed marriage to Mark Milke—his drug and alcohol abuse and his arrests—recounted how she'd gotten pregnant while on birth control and contemplated an abortion, even making an appointment for one, discussed her fear that Christopher was becoming like his father, confessed to a murder conspiracy, characterized the conspiracy as a 'bad judgment call' and solicited Saldate's opinion about whether her family would ever understand. (His view: No.) By the end of the interview, Saldate had more than just cinched the case against Milke; he'd helped her emotionally. According to Saldate, Milke said she was 'starting to feel better and was starting to get some of her self-esteem back.'"

Because Milke had always denied any involvement in her son's murder, and because she took the witness stand at her trial, the core jury issue was credibility. Her denial and his certainty became the ultimate swearing contest. He said she said. She said she didn't. Consequently, "[t]he jury had no independent way of verifying these divergent accounts. Saldate didn't record the interrogation, even though his supervisor instructed him to do so. Saldate didn't bring a tape recorder to the interview, nor did he ask anyone to witness the interrogation by sitting in the room or watching through a two-way mirror. The jury thus had nothing more than Saldate's word that Milke confessed. Everything the state claims happened in the interrogation room depends on believing Saldate's testimony. Without Saldate's testimony, the prosecution had no case against Milke, as there was no physical evidence linking her to the crime and neither of her supposed co-conspirators—Styers and Scott—would testify against her."

Credibility is always a matter for the jury. Judges do not judge credibility, they instruct juries on how to assess it. Nonetheless, and often irrespective of the judge's instruction regarding credibility assessment, witness credibility is resolved in secret during final deliberations by the jury. The only effective mechanism the law provides to test the connection between witness *credibility* and witness *reliability* is cross-examination. In this case, the cross-examiner was a lawyer who could not impeach the witness because the prosecutor refused to disclose impeaching facts about Saldate. The icing on the cake in the state's case was the judge's refusal to allow a full and fair impeachment of the state's only substantive witness.

Witness credibility can be attacked on four distinct grounds: witness veracity, bias, perception, and memory of the event. Some witnesses are competent but not credible. Others are credible but not competent. The 1990 Milke jury presumably found Saldate's version of the confession "credible." Otherwise, they would not have taken just one short day to convict Milke based entirely on what Saldate says she said. Had Milke's lawyer impeached Saldate through pointed cross-examination about his history of confession misconduct, the jury would not have resolved the case in one day. It would have taken the jury much longer to debate the reliability of her confession against the credibility attack on cross-examination. Only one thing explains a one-day deliberation and a quick guilty verdict—they believed Saldate. They thought she confessed. What's there to deliberate? Call the bailiff—we have a verdict. The Ninth Circuit analyzed the jury's *presumption* rather than Saldate's *assumption*. The age-old question of *why* was at the heart of Milke's appellate case. *Why* did the jury so readily accept Saldate's version and so easily disregard hers? Judge Kozinski squarely addressed the why question: "[because] Saldate was an experienced witness and his account of Milke's purported confession proved convincing."

Milke's lawyers did not impeach Saldate because they did not have access to his history. But for the unique factual setting, a jury's resolution of conflicting facts between two diametrically opposed versions of an event is conclusive. Judge Hendrix rebuffed all efforts to impeach Saldate's credibility by introducing exculpatory evidence for that express purpose—the impeachment of Saldate's credibility before the jury. One could argue that Judge Hendrix might not have had access to Saldate's history of blatant misconduct during the initial 1990 trial. But three years later, she got all of it—all 23 cases—attached as Exhibit 12 to the Petition for Post-Conviction Relief on November 1, 1995. She not only did not grant post-conviction relief, she flatly refused to conduct an evidentiary hearing on the massive evidence discovered by Anders Rosenquist and his team of lawyers and law students in 1995. Her dismissive attitude is clear regarding that pivotal exhibit in her November 18, 1996 order:

> Exhibit 12 consists of motions and testimony from other cases in which Det. Saldate was the interrogating officer. It establishes nothing. The filing of a motion to suppress does not mean the police officer engaged in improprieties. The potential benefit from obtaining evidence of Det. Saldate's alleged misconduct with other defendants is questionable because it would not have been admissible to show the detective engaged in the same "misconduct" in this case . . . the information would have been inadmissible extrinsic evidence on a collateral matter . . . If the information was probative of the detective's character for truthfulness, defense counsel might have been allowed to question Det. Saldate about these specific instances, but defense counsel would have been bound by the detective's answers.

Translated from legalese to English, Judge Hendrix's razor-thin excuse for not granting relief for her initial trial court error is that "defense counsel would have been bound by the detective's answers." Maybe so. But the larger point is that the jury would have had the benefit of highly probative evidence regarding Saldate's credibility, in a case where credibility was everything. By denying post-conviction relief after learning of Saldate's history, she caused Milke to spend another 17 years on death row before the Ninth Circuit recognized a clear *Brady* violation by the state, and an unfair trial in her court, based on evidence she certainly did have in 1996.

Courts cannot suppress evidence that is favorable to an accused. When a court suppresses exculpatory evidence, it amounts to a denial of due process. Evidence of misconduct by the state's sole witness is not merely "impeaching." It is exculpatory. It does not matter whether the evidence is material to guilt or to punishment. The due process violation does not depend on whether the prosecution acted in good faith or bad faith. Deliberate deception of a court and jurors by the presentation of known false evidence is incompatible with rudimentary demands of justice. The same result obtains when the state, although not soliciting false evidence, allows it to go uncorrected when it later appears. The Arizona Attorney General's office also got a copy of Exhibit 12 in 1995. It opposed post-conviction relief. It continued to oppose any legal relief up to the time the Ninth Circuit found that Arizona was "constitutionally silent" in 2013.

Suppression of material evidence justifies a new trial irrespective of the good faith or bad faith of the prosecution. When the reliability of a witness may well determine guilt or innocence, nondisclosure of evidence mandates a new trial, if it appears likely that disclosure would have changed the verdict. A finding of materiality of the evidence is required, and a new trial is required if the false testimony could *in any reasonable likelihood* have affected the judgment of the jury.

The Ninth Circuit drove this point home, taking the unusual step of mentioning the trial judge by name in its 2013 opinion. It said, "In reviewing the exhibits attached to Milke's post-conviction petition, Judge Cheryl K. Hendrix, who was also the trial judge, was 'unable to find a reference to the type of evidence that is allowed under Rule 608 to impeach the credibility of a witness.' That is no doubt because she grossly misapprehended the nature and content of the documents that Milke presented. Even though the judge claimed to have reviewed the exhibits, she referred to the collection of court documents as containing mere 'motions and testimony from other cases in which Det. Saldate was the interrogating officer.'" The court went on to say that "Milke presented the state court with hundreds of pages of court records from cases where Saldate had committed misconduct, either by lying under oath or by violating suspects' Miranda and other constitutional rights during interrogations. Had these cases been brought to the jury's attention, they would certainly have cast doubt on Saldate's credibility. In addition to serving as impeachment evidence, they also buttressed Milke's repeated claim that she'd been prejudiced by denial of access to Saldate's personnel file, where more impeachment evidence could be expected to reside."

That Milke's evidence contained court orders, rather than just "motions and testimony," is a significant, objective fact that the state court either misapprehended or ignored. Either way, the court's error resulted in an unreasonable determination of the facts. These overlooked court orders are "highly probative and central to petitioner's claim. Had the state post-conviction judge realized that the documents contained judicial findings of Saldate's mendacity and disregard for constitutional rights, she may well have recognized their relevance as impeachment evidence that had not been disclosed as required by *Giglio*. After all, the judge acknowledged that Milke could have used the court records to question Saldate about 'specific instances of prior conduct' if the information was 'probative of the detective's character for truthfulness.' And this evidence certainly was, though the court seemed unaware of it. While the court held that 'defense counsel would have been bound by the detective's answers' to the questions about these instances of misconduct, the documents would still have been valuable. With court orders in hand, defense counsel would have had a good-faith basis for questioning Saldate about prior instances where he had lied on the witness stand . . . If Saldate admitted the lies, his credibility would have been impaired. If he denied them, he would have exposed himself to a perjury prosecution. If he claimed he couldn't remember, defense counsel could have shown Saldate the documents to refresh his memory. And if Saldate still couldn't recall, the jury would have had reason to doubt, not only his veracity, but his memory. These court orders would have been a *game-changer* for Milke, but the state court failed to grasp their significance because it was apparently unaware that the documents contained judicial findings rather than mere allegations."

Due process of law claims involve three basic constitutional principles. First, due process imposes an "inescapable" duty on the prosecutor "to disclose known, favorable evidence rising to a material level of importance." Second, favorable evidence includes both exculpatory and impeachment material that relates to either guilt or punishment. Third, the prosecutor is charged with disclosing any *Brady* material of which the prosecutor's office or the investigating police agency is aware. Against this backdrop, the Ninth Circuit made three specific factual findings. First, Saldate's personnel file disclosed an Internal Affairs report confirming his taking "liberties in a manner unbecoming an officer" with a female motorist he had stopped for driving with a faulty taillight and lying about it. The report noted, "[Y]our image of honesty, competency, and overall reliability must be questioned." Second, his lies and his supervisor's assessment would have been useful to a jury trying to decide whether Saldate or Milke was telling the truth. The report "discloses a misogynistic attitude toward female civilians and a willingness to abuse his authority to get what he wants." All of this is highly consistent with Milke's account of the interrogation. Third, the court orders Milke's lawyers uncovered were favorable evidence that was available to the state but the prosecution did not disclose. The cases all involved the Maricopa County Attorney's Office and the Phoenix Police Department—the same agencies involved in prosecuting Milke.

To establish a due process claim based on failure to disclose *Brady* material, Milke's appellate lawyers had to persuade the appellate court that the *Brady* violation was a willful or inadvertent failure of the prosecutor. On this point, Judges Kozinski, Farris, and Bea made *seven* additional findings. First, the state eventually produced some of this evidence in federal habeas proceedings. It never claimed it could not have disclosed it in time for Milke's trial. Second, the state also had an obligation to produce the documents showing Saldate's false and misleading statements in court and before grand juries, and the documents showing the Fifth Amendment and Fourth Amendment violations he committed during interrogations. Third, the prosecutor's office no doubt knew of this misconduct because it had harmed criminal prosecutions. The police must have known, too. Indeed, the timing of the suppression order in *Jones* underscores the cavalier attitude of the Maricopa County Attorney's Office toward its constitutional duty to disclose impeachment evidence. Fourth, the prosecution argued against the *Jones* suppression motion on November 16, 1990, and lost, resulting in the suppression of the murder confession. This happened between the time of Milke's conviction on October 12, 1990, and her sentencing on January 18, 1991. Even as Milke's attorney was working hard to stave off a death sentence, the prosecutor's office and the police were actively dealing with Saldate's misconduct in *another* murder case. Fifth, because the *Jones* court suppressed a murder confession, this "must surely have reminded the Maricopa County Attorney's Office and the Phoenix Police Department of Saldate's propensity to commit misconduct. Indeed, Paul Rood, the prosecutor in *Jones*, was also the prosecutor in *King*, where in June 1990 "Saldate had been caught in a lie about violating *Miranda*." Sixth, at about the same time as *King*, Rood also received a suppression motion in State v. Mahler, a Saldate case in which the defendant made what the Arizona Court of Appeals called "an unequivocal invocation to remain silent." The Arizona Court of Appeals held that "Officer Saldate's intent was clear . . . he wanted additional statements from Mahler. This conduct violated Mahler's right to remain silent." Seventh, as the state absorbed the loss of the *Jones* confession in November 1990, it must have occurred to Rood or *someone* in the prosecutor's office or the police department (or both) that Saldate was also the key witness in the high-profile case against Debra Milke—a case where the defendant was still at trial, actively fighting for her life. Yet no one saw fit to disclose this or any of the other instances of Saldate's misconduct to Milke's lawyer.

The Ninth Circuit answered a two-decades-old question. How did the defense acquire the massive exculpatory material on Saldate's long history of misconduct involving confessions? "Milke was able to discover the court documents detailing Saldate's misconduct only after a team of approximately ten researchers in post-conviction proceedings spent nearly 7000 hours sifting through court records. Milke's post-conviction attorneys sent this team to the clerk of court's offices to search for Saldate's name in every criminal case file from 1982 to 1990. Saldate resigned from the police department on July 10, 1990. The team worked eight hours a day for three and a half months, turning up 100 cases involving Saldate. Another researcher then spent a month reading motions and transcripts from those cases to find examples of Saldate's misconduct. A reasonably diligent lawyer couldn't possibly have found these records in time to use them at Milke's trial. Judge Hendrix, perhaps inadvertently, kept out documents that might have revealed Saldate's interrogation history and constitutional violations were suppressed."

In any other case before the Ninth Circuit or any other circuit court of appeals, the reasoning behind the court's decision would have ended the court's opinion. But in this truly unique case, the court had more to say. Besides reversing the denial of habeas relief at the district court level, and granting her a conditional writ, the court instructed the United States District Court for the District of Arizona to do something unique in appellate rulings. "Prior to issuing the writ, the district court *shall* order the state to provide Milke's counsel with Saldate's police personnel records covering all of his years of service, including records pertaining to any disciplinary or Internal Affairs investigations and records pertaining to performance evaluations. This panel retains jurisdiction over any appeal arising from this remand. Upon production of the certification described above or the conclusion of the evidentiary hearing, the district court *shall* order Milke released unless the state notifies the court within 30 days that it intends to retry Milke, and actually commences Milke's retrial within 90 days. The clerk of our court *shall* send copies of this opinion to the United States Attorney for the District of Arizona and to the Assistant United States Attorney General of the Civil Rights Division, for possible investigation into whether Saldate's conduct, and that of his supervisors and other state and local officials, amounts to a pattern of violating the federally protected rights of Arizona residents."

All three panel members concurred in Chief Judge Kozinski's opinion. However, Judge Kozinski also authored a supplemental opinion detailing why he felt the Milke case was "disturbing." This supplemental goes to an issue rarely touched upon at the appellate level—*actual innocence*. Judge Kozinski called the case disturbing because "[t]here's no physical evidence linking Debra Milke to the crime, and she has maintained her innocence since the day she was arrested. Neither of the men who did the killing testified against Milke. Roger Scott refused to testify because his 'testimony would not be what he felt was the truth.' After spending many years on death row, James Styers continued to insist, 'Debbie had nothing to do with it and thats [sic] the truth.' The *only* evidence linking Milke to the murder of her son is the word of Detective Armando Saldate, Jr.—a police officer with a long history of misconduct that includes lying under oath as well as accepting sexual favors in exchange for leniency and lying about it."

"Equally troubling," Judge Kozinski continued, "are Saldate's unorthodox interrogation methods." He repeated the full panel's condemnation of Saldate's practice of disregarding the right to remain silent when invoked by suspects he was questioning. He reminded readers of the link between Saldate's interrogation practice and the complete lack of any physical evidence linking Debra Milke to the crime. And he noted something not included in the majority opinion: "Saldate never asked Milke to put her confession in writing or initial a single sentence acknowledging she had confessed. Nor did Milke sign a *Miranda* waiver. Saldate testified that '[t]here was no document . . . we had available to us' where 'we could have a suspect sign that they waive their rights.'"

What Saldate did not say was that police departments all over America had, by 1989, adopted the practice of having suspects sign the officer's Miranda card. "I never knew that ever happened," Saldate testified. "Never happened with my case or any other case I was involved in." Judge Kozinski could barely disguise his scorn: "This, from an officer with twenty-one years on the Phoenix Police force. Soon after the interrogation, Saldate destroyed the notes he supposedly took while questioning Milke, so we have absolutely *nothing* contemporaneous with the supposed confession."

Judge Kozinski's supplemental opinion includes a rare example of judicial sarcasm:

> Saldate's supervisor asked him to record Milke's interrogation, yet Saldate didn't even take a tape recorder with him. When he arrived in Florence, Arizona, where Milke was waiting for him, he didn't obtain a recorder there either, even though he knew they were readily available. Saldate claims that Milke refused to have the conversation recorded, but admits that he "basically didn't want to record it anyway." And why not? Because "a tape recorder is an obstacle for [him] to get to the truth" and so "it's [his] practice never to use a tape recorder." Of course, being left with no recording is an obstacle for *us* to get to the truth, but Saldate tells us not to worry: "[The] conversation was going to be noted by me in a truthful manner, so there was really no need for tape recording." Right.

Judge Kozinski uses metaphor eloquently in his legal opinions. The Milke opinion is illustrative. "In effect, Saldate turned the interrogation room into a black box, leaving us no objectively verifiable proof as to what happened inside. All we have are the conflicting accounts of a defendant with an obvious reason to lie and a detective whose disdain for lawful process is documented by one instance after another of lying under oath and other misconduct. No civilized system of justice should have to depend on such flimsy evidence, quite possibly tainted by dishonesty or overzealousness, to decide whether to take someone's life or liberty. The Phoenix Police Department and Saldate's supervisors there should be ashamed of having given free rein to a lawless cop to misbehave again and again, undermining the integrity of the system of justice they were sworn to uphold. As should the Maricopa County Attorney's Office, which continued to prosecute Saldate's cases without bothering to disclose his pattern of misconduct."

Everyone involved in, or touched by, the American justice system has reason to note the Milke case. Judge Kozinski lectured all of us about basic fairness. "It's not just fairness to the defendant that calls for an objectively verifiable process for securing confessions and other evidence in criminal cases. We all have a stake in ensuring that our criminal justice system reliably separates the guilty from the innocent. Letting police get away with manufacturing confessions or planting evidence not only risks convicting the innocent but helps the guilty avoid detection and strike again."

His concurring opinion is a jarring reminder that guilt cannot be the sole determinant of due process. "Milke may well be guilty, even if Saldate made up her confession out of whole cloth. After all, it's hard to understand what reason Styers and Scott would have had for killing a four-year-old boy. Then again, what reason would they have to protect her if they know she's guilty? But I seriously doubt the jury would have convicted Milke without the purported confession. Indeed, without the confession, there's not enough evidence to support a conviction. Which is why it's very important that the confession be reliable and lawfully obtained."

The concurring opinion closes on a short, albeit speculative, assessment of Saldate's likely motive in securing such a questionable confession. "This was a high-visibility, high-pressure case, in which Saldate was called in especially and given much responsibility. It is highly doubtful he would have noted an invocation [of Milke's Miranda rights] that would have undermined the alleged confession. Far more likely, Saldate had learned from earlier cases that documenting a *Miranda* violation could result in the exclusion of a confession and make him the object of judicial ire. This may also explain why Saldate so hastily destroyed the original notes from the interrogation. If they contained his habitual documentation of *Miranda* and other constitutional violations during the course of interrogation, he may have thought it wise not to have them available to impeach his official report."

The "take away" from the Ninth Circuit's majority opinion is twofold. It reinforces the due process of law that so eluded the detective, prosecutor, and trial judge and it gives belated hope that confessions might not in the next trial be so highly valued by juries that the total lack of other evidence escapes notice. Unthinkable crimes cannot overpower thoughtless prosecutions.

41

PROOF NOT EVIDENT, PRESUMPTION NOT GREAT: REMAND TO JUDGE ROSA MROZ, MARICOPA COUNTY SUPERIOR COURT—JULY 2013

*J*UDGE ROSA MROZ GOT THE minute entry on July 10, 2013 from Judge Welty—he named her as the remand judge slated to handle the retrial of Debra Milke. The remand order contained two important directives. First, it confirmed the U.S. District Court's granting of a writ of *habeas corpus* for Milke. Second, it noted the state of Arizona's intent to retry Milke and "seek the death penalty." The remand order set a status conference with the new judge and counsel, and ordered Milke "held without bond pending trial."

Rosa Mroz was a good choice. After earning her BS, *cum laude*, from Arizona State University in 1986, she got her CPA credentials, and began adult life as an accountant for Price Waterhouse. She entered ASU's Sandra Day O'Connor College of Law in 1990, graduating *cum laude* in 1993. Arizona Supreme Court Justice Duke Cameron and Arizona Court of Appeals Judge Thomas Kleinschmidt selected her to clerk in their chambers from 1991 to 1994. Following those two prestigious clerkships, she joined one of Arizona's largest law firms, Jennings Strouss & Salmon, as an associate. Later, she spent a little over four years at the Maricopa County Attorney's Office and then another year in private practice before her appointment to the Maricopa County Superior Court in 2004. Along the way, she became a member of, and held leadership positions in, many public service entities. As expected, she moved rapidly through judicial committees and challenging rotations in civil, family, probate, and criminal law.

Perhaps her most notable judicial service, before accepting a criminal bench assignment, was her term as Probate Presiding Judge. In 2013, the National Association of Court Management recognized her by awarding Maricopa County the 2013 Justice Achievement Award. It cited her comprehensive reform efforts over the 2010-2012 time period. Presiding Judge Norm Davis said, "It is clear that over the past few years, the Maricopa County Probate Court has experienced significant reform and innovation under the able leadership of Judge Rosa Mroz." The award honors "outstanding achievement that enhances the administration of justice."

By the time she was assigned the Milke case, Judge Mroz was one of the best on the Maricopa County bench: smart, hard-working, approachable, and not one to "mess with." She would need all that and more in ferreting out the apparent injustice in this case.

After several status hearings dealing with administrative and logistical issues, Judge Mroz held her first substantive hearing on the case on August 8, 2013. She began that hearing with a comment from the bench about what she wanted and what she would not tolerate. Her minute entry stated the obvious:

> Court advises parties that the court found out about the Defendant's motion to disqualify the Maricopa Attorney's office as a prosecuting agency in this case from reading it on

AzCentral.com on July 31, 2013 and notes that the story was posted at *5:02* P.M. The actual motion was not filed with the court until *7:32* P.M. The court admonishes the parties that this case will be tried in the courtroom and not in the media. The court gives a warning that if the parties are going to continue to try this case in the media[,] the court is inclined to issue a gag order to the attorneys in order to preserve the fairness of the trial process.

As it turned out, the parties clarified the filing after the hearing. She surprised everyone on August 9, 2013 by issuing an apology to the parties. She said, "The court misread the e-file certification. The clarification confirms that the motion in question was filed at 3:07:32 P.M., not at 7:32 P.M. The court apologizes for misstating the record at the hearing. . . ." This proved two things. Judge Mroz, like any other judge, can occasionally misread a record. And it proved she had the intestinal fortitude to stand up and publicly apologize when the circumstances called for it. That is a rare trait on the bench. But, she said, "The court remains concerned that the integrity and fairness of this trial will be affected [if] the parties attempt to try this case in the media . . . the court asks that the parties be circumspect . . . it is not just the court's duty to protect the integrity and fairness of the judicial process—it is also the attorney's duty as well."

It would remain to be seen whether either side would "mess with her" by testing her resolve to issue a gag order to inhibit trying the case in the media. The next item of business was a discussion about "the Simpson hearing set for today." Noting that the defense was not willing to waive any conflict, as stated in its motion to disqualify the MCAO, she canceled the hearing, pending resolution of the conflict of interest by the MCAO. That issue would be resolved in due time. Meanwhile she continued the bail hearing, nicknamed a "Simpson" hearing.

A Simpson hearing attempts an early decision on a fundamental question: Should bail be granted or denied? Perhaps the most elementary aspect of such a hearing is the historic presumption of individual innocence. It is often said that "liberty is the norm, and detention prior to trial is the carefully limited exception." The interests served by detention accordingly must be legitimate and compelling because bail cannot be denied for the purpose of punishment. Proposition 103, passed by the Arizona legislature in 2002, permits judges to deny bail only *after* an evidentiary hearing. The standard for such a hearing (proof is evident, presumption great) is historic. The proof must be evident and the presumption great that the accused committed the crimes charged. Although there is no *right* to bail, because of the potential for a compromise of personal liberty, there is a *presumption* in favor of bail. The exception only exists if the proof is evident or the presumption great. Combining both presumptions (of innocence and in favor of bail), the law is clear—to meet due process requirements, the accused must be provided an *evidentiary* hearing, during which she must be given an opportunity to be heard "at a meaningful time and in a meaningful manner." The burden of proving an exception to bail lies with the state. Placing the burden on the accused would force her to prove a negative.

Even though Judge Mroz put the hearing off, she gave the lawyers something to think about in her minute entry. "The court advises the parties that it has already read all of the materials provided. Preliminarily, the court *finds* that (1) the original trial held in 1990 does not take the place of a Simpson hearing because a lot has transpired between 1990 and today; (2) a Simpson hearing is necessary; (3) the Court is inclined to review the documents and transcripts as the evidence for the Simpson hearing rather than take live testimony; (4) the Ninth Circuit opinion in this case is the law of this case; (5) the determination to be made in the Simpson hearing is inextricably intertwined with the issues that will be addressed at the evidentiary hearing on Defendant's motion to suppress confession."

Accordingly, Judge Mroz rescheduled the Simpson hearing, *and* the motion to suppress the confession over a three-day period of time, simultaneously. If the moderate scolding about giving the press copies of court pleadings before giving them to the court was a shot over the defendant's bow, then joining the Simpson hearing with the suppression hearing was a broadside at the MCAO. By connecting the evidentiary issues in "proof evident-presumption great" analysis to the presumption that confessions were involuntary, she was signaling the prosecutor that he'd need his "A" game to deny bail, and maybe a Super Bowl performance to keep the confession in the case. That's because she referenced the fact in her minute entry that the Ninth Circuit opinion was *the* law of the case. Both sides knew what that meant. The Ninth Circuit had thrown out the confession because the MCAO had not provided vital exculpatory impeachment evidence on Saldate's misconduct. She was telling them she would have none of that. Saldate's impeachment evidence was on her desk. Both sides could read the legal tea leaves—without Saldate, there was no confession to suppress; with Saldate, there would be a bloodbath of impeachment evidence. The impeachment via cross-examination would likely discredit Saldate so badly that Judge Mroz would suppress his so-called confession.

At the next hearing, on August 23, 2013, she talked to the lawyers about Saldate. Her minute entry reflects that "discussion was held regarding whether Detective Saldate needs a lawyer to represent him in the suppression hearing because the Ninth Circuit referred him to the U.S. Attorney's office to investigate whether he had committed any civil rights violations." Vince Imbordino, the prosecutor, told her that "to his knowledge" the U.S. Attorney had not taken any action to "investigate anyone out of this case." Imbordino also said he did not think Saldate "wants" an attorney to represent him. On that note, Judge Mroz ordered Imbordino to talk to Saldate and ask him what he wanted.

Regarding the merits of the suppression hearing, Imbordino told the judge he needed more time "to gather evidence to rebut the findings made by the Ninth Circuit about Detective Saldate." The defense also needed more time, saying it intended to move to preclude the evidence the state wanted to offer because it believed the "Ninth Circuit's opinion findings were *the law of the case.*"

Judge Mroz did not offer her own opinion on what would prove a pivotal issue—what is the law of this case. Nonetheless, she granted the prosecutor's motion, resetting the suppression hearing for September 23, 2013.

Three days later, on August 26, 2013, Judge Mroz denied Milke's motion to disqualify the MCAO as the prosecuting agency. The law regarding disqualifying opposing counsel in a case is straightforward. The court should evaluate whether the disqualification is mere harassment, whether the party seeking disqualification will be prejudiced or damaged if the motion is not granted, and whether there are alternative solutions. In the case of a public prosecutor, courts also consider whether the possibility of public suspicion outweighs any benefits that might accrue due to continued representation. At end of the day, the overriding presumption is against disqualification because only "in extreme circumstances should a party be allowed to interfere with the attorney-client relationship of his opponent."

In reaching her decision, Judge Mroz noted the age and complexity of the case. The case is complex not only because it is a capital case, but also because "it has been 23 years since the defendant's original trial . . . witnesses may not be available . . . evidence may have degraded . . . and the state's key witness . . . [may have] lied on multiple occasions and violated various defendants' constitutional rights." Her minute entry also reveals how important the issue was to both sides. Milke, she said, "has made much of current Maricopa County Attorney Bill Montgomery and current prosecutor Vince Imbordino's [relationship since they are] colleagues of Noel Levy."

That relationship was an important factor in the calculus surrounding who should lead the retrial effort. Judge Mroz well knew that Milke's lawyers had attributed to Montgomery, Imbordino, and Levy a desire to "vindicate Levy's and MCAO's reputations." She knew that some thought the MCAO was only retrying this case because "it has a significant political, public, and financial interest in the outcome of this case." But, she said, "[T]here is no indication that Imbordino and Montgomery are even close with Levy." She would not presume that "a prosecutor will seek a defendant's conviction at all costs when the duty [is] to see justice done on behalf of both the victim and the defendant." Judge Mroz sought balance in resolving the 23-year old swearing contest between Milke and Saldate. She came down dead center on the legal teeter-totter. "Neither Imbordino nor Montgomery had anything to do with the prosecution of the defendant in the original trial, nor were they the individuals accused of committing the *Brady* violation." As a final push on the prosecution's end of the teeter-totter, she expressed her belief "that the public can distinguish between bad acts committed over 23 years ago by individuals no longer with the MCAO, or the Phoenix Police Department." In doing so, Judge Mroz accepted the Ninth Circuit's view of the evidence—there were "bad acts committed 23 years ago." What she may not have focused on was the stark reality that Saldate was a legal albatross and Levy a time bomb that would, if there were to be a retrial, explode in her courtroom. While Montgomery and Imbordino may have been in denial, Kimerer and Voepel were not. Losing the disqualification motion was not exactly a loss; it was a glimpse into how Judge Mroz saw the evidence. She chose her words carefully in denying Milke's motion. "The Court finds the facts and circumstances do not raise an appearance of impropriety *sufficient to require* disqualification of MCAO or any individual prosecutor." Sufficiency, like adequacy, often suffers in the delusion of the moment. In time, the connections between the MCAO's "A" team of capital case prosecutors (Levy and Rood) and Saldate's known history of confession misconduct would become ever stronger, perhaps more so because the MCAO "won" the right to lead the debatable effort to re-convict Milke. In the interim, Larry Debus, an experienced and highly successful criminal defense lawyer, agreed to represent Saldate to advise him vis-à-vis his own constitutional rights in the upcoming suppression hearing.

The next battle was infinitely more important—to grant or decline bail. Judge Mroz held a Simpson hearing on August 30, 2013. As expected, she listened intently, but did not rule from the bench. She took the matter "under advisement." For lawyers, taking a motion under advisement was routine, but lay observers find the word curious—who would be *advising* the judge after she'd read the briefs and heard the arguments? While mystifying to those outside the legal circle, when a judge takes a case under advisement, she deliberates with herself, thinks about what she's heard, and announces her decision when she's good and ready. On September 9, 2013, she "found "the proof is not evident, nor the presumption great that the defendant committed the crimes charged in the indictment." Accordingly, she set bail via a secured bond for $250,000.

At that time, there were two women on Arizona's death row, facing an execution no other woman had faced since the state hung Eva

Dugan in 1930. The first media story, by Michael Kiefer of the Arizona Republic, was widely reprinted by the AP in its coverage all over the country. In his 3:04 P.M. posting on September 69 2013, Kiefer described Milke's feelings. "She was stunned and ecstatic to learn she would be released and broke down in tears." Others chimed in. Sheriff Joe Arpaio issued a statement confirming Milke's release "sometime today." Her ex-husband, Arizona (formerly Mark) Milke said, "She's going to get something she's wanted for a long time." Kiefer reported that Milke's supporters would put up the bond money and provide a house for her to live in "as the legal process plays out. Milke has a strong following of people who believe she is innocent, especially in Europe, where she has family."

As part of her rationale for granting bail, Judge Mroz informed the parties that she agreed with the Ninth Circuit's finding that "the only evidence directly linking the defendant to the crimes is the alleged confession." She rejected the prosecution's argument that a jury has "already" convicted Milke. "Much has transpired since [then]," she said. "Back then, the jury did not have the benefit of the information against Saldate." And she now has "all that information." The *Brady* material, she said, "casts serious doubt on the validity of the alleged confession." She decided the bond issue based on the "totality of the *existing* information," not the 1989 version. That information included Arizona cases recounting Saldate's misconduct in extracting confessions from suspects.

Her order required Milke's "submission to electronic monitoring . . . [that she] not initiate contact of any kind with Arizona Milke . . . not possess[] any weapons, or drugs without a valid prescription . . . no alcohol . . . [is not to] drive without a valid driver's license." There were other routine requirements, and a provision that the release order would be sealed to protect Milke's safety.

Judge Mroz knew that the 2013 reality was far from the 1989 perception. Things had changed—evidence had been degraded, witnesses were not available, and Saldate would face vigorous impeachment, at a minimum, *if* he took the stand. That led to the September 12, 2013 minute entry ordering Saldate to appear in court ten days later to "invoke his Fifth Amendment privilege in open court." For obvious reasons, Judge Mroz also vacated the pending suppression hearing, clarified that she intended to rule on whether Saldate had a "right" to invoke the Fifth Amendment, and asked counsel to comment on urgent issues. Michael Kimerer said that since Milke was out of custody, the "urgency to try the case has subsided." Besides, he said, he needed "more time to prepare for trial." Imbordino agreed, on both counts. The court reset everything.

At the October 23, 2013 status conference, Judge Mroz told counsel she had read the motion to suppress the alleged confession and the state's responses. She noted that the state's response contained information "gathered from the Presentence Report and other information presumably obtained from the original trial" in 1990. While that information might relate to a jury in a retrial, it had "no relevance to the narrow issues framed in the motion to suppress." Kimerer limited his suppression theory to an examination of two related issues: First, whether Milke waived her Miranda rights. Second, whether the alleged confession was sufficiently reliable to be admitted in evidence at a future trial. Judge Mroz agreed, saying that the suppression hearing would "not be a mini-trial on whether the defendant is guilty of the charged crime."

That language was apparently of no interest to the media; it was not mentioned in print or on broadcast news. But its importance was not lost on the defense lawyers. The issue of guilt, indeed the presumption of it, pervaded the original trial. Now, the Ninth Circuit's finding of massive *Brady* violations and Saldate's change of heart about testifying signaled the new reality. The retrial, if it ever occurred, would focus on Saldate's credibility. The jury would know of his history of confession misconduct. His misconduct would drive much of the retrial, and Milke's alleged confession would likely become a secondary issue. To crystalize her point, Judge Mroz stated in the October 23 minute entry, "The State requests the court to consider this case's procedural history regarding whether Judge Hendrix was aware of Detective Saldate's disciplinary record related to the 1973 incident during the 1990 trial *or* [during] the 1996 post-conviction relief hearing." If nothing else, this language made clear Judge Mroz's intention that what Judge

Hendrix did in 1996 (ignore Saldate's long history of confession mis-conduct) was not going to be repeated in her courtroom.

Judge Mroz said she had taken note that the "appellate record demonstrates that the 1973 incident was not disclosed to the defendant until 2002." That meant she would likely admit the 1973 incident (Saldate's discipline involving trading sexual favors with a female suspect) as part of the assessment of Saldate's credibility. It also suggested that the state had overlooked the fact that Judge Hendrix had refused to give Milke a hearing on her post-conviction relief petition in 1996. Judge Hendrix denied, without a hearing, Milke's focused claims based on Saldate's misconduct and the long list of judicial errors, not to mention the alleged bias the judge had against Milke.

42

SALDATE TAKES THE FIFTH— DECEMBER 18, 2013

*T*HE BAILIFF SHUSHED THE CROWD with a hand signal as Judge Rosa Mroz entered her seventh-floor courtroom in the "new" Maricopa County Superior Court Tower. She was young, well liked, highly respected, and managed her courtroom with equal measures of openness and sternness.

To her left, the witness chair was empty, as was the jury box. In the pit of the courtroom, and to her right sat Debra Milke, Lori Voepel, and Mike Kimerer. Behind them, in the spectator seats, was a sizeable crowd. Some, obvious friends and supporters of Milke, sat anxiously, while others opened notebooks and jotted initial thoughts. The prosecutor, Vince Imbordino, and a plainclothes sheriff's deputy waited on the jury-box side of the court. Neither side exhibited any visible sign of anxiety, but neither had cause to be hopeful. The issue before the court was unusually important. Judges rarely make case-ending decisions this far in advance of a trial on the merits.

Judge Mroz noted the presence of counsel and the defendant, and gave scant notice to the backbenchers at the rear of the 30 x 60-foot wood-paneled room. Two monitors were on her bench and a half-dozen more spread out for use by lawyers, jurors, and court staff. This courtroom could seat 70 in the back pews, 25 in the pit, and 18 jurors. It had Internet access, PowerPoint presentation screens from every angle, and an audio system that included a white noise facility for private sidebar conferences between the judge and the competing lawyers. The court reporter, court clerk, and bailiff all had separate desks with neatly stacked pleadings, supplies, boxes of Kleenex, and bottles of water. Everything was ready.

Armando Saldate, the subject of this hearing, sat with his lawyer, Larry Debus, a tall, gangly man in his 70s, looking spry and up for the task at hand. His client faced the ultimate dilemma for a long-time cop: stick to your story and lose everything, or take the Fifth Amendment and still lose, but not everything. Saldate took a seat behind the prosecutor's table, which put him behind and to Milke's right side. She never looked back at him. In a few moments, he would come forward to the podium to answer the judge's questions. He did that without appearing to notice Milke's presence. They had faced one another 24 years ago, in an older courtroom a block away. That time she was the only one in trouble. She did not take the Fifth even though it was available to her. This time he was in trouble and had forcefully announced his intention to invoke his privilege against self-incrimination.

His testimony had made the case against her before the grand jury, then at her first suppression hearing, during the first trial, and as a potential witness at her post-conviction review hearing. He had also testified against her in federal court and in two sworn depositions. He never varied from his accusation (she confessed). If his testimony was truthful, he should have no fear of another opportunity to state his case. But if he had fudged the truth, the next time might be fatal to his liberty and his pocketbook. He had also given multiple interviews, signed several affidavits, and written a "paraphrased account" of what he claimed was her true confession. He most likely thought that was enough. And it was, until the Ninth Circuit reversed her conviction on two grounds: the trial judge's error in keeping out relevant impeachment evidence, and the prosecution's violation of its duty to deliver damaging information about him to her.

Prior to March 2013 when the Ninth Circuit reversed Milke's conviction, Saldate had consistently said he would take the stand again. But the Ninth Circuit's findings and its rhetoric changed his mind. This time, the flaws in his testimony and his prior misconduct in other confession cases would be fair game. This time he would face Milke in an entirely different setting. Unlike 1990, this time there would be a new and determined-looking judge on the bench. His old nemesis, Debra Milke, out on bail, would sit in the catbird's seat, on the other side of the courtroom. This time Milke would have much better legal talent, and a unanimous panel ruling from the Ninth Circuit that acquitted her and attacked him. Should he testify again? If so, he might embarrass the state of Arizona by losing a capital case for lack of evidence. And it might give birth to his own criminal charges. Alternatively, he could take the Fifth Amendment, and watch the state's case against Milke swirl down the legal drain.

Lawyers, pundits, and savvy media reps saw it as a *Hobson's choice*—a free choice in which only one option makes sense. Why would he risk charges just to repeat what most saw as a flawed confession at best, or worse—a fabricated one? Instead of a Hobson's (take it *or* leave it) choice, Saldate had a take it *and* leave it choice. He could leave bad enough alone. The prosecutors saw it as more of a *Sophie's choice*—choosing his duty as a law enforcement officer over protecting himself. That was the honorable choice, wasn't it? Duty over self? But Saldate was no Patrick Henry. And Milke now looked less the witch from Salem and more like Joan of Arc.

Judge Mroz invited Mr. Debus and his client to the podium, where she put the questions squarely to Saldate. "Mr. Saldate, do you intend to invoke your Fifth Amendment right against self-incrimination if the State calls you as a witness in this case?

"Yes," the heavily jowled man said, indistinctly, but with his head up.

"And if I do not accept your claim to Fifth Amendment protection, will your testimony be exactly as you stated it in the first trial of this case?"

Saldate nodded, said yes, and looked at his lawyer.

Turning to Debus, Judge Mroz reminded him that the legal issue had been fully briefed by both sides (the state and Milke), but politely offered him the opportunity to speak to the issue. Debus reminded the judge that he'd been in many courtrooms, both as a working police officer before he became a lawyer, and as a lawyer in capital litigation in similar cases. That experience, he argued, gave him a perspective that he'd like to share with the court. She said fine. He talked abstractly about the significance of the Fifth Amendment's several protections, and specifically about Saldate's "genuine and very real" risks. Saldate wasn't much worried, he said, about perjury charges arising out of repeating his earlier testimony. What kept Saldate up nights, Debus said, "was the very real prospect of new witnesses, new litigants, coming from who knows where, and claiming misconduct that might give rise to many civil rights violations based on old cases unearthed by Milke's lawyers and cited by the second-highest court in the land as serious misconduct on the part of his client." Debus implied there could even be some of those possible litigants in the courtroom "this very day." He said he'd spent a good deal of time studying the cases and talking to his client about them. "I fear for my client and I know he is fearful himself," he argued. "I believe he has a right to invoke the Fifth Amendment and I have strongly advised him to do it."

Debus sat down. Judge Mroz nodded at Vince Imbordino. He rose but did not move to the podium, signaling that he would not have much to say. He reminded the judge that his office had no intention of bringing charges against Saldate and that both the U.S. Attorney for the District of Arizona and the U.S. Department of Justice had indicated that they could see no prosecutable offense in the cases cited by the Ninth Circuit. Besides, he argued, the Ninth Circuit was itself in error in many of the cases they relied on. Waving off that argument as inconsistent, Judge Mroz asked for comment by Milke's lawyers.

Mike Kimerer came to the podium and urged the judge to consider the core issue. "This case is before you on retrial because Saldate's misconduct was kept from the jury in the first trial, illegally, and without good cause." Kimerer assured the judge that if the case were retried, he would cross-examine Saldate and "show the new jury exactly why and how they should disregard everything Saldate has to say about a confession that never happened."

Judge Mroz reminded both counsel that the legal issues had been fully briefed, that she'd read all the briefs and cases cited, that she was taking the matter under advisement, and that she intended to rule "next week."

True to her word, three business days later, on December 18, 2013, she issued a seven-page written ruling. It was as momentous as her first, which had granted bail. And it would alter the state's carefully laid plans to retry Milke. Her orders were crisp and she was not afraid to use "all caps" to make her point: (1) "IT IS ORDERED"—denying the state's request to compel Saldate to testify over his Fifth Amendment claim. (2) "IT IS FURTHER ORDERED"—setting a status conference on January 17, 2014. Her two-paragraph conclusion is tightly focused:

> A judge may deny the claim of privilege only where it is *perfectly clear* from a careful consideration of all the circumstances in the case, that the witness is mistaken and that the answer cannot possibly have such tendency to incriminate. This places a heavy burden on the judge who decides to compel testimony over a Fifth Amendment claim. After careful consideration of the totality of the circumstances, the Court finds that it is not *perfectly clear* that Saldate is mistaken and that his testimony could not possibly have the tendency to incriminate him. (Emphasis in the original.)

Her seven-page order is an unvarnished look at the core of what the state wrought by not turning over Saldate's entire file to the defense in 1990. She began by addressing the state's contention that she should have not "asked whether Saldate needed a lawyer before he testifies." While courts rarely inquire if witnesses need lawyers to protect themselves, "this is not a normal case." Here, she said, the Ninth Circuit specifically referred Saldate for "investigation into whether his conduct amounts to a pattern of violating the federally protected rights of Arizona residents." The court needed to ask Saldate if he needed counsel. It would have been "remiss in its duties were it to ignore such an obvious issue."

This obvious issue, and the burden it places on the retrial process, necessitated something even more important than the rights of the state's key witness. It required the new trial judge to determine whether the eight cases cited by the Ninth Circuit can be "challenged" or whether they are "the law of the case." Both sides briefed the issue, but it remained unresolved. Judge Mroz reviewed "the information about these eight cases only to determine the legitimacy" of Saldate's invocation of his Fifth Amendment rights. She said, "[W]hile this court does not fully agree with the [Ninth Circuit's] conclusions in every case, the court finds that Saldate does have a legitimate reason to fear prosecution arising out of these cases."

While perhaps unintended, her point was clear. Had she not asked Saldate if he wanted an independent lawyer, he might not have gotten good Fifth Amendment advice from the prosecutors. Their stated goal was to retry and if possible reconvict Milke. It could not have been lost on Judge Mroz that the prosecutor had also announced an intention to ask for another death penalty for Milke. Saldate's rights conflicted with the state's intention. That's why he *needed* his own lawyer.

Judge Mroz noted that Saldate had been the "main" witness against Milke three times (her original trial, the Rule 32 post-conviction review process, and the federal habeas process). She was right about Saldate testifying three times, but wrong about which three proceedings. He testified at the original suppression hearing, but not at the PCR process because Judge Hendrix had refused to allow an evidentiary hearing. His testimony was "familiar" to her, Mroz said. The prosecutors confirmed in their pleadings that they would ask the same questions of him at the retrial. She could "anticipate questions from Milke's lawyers related to the impeachment materials described by the Ninth Circuit." This history gave her the "factual predicate sufficient to evaluate the claim of privilege." From that vantage point, her analysis was flawless.

The Ninth Circuit clarified that Saldate lied under oath. He disregarded suspects' constitutional rights. It was possible that his conduct amounted to a pattern of violating the federally protected rights of Arizona citizens. All this gave him a "reasonable apprehension of danger." Judge Mroz went through the letters between prosecutorial agencies after the Ninth Circuit ruled in favor of Milke, and found them wanting for clarity and certainty. She evaluated possible perjury charges and noted that the MCAO had declined to immunize Saldate. She observed that the MCAO has no jurisdiction over federal perjury charges. And she was not in the least tentative in her ruling. "The court finds that Saldate *has demonstrated* a reasonable apprehension of danger that, if compelled to answer, he *would face* criminal charges based on his past testimony and/or present disclosures and that the Fifth Amendment affords protection."

This ruling would support only a question-by-question process and would put Saldate on the witness stand, in front of a jury. He and his lawyers wanted more. He wanted a "blanket" assertion of privilege. A protective blanket, preferably made out of legal Kevlar, that would protect him from the machine-gun questions coming from Mike Kimerer if he had to appear against Milke ever again. Judges rarely grant blanket privilege of Fifth Amendment coverage. However, if a judge determines that a witness could legitimately refuse to answer essentially all relevant questions, then a witness "may be totally excused without violating the witness's Sixth Amendment right to compulsory process."

Clarifying that she had "extensive" knowledge about the case, Judge Mroz granted Saldate a blanket Fifth Amendment privilege. Her minute entry confirms that she read "most of the transcripts from the trial, transcripts and exhibits from the 2010 federal court hearing, the Ninth Circuit opinion and records from the eight cases, as well as a number of exhibits submitted by the State and the defense." That gave her more than enough information.

With her order, Judge Mroz pushed what might be a Hobson's choice or a Sophie's choice over to the prosecutor's side of the courtroom. There was no doubt about the efficacy of a case without Saldate's testimony—the state could not prevail without him. So the state's choices were to go through the motions of putting on a case and face

an almost certain directed verdict in Milke's favor, to appeal the ruling, or to try to negotiate a settlement to resolve the case short of
trial. The first choice was unthinkable. The second was a thinly veiled
attempt to buy time. The third choice—throw in the legal towel—
would have political and judicial consequences, not to mention career-
ending implications.

43

THE CORNERSTONE OF
LEGAL CONSISTENCY—
THE LAW OF THE CASE

ALPH WALDO EMERSON, IN HIS essay entitled "Self-Reliance," complained that consistency was the hobgoblin of little minds. But consistency is as important to the law as wind is to sail. Nothing moves forward without a strong, consistent wind, on the water or in the legal system. One of America's most honored appellate judges, Oliver Wendell Holmes, understood legal consistency better than most. He said, "Every opinion tends to become a law." That is why the towering structure we call the American legal system has four cornerstones upon which its impact and its legacy rest: collateral estoppel, law of the case, *res judicata*, and *stare decisis*. Without these four structural deadweights, the tower would fall and the homily of Terence, the third century b.c. Greek poet, would prevail: "As many opinions as there are men; each a law to himself."

There are at least nine important "opinions" in the Milke case. Saldate came up with the first—his December 5, 1989 "paraphrased account" (Milke confessed to killing her own child). Two hours later, Milke gave the second—her version of the Saldate interrogation (she denied confessing). Noel Levy offered the third (he believed Saldate). Levy managed the grand jury's indictment, called Saldate as a witness, and stood firm with him for the next 24 years. Judge Hendrix was fourth in line, authoring many oral and written opinions (she believed Saldate and refused to suppress his version, or admit evidence of his character). The fifth opinion came from the jury (it followed Judge Hendrix's instructions, believed Saldate, and found Milke guilty). The Arizona Supreme Court was next—sixth in sequence (it held Milke's claims of trial court error were not nearly fundamental enough to warrant a reversal, and confirmed her conviction of guilt and her death sentence).

Judge Hendrix re-entered the fray in 1996 in a new role as the post-conviction judge. This counts as the seventh opinion (denying any relief and finding no after-the-fact fault with either Levy or Saldate). U.S. District Court Judge Robert Broomfield offered the eighth opinion in 2010 (holding that Milke had been given "due process of law" and denying habeas relief in the federal system).

The ninth opinion was the game changer. Fittingly, it came from the Ninth Circuit Court of Appeals. Chief Judge Alex Kozinski and Circuit Judges Jerome Farris and Carlos Bea took a deep and serious look at all of the earlier opinions, findings, rulings, dispositions, and orders. The court released a 90-plus-page written unanimous opinion (Milke was wrongfully convicted and denied her constitutional right to a fair trial). It came to this opinion because Saldate's long history of interrogation misconduct should have been given to Milke's jury. Had that happened, the court said, Milke "would likely have not been convicted, or sentenced to death." So, it remanded her case back to Arizona for a new trial. The Ninth Circuit's weighty opinion became the law of the case, binding on all lower courts under the ancient doctrines of *res judicata* and *stare decisis*.

The ultimate decider in this country is the United States Supreme Court. It declined to disturb the Ninth Circuit's opinion, and this made that court's opinion *the law of the case*. That's when the trouble started.

The prosecutor rebelled and said the Ninth Circuit was wrong—wrong on its findings, wrong on its view of the law, and wrong about Saldate. It did the unthinkable—it ignored the Ninth Circuit, insisting that Saldate, the Maricopa County Attorney's Office, and Judge Hendrix were right all along. So much for consistency.

If a prosecutor can ignore the highest decision maker in the case—here the Ninth Circuit—the consistency upon which the law depends becomes legal chaos. The law, writ large, demands coherence and respect. Simple traffic and small claims courts, plus superior and intermediate appellate courts, strive for consistent rulings and outcomes in cases based on identical facts. When one cog in the legal machine, say the prosecutor, refuses to honor either the spirit or the letter of a ruling of the highest court in the machine, the legal risks are enormous—inconsistency on identical facts. The legal machine, like any well-lubricated machine, is a series of opinions that transfer legal consequences up or down the legal system.

As a practical matter, the post-appellate question is how much of the highest appellate court's decision truly "binds" the lower court as it processes the case anew based on the appellate outcome. To address those concerns, the law invokes several doctrines. Each operates in a different way to encourage consistency. Double jeopardy, the law of the case, and the law's most storied doctrine, *stare decisis*, collectively mandate consistency. To achieve consistency requires compliance by all the cogs in the justice machine. If one cog rebels, in this case the prosecutor, the other cogs (the trial judge and the defendant) find little purchase trying to manage a retrial of the case. That is especially true where, as in this case, the appellate court vacated the prior rulings of the lower court and they are no longer binding on the defendant. Consistency demands that the lower court's "new" rulings be consistent with the overruling appellate court.

LAW OF THE CASE

The law of the case doctrine expresses a preference for not reconsidering or changing a ruling made earlier in the same case—consistency from top to bottom. It has two overarching principles. One, called the mandate rule, prevents a lower court from relitigating an issue after a reviewing court has decided the issue in the same case. The other, sometimes called the coordinate jurisdiction rule, provides that a court should not ordinarily reconsider issues already decided by a court of coordinate jurisdiction. This second principle, while not directly applicable to the Milke case, could become applicable if the new trial judge were to adopt the prosecutor's attitude, i.e., ignore the Ninth Circuit. The doctrine regulates the remand court's discretion, but does not deprive it of the power to revisit an issue. However, if the remand court fails to follow the law of the case and issues a ruling inconsistent with the earlier ruling, that decision will be reviewed, again, by the higher-ranking appellate court. For that reason alone, remand courts are especially carefully not to relitigate an issue resolved by the court of last resort, which in this case is the Ninth Circuit.

Sound public and legal policy support the law of the case doctrine. It promotes consistency, efficiency, finality, and conservation of judicial resources. If remand courts freely rendered inconsistent rulings in successive phases of the same case, or disregarded appellate rulings, the parties could not treat any issue as decided, until resolved again on appeal.

At the remand level, Milke's prosecutor (the Maricopa County Attorney's Office) wanted to reopen and relitigate unfavorable rulings and findings of the Ninth Circuit by arguing they were "wrong." Had the remand judge allowed it, this would have injected delay and uncertainty. And it would have unnecessarily consumed judicial resources.

Unlike *res judicata*, the law of the case doctrine applies to rulings *not* embodied in a final judgment. That's because *res judicata* already gives preclusive effect to final judgments. The law of the case doctrine, with its inherent applicability to non-final rulings, provides additional consistency. Some courts have treated the doctrine as having less force, but more flexibility than other rules of consistency. One example is when a party asks a court to revisit a question and advance a new basis for the relief sought. The law of the case doctrine might allow such revisiting. However, if the court finds the question has been resolved by a final order, then *res judicata* would bar further consideration even if the party has new information.

The Milke case is a classic example of how the law of the case doctrine works when the remand issue is whether a confession should be suppressed. It is used in conjunction with *res judicata*. The Ninth Circuit, while criticizing the original trial court's handling of the suppression issue, did not make specific findings that would preclude a new suppression hearing on remand. A new suppression hearing would allow the introduction of evidence the original judge kept out, thus protecting the state's prime witness to the disadvantage of the defendant.

DOUBLE JEOPARDY

The double jeopardy doctrine protects defendants from successive prosecutions for the same offense. Provided that jeopardy attached in the first proceeding, a defendant can invoke double jeopardy to bar further prosecution for the same offense whether the first case ended in conviction *or* acquittal. It also bars further prosecution after a reversal based on prosecutorial misconduct. Unlike the defendant, however, the prosecution cannot invoke double jeopardy and will never be in the position of arguing that double jeopardy bars a defense claim.

STARE DECISIS

Stare decisis, "to stand by things declared," is legal-speak for the ancient doctrine of precedent. Whether a case is precedent determines whether it is binding on other courts, which depends on whether the same points were involved in the prior case. It reflects the judiciary's time immemorial practice of adhering to established legal precedents unless special justification compels reconsideration of earlier decisions. Conceptually, *stare decisis* achieves consistency in the law, implementing the preference for declining to alter judicially defined law governing an issue. Practically, it is woefully inadequate in explaining whether a particular criminal defendant will be bound by the earlier resolution of a legal issue in the defendant's case.

Stare decisis bars an appellate court from overruling or disregarding its prior precedent without adequate justification. It binds trial courts by applying the governing precedent of a higher court in the direct chain of responsibility. And, to prove that nothing in the law is simple, it requires some courts to apply the legal principles already determined by certain other courts. But it does not preclude a party from litigating the facts of the party's own case. Nor does it foreclose the argument that the earlier precedent does not govern the facts of the later case. Finally, it leaves opposing parties free to persuade the court to alter or abandon earlier holdings.

44

JUDGE MROZ RULES ON
DOUBLE JEOPARDY—
JANUARY 2014

O
N JANUARY 17, 2014, JUDGE Rosa Mroz entered her packed
courtroom unannounced. Everyone in front of the bar anticipated her entrance when the staff went immediately silent. But the
less-observant civilians in the back of the courtroom continued chat-
ting as she took her seat.

"All right," she said, after adjusting the stack of papers she carried
and moving the microphone slightly to her right. "This is the time set
for CR 1989-012631, the State of Arizona versus Debra Jean Milke.
Please announce your presence."

"Vince Imbordino, on behalf of the State.

"Mike Kimerer. Good afternoon, Your Honor. I'm here with Lori
Voepel, and Rhonda Neff on behalf of Debra Milke, who is present in
the courtroom at this time."

"All right. The first thing I would like to address is the motion to dismiss on double jeopardy grounds. I reviewed the motion, the response, and the reply. So, Mr. Kimerer, whenever you're ready."

The crowd seated in the pews on the left side, at the rear of the courtroom, were a mix of Milke's friends and family and her customary support group, all bunched into the first three rows. On the right side, separated by culture, mindset, and attitude, were two MCAO law clerks, two Phoenix PD officers, a sheriff's deputy, a half-dozen interested citizens, one of whom would take copious notes, and Arizona Milke, with his skull-headed cane. The back row of the courtroom, on both sides, was unofficially reserved for local press. Typically, a half-dozen print and broadcast media were present at every hearing.

No one paid much attention to Judge Mroz's comment that she *had* read the motion, the response, and the reply. She directed that message straight at Messrs. Kimerer and Imbordino—*don't bother repeating what's in your briefs, guys, just argue your position.* The level of judicial preparation varied widely from one courtroom to the next; some judges were always prepared and looked askance at repetition. Other judges needed a little nudge because the briefs were still sitting unread on their desks. Judge Mroz was decidedly in the former category—always fully prepared—and was open, but knowledgeable. Mike Kimerer knew well her intellectual capacity and her tolerance level.

"Thank you, Your Honor. As you know, we ask that the case be dismissed on double jeopardy grounds. We base that on the ruling in the Ninth Circuit where they found substantial misconduct by the prosecution, which would be a basis for arguing that the double jeopardy standard applies, and that this case should not go to trial again. Briefly. I know we've touched on it in our motion, but I think we need to build the case."

Kimerer took less than a half-hour. He rejected the notion of retrial given the level of misconduct by the police and prosecutors in the case. He referenced the current state of the U.S. Supreme Court rulings, citing Oregon v. Kennedy, a case involving intentional prosecutorial misconduct. He argued the Arizona Supreme Court's ruling in Pool v. Pima County, and Justice Feldman's definition of what it takes in

Arizona to invoke double jeopardy in a prosecutorial misconduct case. He noted Arizona's three-prong test and started to explain it.

Judge Mroz had been patient long enough, "Which I do have," she said, smiling at Mr. Kimerer.

Kimerer got it. "Which I believe you have."

"Right," she said with a small wave of her hand, suggesting he get on with it.

Kimerer did. He jumped pages ahead in his notes and said, "When you look at this case, Debra Milke's case, it [the legal analysis] has been done for us—by the Ninth Circuit . . . They have looked at every aspect of this case, and they have made conclusions that fit those three prongs of the *Pool* case . . . There's certain findings that they make in the *Milke* case . . . if there's any case at all, this is a case where the double jeopardy application should apply."

Kimerer set his notes aside, looking at both judge and prosecutor directly. "The prosecutor here had an absolute duty to disclose, without request, impeachment and exculpatory material. The State is charged with knowledge there was impeachment material in Saldate's personnel file. The Ninth Circuit says the State failed in its constitutional obligation of producing material even without a request . . . by the defense. And they say that the State had a duty to produce the documents showing Saldate's false and misleading statements in court, and before grand juries. Saldate violated other suspects' rights under the Fourth and Fifth Amendments. And the Ninth Circuit also made a finding that the prosecutor's office knew of this conduct because it prosecuted a case where the misconduct occurred: so it knew of the cases. The Ninth Circuit said the prosecutorial misconduct in this case was 'so egregious.' The Ninth Circuit called the attitude of the Maricopa County Attorney's Office cavalier towards its constitutional duty to disclose impeachment evidence. The Maricopa County Attorney's Office was ultimately familiar with Saldate's pattern of misconduct. Your Honor, I know you've read this over and over again. And know all of the history here. At that point in time, there were a whole slew of different cases that had passed through the office certainly, where the conduct of Officer Saldate was questioned. It certainly had to be in the purview of the Maricopa County Attorney's Office to know about what was going on at that time. Some of the cases were before the Milke trial. Some of them were after. But you have to remember *Milke* was the very last case that Saldate had. All of his other misconduct had been floating around there in motions, or whatever and it was [enough,] according to the Ninth Circuit, to trigger knowledge by the Maricopa County Attorney's Office that this was a cop that had a problem."

Judge Mroz entered the fray with another wave of her hand at Mr. Kimerer. "In fact, at least two other judges, and I'm talking specifically about Judge Hendrix and Judge Broomfield, who looked at these issues and decided that really this was not something that needed to be disclosed or given over to the defense. Are those intervening causes that would not make it fit so squarely into the test that's enunciated in *Pool?*"

Kimerer answered, "I don't think so, Your Honor. The Ninth Circuit specifically found that Judge Hendrix was wrong, in her ruling. She should have seen exculpatory evidence, obviously didn't, and did not produce it. They also say, even if she makes a wrong ruling or doesn't see it, that's no excuse for the prosecution not to produce it. They had a duty to produce it and they should know what that *Brady* information was. And there was a lot of it. Just because she made an erroneous ruling and the prosecution still has knowledge of that misconduct, they should still have produced that to the defense at that time. The same situation with Judge Broomfield. He made that analysis and Judge Kozinski totally rejected Broomfield's analysis, when you read the Milke opinion. I think you have to look at how they look at the record in the case—that is[,] the prosecution just had to know about Saldate."

Judge Mroz didn't agree. "Okay. This is what I would like you to address. If the Ninth Circuit really felt this way, why didn't the Ninth Circuit just go ahead and bar a retrial altogether? Why go through this exercise of remanding it down to the trial court to see if a confession should be suppressed or not, and do all of this? When really all they had to do was just say this is so egregious no retrial should be had? I know that in Judge Kozinski's concurrence he went so far as to say that he would have said no retrial. But the other two judges felt differently, which is why there's a main opinion and a concurring opinion. So can you address that?"

As usual, Kimerer had anticipated the question. It was not unusual for state court judges to misunderstand the scope of what a federal appellate court can do under the federal *habeas corpus* statutes. He took the question as a chance to educate Judge Mroz on exactly why the federal court could not just "go ahead bar a retrial altogether." He said, "Of course, your Honor. On a *habeas* review, the jurisdiction of the court is limited to sending the case back. It doesn't have the power to dismiss the case."

Judge Mroz looked puzzled, which prompted Kimerer to expand on his answer. "It could send it back and recommend dismissal. It could send it back for different reasons. But under *habeas* review, it is limited to sending a case back and finding constitutional violations. I know that's the argument that the State makes in their response— Why didn't the Ninth Circuit, under double jeopardy grounds, go ahead and dismiss the case then. They didn't have the jurisdiction under *habeas* law to do it. Also, that issue was not presented to them. And if you look at the other cases, how they [address] double jeopardy—one of the examples is the case I talked about in Oregon. You'll see that it always comes back. If you're sitting there as the prosecutor, and you look at this case when it comes to the office, and you go through that office, you realize the only evidence that you really have is a *he said/she said* case. And it's Saldate saying she confessed, and it's her saying she didn't. It's in state court. The issue is raised there and has to be presented to the court at the state level to make that [a double jeopardy] determination. When you look at all of the things the Ninth Circuit says happened here, and you look at what they're talking about, there is no question that I think the standard is set forth in *Pool*. And it is also mentioned in later in *Minnitt*. It certainly was met in this case."

Kimerer paused, reached for a black three-ring notebook beside the podium, found what he wanted, and continued, looking at the judge over the rim of his reading glasses. "Let me put it in terms of just how we live in this world. And what you see going on. Back in 1990 when this case hit, it was one of the most [highly publicized] cases around. Debra Milke was painted as the most heinous woman; [she] had her child killed on Christmas. The media had been certainly caught up in the hullabaloo of that. She was basically marked in this community as one of the most horrible murderers around. Underneath all of that, if you're sitting there as the prosecutor, and you're looking at this case when it comes to the office, and you go through that office, you realize the only evidence that you really have is a he said/she said case. And it's Saldate saying she confessed without any corroboration, and then she saying she didn't, and she has no corroboration. So the prosecutor's strategy, obviously, if you're going to proceed with the case, is that, you know, it's all going to be about the credibility of your police officer, and about her credibility.

"In terms of the investigation, which was also done by Saldate, he went out, told lies to many witnesses to get them to turn so they would come into court and talk about her character, and malign her character. At that point in time, in that office, and the Ninth Circuit describes why this has to be, when Noel Levy is sitting there looking at this case. He *has to know* about Saldate's questionable background. They have had all of these cases at the trial level, district level, and motions going back and forth.

"I remember at that time going through the office, in the case that the Ninth Circuit describes Paul Rood, for instance, being there. All of these offices are 50 feet apart. They're all in the same section. Everybody talks. It's just inconceivable that Noel Levy at that time doesn't have an idea that, hey, if I'm going to make this case fly, I have got to protect Saldate. Because if this stuff comes out against him, then a jury can question his credibility, and then I'm going to have problems. And what he did from the very beginning in the case is to start blocking any attempt by the defense attorney to get any type of impeaching, exculpatory evidence. And what Ken Ray did, as a good defense attorney would do, he went out with his subpoena and he subpoenaed the personnel records of Saldate. And we know what happens there. They fought that motion. The judge ruled against them. We don't know if she looked at the file. But Noel Levy had to know what's in that file.

"We know there's one thing in that file at this point—that's the incident back in 1973—which is definitely impeaching information. They enter into a stipulation about how to handle the whole thing. But that stipulation is just to look in there for stuff that pertains to Fifth Amendment violations, and it doesn't have anything about looking for impeachment violations. They only produced, I think, one or two years of his personnel file. Well, many of the years weren't even in the records that got produced from what we can ascertain from the record. They would show particular cases that Saldate was working on. You could look at those cases, and if he had had all of that, he would have been able to check out and see what was going on as far as any type of misconduct by Saldate or what was happening in some of those cases. All of that was kept from him. He never received any of that. And then you've got Noel Levy sitting here, obviously, in this office. And I think they talk about it. Paul Rood talking about the situation they had between her conviction and her sentencing where the case comes down, and that there is a finding of misconduct by Saldate. Yet, that is never turned over to the defense. They have none of this information. They're not given anything about places where Saldate has committed any misconduct. To me that shows active participation by your prosecutor in terms of blocking that evidence, and keeping it from getting out. Because he knows if it gets out, he's got a whole different case on his hands. And that's what happened. None of it ever got in trial. That's why the case is here. And the Ninth Circuit says it was very egregious. Horrible misconduct. It rises to that level. We submit that triggers the double jeopardy clause in this particular case."

Kimerer paused again, moved through his briefing book, and settled on a new section. He spent about ten minutes responding to the state's position. Then he closed with this: "Do the people of Arizona feel confident in taking Milke's life when the only thread on which her conviction hangs is [the] word of a policeman with a record of dishonesty and disrespect for the law? Bad cops, and those who tolerate them, put all of us in an untenable situation. And that's what we had happen here. Debra Milke gave up twenty-three years of her life based upon testimony from a dishonest cop. And there's really no other evidence to support this conviction, other than the character evidence, and the negative fashion, which he also was responsible for creating. We would ask that our motion be granted. Thank you, Your Honor."

Kimerer returned to the defense table. Judge Mroz thanked him and turned toward the prosecution table, where Vince Imbordino was standing, ready to move to the podium the second Kimerer vacated it.

"Good afternoon," he said to Judge Mroz.

"Good afternoon," she said, smiling.

"Your Honor, we filed a response upon which I'm still happy to rely. You know[,] I don't have any changes to make to it. I keep hearing from the defense about things that must be true. But upon which there's no evidence that they're true. I've heard allegations that the record demonstrates that Mr. Levy intentionally forwarded, or withheld the personnel file of Detective Saldate. There's no evidence of that. In fact, the record is just the opposite. While we understand that the Ninth Circuit concluded that the State is imputed with knowledge of what they found to be misconduct in his various cases, which you understand by now we disagree with their conclusions, but, I mean, we're stuck with the fact that they've concluded that our office and Mr. Levy is imputed with the knowledge of those cases, and they certainly should have been disclosed. There's certainly no evidence. The Ninth Circuit didn't have any evidence, and counsel keeps referring to—not only to *dicta* in the opinion, but also to the opinion of the—of Justice [sic] Kozinski who was in the minority on one of the primary issues in this case. As you pointed out just a few moments ago. There's absolutely no basis under the facts or the law, for this Court to dismiss this case on the basis of double jeopardy."

With that, Imbordino left the podium and returned to his chair at the defense table.

Judge Mroz noted his early departure with an "okay," and then turned toward the defense table. Nodding to Kimerer, she said, "It's your motion, so you get the last word."

Returning to the podium, Kimerer squared himself to the bench and pushed away his notes. His rebuttal was reflective. He dealt quickly with the few points argued by Imbordino, before ending the hearing on a high note. "The Ninth Circuit reviewed *all* of the evidence in this case, *all* of the transcripts in this case, and came to their conclusions that were supported by that evidence. This is a case, if there ever was one, that should be dismissed on the basis that double jeopardy applies. Thank you."

Kimerer returned to his table, and the court addressed both counsel.

Judge Mroz reminded both lawyers that she'd set this hearing on double jeopardy because she saw it as "separate and apart from whether we need to know if he's going to testify or not."

Imbordino admitted, "[W]e might well be spinning our wheels. That's because the primary issues revolve around his potential testimony."

Kimerer told the judge that he and Ms. Voepel needed something clarified by the court. "If Saldate is not going to testify, we don't see why we would be proceeding with a motion to suppress hearing. There is no other evidence. At that point, we would certainly file some type of a motion to dismiss on this, based on no evidence to even proceed in the case at that point in time. I don't know if that's something we would do now, but it's premature since they say they're going to appeal [on Saldate's invocation of the Fifth Amendment]. But, right now, we don't see how you can practically proceed if Saldate is not going to testify. That is the only place where you're going to get any evidence that connects Debra Milke to this crime."

The judge wanted to wrap up both the hearing on double jeopardy and the debate about the next steps pending a decision by the appellate court.

"Okay. All right. I've reviewed the file extensively now several times. I want to confirm with you all what's pending and get your viewpoints. Is there something I need to do, other than decide this motion on double jeopardy grounds, and the motion for reconsideration?"

None of the lawyers had any objections to staying all other proceedings until they had an appellate resolution on Saldate's invocation of his Fifth Amendment rights. With that, the court staff cleared the court for the next case on the calendar. There were a good many lawyers in the courtroom that day. Several were struck by how odd it was for the Fifth Amendment to be so central to a case, yet so disconnected as a matter of trial procedure.

The lawyers and the court had just spent an hour debating the applicability of the double jeopardy doctrine to the case. The previous hearing had involved Saldate's invocation of his privilege against self-incrimination. The lawyers and the judge so easily accepted the separation of the issues; none seemed to notice their inherent synchronicity. No one connected Milke *to* Saldate on the two principal issues before the court. Was it just a matter of concurrent events in their lives—just a mere coincidence? Or was that December 3, 1989 interrogation something that would later turn out to be incoincident?

By the end of this hearing, the Fifth Amendment and double jeopardy were what this case had been reduced to. They would be the deciding issues at both the trial and appellate courts. The appellate courts would soon pair Milke's double jeopardy issue *with* Saldate's invocation of privilege. The legal premise is the same in both issues: *protection of individuals against governmental authority*. Milke would be harmed by the government's effort to try her twice for the same crime—*Fifth Amendment* protection against double jeopardy. Saldate would be harmed by the government's effort to compel him to be a witness against himself—*Fifth Amendment* privilege against self-incrimination. That's how the legal issues blend for the general public.

But for lawyers familiar with the nuances of the Fifth Amendment, there is a *casual* connection. *But for* what Saldate did (and said), Milke would not have been tried, much less found guilty. The Fifth Amendment protections that both Milke and Saldate were fighting for became the legal life preserver for both. Saldate wanted to "be done" with the case. So did Milke. Did she confess or not? The Fifth Amendment is neutral on truth or falsity. It protects both. Guilt or innocence does not matter. What matters is whether the Fifth Amendment protects both, only one, or neither.

And if the obscure notion of synchronicity were not enough, there is the raw irony of it all. Saldate, the extractor of the alleged confession, now claims Fifth Amendment protection and refuses to repeat the confession. Milke, the victim of the alleged confession, also claims Fifth Amendment protection and says she cannot be tried again. Both positions are tied to a premise deeply embedded in our constitutional framework—individuals need and are constitutionally entitled to protection against governmental authority. Milke's propitious moment occurred at the Ninth Circuit, when her convictions and sentences were overturned. Saldate's propitious moment occurred when Judge Mroz ruled that he was entitled to claim his privilege against self-incrimination. If not a legal consequence, this pairing of issues was certainly not a mere coincidence—it would garner independent review by the appellate courts, and forever tie Saldate to Milke in a way no one could have imagined.

—

JUDGE MROZ DENIED MILKE'S DOUBLE jeopardy motion on January 22, 2014. She wrote a short "Under Advisement Ruling." She penned two pages summarizing why she denied the motion. First, a reversal rarely bars retrial. Second, the Arizona cases (*Minnitt* and *Pool*) do not mandate dismissal on the facts of the Milke case. Third, in most instances, the remedy for prosecutorial misconduct is a new trial. Fourth, winning a retrial was enough. She expressed genuine concern about the Ninth Circuit's reversal, saying, "The Court is mindful that the Ninth Circuit determined that the prosecutor had a 'duty to learn of any favorable evidence known to the others acting on the government's behalf in the case, including the police. . . .'" She said she knew that the Ninth Circuit concluded "that what happened here is more akin to active concealment." She said she had "studied this case extensively."

Nonetheless, "[t]he Court does not have any evidence that the prosecutor's actions constituted active concealment. The Court notes that Judge Hendrix, both at trial and during post-conviction proceedings, guided the prosecutor's decisions regarding dissemination of materials related to Saldate. Judge Hendrix determined that discovery obligations did not implicate the materials sought by the Defendant;

the standard (discovery rather than disclosure) and the decision (not to provide material to Defendant) were determined to be error by the Ninth Circuit. The Court declines to impute bad faith to either the prosecutor or to the trial court."

Trial lawyers reading Judge Mroz's explanations likely noted the references to Judge Hendrix as somewhat surprising. Judge Hendrix had enjoyed a reputation as one favoring the prosecution in criminal cases. Many in the courthouse knew about her rebukes by appellate courts, the judicial conduct commission, and presiding judges. But the larger surprise was Judge Mroz's admission that she used her personal experience as a prosecutor in making her decision.

"The Court is familiar with the manner in which the Maricopa County Attorney's Office (MCAO) functions: MCAO is a very large office with many deputy county attorneys, most of whom have very heavy caseloads. It is not a given that prosecutors know what is going on in each other's cases. The three cases cited by the Defendant were not handled by the prosecutor in this case, Noel Levy. It [sic] was handled by Paul Rood. There is no evidence that Mr. Levy and Mr. Rood shared information about their cases. It is speculative that Levy must have known what was going on in Rood's cases."

Judge Mroz footnoted her own experience in her written order. "This judge was a former prosecutor from 1995 to 1999. As a judge, the Court has presided over [a] countless number of criminal cases prosecuted by [the] MCAO."

All judges bring their own experience into their courtrooms. But in a case involving misconduct *by* the MCAO, where the trial judge rules *for* the MCAO, the decision is at least slightly tainted by recounting her former job *at* the MCAO. Or, as a millennial might put it, TMI.

Presumably, based on her personal understanding of how, or whether, Levy and Rood shared or did not share information, she concluded: "Based on the existing information, the Court cannot conclude that the prosecutor intentionally engaged in conduct which he knew to be improper, or that he did so with indifference, if not a specific intent, to prejudice the Defendant. The Court concludes that the *Brady/Giglio* violation was not sufficiently egregious to implicate the double jeopardy protection afforded by either the Arizona or U.S. Constitutions. The Court further concludes that the remedy imposed by the Ninth Circuit, disclosure of the impeachment materials and a new trial, is sufficient."

And with that, Judge Rosa Mroz denied Milke's motion to dismiss on double jeopardy grounds.

45

THE LAW OF DOUBLE JEOPARDY

$\mathcal{W}$HETHER DOUBLE JEOPARDY LIMITATION ON retrial following prosecutorial misconduct applies is always a difficult
and hard-fought issue. Even calling it "fundamental" minimizes its
impact. When applied by an independent judiciary, it is justice-at-
stake and cuts deeply into the core of government under law. There
is at every level of criminal and constitutional litigation an enormous
imbalance between the prosecutor and the accused. That is a byprod-
uct of giving prosecutors virtually unchecked powers, while holding
public defenders to the poverty line. The government's intrusion into
suspects' lives in criminal cases is at its zenith in cases of prosecutorial
misconduct. Other elected or appointed officials have minimal impact.
But prosecutors control almost every aspect of due process in criminal cases—starting with *whether* to make a charge and culminating
with *what* charge to make. They access vast governmental resources
in investigating and preparing cases. At the proximal end of the pipe-
line, they manage the plea bargaining process for the majority of cases
without any oversight. Finally, prosecutors enjoy great deference and
authority when they rise to stand before juries in cases that do not
"bargain out" and go to trial.

In capital cases, the prosecutor's power and impact shine like a halo around a harvest moon. They are solely responsible, in the most opaque way, for slating defendants for the death penalty. Once the defendants are in line, prosecutors decide which defendant will face incarceration in exchange for tightly scripted testimony against a co-defendant. Once plucked out of the active defendant pool, the co-defendant goes straight to jail and the other defendant goes to trial with her life hanging in the balance. Once resolved, the decision is not reviewable by anyone. And once put into play, it inevitably leads to a negotiation with the accused on the right to life.

With the possible exception of a theater of war, no other government employee controls the depth or breadth of litigation the way a prosecutor does in a capital case. Shoring up this limitless power is the complete absence of control on its exercise. The independence of prosecutors and the absence of a check, much less a balance, makes their broad discretion government policy—a policy largely ignored.

Like judges, prosecutors are not subject to executive or legislative control. But unlike judges, they rarely even attempt to explain or justify their conduct. In theory, prosecutors are subject to disciplinary codes, but in every jurisdiction, formal discipline for misconduct is rare. But when they go to trial, especially in capital cases, their power is subject to a written record. That may be the only light that ever shines on that rare prosecutor hell-bent on securing a conviction at any cost.

Because a written record exists in every trial, cases of prosecutorial misconduct are occasionally viewed through the lens of the single most important constitutional limitation on prosecutorial misconduct—the double jeopardy clause. Its profound essence is plainly stated. Prosecutors can cause no person to be "twice put in jeopardy of life or limb" for the same offense. The key prohibition is *not* against being twice punished. It is against being twice *put in jeopardy* of punishment. That alone makes it the preeminent remedy in constitutional protection for defendants.

In what is arguably the most important U.S. Supreme Court case on this subject, Oregon v. Kennedy, the Court dealt with the thorny issue of a mistrial, short of an acquittal, in a criminal case. The Court held that a defendant who had successfully moved for mistrial based on prosecutorial misconduct could invoke the double jeopardy bar to retrial only if "the conduct giving rise to the successful motion for a mistrial was intended to provoke the defendant into moving for a mistrial . . . prosecutorial conduct that might be viewed as harassment or overreaching, even if sufficient to justify a mistrial on defendant's motion . . . does not bar retrial absent prosecutorial intent to subvert the protections afforded by the Double Jeopardy Clause."

Article 2, Section 10 of Arizona's constitution provides that no person shall be twice put in jeopardy for the same offense. As part of the protection against multiple prosecutions, the clause protects a defendant's valued right to have her trial completed by the tribunal to which it was first assigned. It also protects a defendant from multiple attempts by the government, with its vast resources, to convict an individual for an alleged offense, thereby subjecting her to embarrassment, expense, and ordeal, and compelling her to live in a continuing state of anxiety and insecurity.

In Pool v. Superior Court, the Arizona Supreme Court held that double jeopardy attaches when (1) the prosecutor's misconduct is not merely the result of legal error, negligence, mistake, or insignificant impropriety, but when taken as a whole amounts to intentional conduct which the prosecutor knows to be improper and prejudicial and which he pursues for any improper purpose with indifference to a significant resulting danger of mistrial or reversal; and (2) the conduct causes prejudice to the defendant which cannot be cured.

Double jeopardy bars retrial arising from prior misconduct in a case unless evidence of misconduct subverts the defendant's double jeopardy rights. Courts look at the prosecution's action. Was it sequential? Was it a pattern of repeated wrongdoing, or merely an isolated, perhaps inadvertent, mistake? Almost all trial lawyers live in an imperfect trial world—full of fallible human beings. This fallibility is often the prosecutor's defense to a misconduct charge. One test against a claim of mere fallibility is whether the prosecutor acted in bad faith. The broader test is whether the prosecutor's abuse of power was so egregious as to be "unacceptable and capable of undermining the judge's moral authority." Usually, bad faith or abuse of power lies solely in the eyes of the beholder. A judge without political or experiential history favoring so-called law and order might find bad faith where an ex-prosecutor elevated to the bench might find mere mistake or legal error. After all, judges are as fallible as trial lawyers are.

46

THE AMERICAN PRIVILEGE AGAINST
SELF-INCRIMINATION

*T*O INCRIMINATE MEANS, LITERALLY, TO charge with crime. Figu-
ratively, it means to involve oneself in a criminal prosecution.
While the privilege against self-incrimination dates back to 1791,
the modern origin of the law regarding self-incrimination lies in a
famous 1935 U.S. Supreme Court case—Brown v. Mississippi. The
case involved the murder trial of three black defendants. Their convictions were based entirely on their confessions, which were admittedly
obtained under torture inflicted by white deputy sheriffs. In an opinion by Chief Justice Charles Evans Hughes, the Court unanimously
reversed, noting that while "the State was free to regulate the procedure of its courts with its own perceptions of policy[,] its policies are
limited by the requirement of due process of law. Because a State may
dispense with a jury trial does not mean that it may substitute trial by
ordeal. The rack and torture chamber may not be substituted for the
witness stand."

After Brown v. Mississippi, scores of cases involving convictions
based on coerced confessions (most having occurred in Southern

states) came to the U.S. Supreme Court. The Court repeatedly recognized that coercion could exist even absent physical compulsion,
observing, "There is torture of the mind as well as the body." In Watts
v. Indiana, the Court categorically stated, "A confession by which life
becomes forfeit must be the expression of free choice."

Legally, this idea of free choice, or voluntariness, is a notion separate from coercion. If force or mere coercion is applied to extract a confession, then the confessor's volition is immaterial. While some claim
confusion, it is plain that even a voluntary confession can be coerced,
therefore making it inadmissible. The question can't be dismissed
because the context in which these terms are used is evidentiary, not
linguistic. The law focuses on whether the confession is admissible in
evidence, *not* whether it was given freely. Justice Felix Frankfurter, one
of the giants in judicial rhetoric, put the distinction in a psychologically elegant way:

> But whether a confession of a lad of fifteen is "voluntary"
> and as such admissible, or "coerced" and thus wanting for
> due process, is not a matter of mathematical determination.
> Essentially it invites psychological judgment—a psychologi-
> cal judgment that reflects deep, even if inarticulate, feelings
> in our society.

Two 1958 cases, one from Arkansas and the other from Arizona,
gave the Supreme Court the opportunity to discuss the difficulty of
assessing voluntariness on a case-by-case basis. The Court's opinion
in Payne v. Arkansas reversed the lower court's decision because the
confession was coerced. In Thomas v. Arizona, handed down the same
day, the Court affirmed the lower court's decision because the confession was voluntary.

Affirming or reversing a lower court is easy when the evidence is
fundamentally flawed, but more difficult when the factual nuances are
disputed. In *Thomas*, local ranchers had twice lassoed the defendant on
the day of his arrest; however, the local sheriff had, upon arriving to
arrest him, immediately removed the ropes and waited until the following day to obtain a confession. The defense argued that the ranch-

ers' abuse of the suspect invalidated his confession. But the Court ruled that the confession when given was voluntary, notwithstanding the lassoing on the previous day.

1964 was a seminal year for the Fifth Amendment privilege against self-incrimination. Two cases handed down in June of that year, Malloy v. Hogan and Murphy v. Waterfront Commission, summarily discarded doctrines cemented into the wall of prior self-incrimination cases from 1908, 1931, 1944, 1947, and 1958. In *Malloy*, the petitioner was held in contempt of court for refusing to answer questions in a Connecticut gambling inquiry. The Supreme Court reversed his conviction, holding he was entitled to the protection of the Fifth Amendment privilege against self-incrimination. In *Murphy*, the question was more complicated. The Court decided that a witness granted immunity in one state court could not be compelled to give incriminating testimony that might convict him of a crime in some other state.

Historical constitutional analysis of cases involving the privilege against self-incrimination provides an important context in which to view the birth of America's right to remain silent. That context begins in 1896 with Brown v. Walker, which was largely ignored until 1956, when the Court handed down Ullmann v. United States. In this infamous case, the Court sustained the constitutionality of the Federal Immunity Act of 1950, believing "it was sufficiently broad to displace the protection afforded by the privilege against self-incrimination." In so holding, Justice Felix Frankfurter cited the 1896 case of Brown v. Walker.

That prompted Justice William O. Douglas to dissent, insisting that the Federal Immunity Act left a witness subject to "penalties affixed to criminal acts." Justice Douglas said, somewhat prophetically, that Brown v. Walker should be overruled because "[t]he Fifth Amendment was designed to protect the accused against infamy as well as prosecution . . . [and] places the right of silence beyond the reach of the government."

No assessment of the Fifth Amendment is complete without reference to the second most cited case in American law—Miranda v. Arizona, the historic 1966 case that famously established the Miranda warnings. The first of those four warnings, "you have the right to remain silent," is intertwined with the privilege against self-incrimination. If the suspect is silent, he cannot incriminate himself. The 60-plus-page Miranda opinion is most explicit in detailing the requirements, purpose, and reach of each of the four warnings, and the order in which the warnings should be given—first tell the suspect he has a right to remain silent, then inform him of the other three Miranda rights.

The Court asserted that silence was an "absolute prerequisite in overcoming" the pressures of the interrogation room. "For those unaware of the privilege," the Court wrote, "the warning is needed simply to make them aware of it—the threshold requirement for an intelligent decision as to its exercise." The same reasoning applies , irrespective of the priority of the first warning's placement in the broader scheme of the four warnings. Consequently, it cannot be limited to "[j]ust the subnormal or woefully ignorant who succumb to an interrogator's imprecation [because] the interrogation will continue until a confession is obtained or silence, in the face of an accusation, [becomes in] itself damning [which] will bode ill when presented to a jury." Silence at the custodial stage is also critical because "the warning will show the individual that his interrogators are prepared to recognize his privilege should he choose to exercise it." The opinion also carefully establishes the legal justification for the right to remain silent, with the Court contending that "[t]he Fifth Amendment privilege is so fundamental to our system of constitutional rule and the expedient of giving an adequate warning as to the availability of the privilege is so simple, we will not pause to inquire in individual cases whether the defendant was aware of his rights without a warning being given." Finally, the opinion holds that the lower courts need not bother inquiring into the idiosyncratic variations among suspects:

> Assessments of the knowledge the defendant possessed, based on information as to his age, education, intelligence, or prior contact with authorities, can never be more than speculation; a warning is a clear-cut fact. More important, whatever the background of the person interrogated, a warning at the time of the interrogation is indispensable to overcome its pressures

and to insure that the individual knows he is free to exercise the privilege at that point in time.

Set against this historical backdrop, the ironies in State v. Milke are spectacular. The original accuser, Saldate, now fears self-incrimination and is vigorously pursuing his Fifth Amendment right. The original accused, Milke, having been vindicated on appeal, now wants her retrial barred under the other Fifth Amendment right, double jeopardy. The original prosecutor, Noel Levy, is in the appellate narrative, but is not involved in any aspect of Milke's retrial. The new prosecutor, Vince Imbordino, insists that the court deny Saldate his Fifth Amendment protection against self-incrimination *and* deny Milke her Fifth Amendment protection against double jeopardy. The original trial judge, the Honorable Cheryl Hendrix, denied Milke all rights, not to mention access to her accuser's personnel file. The new trial judge, the Honorable Rosa Mroz, granted Saldate the right to remain silent but denied Milke's double jeopardy claim. The fact that Saldate violated Milke's Fifth Amendment rights by interrogating her long after she asked for an attorney will only be an issue at retrial if Saldate loses his own Fifth Amendment right.

In each ironic twist of the due process chain, the Fifth Amendment is the missing link. Justice Douglas said it best—"the Fifth Amendment protects the accused against infamy as well as prosecution. It should place the right of silence beyond the reach of the government." For 24 years, Milke and Saldate were separated by a Grand Canyon of legal issues, interests, and needs. Now, both are on the same side of the courtroom, each battling a common opponent—the prosecutor, who insists neither can use the Fifth Amendment against the almighty government.

47

THE FIFTH AMENDMENT ON APPEAL: ARIZONA COURT OF APPEALS— APRIL 17, 2014

*T*HE HONORABLE JON W. THOMPSON, Peter B. Swann, and Patricia K. Norris issued a unanimous Memorandum Opinion overruling Judge Rosa Mroz's grant of a blanket Fifth Amendment privilege to Armando Saldate. This decision is inexplicable. The Fifth Amendment provides that no person shall be compelled in any criminal case to be a witness against himself. That may have confused the general public since Saldate was not "on trial." But his retrial testimony against Milke put him in legal harm's way *if* his testimony was perjurious when initially given in 1990, or perjurious when offered in 2015 at the Milke retrial.

Over time, the U.S Supreme Court has expanded the protection provided by the constitutional guarantee of a *right to remain silent*. It is ironic that Milke's prosecutor now argues that Saldate is not entitled to that right, given that he himself denied it to Debra Milke. The old expression "as the worm turns" comes to mind when reading the prosecutor's brief on why Saldate should not be allowed to claim his right to avoid self-incrimination. There was no such argument when Saldate encouraged Milke to incriminate herself in 1989, thus leading to his own personal dilemma in 2014.

The prosecution argued Judge Mroz's ruling allowing Saldate to take the Fifth was effectively an "order *not* to disclose information." That, it argued, was why a so-called blanket privilege should not be granted. It would prevent its witness from disclosing relevant information "essential to the truth-seeking function of a trial." The prosecution argued that Saldate had "no reasonable danger of a federal criminal civil rights prosecution" and that it had "no intention of prosecuting him in state court." His position that he "might" commit His perjury was "unfounded and misguided," it argued.

Saldate responded to the prosecutor's claims by pointing out that the prosecution cited cases and made arguments based on situations in which a defendant seeks testimony from a witness who is invoking the Fifth Amendment. But here, Saldate argued, it was the prosecution "who is desirous of presenting" *his* testimony. He was not the defendant; Milke was the defendant, and her constitutional rights were also at peril if the appellate court overruled the trial judge's findings that Saldate was at risk of prosecution if he testified consistently with his 1990 testimony against Milke. Saldate argued that the "state has no absolute right to call a witness."

Treasure VanDreumel, once the appellate lawyer for James Styers, was now back in the case for Saldate. She argued, "[A]t bottom, Saldate's historic practice reveals the habitual violation of Miranda v. Arizona." Early in the case, when it was initially assigned to Judge Mroz for retrial, the prosecutors asked for an explanation of why Saldate would invoke the Fifth Amendment. His lawyer at that time, Larry Debus, said he was not required to "explain to the prosecutor, or the defense counsel the basis of his invocation. It was only necessary that *the Judge* identify a potential risk of future prosecution." Importantly, Judge Mroz specifically found "that Saldate has provided a factual predicate sufficient for the court to evaluate the claim of privilege."

The same court to which the prosecution was now appealing had long ago answered the question. In State v. Cornejo, the Arizona

Court of Appeals approved the same procedure followed by Judge Mroz: "[The] witness will allude in very general, circumstantial terms to the reasons why he feels he *might* be incriminated by answering a given question. The judge examines him *only far enough* to determine whether there is reasonable ground to apprehend danger to the witness from his being compelled to answer. If the danger *might* exist, the court *must* uphold the privilege without requiring the witness to demonstrate that a response would incriminate him, the latter inquiry being barred by the privilege itself."

The prosecution had a remedy, albeit one it was reluctant to use. When the state wants or needs the testimony of someone who claims a Fifth Amendment privilege, the state may offer an inducement—either transactional or use immunity. Transactional immunity guarantees that the state will not prosecute the witness for anything that relates to his testimony. Use immunity protects the witness against prosecutorial use of any evidence drawn from the testimony. Granting a former police officer immunity from prosecution arising out of his actions as a police officer is probably not something any prosecutor wants to do. And even if the prosecutor did grant immunity, that would not bind the federal government, which may have claims against Saldate.

Saldate's appellate lawyer argued the immunity issues to the Arizona Court of Appeals, saying, "The privilege against self-incrimination does not absolutely bar prosecutors from obtaining incriminatory testimony. The Constitution permits federal and state prosecutors to compel testimony if a grant of immunity ensures that neither the compelled testimony nor its fruits are available for federal and state criminal proceedings." A "limited grant" will not suffice. She told the court that Saldate's requests for immunity had been ignored and argued that any grant of immunity must be "coextensive with the scope of the privilege." In resolving the question in favor of the prosecutor and against Saldate, the court did exactly what the prosecutors had done. It ignored his request for immunity from prosecution and denied his right to claim protection under the Fifth Amendment. Perhaps Saldate was feeling like Milke must have felt when she claimed that she had confessed to killing her son—ignored *and* prosecuted.

The court's April 17, 2014 decision is obtuse, especially given the complexity of the issues. The panel ignored the arguments made by Saldate *and* Milke. It accepted the prosecutor's position without analysis or substantive examination. The decision is premised on the prosecutor's obvious need—without Saldate's full cooperation and extensive testimony, the prosecutor can't prosecute. The MCAO argued that a "blanket" invocation of the Fifth Amendment "should not have been granted." Saldate argued that he had a real and appreciable risk of prosecution if he testified and that both federal and state law supported his position. Milke argued that the trial judge's grant of a blanket invocation was both factually sound and supported by binding Arizona Supreme Court case law. Milke also argued that had the trial judge *not* accepted a blanket invocation, "it would have constituted reversible error by placing Milke in the same position as in her first trial."

The court's response to Saldate and Milke's arguments was revealing. "Nevertheless, based on a *review of the record before us*, Saldate has not shown a real and appreciable risk of prosecution for his claims . . . on this record . . . Saldate may be compelled to testify *truthfully* in the upcoming trial." Therein lies the simplistic response from the appellate court to the trial court—"review of the record" and "testify truthfully." The appellate court, in its limited four-page memorandum decision, did neither of the two things it directed the trial court to do: (1) "review the record" as presented by the prosecution to the appellate court, and (2) compel "truthful" testimony from Saldate.

Without access to a virtual mountain of evidence, all of which Judge Mroz had earlier considered, and without giving the trial court judge, much less the opposing parties, a serious explanation of the basis for its decision, the court held that Saldate was not "entitled invoke the privilege." But it is clear from the record that the appellate panel did not know and could not have known the actual state of the *existing record*. And compelling a witness to testify "truthfully" is virtually impossible. Witnesses take oaths of truthfulness. Whether testimony is truthful or not is always a jury question. It is not a question of law. It is beyond the reach of an appellate court to demand *only* truthful testimony, when the real issue is whether the witness may avoid testimony that would incriminate him. Milke's original jury must have accepted Saldate's testimony as truthful because it convicted her solely based on that testimony. That conviction was eventually overturned because the United States Court of Appeals for the Ninth Circuit granted habeas relief and reversed all of Milke's convictions and sentences. That reversal goes to the heart of the question presented by Milke and Saldate to the Arizona Court of Appeals in February of 2014. The Ninth Circuit called Saldate's evidence "flimsy." It called into question the foundation of the prosecutor's case against Milke, which was based solely on Saldate's testimony. Relying on the Ninth Circuit's analysis and its direction regarding the possibility of serious charges against Saldate, should he elect to testify "again" at Milke's retrial, Saldate invoked his Fifth Amendment privilege and sought the blanket protection, which the trial court awarded.

In its briefing to the Arizona Court of Appeals, the prosecution gave short shrift to the controlling Ninth Circuit opinion—which is considered by all disinterested observers to be "the law of the case." The opinion controls all downstream assessments by all courts and both parties. It also controls how witnesses are evaluated for testimony. The grant of habeas relief in the federal courts was entirely a consequence of the prosecutor's failure to disclose critical impeachment evidence against Saldate. That substantial body of impeachment evidence is precisely what Saldate seeks to avoid revealing by invoking his Fifth Amendment privilege against self-incrimination.

The 2014 Arizona Court of Appeals' decision is problematic for three entirely separate reasons. First, had the critical impeachment evidence Saldate now fears revealing been disclosed by the prosecutor in 1990, the alleged confession would have likely been suppressed, and the case dismissed. We know that now because the Chief Judge of the Ninth Circuit, Alex Kozinski, clarified it in the court's 2013 opinion: "Without the confession, there is not enough evidence to support a conviction. Which is why it's very important that the confession be reliable and lawfully obtained."

Second, no one knows better than Saldate that the vital impeachment evidence is now in the hands of Milke's lawyers. He knows that evidence is a cannonball aimed directly at him. And he knows that if he must testify, it will expose him to a high risk of self-incrimination. That risk includes "judicial findings by Arizona courts, including the Arizona Court of Appeals itself, in eight separate cases in which Saldate lied under oath and engaged in other forms of misconduct, as well as ten other cases alleging misconduct, including some in which Saldate admittedly ignored Miranda violations. Two defendants in the eighteen separate cases are presently on Arizona's death row. Two others are serving life sentences, and one defendant has already been executed. The impeachment evidence includes a woman's allegations of felony extortion, and bribery in 2009. It also includes a 1973 Phoenix Police Department internal investigation that resulted in Saldate's suspension from the force based on 'a similar sexual *quid pro quo*' with a female motorist, in which Saldate also lied to investigators."

Third, if Saldate can only invoke his Fifth Amendment privilege in response to limited questions about impeachment evidence, rather than invoke a blanket protection claim, the legal consequence is clear. Milke's lawyers could not fully cross-examine him at the retrial. We know that because both lawyers (Lori Voepel for Milke and Treasure Van Dreumel for Saldate) took that position before the Arizona Court of Appeals. Milke argued that such a limited application of Saldate's privilege would violate *her* confrontation clause rights under the Sixth Amendment of the U.S. Constitution, and Article Two of the Arizona Constitution. As Milke's lawyers put it, "[a]llowing the State to present its case-in-chief through Saldate [by denying him his Fifth Amendment protection] while preventing Milke from impeaching him in this 'swearing contest' would deny her a fair trial."

Milke's position on Saldate's Fifth Amendment protection was elegantly simple. If the appellate court denies Saldate's Fifth Amendment rights, it will put her back in the exact position she was in during her 1990 trial. Milke argued that the trial judge correctly ruled that Saldate could invoke a blanket invocation in response to all questions put to him at retrial.

Saldate's lawyers argued that his right to invoke Fifth Amendment privilege was absolute. It was centered, they argued, on "the cases . . . which unambiguously document that [their client] had engaged in a pattern of Miranda violations and other [Fourth Amendment]

constitutional violations during interrogations of criminal suspects . . .
While Saldate may disagree, these factual findings borne of the record
before the Ninth Circuit constitute the law of the case . . . the law of
the case is a 'judicial policy' of refusing to reopen questions previously
decided in the same case by a higher appellate court . . . Saldate wisely
proceeds accordingly."

The same court that denied Saldate's Fifth Amendment claim in
2014 had granted identical relief in a 1984 case, saying:

> In short, the state can't have it both ways. It cannot use paid
> [agents] to uncover criminal activity and at the same time
> deprive the defendant of the opportunity to prove his inno-
> cence of that activity because of the criminal involvement . . .
> of their paid agent. This process smacks of such unfairness as
> to deprive the defendant of due process.

By handing the prosecutor a temporary victory—disallowing
Judge Mroz's blanket grant of Fifth Amendment protection—the
court gave the MCAO the right to have it both ways. It could use Saldate to uncover alleged criminal activity by Milke, but the trial judge
could not grant Saldate a blanket privilege to avoid self-incrimination.
That deprived *both* Milke *and* Saldate of their constitutional protections in the retrial. Accordingly, both Saldate and Milke joined forces
and filed special action briefs in the Arizona Supreme Court asking
that court to overrule the Arizona Court of Appeals. The Arizona
Supreme Court exercises appellate jurisdiction over the Arizona Court
of Appeals. It is the court of last resort in the Arizona judicial system.

48

MILKE AND SALDATE PETITION THE ARIZONA SUPREME COURT TO GRANT SALDATE HIS FIFTH AMENDMENT RIGHT—MAY 19, 2014

*O*N MAY 19, 2014, JUST 32 days after the Arizona Court of Appeals issued its perfunctory assessment of Saldate's Fifth Amendment invocation, Saldate and Milke filed simultaneous Petitions for Review in the Arizona Supreme Court.

Irony is a figure of speech rarely used in legal documents. In fiction, irony is often used when characters use words that mean something different from the actual meaning of those words. In nonfiction, irony often depicts a truthful situation that differs from what the characters anticipated. It is the difference between appearance and reality—and Saldate's Fifth Amendment invocation was beyond irony. The reality of his 2013 conundrum bore no resemblance to his 1998 appearance. Back then, he appeared supremely confident that he would be believed when he took the stand. Now he appeared justifiably worried he might be taken at face value again (on direct examination) and then destroyed (on cross-examination). If that happened, the jury would reject his testimony, believe Milke, and he'd face perjury charges, or worse.

Milke's core defense was Saldate's fabrication of her confession. The state's core offense was the mirror image. Truth or fabrication— that's what his new reality would be in a retrial. It would be another swearing contest, but this time the defense would have miles of confession misconduct rope to tie him up with. He could avoid that by not testifying against her, but only if a court allowed him to take the Fifth. The trial court agreed and allowed him to take the Fifth. The court of appeals disagreed and took away that right. The Arizona Supreme Court would resolve the question, for the last time. Maybe.

Lori Voepel, Milke's lawyer, presented two related issues to the Arizona Supreme Court. First, did the court of appeals err in overturning the trial court's Fifth Amendment ruling when it had "only a fraction of the record" on which the trial court based its ruling? Second, did the court of appeals err in effectively adopting a different standard of review for the state's witnesses than for the defendant's witnesses who invoke the Fifth Amendment?

Treasure Van Dreumel, Saldate's appellate lawyer, posed four issues: (1) whether the court of appeals "adopted/employed an erroneous rule of law" to reverse the trial court's order permitting Saldate to invoke the Fifth Amendment; (2) whether the standard of review was "*de novo*, or an abuse of discretion"; (3) whether the case could properly be subjected to *de novo* review or abuse of discretion when the state failed to provide the "totality of the record considered below"; and (4) whether the trial court's finding that Saldate could properly invoke the Fifth based on a "risk of incrimination" for state offenses remains a valid basis for Saldate's invocation.

Both briefs made clear the outcome should turn on whether the impeachment evidence Milke would offer at retrial poses a risk of prosecution to Saldate. Voepel's brief was a direct hit on the evidence the court of appeals did *not* consider. She separated the evidence into three categories, each of which put Saldate at risk of self-incrimination. She argued eight cases involving judicial findings of lying under oath, coercing confessions, and Miranda violations. She argued ten additional cases that involved misconduct claims in cases resolved by plea agreements or dismissal *before* adverse findings were made against Saldate. She argued Saldate's disciplinary record at the Phoenix Police Department, and a 2010 investigation involving sexual misconduct by Saldate with a woman named Belinda Reynolds. She argued that any of these could subject Saldate to perjury charges. Combined, she said, these arguments give Saldate and his lawyer "reasonable grounds to apprehend danger of prosecution if compelled to testify" against Milke.

Van Dreumel repeated Voepel's contentions in her brief, but posed the risk differently and in only two discrete areas. First, she argued, Saldate is at risk if he is compelled to testify because "his responses may incriminate him on state crimes of bribery/extortion on the Belinda Reynolds matter." Second, she argued, Saldate is at risk because testimony in Milke's retrial reveals a "danger of incrimination on a multitude of federal conspiracy offenses, including offenses *currently* under investigation by the DOJ."

Both lawyers cited the same cases supporting Saldate's invocation of privilege. Both noted the "flawed analysis by the Court of Appeals." And both hammered the state prosecutor, who either misunderstood or misrepresented the proper test of Fifth Amendment invocation. They argued that it was the *possibility* of prosecution, rather than the *likelihood* of prosecution, that governs Fifth Amendment availability. The Arizona Court of Appeals had surprised most observers by overturning Judge Mroz's decision favoring Saldate's invocation. But its reasoning was an even bigger surprise. In a short, hastily crafted memorandum opinion, the court of appeals court found Saldate had "failed to show a real and appreciable risk of prosecution . . . since in *its* view, prosecution was unlikely." That was an erroneous standard, and both lawyers pounced on it.

Saldate's lawyer was blunt. "In the face of the ongoing DOJ criminal investigation and the appellate court's acknowledgment that possible conspiracy claims under federal law may not be time-barred, the possibility of a criminal prosecution is not merely speculative or academic, it is a fact."

Milke's lawyer sliced deep into the court of appeals' flawed reasoning. "The Court of Appeals' decision eviscerates the Fifth Amendment . . . its opinion is unsupportable . . . even the State concedes Saldate could still be prosecuted depending on how he testifies in the retrial."

Neither lawyer voiced the layperson's perspective. What are we coming to when an officer of the law is denied the protection of the law? Why is the state forcing its own star witness to testify if there is even the slightest possibility that his testimony will subject him to prosecution? And why, if even a small portion of the impeachment evidence against Saldate were admitted at retrial, does the prosecution think that Saldate could win the swearing contest with Milke? After all, he stands as a disgraced former officer in the eyes of the Ninth Circuit Court of Appeals *and* in the public, given the press coverage across the country. While there is no reliable survey data, most casual observers now believe Milke was wrongly convicted by Saldate, with help from the prosecutor and the judge.

Both aggrieved parties argued that the court of appeals had erred on one of the most important questions before the Arizona Supreme Court—*the standard of review*. While largely misunderstood outside the legal community, the basic principles guiding review of lower court decisions are pivotal to resolving appeals presented to higher courts. There are many ways appellate courts review lower court rulings. One is to examine the sufficiency of the evidence. Under this standard, the appellate judges review the trial court's judgment to determine whether the evidence in the record is strong enough to support the judgment. Under both common and statutory law, appellate courts using a sufficiency of evidence standard look at whether the evidence, if believed, would convince the average person that the prevailing party in the lower court proved the case by either a preponderance of the evidence (in a civil case), or by evidence beyond a reasonable doubt (in a criminal case). In either case, appellate courts do not weigh the evidence or determine witness credibility. Instead, appellate courts accept the trial court's fact-finding and affirm the judgment unless the evidence is insufficient to support the lower court's finding.

Another way that appellate courts review lower court decisions is by an abuse of discretion standard. Under this standard, appellate courts look at whether the trial judge acted in an arbitrary or unreasonable way. If so, they follow that by assessing whether the abuse of discretion resulted in unfairly denying a person an important right, or caused an unjust result.

A third way appellate courts review trial court decisions is under a *de novo* standard. *De novo* is a Latin term meaning "from the new." When an appellate court hears a case *de novo*, it decides the questions presented without reference to the legal conclusions or assumptions made by the trial court. An appeals court hearing a case *de novo* may refer to the trial court's record to determine the facts, but will rule on the evidence and matters of law *without* giving deference to that court's findings. All three review standards articulate the appellate court's authority to review the trial court's conclusions regarding the application, interpretation, and construction of law.

The Milke case morphed into the Saldate case in this special review by the Arizona Supreme Court because both lower courts came to diametrically opposed decisions. That alone was not enough to invoke the supreme court's discretionary review. But this was a death penalty case in which a man who now refused to testify in a retrial had provided the sole incriminating evidence in the first trial. Heightening the criticality of the substantive matter to be resolved (the application of the Fifth Amendment), it was clear to all concerned that the supreme court's decision was not only a matter of statewide interest; it was a matter of life and death for the defendant Milke *and* a matter of crime and punishment for Saldate. This would be an "all in" decision by Arizona's highest court. That is why they call it the *court of last resort*—if the supreme court agreed with the trial judge, then Milke would likely never be retried and Saldate would never be criminally charged. If the court agreed with the appellate panel, then Milke might again face the death penalty. And for the first time, Saldate might face criminal charges for his misconduct in this and other cases. This case would put the Arizona Supreme Court front and center and would test it in a way that few cases do. Affirming the court of appeals would be widely unacceptable because that decision forced a situation no one really wanted (putting Saldate and Milke at risk). Affirming the trial court would be good news for Milke (setting her free) and avoid the risk of prosecution for Saldate (no testimony—no perjury). The MCAO would have an out—it was the court, not us.

As if the death penalty and the risk of new criminal charges were not enough, the Arizona Supreme Court also faced a statewide interest in how this case was resolved because it involved confidential and privileged matters for Saldate. He had been the case agent against Milke. His original cross-examination in 1990 had been ineffective for lack of ammunition. But a 2015 retrial would feature a robust cross-examination by Milke's new heavy-weight and now well-armed lawyer (Mike Kimerer). The forcefully put questions about prior misconduct would elicit answers that would likely incriminate him. The range of charges he might face if forced to testify ranged from state charges of bribery, extortion, and perjury, to federal charges of conspiracy and civil rights violations. The prosecutor had urged in both the trial and appellate courts that Saldate had no real, appreciable risk in either system. But Saldate, on the advice of two of Arizona's best criminal defense lawyers, saw the risk as not merely "appreciable," but as highly likely. They knew many things that the prosecutor not only did not know, but also could not possibly know. That is why the core issues involving confidentiality and privilege were so important to the outcome. It seemed incomprehensible to most legal authorities in Arizona that any court would disallow the Fifth Amendment in these circumstances. Nonetheless, the court of appeals had overruled a trial court judge whose ruling protected both the defendant (Milke) and her accuser (Saldate). The appellate court panel ignored the relevant standard of review and failed to give appropriate deference to the broad evidentiary review conducted by the trial judge. The outcome focused only on the prosecutor's need to make the case, while ignoring the plight of the defendant and the case agent. What seemed to get lost in the brevity and advocacy of the appellate court panel was the right of any witness to assert his privilege against self-incrimination for misconduct. The Ninth Circuit Court of Appeals referred to three prosecutorial agencies. That deficiency will most likely be addressed by the Arizona Supreme Court.

Judicial opinions, like dictionaries, come with explanatory notes. For dictionaries, the notes are important in using the text; for opinions, the notes are important in understanding how the court arrived at its decision. In judicial opinions, the explanation takes the form of a court recitation as to "how" the case was presented to it, "why" the court can resolve it, and "what" standard of review it used to resolve the case.

The Milke case was reviewed by four courts between 1989 and 2013 (the Maricopa County Superior Court, the Arizona Supreme Court, the U.S. District Court for the District of Arizona, and the United States Court of Appeals for the Ninth Circuit). In each review, the court carefully delineated its jurisdiction, what issues it resolved, and the standard of review it used in reaching its decisions. Unfortunately, in 2014, the Arizona Court of Appeals did not identify which of several standards of review it utilized in overruling the Maricopa County Superior Court. Nor did it carefully articulate its reasoning or its precedent. Accordingly, Milke and Saldate sought appellate relief at the Arizona Supreme Court. They were quick to pose the evocative issue: "The court of appeals' failure to indicate what standard of review it applied is a huge problem, given the parties' dispute over the standard and the law's ambiguity."

Before the court of appeals, the prosecutor argued for a *de novo* review. Saldate and Milke argued for an *abuse of discretion* standard. All three briefs cited relevant case authority in their favor. But no one knows which standard the court of appeals used to resolve the case because it did not identify it. That failure, coupled with the court's overruling the trial judge based on a small fraction of the evidence she reviewed to reach a contrary decision compounds the appellate error.

Milke argued to the Arizona Supreme Court that the court of appeals rendered a narrow ruling based on its review of only part of the underlying record. The court of appeals identified one risk facing Saldate (a conspiratorial agreement). But the trial judge identified three other prosecutorial risks facing Saldate: (1) judicial findings of misconduct in eight Arizona cases; (2) continuing violations against Milke in a scheduled retrial; and (3) the 2009 Belinda Reynolds investigation. Those three were ignored by the court of appeals.

The dichotomy between how the trial court resolved Saldate's privilege against self-incrimination argument and how the appeals court dealt with it gave the supreme court a perplexing challenge. Are there two different standards for invoking and compelling testimony in a criminal case? Does the standard depend on whether the person invoking the privilege is a defendant or merely a witness? Put differently, if you're *on* trial, does a witness against you get a different version of the Fifth Amendment than the one that's available to you? The court of appeals based its opinion, at least in part, on oral and written representations from the same prosecutorial office that was prosecuting Milke and might prosecute Saldate. That, Milke argued, "effectively equated such representations with a court-approved immunity agreement." To support that argument, Milke reminded the supreme court that one of the court of appeals judges had remarked during oral argument, "If I was a Mack truck, I think I could probably drive right through both of those letters." A different appeals judge suggested at that same oral argument that "statements by the prosecutor in oral argument might cause a waiver of the State's later right to prosecute Saldate." In combination with the failure of the appeals court to identify which standard of review it used to reverse the trial judge, these comments give the appearance that Saldate is treated differently because he's a witness than Milke is treated because she's a defendant. The state conceded Milke's point that Saldate could be prosecuted depending on how he testified in the scheduled suppression hearing on Milke's alleged confession, or at her upcoming retrial. That alone makes the trial judge's decision correct and the court of appeals decision incorrect. The trial judge accepted the possibility of prosecution and the court of appeals ignored it. The only solution, Milke's lawyer argued, was to apply the same standard to both state and defense witnesses. He said, "The appeals court's solution alters the standard for prosecution witnesses, which leaves Saldate exposed, but gives the State an unfair advantage in compelling its primary witness to take the stand against Milke, without requiring an immunity agreement."

Saldate's lawyer, Treasure Van Dreumel, used her brief in the supreme court to define the deep dilemma facing the state's chief witness. With the mountain of misconduct evidence it had, Milke's lawyers would have, she said, "a good faith basis for questioning Saldate about prior instances where he lied on the witness stand. If he admits to previously lying under oath, a basis for state perjury charges arise[s], prosecutable under Arizona's discovery rule embedded in the statute of limitations . . . conversely, if he denies them he will [also] expose himself to a perjury charge." Either way, Saldate's lawyer argued, "the State has the authority and the duty to prosecute where there is probable cause to believe a criminal charge has been committed."

Van Dreumel's other argument challenged the language used by the appeals court in overruling the trial court; it found "no reasonable ground to apprehend danger where prosecution was *unlikely*." However, courts *must permit* invocation of the privilege unless the court can be *certain* that anticipated questions will adduce no potentially incriminating responses where prosecution is possible under the law. Saldate's position was clear: "It is the danger *of incrimination* and the *possibility, not the likelihood* of prosecution which governs the inquiry."

Driving the point home, Saldate accused the appeals court of forgetting a fundamental principle it announced three decades ago: "The right against self-incrimination must take precedence [over a citizen's duty to testify in a criminal case,] for a citizen should not be faced with a criminal prosecution in order to prove the guilt or innocence of a third party."

49

PROSECUTORIAL MISCONDUCT AND THE LAW OF IMPEACHMENT: INTENTIONAL VIOLATION OF THE BRADY AND GIGLIO DOCTRINES

*W*HILE NATIONAL STUDIES ARE LIMITED, the consensus view is that 80 to 90 percent of mothers who murder their children are driven by psychiatric conditions. Their situations feel so unbearable that they can fathom no other remedy except to kill their children—the ultimate depravity in any society. In both law and psychiatry, it's called *maternal filicide*. To the rest of the world, it's unthinkable. Even so, prosecuting a woman who the police believe killed her child requires full compliance with the rule of law. The prosecutor cannot simply believe the police and protect them because the crime is unthinkable. Violent crime—especially child murder—must be prosecuted to the fullest extent of the law. Prosecutors trying those cases perform a vital service. They are held up to high commendation. But they must be equally vigilant that zeal to convict does not violate a defendant's civil rights. The trial cannot be all about the victim. It must also be about the defendant. When prosecutors fail to follow the law, courts cannot balance the needs of the community with the defendant's constitutional right to a fair trial.

Under the landmark case of Brady v. Maryland, prosecutors are constitutionally obligated to disclose "evidence favorable to the accused . . . that is material to guilt or to punishment." This prosecutorial duty is grounded in the Fourteenth Amendment: states shall not "deprive any person of life, liberty, or property without due process of law." *Brady* ensures that criminal trials are fair and that a miscarriage of justice does not occur. Placing the burden on prosecutors to voluntarily disclose exculpatory or favorable information to the defense illustrates the special role that American prosecutors play. We trust our prosecutors to turn over evidence to the defense because we believe their interest is not merely to win the case, but that justice should be done.

Prosecutors have not only a legal duty to turn over exculpatory or favorable evidence to the defense, they also have a broader ethical duty to "make timely disclosure to the defense of all information known to the prosecutor that *tends to negate* the guilt of the accused, or mitigates the offense. . . ." From an ethical perspective, prosecutors are specially responsible, because they are ministers of justice, rather than mere advocates for the state. This entails an obligation to see that the defendant is accorded procedural justice and that guilt is decided upon the basis of sufficient evidence. Precisely how far the prosecutor must go in this direction is debatable. A knowing disregard of ethical obligations or a systematic abuse of prosecutorial discretion can constitute a substantive violation such that the prosecutor can be disbarred. Disbarring a lawyer requires clear and convincing evidence of conduct that is prejudicial to the administration of justice. Which, some say, is the trap door in the floor of prosecutorial misconduct.

On the legal side, a *Brady* claim of professional misconduct only requires proof by a preponderance of the evidence that (1) the evidence at issue is favorable to the accused, either because it is exculpatory or because it is impeaching; (2) the evidence was suppressed by the state, either willfully or inadvertently; and (3) prejudice to the defendant must have ensued. Favorable evidence is not limited to just exculpatory evidence; it extends to information that impeaches a prosecution witness.

The best-known case on impeachment evidence is Giglio v. United States. There the government's case depended almost entirely on one witness, yet the prosecution failed to inform the defense that the witness testified in exchange for a promise from the government that he would not be prosecuted. The court held that the prosecutor had to disclose that fact because it "went to the witness's credibility and the jury was entitled to know of it." The similarities between *Giglio* and *Milke* are striking, "because if the prosecution is in a unique position to obtain information known to other agents of the government, it may not be excused from disclosing what it does not know, but could have learned." The prosecutor's obligation under *Brady* is not excused by the defense lawyer's failure to exercise diligence regarding suppressed evidence.

50

DEBRA MILKE'S RESPONSE TO THE STATE OF ARIZONA ON DOUBLE JEOPARDY—JUNE 19, 2014

*D*EBRA MILKE'S APPELLATE LAWYER, LORI Voepel, filed her reply in support of her petition for special action in the Arizona Court of Appeals on the double jeopardy issue on June 19, 2014. As required, she did not repeat her initial arguments that double jeopardy had attached and barred any retrial of her client. Instead, she adopted an issue-by-issue rebuttal of the state's position.

> The State spends three pages arguing against what it mischaracterizes as Milke's "'far reaching position'"—that a *mere Brady* violation is sufficient to bar a retrial under the Double Jeopardy Clause. That is not her position. Ironically, by misstating Milke's argument, the State fails to respond to the bulk of the Petition. As a result, it never even addresses the extensive, specific findings by the Ninth Circuit regarding the

prosecution's knowledge of Saldate's misconduct, which . . . are *binding* in these retrial proceedings.

The State also misstates the applicable double jeopardy standard as requiring a showing of "specific, egregious, intentional misconduct by the individual prosecutor." It further claims that for double jeopardy to bar retrial here, "Milke must prove that Mr. Levy intentionally and egregiously suppressed evidence, and that he did so with the intent to prejudice her." Not only do these formulations of the standard leave out the prejudice prong of the test (as does the sState's analysis), but they also omit that double jeopardy attaches where the conduct is pursued for any improper purpose with indifference to the danger of mistrial or reversal. The sState's articulated standard and analysis also focus on the *subjective* intent of Noel Levy, which is not the standard under either federal or Arizona law. Because the sState's entire argument—— and the trial court's ruling—— focus exclusively on Levy's subjective intent, while ignoring the extreme prejudice suffered by Milke, and leaves out important portions of the test, they are both clearly erroneous."

The State of Arizona had focused on the Fifth Amendment's double jeopardy clause as though it were controlling law on Milke's retrial. Voepel argued that Arizona's double jeopardy clause was broader than the federal version. The federal version "protects against multiple prosecutions for the same offense," she said. But the Arizona version is narrow: "no person shall be twice put in jeopardy for the same offense."

Next, Voepel argued that the sState and Judge Mroz relied on a Ninth Circuit case that conflicts with Arizona Supreme Court case law and is factually distinguishable. United States v. Lewis, she argued, is not applicable to Milke's case. *Lewis* concluded that double jeopardy did not attach to a prosecution's *Brady* violation. That does not apply here because *Lewis* exclusively applied the dDouble jJeopardy cClause ofunder the U.S. Constitution and the *Kennedy* test. Applying what it called the "narrow exception" under *Kennedy*, *Lewis* held that double jeopardy bars retrial only where "the government engages in prosecutorial misconduct 'intended to provoke the defendant into moving for a mistrial.'" Because the defendant in *Lewis* did not even allege that the prosecution provoked him into moving for a mistrial, and because the record there did not suggest prosecutorial misconduct, the Ninth Circuit held that the double jeopardy exception under *Kennedy* was inapplicable. She argued that, the *Lewis* court "concluded that the Double Jeopardy Clause did not apply because no mistrial occurred."

Arizona's test is much broader. "First, it also applies to reversals caused by the prosecution's improper conduct in the first trial. Second, it is not limited to the prosecutor's subjective intent to cause a mistrial." Moreover, Milke's case could not be more factually distinct from *Lewis*. In *Lewis*, the defendant's conviction was reversed just two years after sentencing based on the district court's erroneous exclusion of a report. At a status hearing after remand, the government revealed two pieces of potentially exculpatory material it had just learned about. Both pieces of evidence were available for the defendant's use at his second trial. There was no indication that the prosecution had previously known or should have known about the exculpatory material. "In contrast, 24 years have passed since Milke's first trial. All of Saldate's personnel files have since been destroyed, so any additional *Brady/Giglio* evidence has now been forever placed out of Milke's reach by the State."

The Ninth Circuit made extensive findings.—"All binding in these subsequent proceedings"—regarding the improper conduct of the prosecution in Milke's case. Its specific factual and legal findings of the prosecution's knowledge and suppression of Saldate's pattern of misconduct (and its indifference to the risk of reversal from doing so) were based on its exhaustive review of the vast record in Milke's case and the other cases in which "Saldate was found to have committed misconduct, including lying under oath."

Those findings are "the law of the case [here and subject to the doctrines of] *res judicata*, and collateral estoppel. In the case before this Court, the previous habeas corpus proceedings are *res judicata* on the issue of the lack of the voluntariness of defendant's absence in his previous State trial. The State had its opportunity to challenge the Ninth Circuit's legal and factual findings through a petition for rehearing en banc (which was denied) and a petition for writ of certiorari to the U.S. Supreme Court, which it chose not to file. As a result, the Ninth

Circuit Opinion—which is the final decision issued in Milke's case—
became law of the case. Here, both the issues of Saldate's misconduct
and of MCAO prosecutors' knowledge of that misconduct during
Milke's initial trial were actually litigated in the federal habeas proceedings, and in the state post-conviction proceedings, which began in
1995. Clearly, 18 years provided the parties more than a full and fair
opportunity and motive to litigate these issues.

In claiming Milke has 'twisted' the State's words regarding its con-
cession of Levy's personal knowledge, the State ignores its own lower
court pleadings admitting that Levy obtained actual knowledge about
the contents of Saldate's personnel files once Judge Hendrix conducted
her *in camera* review. As to the second admission in its Response to the
Double Jeopardy Motion, the State now claims it meant "'State'" in
the broadest sense to include PPD. However, one need only look at the
context of the State's argument to see it was clearly intended to counter
Milke's claim that Levy and MCAO intentionally "'hid, destroyed, or
otherwise intentionally prevented the disclosure of evidence'" and to
support its own argument it acted in 'good-faith' by "'provid[ing] the
file when the trial judge considered Defendant's subpoena.'" Presumably, MCAO knows that Levy became aware of Saldate's personnel
files during the 1990 *in camera* review process, or it would not have
defended against Milke's arguments in this manner. Regardless, as
noted in Milke's Motion to Strike, it cannot now assume a different
position for the first time on appeal or try to support its new argument
with documents not presented to the trial court on this issue.

"In any event, the State's new theory on appeal that Levy 'knew
nothing' about Saldate's misconduct simply doesn't pass muster, given:
(1) the reality of how *in camera* reviews of police records of central State
witnesses are conducted; (2) the fact that Levy was one of MCAO's
most experienced homicide attorneys whose high profile case against
Milke turned solely on Saldate's credibility; and (3) the fact that Levy
was handling this high profile case at the same time numerous successful challenges to Saldate's credibility, honesty, and tactics were
being made in other MCAO cases handled by Levy's homicide division colleagues. These realities, together with the State's own admissions in the trial court, lead to only one logical conclusion: Noel Levy

had actual knowledge about Saldate's pattern of misconduct and, at the very least, those incidents of misconduct contained in Saldate's personnel records."

In her response, Voepel connected the dots between Levy's knowledge of Saldate's personnel records and Milke's resulting extreme prejudice. "The personnel records Levy knew about contained, at a minimum, the powerful *Brady-Giglio* impeachment evidence that Saldate had engaged in a "'sexual quid pro quo'" with a female motorist, lied about it to his supervisors, and then finally confessed after failing a polygraph test. Notwithstanding the State's attempts on appeal to downplay the significance of this evidence, the record speaks for itself. The written reprimand by Saldate's supervisors—which was signed by the City Manager and Chief of Police—stated, "'because of this incident, your image of honesty, competency, and overall reliability must be questioned.' As noted in the Ninth Circuit's Opinion, it is hard to imagine more powerful impeachment evidence in a 'swearing contest' between then 25-year-old Milke and 22-year-long detective Saldate over whether she "'confessed'" within 30 minutes, in a room with just the two of them, where there was no witness, no recording, and no other corroboration. As the Ninth Circuit noted, these records also included evaluations with names of at least six cases Saldate had handled, which the defense could have researched for additional impeachment evidence back in 1990, *when it counted*. The suppression of the personnel records thus 'ran together' with suppression of the court documents. The State's attempts to blame Levy's suppression of these materials on the initial trial judge are meritless. As the Ninth Circuit specifically found, Levy had an independent duty to turn over this evidence of Saldate's misconduct . . . The fact that Milke had to request and was denied access to Saldate's file did not excuse MCAO and Levy from their constitutional obligation to disclose this critical impeachment evidence . . . Contrary to the State's assertion, the 'usual' remedy under *Brady* of disclosure of the materials and a new trial cannot cure this level of prejudice."

Voepel also addressed a new position taken by the state—that Kenneth Ray, Milke's firstinitial attorney, did not need the sState's assistance to locate these other court cases because they were public records. That, she said, "reflects a complete naiveté regarding how such records were kept and accessed back in 1990. There was no Internet, nor any electronically available records. As detailed by the Ninth Circuit, Milke's post-conviction team was only able to discover what they did find on Saldate through a 7,000-hour long search on microfiche in the Clerk's Office conducted by 10 researchers working 8 hours a day for 3 ½ months. Clearly, the 'continual state of anxiety and insecurity' the double jeopardy clause is designed to prevent would encompass not forcing someone to face retrial after having already lived half her life in a 12 by 7 foot 'home' under the perpetual threat of death."

In its response to her special action, the state argued for an evidentiary hearing on the matter. But Voepel rebutted, saying, "It is, and always has been, Milke's position that an evidentiary hearing is not necessary to find that double jeopardy bars retrial under *Pool* and *Minnitt*, in light of this record and the Ninth Circuit's detailed findings ... One is hard-pressed to find a more scathing indictment of prosecutors than that contained in the Ninth Circuit Opinion regarding the conduct of the prosecution in Milke's case. As if the findings weren't enough, the Ninth Circuit referred this case to the Department of Justice and U.S. Attorney's Office for investigation into whether the conduct of Saldate, his supervisors *and other state and local officials'* amounts to a 'pattern of violating the federally protected constitutional rights of Arizona residents' ... Besides Saldate and his superiors, there are no state and local officials discussed or even referenced in the Opinion other than prosecutors within MCAO. Presumably, the second highest court in the land would not refer prosecutors or police for possible federal investigation if, as the State alleges, the court 'found only that the State violated *Brady* ... not intentional misconduct or intentional nondisclosure by the State.'"

Voepel turned the sState's argument to her advantage. "At a minimum, if the Court orders an evidentiary hearing, it should be with two conditions: (1) the Court should instruct the trial court that it is bound by the Ninth Circuit's findings regarding MCAO prosecutors' knowledge and Saldate's misconduct; and (2) it should find that the State is bound by its prior admissions of Noel Levy's knowledge of the contents of Saldate's personnel files."

The court had asked what the parties would deem an appropriate remedy if it remands for a hearing and finds that the Respondent Judge should not have considered her personal experiences with MCAO in deciding this issue. Voepel responded, "Due to the exceptionally high stakes in this case, Milke believes it would be best for a new trial judge to preside over further proceedings on this issue only. Milke believes Respondent Judge acted in good faith in making her rulings on this issue. She feels it is important, however, to preclude any possibility that Respondent Judge's original decision and experiences with MCAO might color any further decision on this critical issue."

EPILOGUE:

2015—NEITHER LIFE NOR LIMB

*I*T TOOK 25 YEARS FOR the judicial system to unravel the Debra Milke case and dissect her so-called confession. What began as the ultimate tragedy, a mother found guilty of arranging the murder of her four-year old son, ended with a dismissal of all charges against her. She would never again face a jury that took the word of a police officer with a checkered past over hers. And because of the circumstances that set her free, the people of Arizona could also claim an important victory. We all win when the rule of law exposes corrupt cops and prosecutors who ignore the law. Child murder morphed into something even more terrifying, a mother's wrongful conviction of that murder. Her conviction was the consummate product of police corruption and prosecutorial misconduct.

Milke's guilt or innocence played no role in her ultimate appellate victory. But, the court of public opinion redounded in her favor, granting her the presumption of innocence she did not get 25 years ago. The end of her case is historic because, on December 11, 2014, the Arizona Court of Appeals ordered the dismissal of all charges against her. The court's opinion was not merely decisive and dispositive on all issues in the 25-year appellate saga, it delivered a rare and scathing rebuke of the entire process. The court was blunt in blaming the prosecutor and the police for advancing a judicial process that protected Saldate and accepted his presumption of Milke's guilt. Everyone could see the case as one of those rare but sadly recurring cases where police get the benefit of the doubt and the defendant gets a seat on death row.

On January 12, 2015 the MCAO filed a petition for special action seeking reversal of the Arizona Court of Appeals' rebuke. The MCAO made two arguments in favor of reversal. First, it argued that Arizona's double jeopardy clause did not bar retrial for *Brady* violations. Second, it argued that in retrials, the law of the case doctrine did not require Arizona courts to adopt findings from the Ninth Circuit Court of Appeals and did not prevent the MCAO from considering additional evidence or making new findings. Both sides filed voluminous briefs. Unsurprisingly, the Arizona Supreme Court did not accept the petition, denied review, and allowed the court of appeals' decision to stand. Judge Rosa Mroz dismissed all charges on March 23, 2015. That ended all criminal case issues against Milke arising out of her son's murder. The final order was issued *with prejudice*, meaning the case is dismissed permanently—over with—done. But as everyone knew, dismissing the criminal case would commence the civil litigation.

On Friday, March 13, 2015 (ten days before the official end of her case) Milke's lawyers filed a 72-page federal civil rights action against the city of Phoenix, Maricopa County, Maricopa County Attorney William Montgomery, in his official capacity, and Armando Saldate, Jr. The suit also named ten former police officers, a forensic anthropologist, a crime lab criminalist, and an assistant medical examiner employed by the city of Phoenix. The federal court suit, casually referred to as a Section 1983 case, is premised on the legal theory allowing civil redress for "deprivation under color of law" of Milke's rights "as secured by the United States Constitution." Milke's lawyers requested compensatory damages, punitive damages, pre-judgment and post-judgment interest and recovery of costs, including reasonable attorney's fees under federal law.

The dramatic dismissal of all charges against Debra Milke was based on the Arizona Constitution's protection against double jeopardy. The federal version's quaint language—"nor shall any person be twice put in jeopardy of life or limb"—is a linguistic leftover from the eighteenth century. But its applicability in twenty-first-century America has even deeper roots. The principle is one of the oldest in Western civilization, stemming as it does from ancient Greek and Roman law—when rulers cut off wrongdoers' limbs, lest they steal another loaf of bread. Those were the pre-prison days. Now we just lock up people for slightly more serious crimes. In nineteenth-century America, we hung murderers from stout tree limbs. Some of those lynched were innocent but could not convince the sheriff. Perhaps one of those old-time sheriffs made up a story to secure the lynching, lest the scoundrel, whom he *knew* was guilty, go free for lack of hard evidence. Who dared doubt the sheriff back then? By the late twentieth century, when Debra Milke took her assigned seat on death row, we were long past the *limb* era and well into the *limbo* stage. Prisoners wait for decades to hear a court finally declare prosecutorial misconduct for what it is—a denial at every stage of the defendant's presumed innocence. When the jury easily accepts a police officer's word as truth, and hears nothing from the bench or the witness stand about the police officer's unsavory history, a one-day deliberation becomes a wrongful conviction.

Presiding Judge Patricia K. Norris, Judge John C. Gemmill, and Judge Peter B. Swann delivered the court's opinion in the Milke case on December 11, 2014. Their 12-page opinion began with an explanatory note about Arizona judicial process. The Arizona Supreme Court expects the intermediate court of appeals to exercise special action jurisdiction over capital cases. Defendants in capital cases file petitions for special action in the court of appeals *before* filing in the supreme court. Some think intermediate appellate judges, who work in the same building and have close relationships with supreme court justices, usually decide cases consistent with what they think the court of last resort will do when it considers whether to even review their decision. That soft understanding seems borne out because there are scant reported cases where the Arizona Supreme Court overturns a well-reasoned and presumptively correct decision in a capital case. By the time her case reached the Arizona Court of Appeals on the double jeopardy argument, Milke had already secured a transient victory at the United States Court of Appeals for the Ninth Circuit. In December 2013, that court reversed Milke's state court conviction, giving the prosecutor the option to retry or release Milke. But a year later, the Arizona Court of Appeals took the retrial option off the table and ordered her dismissal. And, as noted above, the Arizona Supreme Court allowed that decision to stand by denying review to the Maricopa County Attorney's Office.

Predictably, the MCAO had announced it would retry her, while vigorously rejecting the factual and legal findings in the Ninth Circuit's opinion. That ill-advised position caused the Arizona Court of Appeals to school the prosecutor on hornbook law. "When certain facts have been determined by the Ninth Circuit's collateral attack on the defendant's conviction following the first state court trial, the decision of the federal court becomes the law of the case."

The Arizona Court of Appeals was bound by Ninth Circuit's clear finding of a *Brady/Giglio* violation by the prosecution in Milke's original 1990 trial. The law of the case doctrine applies with equal force to the retrial judge and the intermediate court of appeals. Saldate's "numerous prior acts of improper and deceitful conduct" and the prosecutor's "intentional failure to disclose that history" gave Milke a solid double jeopardy defense. The court noted that by the start of her trial in 1990, "at least seven cases involving instances of Saldate's misconduct had been or were being litigated, yet the State failed to disclose any such information to Milke and her attorney." The Ninth Circuit had described that failure, and more, as the state of Arizona remaining "unconstitutionally silent."

The Ninth Circuit's conclusion, "that the State knew of Saldate's misconduct and failed to disclose it in a timely manner," was binding law on the Arizona Court of Appeals. But it did not merely accept the finding; it expanded the state's failure significantly. It said that the state "knew about Saldate's extensive misconduct record," and cited in its opinion the federal court's notion of "the State's actions as more akin to active concealment."

The Arizona Court of Appeals carefully explained how the double jeopardy clause in the U.S. Constitution differs from the double jeopardy clause in the Arizona Constitution. It also established why that difference matters in the Milke case. "Our supreme court has determined that the Double Jeopardy Clause of the Arizona Constitution affords even greater protection than the federal Constitution, barring retrial where there are instances of egregious prosecutorial misconduct that raise serious concerns regarding the integrity of our system of justice." With this language, the court of appeals gave fair notice to all prosecutors that there was more at stake here than just reversing Debra Milke's wrongful conviction. Arizona's integrity was at stake.

Citing three Arizona Supreme Court cases that collectively frame a clear doctrine, the Arizona Court of Appeals held, "[D]ouble jeopardy bars retrial when the prosecution *deliberately* fails to disclose significant impeachment and exculpatory evidence during the defendant's initial trial. The State's severe and prejudicial *Brady* violations in withholding impeachment evidence prevent a fair trial and result in the reversal of a conviction."

The opinion cites seven Arizona trial court cases, ranging from 1983 to 1990. Each case was resolved against Saldate and in favor of the individual defendants. Judges Norris, Gemmill, and Swann displayed other examples of Saldate's record, none of which was known by Milke's original jury. They made particular note of the undisputed fact that the "Police Chief and Phoenix City Manager questioned Saldate's character, stating that [his] image of honesty, competency, and overall reliability must be questioned."

The duration of the state's failure to disclose was particularly disturbing to the court of appeals. "The nondisclosure by the State of the evidence impeaching Saldate persisted for years after the conclusion of the state court proceedings." These nondisclosures "remained unresolved and uncured, thereby exacerbating the constitutional harm from the original *Brady* violations." It was not just the magnitude of the violations, or the 23-year failure to disclose those violations, that stunned the Arizona Court of Appeals. It was also the state's inexplicable defense of its misconduct by arguing that "the prosecutor in Milke's 1990 trial did not *personally* know of Saldate's misconduct." That argument "misses the mark," the court said. The unanimous court reminded the prosecutor of his "duty to learn of any favorable evidence known to others acting on the government's behalf in the case, including the police." And they instructed him that the "prosecutor's office cannot get around *Brady* by keeping itself in ignorance or compartmentalizing information about different aspects of a case . . . The extent of any individual prosecutor's knowledge of the misconduct is immaterial. Though in some cases an individual may be the focus of the inquiry, it is the duty of the *State* as a whole to conduct prosecutions honorably and in compliance with the law." (Emphasis in the original.)

Tying the disclosure duty to the state *as a whole* is an abstract proposition. But there was nothing abstract in the Milke facts. "The Maricopa County Attorney's Office was aware by the time of Milke's trial in 1990 of Saldate's improper conduct, as several of its prosecutors had been forced to address the subject in other prosecutions. The court documents from these other prosecutions and the information in Saldate's disciplinary record 'fit within the broad sweep' of *Brady/Giglio*. It was the State's obligation to discover and disclose such information regardless of whether the information was possessed by other prosecutors, or the police." Instead of a "don't ask, don't tell" mantra, the MCAO apparently had a "don't ask, don't disclose" policy for individual prosecutors within the office.

While prosecutors often take umbrage at being judged in hindsight, hindsight is always right. In the Milke case, hindsight by the Arizona Court of Appeals was not just right, it was imperative. "We are unable to conclude that the long course of *Brady/Giglio* violations in this case are anything but a severe stain on the Arizona justice system. Nondisclosure of this magnitude calls into question the integrity of the system; it was highly prejudicial to Milke." And with that clear statement of how unique the Milke case was in Arizona legal history, the court of appeals remanded the case to Judge Mroz at the Maricopa County Superior Court "for dismissal with prejudice of the pending charges against Milke."

—

THERE IS A MUCH LARGER question in *Milke's* appellate history. Some might be tempted to argue she was freed on a legal technicality. That specious argument won't work because her conviction was wrongful. What happened to her could happen to anyone, irrespective of guilt, innocence, happenstance, or bad luck. She was a victim not of her own environment or anything she did, legal or otherwise. A potent trio—police officer, prosecutor, and trial judge—placed enormous confidence in and fealty to the doctrine of *prosecutorial discretion*. At the same time, they disregarded the doctrine of *presumed innocence*.

Our judicial system gives prosecutors complete and unfettered discretion to initiate and conduct criminal prosecutions. The common wisdom is that a good prosecutor could "indict a hamburger," if he or she wanted to. Another common belief is that prosecutors will never indict police officers. Both may be urban myth, but even if true, they disguise the larger issue. Is unfettered prosecutorial discretion wise legal policy?

Giving one player in a complex judicial system exclusive discretion is arguably justified by a narrow view of the separation of powers doctrine. It also stands on a never-vetted proposition that prosecutorial decisions are ill-suited to judicial review. The consequence is that prosecutors decide, without permission or consent, what charges to bring, when to bring them, and where to bring them. Prosecutors have unsupervised and far-reaching authority to decide whether to investigate, grant immunity, negotiate a plea bargain, or dismiss charges. They have the prerogative to recommend downward departures from sentencing guidelines for some defendants, while enhancing prison terms for others. Although prosecutorial discretion is broad, it is not unlimited; courts should protect individuals from bad or legally deficient prosecutorial decisions. State and federal courts presume that prosecutors act in good faith. Any defendant who thinks otherwise bears a heavy burden of proving facts sufficient to overcome prosecutorial discretion *and* prosecutorial presumption.

In part, the burden is heavy because of the symbiotic relationship between police and prosecutor at trial. The police, through an assigned "case agent," do the pretrial work of building the case witness by witness. Saldate was that case agent. The prosecutor does the courtroom work, including putting the "case agent" on the witness stand. Levy was the prosecutor. The prosecutor decides trial strategy and evaluates trial risk, with the case agent close at hand, usually at the same court-room table. The risk of loss is beyond *heavy* if the prosecutor discloses impeachment evidence that would discredit the case agent. Any prosecutor would be reluctant to sink his or her own case by facilitating the impeachment of his star witness. That natural reluctance reaches Titanic proportions if the entire case depends on the case agent's credibility. In *Milke*, the iceberg that would sink the prosecution was disclosure of Saldate's confession misconduct history. The Milke case and the three other double jeopardy cases cited in the court's opinion point out but do not solve the underlying problem—exclusive prosecutorial discretion, when abused, results in unfair trials and wrongful convictions. There is little doubt on either side of the case that a jury would never have convicted Milke had the members known of Saldate's long history of confession misconduct. Moreover, producing that evidence might have risked losing the cases of all three defendants—Milke, Styers, *and* Scott.

Saldate made the case against Scott and Styers when he persuaded Scott to confess his involvement and name Styers as the shooter. Styers then turned on Scott and accused him of being the shooter, thus placing both at the murder scene. Both refused to testify against or implicate Milke beyond the soft connection Saldate initially extracted from Scott. There was considerable forensic evidence against both men, but none against Milke. The missing piece in the conspiracy case not satisfied by the forensic evidence was motive. Why would Styers or Scott kill Christopher Milke? The answer to that, from a prosecutorial discretion perspective, was the presumed conspiracy between them and Milke to kill her son. But absent a confession from her, the conspiracy case was doubtful. In every sense of the word, the prosecutor *needed* Milke's confession. Without it, the conspiracy murder count against Styers and Scott would likely collapse. Because the police believed in Saldate's ability to get almost anyone to confess, he became the answer to the problem. He broke Scott in an hour but it took him only 30 minutes to get what they needed from Milke, so he said. She said she never confessed, setting up the swearing contest in court. Prosecutorial discretion won out. The grand jury indicted all three defendants on the strength of Saldate's testimony presented by a prosecutor who would not disclose Saldate's confession misconduct, either to the grand jury or to the *petit* jury at trial.

The eventual impact of Saldate's decades-long misconduct will likely take years to be fully known. There will undoubtedly be civil rights litigation by Milke and perhaps by other victims of Saldate's misconduct. There might be ramifications in the ongoing criminal cases involving Styers and Scott. And there should be policy review and perhaps more judicial intervention into the larger questions the Milke case raises: prosecutorial discretion, police assumptions, and the presumption of innocence.

The short-term consequences of the double jeopardy decision were predictable. Bill Montgomery, the Maricopa County Attorney, vowed to take the case to the U.S. Supreme Court, saying, "This office today bears the burden for trying to get justice for Christopher Milke." Laurie Roberts, a widely read columnist for the Arizona Republic, said, "Phoenix's heart is squeezed once again as a woman who may have ordered the murder of her son is declared a free woman—not because she is innocent (although she may be) but because a former cop couldn't be trusted and a prosecutor cut corners."

The larger question of the intersection between prosecutorial discretion and prosecutorial misconduct was answered in *Milke, albeit* indirectly. The Arizona Court of Appeals said, "In these circumstances, which will hopefully remain unique in the history of Arizona law, the most potent constitutional remedy is required." By "these" circumstances, the court likely meant Detective Saldate's long and sordid history of confession misconduct in a case where the confession was the only probative evidence against the defendant. But what will happen in the many other Arizona cases where a confession is the only probative evidence, but double jeopardy does not attach? The justice community will roundly applaud the court's opinion in *Milke*. But the decision could not and does not address the wide variety of *different* circumstances resulting in wrongful convictions produced by prosecutorial misconduct.

There are scores of cases each year arising out of the intersection between prosecutorial discretion and prosecutorial misconduct. Unfettered discretion will always tempt a prosecutor whose "win" depends on protecting the credibility of a pivotal witness. That's the intersection we ought to address from a policy perspective, not just by deciding one case at a time. The fact that it took a federal appellate court to point out the obvious ought to force us, as a state, to re-examine the broader consequences and circumstances of prosecutorial misconduct. The "hope" expressed by the court of appeals is heartening, but perhaps unwarranted. As long as prosecutors exercise unfettered discretion over capital decisions, and then advance that decision by also deciding what to disclose and what to hide in criminal cases, the state's "integrity" will remain "at stake."

ACKNOWLEDGMENTS

THIS IS MY THIRD BOOK about the presumptions, assumptions, and rationalizations imbedded in the American criminal justice system. All three books dissect the core impact of confessions in criminal cases. When a police officer extracts a confession, it becomes the ace of spades in the prosecutor's hand. But when that card is dealt from the bottom of the deck, everyone loses. My first book in the series (*"Miranda—The Story of America's Right to Remain Silent"*) is about guilty suspects giving *unwarned confessions*. The second (*"Innocent Until Interrogated"* is about innocent suspects giving *false confessions*. This book is about a woman convicted and sentenced to death for murdering her child based solely on a confession I believe *she never gave*. It is not about innocence or guilt. It is about something infinitely more important—the presumption of innocence that some defendants never get. The judge at Milke's trial failed to admit in evidence vital impeachment information about the police, because in part, the prosecution hid it. That judicial failing mushroomed, trumping Milke's presumed innocence at every level by presumed guilt solely because a police officer *said* she confessed.

The first person I want to acknowledge is Debra Milke. She consistently maintained her innocence, and always denied giving any confession. That took courage and endurance. I acknowledge the brilliant analysis and the courage of the judges on the United States Court of Appeals for the Ninth Circuit, the Arizona Court of Appeals, and the Maricopa County Superior Court. Collectively, they took Debra Milke off death row, and spared her a retrial in a case where proof of her guilt was "never great, nor was the presumption evident." Judges Kozinski, Farris, Bea, Norris, Gemmill, Swann and Mroz rendered well-stated, insightful opinions and reached the right result for the right reason. That also took courage and endurance.

I also want to acknowledge the many excellent lawyers, legal assistants, investigators, witnesses, and former police officers who helped me figure out the convoluted saga that the Milke case became. Collectively, they worked tirelessly to get Debra Milke's convictions and sentences overturned. They are too numerous to name here, and some helped only on my assurance they would remain anonymous. Over a two-year span, the named and unnamed sources for this book helped me understand how and why Debra Milke spent 23 years on Arizona's death row based on a confession she never gave. Anders Rosenquist led a team of law students that discovered the evidence ultimately used to free her, and filed the initial habeas petition. Jess Lorona, John Edward Charland, and Elizabeth Hurley were co-counsel. Michael Kimerer and Lori Voepel took over as lead counsel in the late 1990s and successfully led the federal habeas corpus effort. Kimerer and Voepel also managed the retrial process in Arizona, ultimately securing a complete dismissal of all charges with prejudice. The Ninth Circuit briefing was aided by Larry Hammond, Steve Drizin, Amy Lynn Nguyen, Angela Lynn Polizzi, Pamela Kilpatrick Sutherland, Rudolph Gerber and Daniel Pocheda. I would be remiss if I did not acknowledge Anders Rosenquist's insight into his team's post-conviction relief efforts. Without his insight and help, I might not have penetrated the cover laid down by the prosecution. And without Dr. Richard Leo's legal and social science skills, and his voluminous work on this case, I might not have understood how remote the possibility is that Armando Saldate ever "took" a confession, much less that Debra Milke ever "gave" one. Kirk Fowler vigorously investigated the case for many years and gave me an insider's context into the web of manipulation that ensnared Debra Milke.

My most profound acknowledgment goes to Mike Kimerer and Lori Voepel. Without their gracious and continuous help this book simply could not have been written. Their commitment to Debra Milke gave me broad access to their files, memories, and opinions. Larry Hammond, Bob McWhirter, and Judge Craig Blakey consulted with me on many aspects of criminal law and procedure. They frequently commented on the structural organization of my manuscript—what to include and what to ignore. They helped me avoid rabbit holes in the evidence and quicksand in the habeas process. They were always cautious and gave me good advice about both context and impact. Ginger Stahly and Rhonda Neff were always available and bore my incessant calls for more files with grace and good humor.

Jon Malysiak and his exceptionally talented staff at ABA Publishing, pushed the manuscript and believed in it from day one. Mr. Malysiak became a vigorous advocate for the strength of this book and the necessity of getting it all down, tightly, and in a narrative everyone could understand. Last, and as always, I want to thank my wife, Kathleen Stuart, for giving me the freedom to write and putting up with the thousands of hours I spent at my computer desk.

GARY L. STUART

GARY STUART SPENT 32 YEARS as a partner at Jennings, Strouss & Salmon, PLLC, in Phoenix, Arizona. He now practices part time as Gary L. Stuart, P.C. He earned degrees in Finance and Law at the University of Arizona. Martindale-Hubble lists him as an A-V lawyer and a Premier American Lawyer. He was profiled in *Who's Who in American Law* (first edition). He is a sustaining member of Best Lawyers in America, Arizona's Finest Lawyers, and Southwest Superlawyers. The Maricopa County Bar Association inducted him into its Hall of Fame in October 2010. The National Institute of Trial Advocacy honored him with its *Distinguished Faculty* designation in 1994. He holds the juried rank of Advocate and served as President of the American Board of Trial Advocates (Arizona chapter). Stuart completed an eight-year term on the Arizona Board of Regents, and served as its President in 2004-2005. He taught as Adjunct Faculty at the University of Arizona James E. Rogers College of Law (2000-2005). He has been on the Adjunct Faculty at the Sandra Day O'Connor College of Law since 1994, where he continues to teach Legal Ethics, Legal Writing, and Appellate Advocacy. He also serves as Senior Policy Advisor to the Dean at the Arizona State University College of Law. He limits his part-time law practice to legal ethics, bar admission, professional discipline, law firm consulting, and expert witness work in legal malpractice and ethics cases. He served three terms on the Arizona State Bar Case Conflict Committee as its Probable Cause Panelist and is a current member of the Arizona Supreme Court Attorney Disciplinary Panel, which hears disciplinary cases. He was a member of the Arizona State Bar Rules of Professional Conduct Committee for 23 years and served as its chair for ten years. He has written more than 50 ethics committee opinions. He served on numerous ethics-related committees at the state and national levels. He has written two published books on ethics, and more than one hundred law review and journal articles, op-ed pieces, essays, stories, and CLE monographs. His ten published books are: *The Ethical Trial Lawyer,* State Bar of Arizona, 1994; *Ethical Litigation,* Lexis-Nexis Publishing, 1998; *The Gallup 14,* a novel, University of New Mexico Press, 2000; *Miranda—The Story of America's Right to Remain Silent,* University of Arizona Press, 2004; *AIM for the Mayor—Echoes from Wounded Knee,* a novel, Xlibris Publishing, 2008; *Innocent Until Interrogated—The Story of the Buddhist Temple Massacre and the Tucson Four,* University of Arizona Press, 2010; *Angus—Riding the Rio Chama,* a novel, Amazon Publishing, 2012; *Ten Shoes Up,* a novel, Gleason & Wall Publishing, 2015; *The Valles Caldera,* a novel, Gleason & Wall Publishing, 2015; and *Anatomy of a Confession—The Debra Milke Case,* ABA Publishing, 2016.